THE
GUN DIGEST BOOK OF
SHOTGUN
GUNSMITHING

By
Ralph T. Walker

Edited by Jack Lewis

DBI BOOKS, INC., NORTHFIELD, ILLINOIS

ABOUT OUR COVERS

The gunsmith who works with shotguns couldn't begin to do the specialized work required of him without the tools that Frank and Bob Brownell provide — it's that simple!

Of course, it must be said that the selection of Brownell's tools seen on these covers is only a small representation of what that company sells to gunsmiths worldwide. Also worthy of mention is the fact that Ralph Walker, the author of this book, is directly responsible for the design of many of the tools seen on our covers and throughout this book. He, like Frank and Bob Brownell, has spent a lifetime improving the tools and techniques of his craft. (The Winchester Model 42 receiver is courtesy of Tom Goss, The Fixit Shop, Northfield, Illinois. Photo by John Hanusin.)

PUBLISHER
Sheldon Factor

EDITORIAL DIRECTOR
Jack Lewis

ART DIRECTOR
Sonya Kaiser

ASSISTANT ARTISTS
Dana Silzle
Kristen Tonti

PHOTO SERVICES
Cynthia Forrest

PRODUCTION
Betty Burris

COPY EDITOR
Dorine Imbach

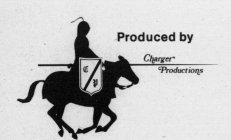

Produced by

Charger Productions

Dedicated to
BETTY RHEE DuBOSE WALKER
*for thirty years past and all the years to come
my partner in life and my wife*

ISBN 0-910676-54-2

Library of Congress Catalog Card #83-70144

CONTENTS

INTRODUCTION

When you first begin to read this volume, you may begin to wonder whether it really is a gunsmithing book at all. You will note that there are chapters that appear to cover shotshell design, gun design and even how to shoot.

Well, call that background, if you will. The author, who is one of the nation's top shotgun experts when it comes to design and correcting a gun's faults, is a firm believer in the fact that you can't work on a shotgun unless you fully understand how it functions and why. And interspersed with what might be a review of old knowledge are countless tips on gunsmithing that can be of value both to the amateur and the professional.

Much of the information contained in this volume never has been published before and is based upon the hard-learned lessons of the author. In the writing he manages to explain fully some devious facets of the shotgun that are poorly understood by the average shooter. His chapter on choke forcing cone length, as an example, covers a subject from which other gun writers tend to shy away, since they don't understand the subject and would be hard put to explain it to one seeking such knowledge.

This is a labor of love for the author, since he has been keeping notes on his findings for more decades than some readers have been alive. He has verified and reverified his findings in some of the obscure areas of shotgunning and shotgun gunsmithing before passing on the information to those with less experience.

We think you'll find this a worthwhile book in all respects.

Jack Lewis
Editor

Chapter 1

There was a period in history when shotguns were used for food harvesting in the U.S. while Britain utilized the scattergun primarily for sport.

THE AGE OF SHOTGUNS

The Basic Premise Of Design Has Not Changed All That Much Through The Centuries

THE SHOTGUN is the oldest of all types of sporting firearms and its history can be traced back to the beginning of hand-held guns. Yet its fascinating story usually takes a back seat in any history of firearms with the limelight cast upon the rifle and the handgun. Nonetheless, one should be fully familiar with any firearm upon which he intends to perform gunsmithing chores. The shotgun certainly is no exception.

The first shotguns were early hand cannons which consisted of little more than an iron tube sealed at one end, open at the other. To the sealed end was attached some form of handle, usually nothing more than a wooden rod. As with all muzzleloaders, an early crude form of black powder went in first with some type of projectile pushed down upon the powder. Ignition was achieved by placing fire to a small open hole at the sealed end of the rough tube. If all went according to plan, the powder was ignited and dispatched the shot in the general direction of the selected target.

The tube's bore was smooth as rifling was somewhere in the distant future. It is not beyond belief that some disgusted shooter, after failing to place his projectile into a target, made the monumental breakthrough of increasing the chances of a hit by simply increasing the number of projectiles he crammed down the bore. Thus was born the shotgun.

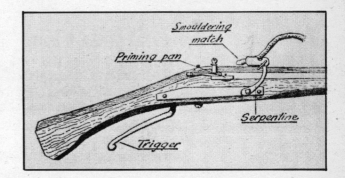

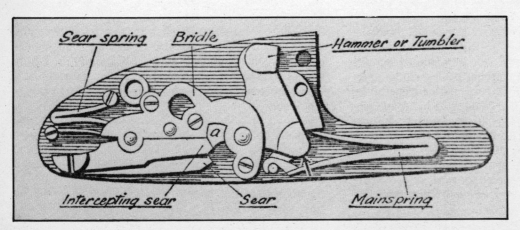

Above: Tudor matchlock was used in England in the 15th Century as a means of taking game. (Left) Sidelock was a later development that made the shotgun more efficient in its uses.

One of England's top gunmakers in the last century, Robert Churchill was an early advocate of a short-barrel shotgun in the era when 30 to 34 inches was common.

The first step up the ladder of development was the matchlock. The smoothbore tube became longer to burn the black powder more fully and, as a side advantage, increase range. The longer barrel also allowed more precise aim. A rough form of a stock took the place of the wooden rod and the shooter could hold his scattergun against his shoulder, adding to overall advantage. Instead of carrying around a flaming torch, he now lit a slow burning section of rope which was clamped to a device attached in the center with a pin to the gun. By pulling on the bottom part of the device, the top pivoted forward and forced the burning match (rope) into the open touch hole to ignite the priming powder charge.

While the shooter could aim with some reliability at the target, lock time was somewhat on the slow side. Game-getting potential limited, shooting was done preferably while sitting perfectly still. Wing shooting? I doubt that it was even remotely considered; if so, it was strictly a daydream.

Around 1525 the wheellock came upon the scene. This operated somewhat like a modern cigarette lighter. A clock-like spring was wound with a key to compress the spring and store power. The spring was attached to an iron wheel resembling the cigarette lighter wheel of today. A pull of the trigger released the sear to release the spring which, in turn, spun like crazy. A piece of iron pyrite or flint was

The Churchill gun works in London became a mecca for a line of sportsmen who desired the best in a shotgun.

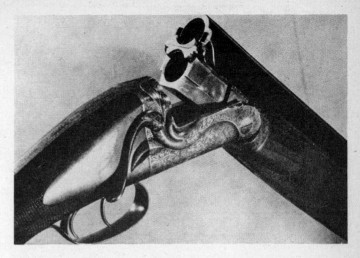

This early shotgun of over/under design featured a side-break lever that was clumsy but still efficient.

A style that quickly became a favorite with European shooters, and later those in this country, was Churchill 12-gauge, double barrel, self-ejector sidelock model.

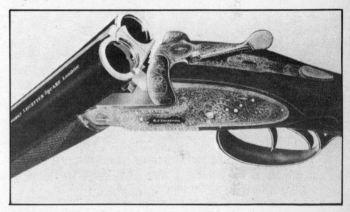

pressed against the rotating wheel and sent a shower of sparks downward into the pan to ignite the priming charge.

While the wheellock was a definite advantage over the old matchlock, the main fault was expense and easily broken parts; only the rich could afford them. The military stuck to the old, less expensive matchlock, as did the general public.

The really giant step forward was around 1550 in the form of the snaphaunce, which in its final form, the flintlock, was to last over three hundred years with improvement along the way. The flintlock was more simple than the wheellock, more rugged and — most importantly — more reliable. Basically it consisted of a hammer holding a bit of flint under pressure from a main spring. When released by its sear the hammer went rapidly forward with the flint striking a spark on the top part of the pan containing the powder charge to ignite a main charge in the barrel. The top of the pan was spring loaded and went back, exposing a steel striking surface and at the same time opening the pan to receive the resulting shower of sparks.

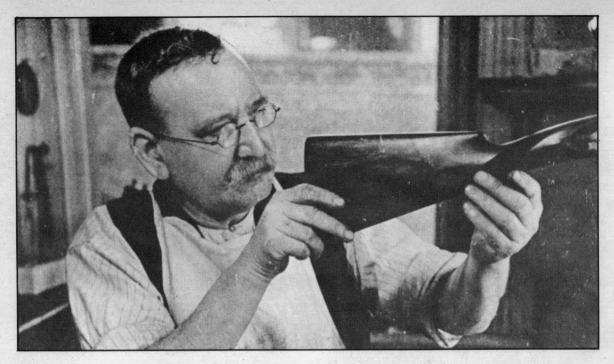

The English gunsmiths of the last century were top craftsmen, undergoing extensive apprenticeships.

This approach resulted in much faster lock time from trigger pull to muzzle exit of the projectile or projectiles. Practical shooting of game on wing finally was possible.

Equally important was the overall change in design. The gun became more streamlined. Stocks became more efficient, barrels thinner to reduce weight. Shotgun locks were refined in size and shape. During this period another step was taken by joining two barrels side by side with two lock mechanisms on the same gun. This second shot made shotgun shooting an art form.

These refinements reached the common hunter many years later with the beginning of the classic flintlock side-by-side around 1750-1800 in England. The average shooter used a single-shot called a fowler. It was between five and six feet in length with a fifty-inch barrel length! Most of the locks were taken from the same batch used on military muskets of the period. In most collections a flintlock fowler is rare simply because most of them were worn out with constant use.

The military muskets of the period were really shotguns to be technical. Barrels were smoothbore to ease loading; rifles were in a small minority. With a single projectile they were so inaccurate that a British colonel named Hanger said in 1814, "A soldier's musket will strike a figure of a man at eighty yards, maybe at even one hundred yards, but a soldier must be very unfortunate indeed to be wounded at 150 yards." The common load was buck-and-ball, consisting of a single projectile and four buckshot about #1 size (.30). Even this was considered impractical by many and the load was twelve buckshot of the above size.

The average person used something resembling a musket for his daily shooting of Redcoats, Indians and others who would deprive him of life. Just the ticket to bring in a deer for the table was the buckshot load and the musket was equally sufficient with small shot for the more easily found small game such as rabbits and squirrel. If there was a really accurate way of testing, I would give odds that the common man's multi-use musket fired more times with a shot charge than with a musket ball or buckshot.

We have come to think of the Minute Man and his flintlock rifle as a national symbol. Yet many of the flintlock rifles were smoothbored for the same reason as the more

Parts for Churchill and other quality shotguns were individually matched by hand, making each firearm a one-of-a-kind, but repairs could be expensive, as it often required hand-making new parts to fit the gun.

common multi-use musket. The over/under shotgun was born as the Pennsylvania/Kentucky rifle which was smoothbored more often than rifled; when rifled, one barrel usually was smoothbored.

Englishman Joshua Shaw is credited with inventing the percussion cap around 1815, but it was not until he migrated to the United States and secured a patent in 1822 that the percussion cap came into its own. This was another big step forward, offering many advantages over the flintlock. The percussion cap was more waterproof and more immune to flash fire (firing both barrels) than the flintlock. Lock time reduction was the big gain for shotguns which meant more practical wing shooting.

The British must be given the blue ribbon for taking advantage of this technical gain, for they were not long in switching from the flintlock to development of the side-by-side shotgun. The English double became a class symbol all over the world with its roots in the percussion period. Europeans, especially Belgians, jumped on the bandwagon of exported doubles. Sad to say, there were no American double-barrel shotguns in this period.

By the same token, American single-barrel shotgun development went a different but equally interesting route. The flintlock fowler underwent a technical change to percussion, but remained basically the same gun except for a bit of barrel shortening. This was the common man's gun and saw the most day-to-day use, taking the place of the old musket.

Today double-barrel percussion shotguns are relatively common on the collector market, single-barrel percussion shotguns breed rare. Why? The single-barrel saw more use and simply wore out, hence fewer survived, although they

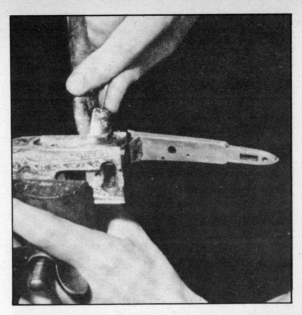

European craftsmen, especially the English, looked upon the shotgun as an extension of the shooter's personality, often using specific engraving motif.

probably outnumbered the doubles ten to one in the hands of the average man. Remington offered a single-barrel percussion shotgun from 1840 through 1880.

One of the most interesting shotguns of this period is the Sharps Model 1853, more famous as a rifle. This Sharps fired a caseless cartridge, the breech block shearing off the rear of the paper cartridge that contained powder and shot

The shop area of Churchill's looked more like a junk shop than gun factory in the firm's heyday.

seprated by a wad. This shotgun never got off the ground production-wise; with the beginning of the Civil War came the total switch of Sharps to carbine production for the military.

The first successful double-barrel breech-loading shotgun was the French LeFaucheaux that utilized the pin-fire shotshell. This was a shotshell with the firing pin built into the shell. The pin, protruding through a notch at the rear of the barrel, was struck by a hammer. After firing, the pin also served as a method of extraction. It was a simple system and was well received worldwide and remained popular in Europe well into the Twentieth Century.

In 1860 Colt introduced the 1855 revolving shotgun based on their 1855 Revolving Carbine. Each of the five chambers accepted a powder charge contained in a tight paper unit that was totally consumed in firing the gun. In front of this went the shot charge in a separate container. With all five chambers loaded by the conventional attached rammer, the nipples were capped and the gun was ready to fire. The only problem was the flash which required that the left hand be held behind the chambers rather than extended to the forearm position. Sold in 10- and 20-gauge from 1860 to 1863 with barrel selection from twenty-seven to thirty-six inches, it was quite popular during this transition period.

The self-contained cartridge went through rapid technological advancement during the War to Establish the Southern Confederacy (or Civil War if you are of Northern persuasion). At war's end there was an abundance of surplus rifles and little commercial market for the many manufacturers to share. So they turned to the shotgun market introducing self-contained cartridge technology to shotshells.

One of the first was the Roper repeating shotgun with a revolving chamber. This used iron shotshells loaded with black powder, wad, shot and an over-shot wad; ignition was a form of percussion cap. Patented in 1866, it was a step forward, but saw little public acceptance. It is best remembered as the first shotgun with a detachable choke, which was a ring that screwed onto the barrel. Removal of one ring and substitution of another offered instant selection of choke.

Sylvester Roper was associated with Christopher Spencer of Spencer repeating rifle fame. In the early 1880s they produced the first successful slide-action shotgun. Alexander Bain had developed a slide-action in 1852, but Roper and Spencer put the idea to practical and production application. The gun incorporated a tubular magazine that held shells. Slid to the rear, the breech block dropped and picked up the next shell, which was inserted into the waiting chamber. It was different in two interesting respects: The fired shell was ejected upward and the trigger group contained a second forward trigger to recock the mechanism should the gun misfire.

A repeater that was in the limelight for a few years was the John Browning-designed lever-action shotgun, first produced by Winchester in 1887. Massive and clumsy, it was widely accepted for its rugged construction and the ability to digest the big 10-gauge shells both of home-grown variety — as most were — and the commercial versions. It was continued in the Winchester line for these reasons until 1920.

L.C. Smith was one of the first Americans to attempt to duplicate English quality in his line of scatterguns.

Perhaps the most famous side-by-side of the last century was the famous Parker shotgun that remained in production until World War II, with a few even made afterward. Charles Parker was in the hardware business, but contracted to manufacture rifles during the Civil War. He later switched to shotgun production, marketing the first model in 1868. This was later refined with a bolting action designed by one C.A. King, which featured a dolls-head extension between the barrels and a hardened sliding wedge just below the barrels. This design made the Parker shotgun famous.

Remington followed shortly with their Model 1874 double-barrel and steadily refined the basic design. They read the market right and made the gun available in a seemingly endless variety of models with something for every hunter.

Also aiming at the shotgun market in the post-Civil War days was William H. Baker. An interesting feature of his double shotgun was that the forward trigger operated the

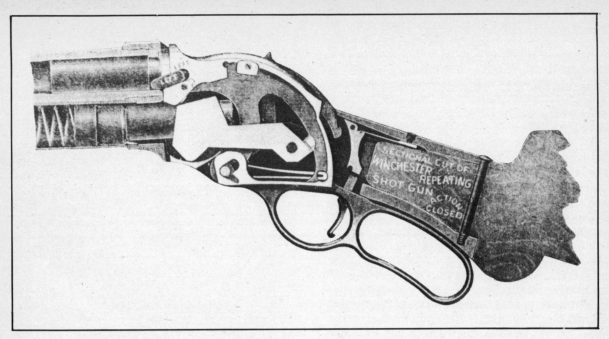

The Winchester lever-action shotgun was derived from many basic design features of Model 73 carbine.

unbreaching system. His firm was purchased by Lyman C. Smith in 1870 and the famous L.C. Smith shotgun came on the scene. This was a sidelock hammer double with barrels made in Europe. The rotary locking system of the L.C. Smith was designed by Alexander Brown. The side hammer system was dropped, but the side plate action remained an L.C. Smith trademark until the end of production just after the end of World War II. Marlin, who purchased the L.C. Smith firm, reintroduced the shotgun in mid-1960, but high costs of production could not be overcome and the design was dropped.

The Ithaca Gun Company also was founded by the same William H. Baker at Ithaca, New York, and produced their first side-by-side double in 1883. One of his partners in the firm was L.H. Smith, brother of Lyman C Smith. Another famous name of this period was D.M. Lefever, who introduced the hammerless double-barrel shotgun to the American market in 1878. Forced out of the first company, The D.M. Lefever Co., he quickly founded D.M. Lefever, Sons and Company, which included his five sons. His death in 1906 resulted in the company being sold to Ithaca, which continued the Lefever shotgun name for many years.

During this period the single-barrel shotgun was not neglected. Remington introduced the Remington-Rider No. 1 rolling-block shotgun in 1867. This was based on their rolling-block rifle action that had found acceptance worldwide in its military configuration. This simple, rugged shotgun was well suited for a young nation pressing Westward and the sod busters who looked upon a shotgun as a tool.

Nevertheless, it was a tough market for single barrels during this period. Surplus military muzzleloading rifles left over from the Civil War were as numerous as ex-soldiers of both sides. Many were carried westward or used for hunting throughout the country. Others were customized by chopping off a bit of barrel, shortening the wood forend. But the majority were bored out to become single-shot muzzleloading shotguns at less than two dollars each. This altered shotgun was still selling in 1900.

Stevens Arms Company jumped into the game in 1870 to introduce the first of the single-barrel shotguns that made the company famous. A simple break-open single-barrel attracted other gun companies, including Remington and Lefever.

Imported doubles bearing every trade name imagineable were competing for the American dollar. If a hardware store placed an order for a dozen guns, the store's name went on the gun. This explains why many shotgun brands simply cannot be identified. Bob Hinman's book, *The Golden Age of Shotgunning,* identifies many, however.

The double-barrel side-by-side bit the dust because of the high cost of hand labor necessary to its production. Many remained on the market up until 1941 and a few were reintroduced with the end of the war in 1945, but only two survived into the 1950s. Both had their beginnings in the 1920s. Probably the most famous of the two is the Winchester Model 21, still in limited production. Winchester designers set out to build the finest side-by-side shotgun made. That they succeeded is reflected in the fact that it has lasted in the basic original design all of these years. Not introduced until 1930, it contained many unique features, the most noteworthy being the method of key locking the two barrel tubes together. Even at the beginning it was not the gun for the average citizen, price-wise; this has not changed.

The combination Savage-Stevens-Springfield-Fox double is the same simple, rugged design built originally by Savage Arms at their Westfield, Massachusetts, factory. It has survived because the design is simple, efficient and reasonably easy to manufcature. Also continuous research utilizing modern equipment and techniques have kept it within reasonable price for the average shooter. This translates to a large number of sales each year which, in turn, reduces the per-gun production cost.

America has long been known as the land of the repeater shotgun; no other country accepts this type so readily. The man who can accept most credit was John Moses Browning of Utah. He designed the Winchester Model 1893 actually two years earlier and Winchester promptly purchased the plans. This was the beginning of the Winchester pump-action shotguns with over 34,000 being produced before the introduction of their refined version which was termed the Model 1897. The '97 contained many factory refinements as well as John Browning's ideas for improvement. Regardless of the changes, which continued throughout production, the 1897 was The Pump for many shooters and remained in production until 1957 with 1,024,700 produced!

Marlin issued their Model 1898 pump as competition to the Winchester 97. With modifications and model number changes it too passed the one million production mark before the gun was discontinued in 1935.

John Browning designed another pump, the Stevens Model 520, in 1904. The first hammerless slide-action on the American market, it remained in production until 1930. As a note of interest, this was the first shotgun offered for a 20-gauge three-inch shell.

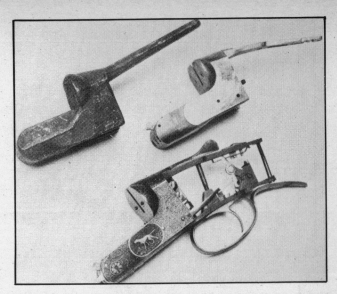

The three stages in manufacture of the frame and breech mechanism of an early Ithaca shotgun are illustrated.

Remington introduced the Model 10 pump in 1907, but never really solved some design problems. They sold the design to Ithaca which redesigned the gun into their famous Model 37 pump. The design was unique in that it both loaded and ejected via an opening in the bottom of the receiver, making it a favorite for southpaw shooters.

John Browning's Remington Model 17 pump incorporated many of the good features of the Model 10, which were adopted also into the Remington Model 29 as well as the Ithaca Model 37.

In 1912 Winchester introduced another pump, the Model 12, which racked up an impressive 2,000,000 sales in its sixty years in the standard line. Why it sold so well is in the

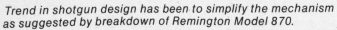

Trend in shotgun design has been to simplify the mechanism as suggested by breakdown of Remington Model 870.

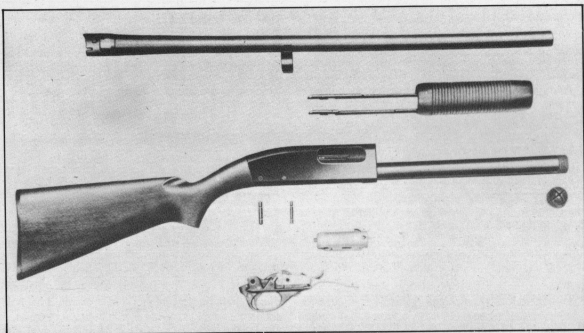

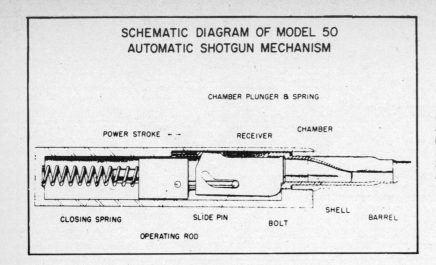

SCHEMATIC DIAGRAM OF MODEL 50
AUTOMATIC SHOTGUN MECHANISM

CHAMBER PLUNGER & SPRING

POWER STROKE - - RECEIVER CHAMBER

CLOSING SPRING SLIDE PIN BOLT SHELL BARREL

OPERATING ROD

Left: Winchester Model 50 shotgun was later redesigned to become Model 59. (Below) The design of the Browning five-shot self-loader has served as the basis for numerous other models made both in the U.S. and abroad.

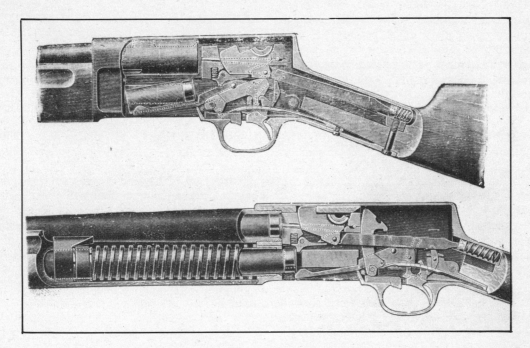

outline of the gun. The balance is almost perfect and weight distribution makes it come to the shoulder like a shotgunner's dream.

I realize I am about to start a small revolution with the following statement: The Model 12, from a design standpoint, is a turkey! In fact, it is probably the worst-designed gun mechanically and a nightmare to produce. To interchange barrels one has to replace the complete front of the gun including barrel, magazine tube assembly, slide assembly, et al. No other pump from 1930 forward requires this much to change barrels. If you changed often, the joint became so slack it was necessary to install a take-up sleeve on the barrel! It would require a full book to list all of the faults in the design.

Gun companies, however, make the gun that sells and the Model 12 sold like Long Johns in the Arctic. But time caught up with the Model 12 and in the final years of production Winchester lost their proverbial shirt each time one went out the door. More modern guns were available and I remember well when the last ones stayed in the gun racks for less than a hundred bucks.

Remington's new pump introduced in 1931 had a simple interchangeable barrel system. One simply rotated a knurled nut at the forward end of the magazine tube and the barrel rotated a quarter turn, free for removal for cleaning or another barrel choice. The Ithaca Model 37 refined this system as did several other pumps marketed in the late 1930s. The Model 31 was discontinued in 1949 with the 870 taking its place for another classic design.

The Remington Model 870 is the father of modern pump shotguns. The simple design features translate into one of the most dependable shotguns ever and it still is going strong. Barrel take-down is similar to that of the Model 31, but the breech bolt locks directly into a barrel extension, a key feature on all modern pumps and semiautos. Push two pins and the complete fire control system can be removed for cleaning. Pull forward on the slide with the barrel removed and the bolt is clear for cleaning.

With the demise of the Model 12, Winchester introduced their current Model 1200 pump. The bolt with rotary lugs locks directly into a barrel extension. Barrel change is as simple as with the 870 and removal of the fire

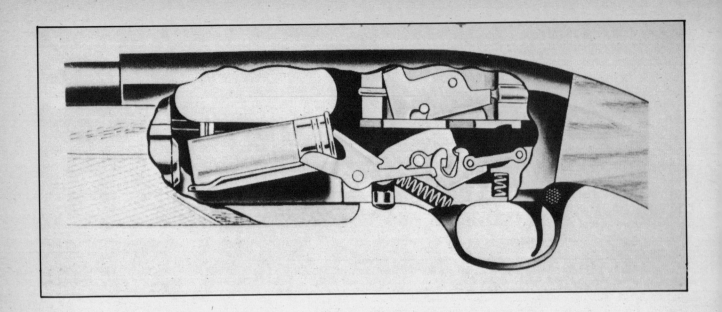

The approach to movement of the shotshell from magazine to the chamber of autoloaders, pump-actions has remained basically the same, no matter what the make of gun. Above is Marlin Premier model; below, Winchester Model 12.

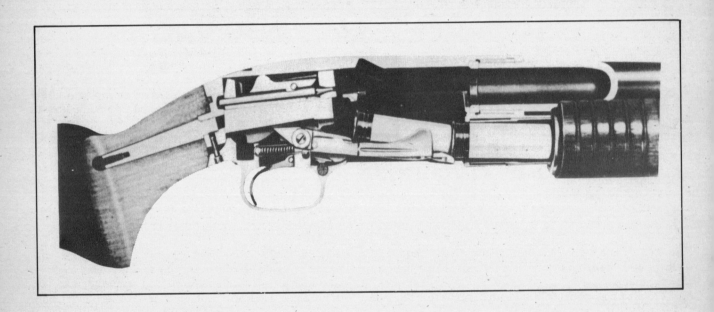

control mechanism and breech bolt is a snap. Winchester, in my opinion, is ahead of competitors in one department at this writing. The screw-in WinChoke system allows choke change with only the removal and insertion of assorted choke tubes instead of the complete barrel. It makes a lot more sense to pack along several choke tubes than to carry a spare barrel in a hip pocket!

The High Standard pump line came and went and is best known for the zillion sold by Sears under their trade J.C. Higgins brand name. One excellent feature of these guns is the simple shell lifter.

I was in the Philippines a couple of years ago doing some redesign work for a gun manufacturer whose action was a nut for nut, bolt for bolt copy of the old High Standard

pump! Thus the design is still on the market with a few updates in production techniques and a change here and there for the better.

Savage Arms' old Model 67 pump was nothing fancy; just a solid design that worked just short of forever. The firm did a bit of update recently with a simple interchangeable barrel in the Model 30. To illustrate how strong that action is they used the .410 model as the basis for a pump .30-30 rifle and you would be surprised at how few design changes were required. That has to be a compliment for a rugged, dependable pump shotgun.

When it comes to a good design that incorporates the best of all modern pumps, the Marlin Model 120 introduced in 1972 deserves the blue ribbon. One would have to look hard for original thought as there are so many field-proved features that it was a success from Day One with the shooting public.

John Browning started working on a recoil-operated self-loading shotgun around 1890 and spent the next ten years perfecting the design. In 1900 he carried the gun to Winchester at New Haven and Tommy Johnson drew up the patent features. Browning departed from past procedure of outright sale and asked for a royalty arrangement. Winchester refused and Browning took the next ship to Europe, where Fabrique National of Belgium met his terms to produce one of the world's most famous shotguns. In Europe the gun still is known as the Browning FN. It gained rapid acceptance in America as simply the Browning and was *the* semiauto. After more than half a century it is still going strong.

Remington worked out a royalty arrangement with Browning and started production of the home-grown version in 1911 with only minor modifications to the original design. Both versions built a reputation that was hard to match in the field of reliability. What few modern shooters realize is that both guns had to function with shotshells loaded with black powder for quite a few years, which says something for the design capability to use a wide range of shotshell types. The first semiautomatic to handle the 12-gauge three-inch magnum shell was a Model 11 Remington modified by Arthur Kovalosky of California.

Thomas Crossly "Tommy" Johnson of Winchester was given the task of designing a recoil-operated semiauto shotgun. He was extremely qualified in two ways, having been the chief designer at Winchester for a number of years and the engineer who had worked with Browning in drawing up the patents for Browning's design. His efforts resulted in the Winchester Model 11 self-loader which was a success primarily in not getting Winchester into court, but it never really was competition to the Browning or the Remington Model 11. The Winchester 11SL was worked over in 1940 and given a new model number, but with war being declared a year later and suspension of sporting arms being declared a year later and suspension of sporting arms production there was only the death bell for this semi-auto.

With war's end, most manufacturers started producing guns that had been in their lines before the hostilities, although some were dropped due to high production costs. After the Germans seized the Browning manufacturing facility in Belgium in 1941, Remington began producing the Browning A-5 for Browning, continuing until 1946. Much of the European tooling was lost during the war, so Browning was slow in beginning post-WWII start-up there.

The first new-model semiauto was the Remington 11-48, the old Model 11 in new dress with modern production technqiues necessitating some action redesign. It was still a recoil-operated shotgun, but with a modernized sloping receiver instead of the old square-back design. It was later produced as the Mohawk 48 by Remington and was the basis for several European shotguns such as the Franchi.

The success of the M-1 Garand gas-operated rifle and the M-1 Carbine turned gun manufacturers to the question of how to harness gas energy to function a shotgun action. The first was Winchester's Model 50 in 1950 which utilized a separate gas chamber. Gas pressure between the floating chamber and the main section of the barrel gave a quick backward shove to work the action. They produced about 200,000 before the gun was redesigned to become the Model 59 with an aluminum receiver and a unique barrel wound with fiberglass. It remained in the line until 1965. Owners fell into two categories, one praising its light weight and handling ease, the second swapping it at the first opportunity. There seemed to be no middle ground with the 59.

The first commercially produced shotgun that tapped gas via small holes from the bore was manufactured by High Standard under exclusive contract for Sears, Roebuck. Several years later High Standard obtained the rights to market the gun under its own name. As the first true gas-operated semiauto, its system was a manufacturing night-

Stevens Model 9478 10-gauge magnum reflects the modern trend toward simplicity of design, featuring clean lines.

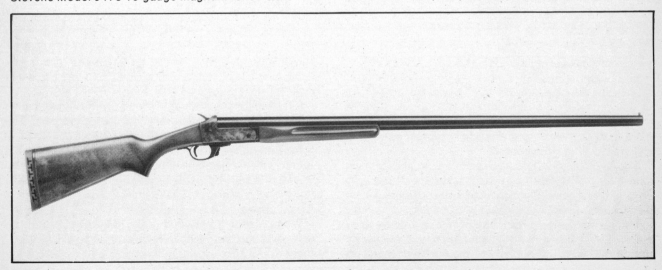

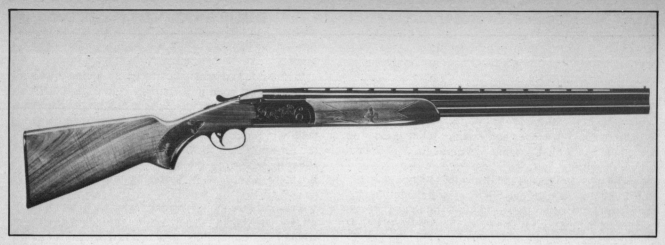

Savage Model 333 followed the trend set by earlier models of over/unders, incorporating good handling qualities.

mare, but one must remember that this was the first design of its type. Its original designer was Gus Swebelius and the introduction was in 1955.

A year later Remington marketed its own gas-operated design which had been under development for several years. The Sportsman-58 featured a device in the magazine cap to allow either a light or heavy setting causing the action to cycle at constant speed with various shotshells. Remington brought out an improved model in 1959 that corrected many of the original problems. This new gun, the Model 878, was to father the gas-operated semiautomatic shotgun, the Remington Model 1100. Introduced in 1963, it has gone through numerous modifications and today is the top seller in the gas-operated category, the gun to which all others are compared for simplicity of design and reliability.

In 1963 Winchester introduced a gas-operated self-loader with the assigned model number of 1400. Similar in appearance to their pump Model 1200, the key design feature of the 1400 is the self-compensating gas metering system which bleeds off unwanted gas pressure through the magazine cap's front end. Add the WinChoke system to

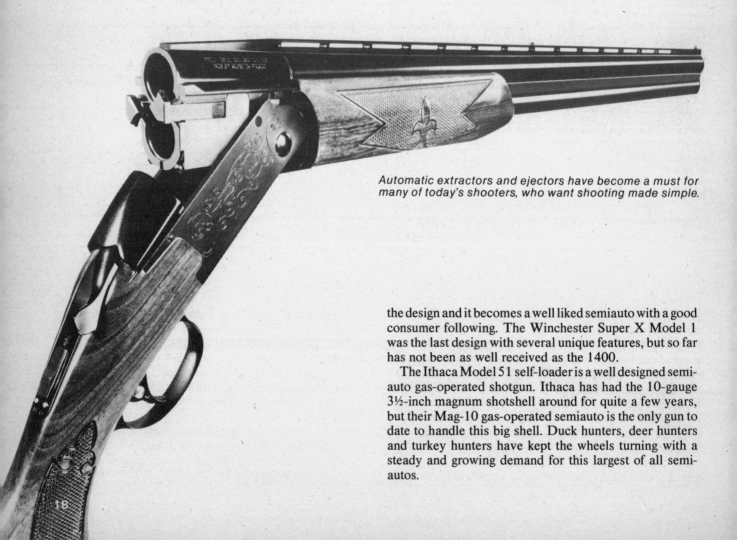

Automatic extractors and ejectors have become a must for many of today's shooters, who want shooting made simple.

the design and it becomes a well liked semiauto with a good consumer following. The Winchester Super X Model 1 was the last design with several unique features, but so far has not been as well received as the 1400.

The Ithaca Model 51 self-loader is a well designed semiauto gas-operated shotgun. Ithaca has had the 10-gauge 3½-inch magnum shotshell around for quite a few years, but their Mag-10 gas-operated semiauto is the only gun to date to handle this big shell. Duck hunters, deer hunters and turkey hunters have kept the wheels turning with a steady and growing demand for this largest of all semi-autos.

Although the mechanism involved with this Savage hammer model may appear complicated at first glance, number of parts is minimal. (Below) Engraving, gold-inlaying is becoming a lost art in this country, but not in Europe.

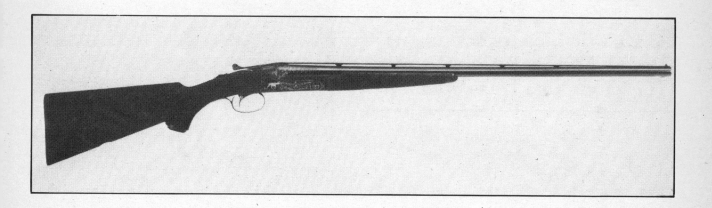

There have been numerous good gas-operated imports such as the Beretta A-301. Several Japanese designs are marketed by various firms, the most noteworthy being the Browning B/2000 and the new version, the B-80. The best to come out of the Land of the Rising Sun is the Kawaguchiya or KFC Model 250. This is a new design and not a copy of another basic idea. A short piston stroke via an independent rod imparts a sharp blow to the bolt, thus unlocking it from the barrel extension and starting it on its way rearward for extraction, ejection and loading of a new shell.

Last, and appropriately placed, is the bolt-action repeating shotgun. This all started with the Germans converting old Mauser 98 actions left over from the First World War into something resembling a shotgun. Three American companies — Savage, Mossberg and Marlin — began manufacturing a better version in the late 1920s and they have been around ever since in various model numbers. I have always felt the hunter was better off with a good break-open single-barrel in both function and speed of the second shot. The only claim to fame for the bolt-action shotgun is low cost.

For the hobbyist or professional gunsmith, historical knowledge and understanding of mechanisms of various shotguns is an absolute necessity if any skill of shotgun smithing is to be acquired.

Chapter 2

HISTORY OF THE SHOTSHELL

WHETHER YOU are interested in shooting a shotgun, reloading a shotshell, cleaning and maintaining a shotgun or repairing a shotgun, knowledge of its historical development is essential. For example, how do you make a full choke barrel shoot modified patterns without boring the choke out or developing a special spreader reload? How do you use the same barrel and choke to obtain a cylinder choke pattern? The answer is knowing the history of shotshell development.

To fully appreciate the modern shotgun shell it is necessary to know what was involved in its slow evolution over the past 130-odd years. While some components go back even further, shotshell evolvement paralleled that of the breechloading shotgun.

Today's Version Didn't Just Happen; A Great Deal Of Thought, Even Genius Has Gone Into Development

Practice through the decades has been to pour molten lead from top of shot tower into a vat of water after lead has passed through a perforated pan.

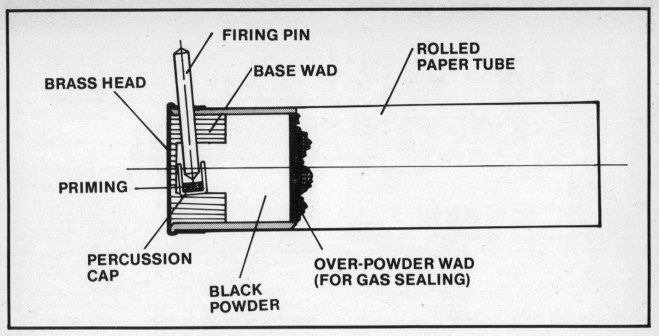

FIRING PIN

BASE WAD

ROLLED PAPER TUBE

BRASS HEAD

PRIMING

PERCUSSION CAP

BLACK POWDER

OVER-POWDER WAD (FOR GAS SEALING)

One of the earliest innovations in the design of self-contained shotshells was the pin-fire, which was short-lived.

William Watts of England is credited with the major development of modern shot with erection of the first shot tower in 1769. Prior to that shot had been moulded individually, only the larger shot sizes being possible. Smaller sizes were made by sprinkling molten led onto an angled and greased flat surface. This was commonly known as "swan shot" due to the lead "tail" attached to each of the pellets. Another system for creating shot was simply to cut small squares from a sheet of lead. This can still be done and will result in a cylinder choke pattern when fired through a full choke barrel. These flat shot are scattered widely as they encounter air pressure on the way to the target.

Drop or soft shot is pure lead. Hard shot or chilled shot is made from lead to which has been added a percentage of antimony as the hardener; the higher the percentage, the harder the shot. The term "chilled shot" came from a German inventor who blew cold air across the newly formed shot in an effort to add hardness. Plated shot, as the name implies, refers to hard shot that receives an outer coat of nickel or copper to achieve even harder shot. The purpose of hard shot is to prevent pellet deformation during the trip through the barrel; thus more shot stays with the main charge on the way to the target and results in a higher pattern percent.

Even during the flintlock period and into the percussion era the muzzleloading shotgun used some form of a powder wad to hold the powder in place and separate it from the shot. Someone discovered that if a felt wad or one of a similar material was added on top of the powder wad as a cushion, fewer shot were deformed by the initial shock of the powder pressure. For a hundred years a thin paper wad was used over the shot to keep it in place.

The oldest form of self-contained shotshell is the pin-fire shell designed by Houiller and improved to the point of actual use by the Paris gunmaker Lefaucheaux and patent-

ed in 1836. The pin-fire shell was widely adopted by English shotgun makers. Although still in production, the pin-fire has many disadvantages when it comes to sealing the rear of a chamber completely. An Englishman named Lancaster did away with the pin of the pin-fire and used a priming mixture at the rear end of the shell, a thin copper disc covering the mixture. The firing pin was blunt on the end, but sufficient force from the firing pin ignited the primer mixture and fired the shell. A thin brass head at the rear provided better chamber sealing and also a better method of extracting the fired shell. Lancaster patented this in 1852 and the system was used in many English guns.

In 1855 a French designer, M. Pottet, patented a center-fire shotshell that utilized a single primer unit much like the primers in use today. Daw of England introduced the design with some minor modifications that placed an anvil inside the primer as we do in modern primers. He secured a British patent and the shell was accepted by gunmakers all

English made a few guns with a short section of rifling at the muzzle. These guns fire shot charges as well as slugs such as this Holland & Holland Paradox slug load.

over the British Isles. Soon break-open shotguns using this shell design were in common production. The Ely brothers obtained patent rights and started production of shotshells in 1861 using the primer perfected by Daw.

The Ely shotshell was in wide use in England and the Continent during the turmoil of the Civil War in America, so few were imported into this country during these years or the years following the war.

The Ely shotshell with its paper body was expensive and almost impossible to reload. Hence most American sportsmen continued using muzzleloaders during this period; loose powder and shot was inexpensive.

While Americans were eager to embrace the new breech-loading system with its self-contained-shotshell concept, the Ely-type shell was too expensive to purchase, shoot once, then throw away. Reloading was important as sporting goods stores then were few and far between, hence shotshell development took a different road.

Edward Manard developed a reloadable shotshell that was widely used. This consisted of a drawn brass shell body and head with a primer that was pressed into the center upon a built-in anvil. Initially developed in the late 1860s, it was perfected in 1873. The only problem was the 410-grain-empty weight! The primer was of the large, flat Berdan type, but unlike modern Berdan-primed cases, which use two side flash holes, the Manard used a large single center flash hole. This resulted in primer setback when the shell was fired.

W.H. Wills patented another brass shotshell in 1864 which was marketed by Draper & Company. The body was machined from brass and thin at the front. The rear was threaded to accept a separate brass head. Ignition was

The Winchester-Western firearms empire was founded in East Alton, Illinois, where corporate headquarters remains today. The Western Cartridge Company did much to improve the shotshells of the era. This photo is of the 1900 period.

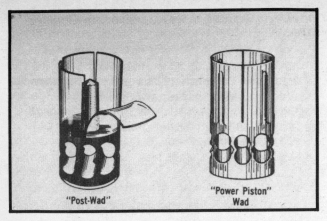

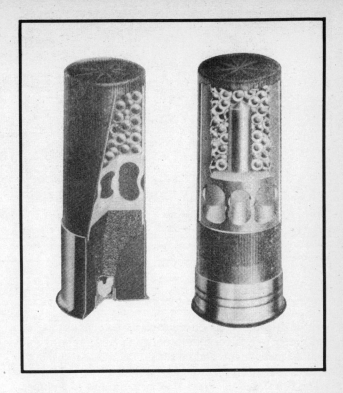

Above: Design of Remington-Peters Post Wad and Power Piston are shown. (Right) In shell at right, Post Wad is installed. Other shell is equipped with Power Piston.

via a percussion cap on a steel nipple in the shell case body; this was held in position by the screwed-in head. The advantage is that these cases could be disassembled, washed, a new common percussion cap installed and used almost indefinitely.

Remington developed the solid brass drawn shotshell case which reduced weight and cut costs drastically. The case, easy to reload with even primitive tools, gained in popularity back in the pine thickets or in the wastelands. In the 1870s, when the shell was developed, and for many years to follow, the Remington brass shotshell was welcomed by shotgunners. Winchester introduced an all-brass drawn shotshell in 1877 with similar results.

I cut my teeth on brass 10-gauge shotshells in my grandfather's double-barrel hammer Parker. He purchased the gun new in 1900 with 150 new Remington all-brass shells. Only forty-odd shells had been discarded by the early 1940s when he sold the gun! Remington continued manufacturing this shell up until 1957, which attests to its popularity.

Also in 1877 Winchester introduced a paper-body shotshell with a brass head. These were sold empty to be loaded by individuals or one of the thousands of private commercial shotshell loaders who then marketed the product under an equally bewildering number of trade names. Winchester brought out its own loaded paper-bodied shotshell in 1886 under the brand name Rival.

Black powder shotshells remained in production much later than most sportsmen realize. This was for a number of reasons, the primary being pressure.

Smokeless powder, developed by the French in 1880, was used primarily in rifle cartridges in which much higher pressure could be contained by the thick barrel. Smokeless powder creates a peak pressure curve roughly four times faster than black powder and the pressure peak is much higher.

Powder ignition proved to be another problem. The

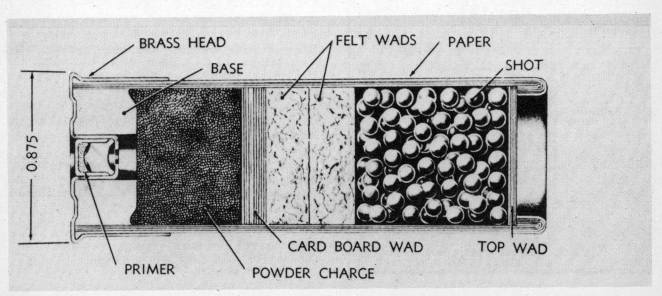

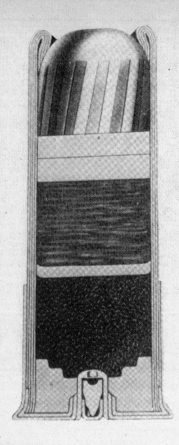

From left: The early rifled slug used a flat nitro overpowder wad. Winchester Mark V (center) was the first shell to use a plastic wrap-around of the shot rather than the plastic shot protector. This transition shell still used felt cushion wad, paper cup overpowder wad. (Right) One of the short-lived innovations was Winchester's tracer shell.

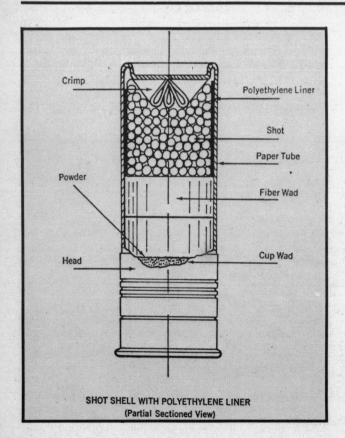

SHOT SHELL WITH POLYETHYLENE LINER
(Partial Sectioned View)

same primer could be used for rifles, pistols and shotguns if black powder was used. Black powder is ignited so easily that a small bit can be used as a priming compound. The common toy cap pistol uses a pinch of black powder between two pieces of paper. When struck a blow, the powder ignites. With black powder shotshells a simple priming system was adequate.

A shotshell requires four times as powerful a primer as a rifle in order to ignite smokeless powder due to complicated internal ballistics. Early reloaders partially solved the problem by inserting a small amount of black powder right over the primer, then adding the main charge of smokeless powder. The primer ignited the small amount of black powder, which in turn, ignited the smokeless powder.

A hotter primer was used, but the thin head of the shotshell could not support the new primer. The end result was the battery cup for the primer which remains in use today.

When smokeless powder was introduced every shotgun had Damascus barrels designed for black powder pressures. A smokeless powder shell would literally turn a

The introduction of the polyethylene liner in the Mark V Winchester shell was another development aimed at the continuing problem of reducing distortion of lead shot.

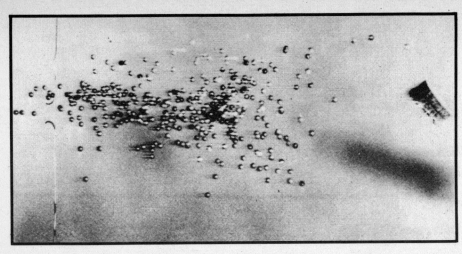

The high-speed photos show the shot pattern from shell without a plastic protector.

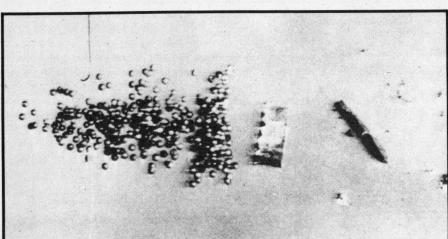

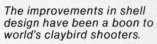

The improvements in shell design have been a boon to world's claybird shooters.

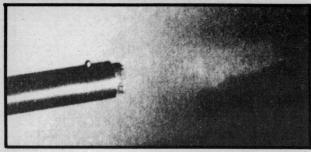

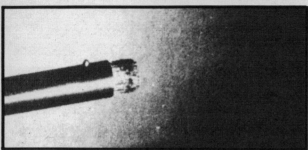

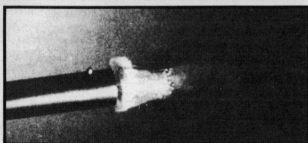

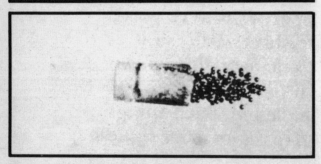

Damascus gun into an instant grenade. To this was added the reloading problem. Many Americans of that time reloaded their shotshells and thousands of independent firms loaded shells for local customers.

So, how do you get all of these people to understand that smokeless powder cannot be loaded in the same volume as black powder, but must be weighed carefully. All of this helped to retain black powder shotshells well up into the 1920s.

The dram method of shotshell measurement is by volume in both loading and stating the "power" of a shell, so the first smokeless powder shotshells constituted a compromise. This was DuPont Bulk Smokeless Shotgun Powder, which could be loaded by the dram — volume for volume with the black powder charge — but it eliminated the huge cloud of smoke generated by a black powder shell. Even today shotshells are marked *dram equivalent* as a method of stating relative power. Every box of modern shells still carries the warning against firing them in Damascus barrels.

By 1900 the paper shotshell was a waterproof paper tube sealed on one end by a brass head. The inside base head had been improved in shape, but still consisted of a

separate unit of heavy paper. The over-powder wad or nitro wad was a thick round paper disc treated to withstand the burning powder. Next came one or more felt or fiber wads that cushioned the shot. The shot charge was on top of the filler or cushion wad. Then a thin over-shot wad held the shot in place in the shell. The edges of the shell body were rolled or turned at the front to hold the over-shot wad in place. On the other end a primer in a battery cup fitted into the thin brass head of the shell. Numerous individual improvements to the basic components followed, but with no drastic changes. In 1924 James E. Burns developed a non-corrosive primer and promptly joined Remington to evolve their Kleenbore non-corrosive primer. In 1930 Western offered a non-corrosive primer of their own, followed shortly by Winchester.

Smokeless powder went from the multi-charge of black and smokeless previously described to a true smokeless variety. Bulk smokeless was used less by the manufacturers as better powder was introduced.

Felt wads were phased out slowly and cork became the main filler wad. Later a composition wad eliminated break-up in firing. Nitro wads were refined also. The combustion chamber for the powder was redesigned through the years for better, more uniform powder burning. The paper base wad was joined better with the paper body and brass head to eliminate splits, burn-through and the problem of the base wad tearing loose and entering the bore. If this happened the next shot hit the base wad and the barrel tended to open like a bird cage as it split.

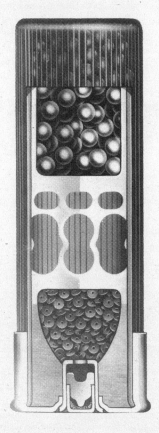

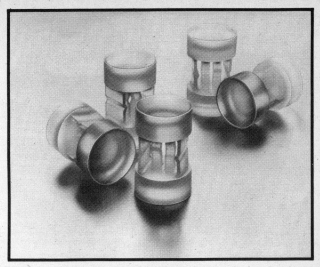

Plastic innards, in one form or another, now are used by virtually all of the major shotshell manufacturers.

By 1940 Remington was beginning to experiment with plastic-body shells, but during World War II everything came to a grinding halt.

Shotshell availability went from abundant to scarce quickly during the war. Each shell was spent with care for a replacement was not to be had. One friend of mine actually traded one of his two fine bird dogs for six boxes of shells.

During the late 1920s and the '30s cheap but high-quality shotshells had dealt reloading a blow. Hardly anyone reloaded. This changed during the war years as old reloading equipment was dusted off and pressed into service. The man who owned several boxes of brass shotshells was lucky indeed. Any type of powder was quickly snapped up and most of the long-obsolete black powder vanished from shelves and storerooms.

With war's end, sportsmen were ready for any type of shotshell. Returning GIs anxious for sport shooting swelled the ranks. Ammunition manufacturers quickly began to turn out pre-war shotshell types. Anything that went bang and spewed shot out the end of the barrel was snapped up by shell-hungry sportsmen.

Modern buckshot also is being loaded with plastic cushion material as an aid to reducing deformation of pellets.

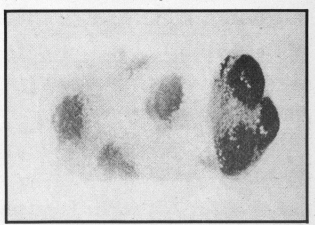

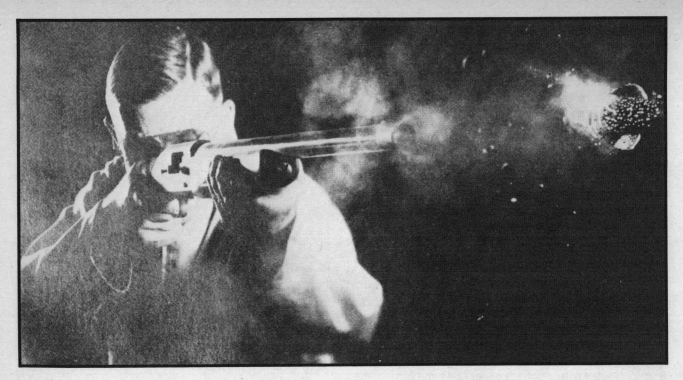

This old photo shows the shot charge and wads leaving the muzzle of a Winchester Model 59. The stop-action was able to catch the charge as the polyethylene collar was separating from the charge of shot at the upper right.

Development had not halted entirely during the war years and Winchester took an important step in 1946. The nitro or over-powder wad had previously been a flat paper disc. Winchester now cupped the rear edges until they folded back over the powder. When the shell was fired, the gas pressure pushed the cupped edge firmly against the inner shell body. It was a more efficient gas seal and hence gas leakage into the filler wads and shot diminished.

Next came elimination of the over-shot wad. When fired, the shot pushed the over-shot wad outward to remain in front of the shot initially. As air pressure built up, the wad was slowed and the heavier shot ran into the wad, dispersing around it. To solve this problem the front of the shell was folded into a pie crimp; since there was no

This series of photos illustrates the effects of protective collars on shot at various distances from the muzzle. Above, the range was at 18 inches. Left photo has shot protector, right is without. Below: same sequence, 36 inches.

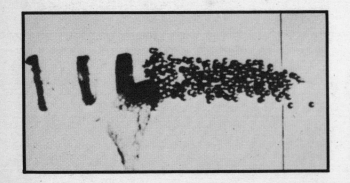 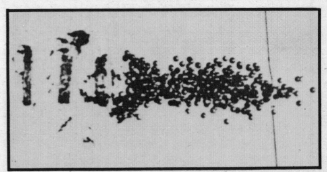

Left: Western Mark V trap load with polyethylene collar at nine inches from gun's muzzle. (Below) Effect of a cylinder bore and full choke (bottom) are shown on shot patterns. Cylinder bore offers much shorter shot column.

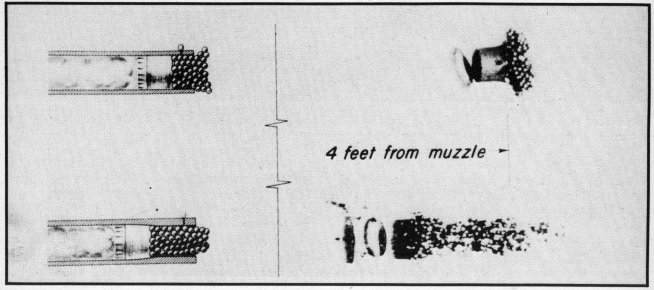

4 feet from muzzle

over-shot wad, the result was a gain in pattern percentages. In rapid succession all major manufacturers adopted the new pie crimp.

In the early Sixties Winchester wrapped a length of polyethylene plastic around the shot. This protected pellets from being scrubbed against the sides of the bore during passage up the barrel. This jumped pattern percentage at forty yards about ten percent as the formerly-deformed pellets now went along with the rest of the shot. Deformed

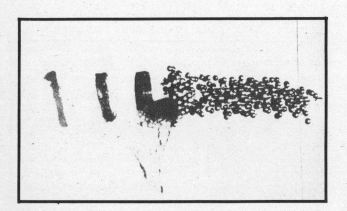

pellets offer more and various angles to wind resistance and become fliers outside of the normal pattern. The polyethylene stripped away from the shot on the way to the target.

The standard shell then became a paper cupped over-powder wad for a better seal, improved filler or cushion wads, polyethylene around the shot to protect it from being scrubbed against the bore and a pie or star crimp eliminating the over-shot wad. In a few short years the standard production shotshell had undergone more technical advances than had taken place in the previous half century.

Alcan introduced an "air wedge" plastic-cupped over-shot wad about 1960. Reloaders were warned to reduce powder charges ten percent to compensate for the better-sealed gases. About the same time they brought out the "quick cert" for reloading. This was much like the Winchester wrap, but had a circular section on the bottom and two wide wings that folded together to surround the shot. Felt filler wads still were used.

At 36 inches from the muzzle, the polyethylene collar is being dropped from 12-gauge Western Mark V trap load. This particular shot was from a full-choke shotgun.

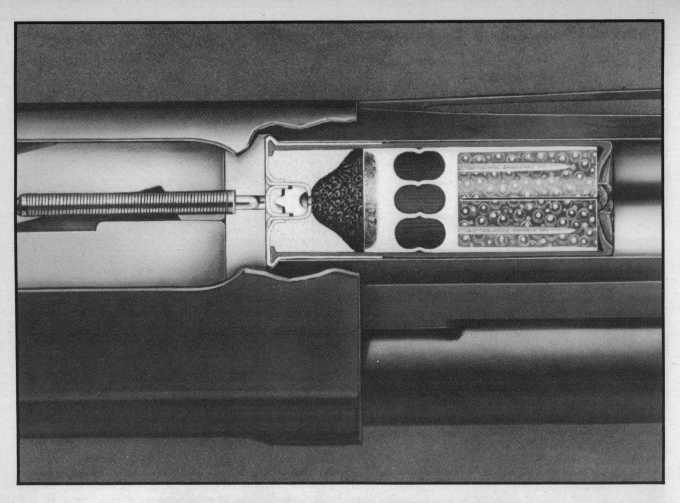

This series of artist's illustrations prepared by Remington shows how the shotshell primer is struck by firing pin causing the gun to fire.

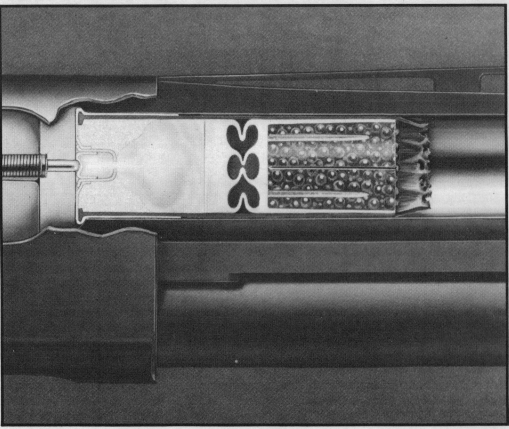

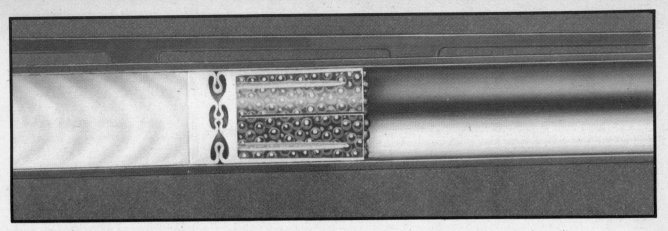

The shot is retained in the polyethylene collar as it is driven down the bore of the gun by gases from the ignited powder. Although this is an artist's concept, it follows theory for a gun that is cylinder bore.

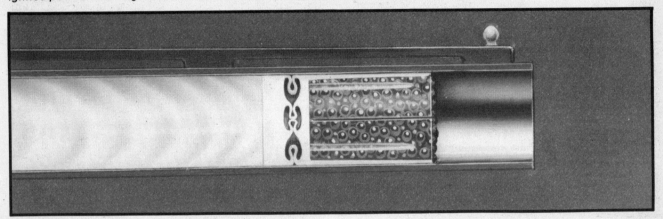

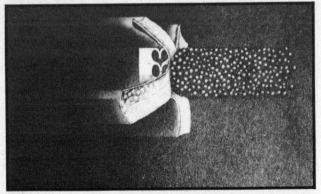

As the load reaches the muzzle, the petals of Power Piston peel back, starting to release shot string.

Remington introduced their combination consisting of the more efficient plastic-cupped over-powder wad, then a plastic cushion wad to take the place of the old felt wad; a plastic cup protected the shot, thus the whole wad was one single unit! Remington also introduced the all-plastic shotshell body. The one-unit wad was added to the combination. Eliminating the old paper base wad that held the powder as it was ignited, Remington made this unit of plastic also, bonding it to the plastic shell body.

Winchester, also deeply involved in the quiet shotshell revolution, made shotshells by the ejection mould process instead of bonding a separate plastic base wad and a plastic shell body together. Thus was born the Winchester AA shell that is so well known today. Remington added a similar shell and was followed shortly by Federal. All prompty adopted single unitized wads similar to the proven Remington Power Piston.

Few shotgunners realize that the plastic section that replaced the old felt wads was, in itself, a revolutionary improvement. Cushioning of the shot is extremely important as the shot at the rear is quickly jammed together in its quick acceleration from dead zero to roughly 10,000 psi pushing on the shot at the rear. This plastic section actually "gives" in this millisecond of time to prevent pellets from being compressed together; this results in fewer shot pellets being deformed. Any time shot pellets are not deformed out of round, these pellets remain with the main group and are more effective in striking the target.

The latest technique for reducing pellet deformation is to mix small plastic "balls" with the shot itself. This adds even greater cushioning effect during the shot compression as it starts to move and in its trip up the bore. Winchester first introduced this technique with buckshot, but now both Federal and Winchester use it for smaller size shot down to #4. Actually this is an old principle, as early reloaders mixed wheat flour with the shot to achieve the same effect. The new plastic balls simply do the old job more efficiently.

Today virtually every shotshell manufacturer utilizes the new technical evolutions outlined in the production of better grade shells. There has even been an improved powder charge and some improvements in the primer. Combined with high antimony or plated shot, the shotshell of today hits with peak performance.

Matching your gauge and shot load to the type of game you are going to hunt can make the difference when it comes to the amount of game you take in the field.

Chapter 3

THE SHOTGUN GAUGES

Magnumitis Continues To Affect Our Choices In Guns And Loads

THE CORRECT spelling when referring to shotgun bore size is often a point of confusion. The earliest spelling is G U A G E and will be found in early texts, especially those from the British Isles and occasionally in a translation. For all practical purposes it is identical to the correct spelling, which is G A U G E. A word often used incorrectly and one that has an entirely different meaning is *gage*. This term concerns taking a measurement, such as "to gage a barrel." Adding to the confusion are shotgun barrels marked *12 Caliber* or *12 Calibre* as often encountered on import guns. *Caliber* is a dimension expressed in hundredths of an inch such as .30 caliber. Technically incorrect, 12 Caliber simply means 12-gauge.

The term *gauge* is an old method of expressing a barrel or bore diameter and was used quite often for smoothbore cannon. A round ball of solid cast iron that would just pass through the bore was weighed. If the weight was, say, six pounds, the gun was termed a "six pounder" or, as abbreviated "6 pdr." Actual measurement per inch in diameter for this weight of cast iron ball was about 3.5 inches, but bore diameter was 3.6 inches, the added .1 inch being allowance to move the iron ball down the bore amid assorted residue. The allowance, incidentally, was

The range of shotgun gauges covers a broad span, ranging from the .410 bore at left up to the mighty 10-gauge (right).

Close-up of the markings on this barrel shows it was made in .410 bore, but also was marked in metric as a 12mm.

termed *windage*, meaning to allow air to escape as the ball was loaded.

With the advent of a smoothbore being attached to a wooden stock and held to one's shoulder, a similar system was used, with the bore-filling projectile a solid lead round ball. Thus a *1 bore* or *1 gauge* occurred when this solid lead ball weighed one pound. A 2 bore or 2 gauge was indicated when the ball weighed one-half pound or there were two balls to the pound. So, a 12 bore or 12-gauge simply means that a bore-filling round lead ball would weigh 1/12 pound or twelve balls per pound; likewise, sixteen to the pound, for 16 and twenty to the pound for 20-gauge.

This holds true until one reaches the .410 bore shotgun or shotshell. This is a caliber expression of .41 inch and the bore diameter is thus .410 inch, but the word *gauge* is sometimes added in common usage. If the gauge system were correctly used for this size, then the .410 would actually be 67-gauge.

This seemingly foolproof system of measuring shotgun barrel bore diameters ended up in a mass of confusion for various early gunmakers. Why, I do not know, but actual bore diameters depended upon individual makers. I guess it was caused by lead impurities. The English standardized shotgun bore diameters in the 1800s was based on a one-hundred-percent pure lead ball, the end result being:

10-gauge	.775 inch diameter
12-gauge	.729 inch diameter
16-gauge	.662 inch diameter
20-gauge	.615 inch diameter
28-gauge	.550 inch diameter

This leaves out the assorted odd-ball gauges no longer

in use and does not include the American addition of the .410 bore. This system seemed to please everyone, for it is still the accepted standard. Even those on the metric standard used the specifications, translating their specifications of millimeters from this standard to metric. If you convert a bore in millimeters back to inches, you will find that the gauge matches this table in inches.

If you were to ask most sportsmen to name the smallest shotshell currently in production, ninety-nine percent would answer ".410." Not so, as there are actually two smaller than the .410 and even more found in certain sections of the world, especially in South America.

The smallest is the .22 shotshell and I do not mean the .22 Long Rifle cartridge crimped at the mouth for what is commonly called the .22 rat shot. The .22 shotshell is a true shotshell with a brass head and a paper body. They are specifically designed for use in a smoothbore gun, usually a .22 barrel minus the lands and grooves. Winchester produced them for quite a few years and they were intended for pests up to ranges of twenty feet. This version is not currently produced in the U.S., but is quite common in Europe. The current American version is actually a .22 Long Rifle brass case with the mouth crimp and contains #12 shot pellets without a top shot wad.

More common is the European 9mm shotshell (.36 caliber) which is gaining popularity in America in recent years. Winchester produced a modified smallbore rifle in this boring around the turn of the century. It is more powerful than the rat shot .22 for dispatching vermin without blowing a hole in walls.

Virtually every pistol caliber either was or is available with a shot loading instead of a single projectile. These are not true shotshells.

The smallest of the current common gauges is the .410 which can trace its ancestry back to the .44-40 handgun and rifle cartridge. They were used primarily by exhibition shooters such as Doc Carver, Annie Oakley and others. They could break glass balls tossed in the air in a

This was the author's first shotgun, given to him on the day of his birth. It's .410 H&R chambered for 2½-inchers.

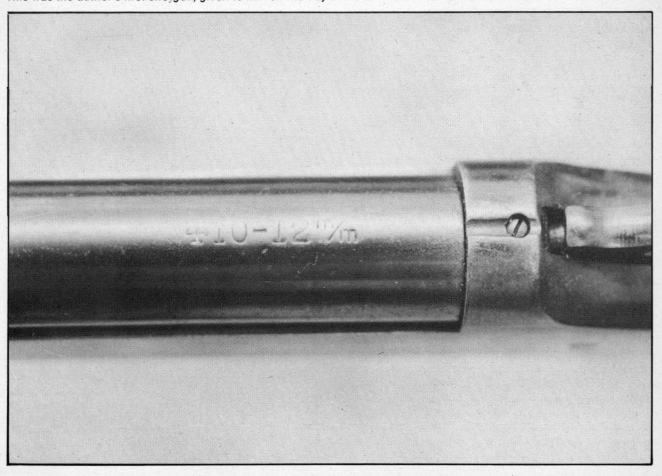

WESTERN SHOT SHELLS

Load	Gauge	Shell Length	Powder Dr.-Eq.	Shot (oz.)	Shot Sizes	Muzzle Velocity (fps)
Super-X	10	2⅞	Max.	1⅝	BB 2, 4	1330
Super-X	12	2¾	Max.	1¼	BB, 2, 4, 5, 6, 7½	1330
Super-X	12	2¾ mag	Max.	1⅜	2, 4, 6	1315
Super-X	12	3 mag	Max.	1⅜	BB, 2, 4, 6	1315
Super-X	12	3 mag	Max.	1⅝	BB, 2, 4, 5, 6	1315
Super-X	12	3 mag	Max.	1⅞	BB, 2, 4	1250
Super-X	16	2-9/16	Max.	1⅛	2, 4, 5, 6, 7½	1240
Super-X	16	2¾	Max.	1⅛	2, 4, 5, 6, 7½	1295
Super-X	16	2¾ mag	Max.	1¼	2, 4, 6	1295
Super-X	20	2¾	Max.	1	2, 4, 5, 6, 7½	1220
Super-X	20	2¾ mag	Max.	1⅛	2, 4, 6	1220
Super-X	20	3 mag	Max.	1⅛	6 (Lub.)	1295
Super-X	20	3 mag	Max.	1³/₁₆	4 (Lub.)	1295
Super-X	28	2¾	Max.	¾	4, 6, 7½	1295
Super-X	28	2¾	Max.	¾	9 (Skeet load)	1200
Super-X	.410	2½	Max.	½	4, 5, 6, 7½	1135
Super-X	.410	3	Max.	¾	4, 5, 6, 7½	1135
Super-X	.410	2½	Max.	½	9 (Skeet load)	1200
Super-X	.410	3	Max.	¾	9 (Skeet load)	1150
Xpert	12	2¾	3	1	4, 5, 6, 8	1235
Xpert	12	2¾	3	1⅛	4, 5, 6, 8, 9	1200
Xpert	12	2¾	3¼	1⅛	4, 5, 6, 8	1255
Xpert	12	2¾	3¼	1¼	7½, 8	1220
Xpert Super Target	12	2¾	2¾	1⅛	7½, 8	1145
Xpert Super Target	12	2¾	3	1⅛	7½, 8, 9	1200
Xpert	16	2-9/16	2½	1	4, 5, 6, 8, 9	1165
Xpert	16	2¾	2¾	1⅛	4, 6, 8	1185
Xpert Super Target	16	2¾	2½	1	9 (Skeet load)	1200
Xpert	20	2¾	2¾	⅞	4, 5, 6, 8, 9	1155
Xpert	20	2¾	2½	1	4, 6, 8	1165
Xpert Super Target	20	2¾	2¼	⅞	9 (Skeet load)	1200

arrive at .47244, or .47 caliber. Confusing isn't it? Nevertheless, some early .410-bore shotguns have the 12mm designation. My grandfather gave me a shotgun the day I was born, a single-barrel Harrington & Richardson so marked.

Actually the 2½-inch .410 shell is the better of the two choices as far as actual pattern performances go and is the designated length of skeet shooters. We are a nation afflicted with magnumitis and not content to let well enough alone, so answering the call of the paying public, Winchester introduced the .410 three-inch shotshell in 1932 and this has been the common chambering ever since.

Every season well meaning parents purchase guns in this gauge for budding young sportsmen based entirely on the idea that "it looks about right for junior." It is the

circus tent without perforating said tent or endangering paying customers.

To gain more shot pellets in the load, the .44-40 case was lengthened to become the .44 XL (Extra Long). This was further lengthened and changed to a true shotshell with a brass head and paper body to end up with the .410 designation. This was a two-inch case but changed further to a standard 2½-inch length.

Quite a few early single-barrel guns were made in this gauge by both American and European manufacturers. To further add to the dimension of bore puzzle, they were often stamped for the 12mm shotshell or 12mm gauge. If one converts the 12 millimeter (multiply by .03937), you

CONVERSION CHART
Millimeters to Thousandths Inch

Millimeters	Thousandths	Millimeters	Thousandths
18.5	.729	15.7	.619
18.4	.725	15.6	.615
18.3	.721	15.5	.611
18.2	.717	15.4	.607
18.1	.713	15.3	.603
18	.709	15.2	.599
17.9	.705	15.1	.595
17.8	.701	15	.591
17.7	.697	14.9	.587
17.6	.693	14.8	.583
17.5	.689	14.7	.579
17.4	.685	14.6	.575
17.3	.681	14.5	.571
17.2	.677	14.4	.567
17.1	.673	14.3	.563
17	.669	14.2	.559
16.9	.666	14.1	.555
16.8	.662	14	.551
16.7	.658	13.9	.547
16.6	.654	13.8	.543
16.5	.650	13.7	.539
16.4	.646	13.6	.536
16.3	.642	13.5	.532
16.2	.638	13.4	.528
16.1	.634	13.3	.524
16	.630	13.2	.520
15.9	.626	13.1	.516
15.8	.622	13	.512

Chamber dimensions have varied considerably over the decades and shotshells have been redesigned for that reason. However, chamber dimensions now are standardized in the industry and today's shells follow the same specifications.

worst possible shotgun choice, for the .410 is an expert's gauge and even they have difficulty with consistent hits. One has but to watch a skilled shooter use a 12 or 20 at skeet with no difficulty, then the 28-gauge with similar results, but start to miss when he switches to the .410 class.

The 28-gauge had its beginning back in 1903 when it was introduced by the Parker Gun Company as the ideal light guage for young sportsmen and the ladies. The first chambers were 2½-inch length and fired a ⅝-ounce shot load.

In 1930 the length was changed to a standard 2¾-inch length and the shot charge boosted an additional ⅛-ounce to ¾ ounce of shot where it remained as the standard loading until 1950 when the shot load went up to a full ounce, thus "magnumizing" the 28-gauge into the light 20-gauge load class.

There also was an effort to stretch chamber length of a

few 28-gauge guns to a 2⅞-inch length, but for once common sense prevailed and the chamber length was dropped back to the current 2¾-inch length. Guns in this chamber length and using the ¾-ounce shot charge are racy little lightweight devils that soon will win the heart of one who admires the upland-game shotgun. The current market is seeing a surge in the popularity of the game-style shotguns in 28-gauge, especially the imported side-by-side doubles.

The 20-gauge is considered by many as the finest upland-game gauge available and they get no argument from me. It is the best selection for a young shooter and when used in conjunction with the ⅞-ounce shot load will give no more recoil than the ill-chosen .410 bore. As the need for a heavier shot load is desired, the same gun will handle the excellent one-ounce load.

Muzzleloading shotguns were available in 20-gauge bore diameter and when the change came to the breechloader and a self-contained shotshell, the 20 was a natural. It was first made in a two-inch chamber length, but was quickly changed to 2½-inch length and a ½-ounce shot load. Quite a few of the early breechloaders and a few pumps will be found in this chamber length and the latter 2¾-inch shell should not be fired in such chambers. In the years following World War I, the shot load went up to ⅞ ounce. In 1926 the chamber length was standardized at 2¾ inches and the one-ounce shot load became common.

Magnumitis reared its head and the 20-gauge went up to three-inch chamber length prior to World War I, with several double-barrels being offered in this length; Stevens even brought out a pump in this chamber length. It died on the vine but was resurrected by Winchester in their Model 21 double-barrel. The first loading of the three-inch shells was 1⅛ ounces of shot, but this climbed to 1-3/16, then to 1¼ ounces, which put it into the 12-gauge field load category.

The 16-gauge has its largest following in two locations: Continental Europe and our Southeastern states. It is an old gauge with its beginning rooted in the days of the muzzleloading shotgun, for many "light game guns" were bored in this gauge. Until 1926 the standard chamber length was 2-9/16 inches, but was changed to the current 2¾-inch length. It has remained in the shorter length in much of Europe with the designation of 65mm.

There is an item that should be closely checked by 16-gauge owners. The early American 16s are stamped simply *16 gauge* while the longer chamber is always stamped as *16 gauge 2¾ inch*. Conversion to the longer chamber is no problem and it will readily accept the 2¾-inch shell. The mad dumping of double-barrel 16-gauge guns of European birth during the 1950s and '60s found most of them with the 65mm short chamber length and kept a lot of us in beans converting them to the 2¾-inch chamber, which is 70mm.

The primary advantage of the old 16-gauge guns is that

The variations in shotshell sizes to match gauges and the loads they carry should meet almost any game contingency.

Becoming familiar with the capabilities of specific gauges and shotshell loads is a must for good hunting success.

most were made on 20-gauge frames or a frame between the 20 and 12 in weight, thus resulting in a light shotgun that could handle all of the 20-gauge loads and up to the field load 12-gauge of 1¼ ounces of shot. Alas, it is a dying gauge primarily because most modern 16s are built on the heavy 12-gauge receiver or frame, thus eliminating one of its practical advantages.

The increasing popularity of the 20-gauge shotgun with the three-inch chamber duplicates in essence the load capability of the 16-gauge and adds to its demise. What few realize is that the 16-gauge will give about ten percent better pattern efficiency with the same load as the three-inch 20-gauge, load for load. This is due to the larger bore diameter handling the shot charge with less pellet deformation to rob the shot pattern of usable pellets.

The 12-gauge is the most popular of all the gauges on a world-wide basis. Regardless of whether you are in a desert or jungle, if there is a local store selling shotshells, they invariably have something in 12-gauge. It is number one in sales in the U.S. and most other countries through-

out the world and has held this position year after year with no change in sight. Probably one reason for this popularity is the versatility of available shells that range from the stubby English two-inch length up to the popular three-inch length with just about every shot size and load available from some company.

Oddly enough, in the muzzleloading era and the early period of the breechloader, the 12-gauge was considered a ladies' gauge. Any man caught afield with one was promptly called a sissy. The big gauges reigned supreme all the way up to the 2-gauge, with the 10-gauge considered as the standard for normal hunting. One of the primary reasons for this was that most guns were straight cylinder bore. Without choke, to increase range one increased gauge and thus the shot load that the bigger bore would handle. Although Fred Kimbel developed choke boring as early as 1867, it remained for W.W. Greener to put it into practical use and production around 1874. Like most new ideas, it required time to filter down to the average shooter.

The early breechloaders were chambered 2½ inches

Walker has settled on what he considers his favorite loads for claybirding or field. Two upper boxes at left were made in Japan under contract for Ely. Center box at bottom is of Polish make; others are American-made.

and some 2⅝ which became the accepted standard up until 1926 when the 2¾-inch chamber length was adopted. Shotguns in 12-gauge with a birthdate prior to 1926 should be checked with a chamber depth gauge for the same reasons explained previously in regard to the short-chamber 16-gauge.

The 12-gauge 2¾-inch chambered shotgun has become the standard by which all other gauges and chamber lengths are measured. The British have brought this chambering to near perfection and refined the shotshells for it to close to maximum performance with the 1¼-ounce shot load being about their maximum and often referred to as the Express load.

Americans seemed obsessed with the notion that hits are in ratio to the number of shot that one can cram into a given space and we have magnumized the 2¾ to the short magnum load of 1⅝ ounces of shot. In my thinking, this becomes a matter of having your brains kicked out, obtaining an inferior pattern, then paying for the privilege!

In the early 1920s the three-inch chamber length was perfected for double-barrel guns and saw some acceptance primarily among duck hunters. In 1935 Winchester brought out their 12-gauge pump with a three-inch chamber and termed it a heavy 12-gauge duck gun. Everybody then jumped on the bandwagon and there is hardly a 12-gauge model gun that cannot be obtained for the 12-gauge three-inch shell.

Many hit upon the idea that the all-purpose gun would be one chambered for the three-inch 12, then have a choice of using either the 2¾-inch shell in light loads up to the short magnum or the full-blown three-inch shell with its 1⅞ ounces of shot. Sounds good, but there is a fly in the pudding. Weight must be taken into consideration, for all three-inch chambered guns are beefed up in certain places to take the constant pounding. So you end up with a heavy gun to lug around to fire a shell that was in reality designed for a gun weighing about two pounds less.

At least five thousand people have asked me at one time or another if their 2¾-inch 12-gauge could be rechambered to take the three-inch shell and would it be safe. Most guns can be rechambered for the longer shell and safely contain the charge. But the action was designed for the lighter shell and it is only a matter of time before the constant pounding batters the gun and its action into a hopeless state. The same is true for the 20-gauge chambered for the 2¾ shell.

The three-incher has its place: to handle about 1½-ounce loads maximum. Beyond that, one should switch to the 10-gauge. Its buckshot loading has its place in the game, but personally I prefer two separate guns: one for light 2¾ shotshells, the other for heavy loads such as buckshot.

The original chambering for the 10-gauge was 2⅞, but in the early 1930s Ithaca brought out their double for the new 3½-inch chamber length and shotshells. The shorter chamber brought the big 10-gauge to maximum efficiency starting with its 1¼-ounce shot load, working up to a maximum load of 1⅝ ounces. It held sway as the best long-range combination for many years, until the three-inch 12 shell pushed it aside with an identical loading.

The 10-gauge with the 3½-inch chamber will handle the two-ounce shot load with amazing pattern efficiency. For many years hunters were saddled with shot size only in the larger selections and developed for long-range duck and geese. Finally, with the gain in popularity of the 10-gauge, more shot size selection was made available. Oddly enough there were no buckshot size offerings,

although it was a natural. Hunters were forced into removing standard shot from their shells and substituting buckshot, hardly a safe practice!

Ithaca gave the 10-gauge a big boost when they introduced their Mag-10, the only semiauto that handles the big shell. It has gained a large following and is being used for turkey and deer as well as waterfowl. This is the second time that this firm has been a leader with the 10-gauge 3½ chambering. There is one man who has been like a lone voice in the wilderness in his steadfast boosting for the 10, 3½ load. Elmer Keith has been a 10-gauge supporter for more years than most shooters have lived. I remember being literally dragged from a talk with friends so he could show me a new over/under for the big gauge at a trade show.

There is no single gauge that will cover all hunting requirements. Once this decision is reached and the search for the illusionary all-purpose shotgun is abandoned, one can start selecting the gauge or gauges that will perform the hunting requirement with maximum efficiency.

The more you learn about shotgun gauges, their good points and their limitations, the better armed you are to make a sensible selection.

The author contends — and many agree — that the best home or store protector is a good 12-gauge riot gun.

Chapter 4

MATCHING SHOTSHELL TO GUN

Arriving At The Best Combination Can Take Time, A Lot Of Shooting

THE BIGGEST single failing of shotgunners is in matching their shotshells to their guns and to the intended game. Lack of knowledge is one factor, of course, but the underlying fault is simply the effort to buy proficiency.

I doubt whether any golf enthusiast would think of taking his clubs out three months out of the year, leaving those clubs in the hall closet the other nine months, then expect to play well. Yet this is precisely what the average shotgunner does. Then when he fails to bag game, the fault is the gun or his shells, never is it his lack of practice. Out he goes to buy the latest gun and the most powerful shotshells on the market. He expects to gain proficiency with the shotgun by emptying his wallet.

Sometimes a different train of thought comes into play. Take the current crop of so-called "game loads" available at just about any outlet selling ammunition, and which are seen on the floor of mass merchandisers still in the carton at the "lowest price in town." The shell body is paper, the internal base wad is made from something resembling paper mache partially stuck to the shell body. It is displaced easily — often into the gun bore — which results in a split barrel on the next shot. There is some form of thin cup paper wad over the powder. The powder is some unknown mixture, purchased at wherever price was lowest. The filler wads resemble a mixed felt and paper composition. Some have shot protectors, some do not. Those that do, use plastic or some cheap cup. Pie or star crimps are erratic in shape giving the impression that anything is acceptable if the shot does not roll out.

To buy these cheapies is taking a step backward in shotshell technology to 1955. The shot is of the dropped or chilled variety with emphasis on cost saving; one ounce is standard in most 12-gauge loads. When you consider all of the money spent to get to the game field, associated equipment, and how few shots one really gets at wild game, the whole thing gets a bit silly. If you doubt this, shoot a few patterns at paper with these shells and compare hits with those from a good shell. Even at dove shooting, where shots are fast and furious, one seldom expends more than two or three boxes of shells. With the cheapies the chances of a hit are reduced about fifty percent or more per shot. So what is the actual cost per bird and what monetary saving was actually effected?

British sportsmen lead the pack in resisting any change in tradition. They have a love affair with the side-by-side shotgun and little good to say about any other form of shotgun. The 12-gauge dominates their thinking, but when it comes to matching a shotshell to the game, they are hard to beat!

The British standard 12-gauge shotshell is 2½ inches in length. Their light field load consists of 3-dram equivalent with one ounce of shot. The standard field load is 3-dram equivalent with 1-1/16 ounces of shot. Both loads give velocity of 1150 to 1200 feet per second (fps) with about 8500 pounds per square inch (psi) breech pressure. When used in their light 6- to 6½-pound shotguns, recoil is well within acceptable limits and the guns are a joy to use in a full day of hunting. The British consider 3 drams equivalent and 1⅛ ounces of shot as a heavy field load and it is used only in guns that weigh seven pounds or a bit over. The 3¼-dram equivalent and 1¼ ounces of shot is considered an express load and is fired only in a 7½- to 8-pound shotgun.

This is a far cry from the American sportsman's usual selection of a shotshell. Our lightest 12-gauge is 2¾ inches in length and loads 3 drams of powder and 1⅛ ounces of shot. These are considered target or light field loads. The 3¼ dram equivalent with 1¼ ounces of shot is our standard field hunting load. Our short magnum shells usually contain 3¾ dram equivalent of powder and either 1½ or 1⅜ ounces of shot. Most of our shotguns are chambered for the 12-gauge three-inch shell which carries 4 dram equivalent powder behind 1⅝ ounces of shot while the real heavies go 1⅞ ounces of shot!

The average American sportsman seems to have an unending love affair with anything that has the word magnum associated with it in shotguns, but few know how to use it properly on select game. Most are lousy shots due to the anticipated heavy recoil from the shells. Add to this the slower swing with the heavier magnum shotguns, and it is not a picture of competent shotgunning on the game field!

If the average shooter takes the time to shoot a few patterns on paper with both the magnum and standard shells, it is a revelation. He will shoot more efficient patterns with the lighter loads. In a proper weight shotgun the load would balance with the gun and the result would be more game per shot.

Matching shotshell to gun and game is not complicated and is beneficial in all of the gauges. The trick is to make one's decision based on facts gained from actual pattern results and not on something read or heard.

Take the lowly .410 bore which is available in either the 2½-inch or the magnum 3-inch shell. Which will deliver the best pattern? The 2½-inch is the correct answer. Why? The 2½-inch normally is loaded with one-half ounce of shot, the three-inch with three-quarters or eleven-sixteenths ounce. This is a shotgun with a bore diameter of .410-inch, hence when the shot weight is increased, the shot column length increases in much greater ratio than a similar gain within a greater bore diameter. What is not known is that chamber pressure really climbs with this small diameter, some creating more than a 12-gauge three-inch! So the shot is mashed, becomes out of round and hence a weaker pattern percent. Those who doubt should shoot some patterns and learn.

Also remember that the .410 is a twenty-five-yard shotshell. With a weak pattern due to the small amount of shot that must be used with any efficiency, #6 shot is about the smallest practical for game birds with 7½ size stretching things. But in the hands of a real good shooter who knows the effective range and picks his shots, it will do well. One fellow I know delights in using the 2½-inch shell with one-half ounce of #6 and makes fools of a lot of shooters on the dove field. But every shot is well within that twenty-five yards. He simply uses the most efficient shotshell and knows the range limitation of the shotgun.

As stated before, the 28-gauge is a beautiful little gun on upland game provided one steers clear of the magnum one-ounce loads. I hunt quail with a fellow who constantly shoots a beautiful little 28 side-by-side. He sticks to the three-quarter-ounce load with #7½ shot and he can best be summed up in one word: deadly. When using a 20- or a 12-gauge he is a firm believer in #8 shot. Why the change in shot size? Pellet penetration becomes extremely important with any smaller gauge that limits pellet load to gain pattern efficiency, so each hit has to be hard to anchor game.

For some reason I have never understood fully, just about every 28-gauge is choked too tight for practical shooting. I remember one above-average shooter who either missed quail completely or put so many pellets in one that it looked like a screen door. I checked the boring on his double and found both barrels had tight full chokes. As the owner had given me full authority to do what I thought best, I rechoked the gun to improved cylinder in one barrel, modified in the other.

With the pattern board placed at the appropriate distance — thirty yards in the case of the 28-gauge — I fired several tests patterns with each barrel and found a big

There is high satisfaction in knowing the capabilities of a gun and its load before venturing into the field.

The introduction of increasingly more powerful loads has caused a reevaluation of the relationship between some models and the loads.

improvement with an even distribution of the pellets in the thirty-inch circle. On the game field the result was a dropped bird at about every shot. All loadings were tested with several shot sizes. In this specific gun the best results were with the three-quarters-ounce load and #7½ shot, but I have seen similar guns give better results with the only a change in shot size to 8s. You have to shoot each gun with each load to determine maximum performance.

The 20-gauge 2¾-inch shotshell is a jewel to shoot and use when the dram equivalent is lowered and the shot weight reduced much more than is commonly believed. I refer to the 2½-dram-equivalent with the seven-eighths-ounce shot load. This is hard to find in anything except a skeet loading, but if you choose to reload, it is no problem to deposit the chosen shot size in the hull. In an ultralight 20, it is not far from the 28-gauge in weight or recoil, but delivers a much more efficient pattern.

Alas, the public does not like light loads and manufacturers sell what the public desires, so we are left with the 2½-dram-equivalent load and a full ounce of shot. Even this is a high-quality selection although recoil is a wee bit more. You can find about any shot size you want in this shot selected weight. I would only recommend trying the various sizes to learn what an individual gun patterns best. When you go up to 2¾ drams equivalent and a 1⅛-ounce shot load you are getting away from the whole purpose of the 20-gauge shotgun and trying to turn it into a 16- or a 12-gauge. If you take the time to shoot a few patterns with both

This old Browning was built to handle shells with light loads. When it was fired with short magnums, the action spring tube was broken from the rear of the receiver. The constant pounding of heavy loads will damage any shotgun.

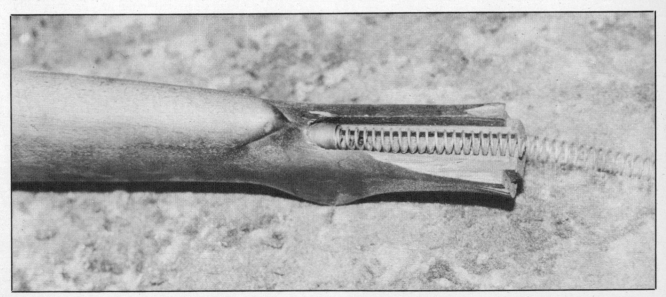

the 1- and 1⅛-ounce loads, same shot size, you will find the one-ounce load gives more efficient patterns with better pellet penetration.

I personally have an intense dislike for the 20-gauge three-inch magnum and make no apology. It is a miserable gun to shoot, recoilwise, in all but a weight that would tend to convince one he was lugging a 12-gauge all day! In any weight approching what one would expect in a 20-gauge, or even a light 16 for that matter, it is unpleasant to shoot more than once or twice. I am not overly sensitive to recoil, having spent a half century with all types of firearms, but I see no reason to absorb unnecessary recoil.

So if you are going to carry a gun with 12-gauge weight, yet shoot only the field load of 3¼-dram-equivalent — 1¼-ounce which, incidentally, is what the 20-gauge three-inch shoots — they might as well carry a 12-gauge and gain the advantage of a larger bore diameter which will increase the pattern percentage by ten percent or more! Most shotgunners never learn that the bigger the bore diameter, the more efficient it will shoot a given shot weight or shot pellet size. So what is the reason for the three-inch 20-gauge from a practical field shooting position? None that I have ever learned, provided the usual load of plain bull is shoveled away to reveal plain facts!

Few modern shotgunners have ever seen a 16-gauge in all of its glory. Should you pick up a modern 16 for a close look, you will see that almost without exception it is simply a 12-gauge modified to 16 with all the weight and handling characteristics of the heavier 12 of the same model. The only thing gained is a slightly lighter shotshell. Few shooters really get a good impression of the 16-gauge in this format and I do not blame them for turning the thing down and buying a 12-gauge at the same price.

But, pick up one of the older Browning Sweet Sixteen autoloaders and compare it to a same model 12-gauge. You will start to get a much clearer idea of what a true 16-gauge shotgun should look and feel like when put to one's shoulder The same can be said for the early Remington Model 11-48 semiautos; they too were built on a much lighter frame and gave that light feel when mounted to the shoulder. Some of the early classic side-by-sides such as the Fox Sterlingworth and L.C. Smith had the same "true 16-gauge feeling."

Occasionally you can pick up one of the fine European side-by-side 16s that were sold by the carloads in the United States in the 1960s as surplus. These normally have the European 65mm chambers that must be run out to 70mm (2¾-inch), but most important is the fact that the gun was built for the true 16-gauge shell. One gets the impression that the gun he is holding is a slightly heavy 20-gauge, but with a clean swing.

You can go back to the lightest of 16 loads which is 2½ dram equivalent and one full ounce of shot, thus placing the gun in the 20-gauge class. The finest load ever develop-

The increasing popularity of claybird games has made the match-up of gun to ammo a preoccupation with many of today's shooters. Ammo has been improved drastically.

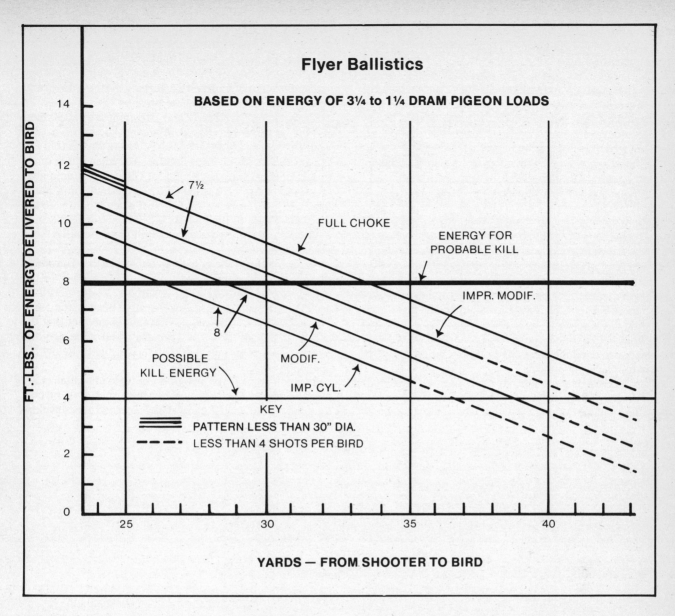

Flyer Ballistics

BASED ON ENERGY OF 3¼ to 1¼ DRAM PIGEON LOADS

(chart with Y-axis: FT.-LBS. OF ENERGY DELIVERED TO BIRD, X-axis: YARDS — FROM SHOOTER TO BIRD)

7½

8

FULL CHOKE

ENERGY FOR PROBABLE KILL

IMPR. MODIF.

POSSIBLE KILL ENERGY

MODIF.

IMP. CYL.

KEY
PATTERN LESS THAN 30" DIA.
LESS THAN 4 SHOTS PER BIRD

ed for the 16-gauge was the 2¾-dram-equivalent with 1⅛ ounces of shot. This delivered a pattern that was beautiful to see and the recoil was at absolute minimum. Three drams of powder with the same 1⅛ was available, but there was no practical need for the extra powder.

The love affair with the magnum load pushed the 16 past where it should be and little was gained except more profit for shotshell makers. Couple this fact with the already stated placing of a 16-gauge on a 12-gauge frame and you have the answer to the demise of the 16-gauge shtogun in the United States.

The big 10-gauge is, in my opinion, the sleeping giant of

The old shotgun was built to handle lesser loads than today's magnums. When magnums were fired in it, forend split, locking lug broke and bolt jammed to rear.

Free Recoil Energies In Foot Pounds Shotshell Loads

Load	Gun Weight in Pounds										
	5	5½	6	6½	7	7¼	7½	7¾	8	8½	9
12 — 4¼-1⅝	83.5	76.0	69.5	64.5	60.0	57.5	55.5	54.0	52.0	49.0	46.5
12 — 3¾-1¼	50.0	45.5	42.0	39.0	36.0	34.5	33.0	32.5	31.5	29.5	28.0
12 — 3¼-1⅛	40.0	36.5	33.5	31.0	28.5	27.5	26.5	26.0	25.0	23.5	22.5
12 — 3-1⅛	34.0	31.0	28.5	26.5	24.5	23.5	22.5	22.0	21.5	20.0	19.0
12 Skeet	33.0	30.0	27.5	25.5	24.0	22.5	22.0	21.5	20.5	19.5	18.5
12 — 3-1	28.0	25.5	23.5	21.5	20.0	19.0	18.5	18.0	17.5	16.5	15.5
16 — 3-1⅛	38.0	34.5	31.5	29.0	27.0	26.0	25.5	24.5	23.5	22.5	21.0
16 — 2¾-1⅛	36.5	33.0	30.5	28.0	26.0	25.0	24.5	23.5	23.0	21.5	20.5
16 — 2½-1	25.5	23.5	21.5	20.0	18.5	18.0	17.5	16.5	16.0	15.0	14.5
16 Skeet	27.0	24.5	22.5	21.0	19.5	18.5	18.0	17.5	17.0	16.0	15.0
20 — 2¾-1	24.0	22.0	20.0	18.5	17.5	16.5	16.0	15.5	15.0	14.0	13.5
20 — 2¼-⅞	19.0	17.0	16.0	14.5	13.5	13.0	12.5	12.0	11.5	11.0	10.5
20 Skeet	21.5	19.5	18.0	16.5	15.5	15.0	14.5	14.0	13.5	12.5	12.0
28 — 2¼-¾	21.0	19.0	17.0	16.0	15.0	14.5	14.0	13.0	13.0	12.0	11.5
.410 — 3"	13.0	12.0	11.0	10.0	9.0	9.0	8.5	8.5	8.0	7.5	7.0
.410 — 2½"	6.5	6.0	5.5	5.0	4.5	4.5	4.5	4.0	4.0	4.0	3.5

shotshells and is just now starting to come out of deep hibernation to take its rightful place. In the old 2⅞-inch case length it still will do everything the three-inch magnum 12-gauge will and do it a lot better. You have the gun weight to easily absorb the extra powder of such loads and that larger bore diameter will pattern the same identical weight of shot into a closer pattern and with much better pellet distribution within the accepted thirty-inch pattern circle. In other words, when you leave the shot weight bracket of the standard 12-gauge, the 10-gauge shotshell in 2⅞-inch length takes over to deliver that heavy weight of the shot load with maximum efficiency. Step up to the more common 3½-inch case length and you also step up to the shot weight of the heaviest of the 12-gauge three-inch

magnum loads of 1⅞ ounces of shot, handling it efficiently. The full and common two-ounce load is about the same as the standard 12-gauge 2¾ load as far as efficient patterns are concerned. The 2⅛-ounce 10 load is also easily handled. With the 10-gauge 2¼-ounce load, which is current maximum, you are about at the same efficiency level as a 12-gauge with 1½ or 1⅜ shot weight. In my opinion, one could consider the 2½-ounce load as absolute maximum in a 10-gauge bore diameter.

Reloaders are teaching ammunition manufacturers what the 10-gauge is capable of doing and the latter are playing the catch-up game in technology. With the addition of *graf* or powdered plastic to the lead shot pellets, especially in the larger size of shot, this load is fantastic in

SUGGESTED SHOT SIZES
FOR TARGET AND GAME

UPLAND SHOOTING

Woodcock, Snipe, Rail and small shore birds.	#8 or #9
Dove, Quail (Grouse during the early part of the season when ranges are short)	#7½ or #8
Pheasant, Prairie Chicken, Rabbit, Squirrel (Grouse in the latter part of the season when ranges are longer)	#4, #5, #6
Turkey	#2 or #4

WATER FOWL SHOOTING

Ducks (over decoys)	#5 or #6
Ducks (pass shooting)	#4
Geese	#2 or #4

TRAP SHOOTING

For all Trap Shooting	#7½ or #8

SKEET SHOOTING

For all Skeet shooting	#8 or #9

APPROXIMATE NUMBER OF PELLETS IN A GIVEN CHARGE

SHOT SIZE	OUNCES OF POWDER										
	2	1⅞	1⅝	1½	1⅜	1¼	1⅛	1	⅞	¾	½
#2	180	169	158	135	124	113	102	90	79	68	45
#4	270	253	221	202	195	169	152	135	118	101	67
#5	340	319	277	255	234	213	192	170	149	128	85
#6	450	422	396	337	309	281	253	225	197	169	112
#7½	700	656	568	525	481	437	393	350	306	262	175
#8	820	769	667	615	564	513	462	410	359	308	205
#9	1170	1097	951	855	804	731	658	585	512	439	292

Note: The exact number of pellets can vary depending upon brand and lot.

long-range shooting, easily reaching fifty yards and beyond! It is only in recent times — no more than two years — that ammunition manufacturers brought a 10-gauge shell to the marketplace with anything but the old two-ounce loading of very heavy shot. Reloaders passed this five years ago. Buckshot in a 10-gauge was a wild dream except when a shooter could find some of the older 2⅞-inch shells as no buckshot was available in the 3½-inch shells. Today, it is available, but to the best of my knowledge not one manufacturer is offering a 10-gauge slug. It is available from the mould makers if you wish to cast your own. I would give odds it will be available commercially within two or three years.

As previously stated, no gauge compares with the 12 in popularity and probably more design work has gone into this gauge than any other. Most of the development work on this gauge has been done in Great Britain and the United States. The British lean toward the lighter loads and consider the 3¼-dram equivalent and 1¼ ounces of shot as about maximum. Our own shotgunners consider the foregoing a medium load and press forward to the short magnum loadings in 2¾-inch chambering.

A few years ago, one would have activated a hornet's nest to suggest the short magnums were too much. However the high cost of such shells has caused American sportsmen to take a good hard second look at the situation. Most target shooters, who fire more shells in a weekend than most shooters do in a lifetime, have led the way in backing away from unnecessary heavy loads. The 3-dram-equivalent with one ounce of shot has gained immense popularity and even the 2¾-dram equivalent with one ounce has a big following. These shooters are discovering extra powder and shot are not necessary to break targets. Most field shooters go a bit heavier in general, but the target shooter is the pathfinder to change.

So what we are seeing is steady withdrawal from the heavy loads with the best of technology in shotshell construction. Reloaders often lead the way for the commercial ammo manufacturers. Less than a year ago you could not find a wad with a one-ounce shot capacity. It was necessary to use some sort of filler to take up the extra space in a shot cup that was for 1⅛ ounces of shot. Today several 12-gauge one-unit wads are on the market with a shot cup capacity of exactly one ounce!

I often have felt like a lone voice crying in the wilderness in stating that the heavy short magnum 12-gauge shells were not necessary for fully ninety percent of the field needs of American sportsmen. For years I have shot only the 12-gauge 2¾-inch shell loaded with a 3-dram equivalent and 1⅛ ounces of shot. These shells and components always have been the most advanced on the market. I have held steadfast to the notion that only the high-antimony shot such as the excellent Lawrence Magnum shot and the nickel and copper plate was worth loading. It is a reassurance to see more and more shooters take this path.

The British long have held that 2¾-dram equivalent and one ounce of shot were sufficient for most needs. When a bit more was needed, they used the 3-dram equivalent and 1-1/16 ounces of shot. This is only a minor difference and I am not convinced that difference has any actual merit. A jump of one-eighth ounce makes more practical sense to me. The British jump from 1-1/16 up to 1¼ ounce of shot and I feel the American system of 1, 1⅛ and 1¼ ounces, which is a one-eighth bracket, is more practical.

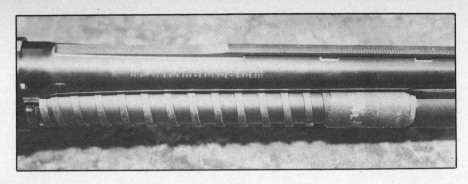

This early Remington Model 11 is equipped with original flat recoil spring. To use modern shotshells, spring should be replaced with a currently made round spring.

The British have maintained that 1¼-ounce of shot was the maximum capacity for the 12-gauge bore diameter and I agree. The 1¼-ounce load is the International trap and live pigeon load where shots can mean thousands of dollars in side bets. Trap gunners often shoot for money and have no qualms about spending extra bucks if it gets the job done. For those who would sit in an armchair and pour forth a volume of hot air on the subject, I suggest shooting one box of each load at a pattern paper, counting pellet holes. My own experience is that when you pass 1¼ ounces in a 12-gauge you start to lose efficiency. Figure the percentage of the pellets that you add. Now do an actual percentage count of a shot pattern and you will see little is gained in added pellet count in the pattern. You also will find that most guns deliver a much better pattern with lighter loads. This does not even consider the flinching from heavy recoil that is a part of every shot in the field.

It's an exercise in futility to go afield with regular drop or chilled shot if you consider the few times you actually shoot at game and the money you have spent just getting there You will gain about ten to fifteen percent in pattern efficiency plus a more even distribution of the pellets with high-antimony shot of identical size. The only place drop or chilled soft shot is an advantage is when shooting skeet and you want as much shot scatter as possible in order to break birds. You are wrong if you think such shot would be good for close-in rising birds; penetration is a key factor in downing a wild game bird and only the high-antimony shot pellet will give the desired penetration.

Pellet size selection is more a practical need and personal choice than anything else. Most shotshell manufacturers and gun manufacturers publish a list of the shot size by type of game and that is hard to beat for the beginner, but one should base his final judgment on actual field experience. The fact that one shotgun may shoot size 7½ fine and not deliver the same quality of pattern with 8s in the same type load will be a key in selection.

I do not think that #9 shot has any place on a game field and should be confined to skeet. For quite a few years I used this size in the open bottom barrel of a fine over/under 12-gauge with 7½ in the tighter-choked top barrel. After retrieving more feathers than birds I dropped this habit and went to #8 with a bit more gain, but finally dropped the whole two-shot-size idea and went to 7½ for all game birds except ducks and the larger size. I prefer to rely on the chokes to get the pattern rather than the shot size and for the last twenty years I have had no regrets.

Number 6 shot is often recommended for rabbit and squirrel type game and I feel this is good advice. Number 7½s result in too many holes in the game and have a lack of stopping power at longer range. For the past few years I have favored #5 shot size for this type game; while pellet numbers are a few less than #6, you gain in range and anchoring the game better. Shot size 5 seems to be the exact medicine for our local ducks. As for geese, as soon as I have shot the next one that will make a total of one, so I pass on this as far as comments are concerned. The same goes for pheasants. I have never shot one in my life.

Alabama has an abundance of wild turkey and you will find ten dozen ideas on the correct shot size for the same. Based on my own experience and that of quite a few ardent turkey hunters, the use of large size shot is a mistake on these old rascals. One must remember that the only target is the turkey's head and his neck. You can shoot one clean through with a .30/06 and he will fly away; a body hit is a poor shot. But with 7½ high-antimony and a head shot they drop on the spot. The more shot in the head or neck, the better. The 3¼-dram equivalent load with 1¼ ounces of high-antimony hard shot, nickel or copper plated will drop more turkeys than any other load I know.

Our deer season lasts about three months and the legal limit is *one per day*. The Old South tradition of dog hunting of deer with hunters on an assigned stand is slowly dying, but still is popular in most places. The best buckshot size I have found is #1 buck and I do know that the larger size is impossible to custom choke for and get a consistent pattern. I have choked guns that would put all sixteen pellets within a two-foot circle at forty yards time after time, but have never been able to get a consistent pattern with 0, 00 or the new 000 buckshot. The three-inch magnum shell possibly has a place in this ball game, but most of the local hunters who do quite a bit of this style shotgunning for deer have gone to the 10-gauge 3½-inch shell.

A close friend in Birmingham has done more of this type deer hunting than anyone I know. A handloader supreme, who takes no one's word, he does his own testing on targets and afield. On numerous occasions he has stated that in over fifty years of such hunting he has found the #1 buck the best, but he will not use standard factory loads. He uses a .30 caliber round ball mould and common wheel weights melted down to get the hardest pellet he can obtain. I have seen pellets of this type drive completely through a deer at twenty-five yards and half-way through at twice the distance. Bones offer little resistance to these extra-hard pellets. Recently this individual has started adding graf or the round plastic balls to the shot to obtain a better pattern. I think he has the answer to the most efficient buckshot available.

Chapter 5

The author displays the proper position of the body for shotgunning. In this case he is using a custom-built KFC semiauto.

HOW TO KNOW WHAT YOU'RE SHOOTING

The Author Insists A Gunsmith Must Be Able To Shoot A Shotgun Properly Before He Can Evaluate Its Problems

REGARDLESS OF whether you are trying to repair, modify or alter a shotgun or simply trying to shoot it more efficiently, it is essential to establish a correct shooting method. A rifle may be held in a machine rest or fired from a bench to establish accuracy or to check performance. Not so with the shotgun as its efficiency must always take into consideration the human factor.

The shotgun is related directly to this human factor, as it depends so much on human instinct for ultimate performance. The primary reason for this lies in the fact that a shotgun is devoid of any form of a mechanical rear sight. With a shotgun the shooter's eye is the rear sight.

To fully appreciate this it is only necessary to remove the rear sight from a common .22 rifle. Now draw a thirty-inch circle around the target's bullseye and place the target thirty to forty yards downrange from the firing point. Hitting the bullseye under this condition becomes a matter of pure luck. Even keeping the bullet within the thirty-inch circle is extremely difficult at first.

However, it is not impossible; in fact, if the shooter can see where his bullet is hitting, he can slowly but surely bring his hits well within that circle. He has changed from depending on a mechanical rear sight, as in a rifle, and is becoming dependent on his instincts whether he realizes it or not. In essence, he is duplicating the system used by trick shooters and eventually can learn to hit even small targets with remarkable success.

This method can be used to teach beginning shotgun shooters. Another method is to use a BB gun with the rear sight removed. The target is placed on the ground at first in order for the shooter to see the impact of the BBs in the dust. With practice, the shooter starts hitting the target consistently. Next, the target can be suspended from a tree limb with a string, and when hits become consistent the targets are thrown. One of the best shotgun instructors I know uses this method to teach beginners how to shoot a shotgun accurately; it is amazing how quickly the new shooter starts to pick up instinct shooting which later is used to teach actual shotgun shooting by going through the whole sequence again and again.

The ability of the human body and the brain to cooperate in such an effort to perform a given task is nothing short of amazing. We often stand in awe of the abilities of modern computers. Yet, using the most up-to-date technology and the most sophisticated circuits with miniaturized components, even the most advanced computer can perform only a pitiful fraction of the capabilities of the human brain. Combine this with the best mechanical automated equipment and the ability to perform a given task is a poor copy of even an untrained person.

This partially explains why and how a beginner can learn to shoot a BB gun or .22 rifle sans sight and consistently hit a target. In essence the brain says it itself, "The last time we had this task and saw this sight picture, we gave certain instructions to the thousand and one muscles involved to perform the task." Then, using its memory banks, the brain tries to duplicate the previous success. It can even make adjustments based on a set of circumstances that resulted in a total miss. All of this takes place within milliseconds and requires no effort either mentally or physically on the part of the shooter. In fact, conscious thought and effort on the part of the shooter can override the automatic efforts of mind and muscles and result in less efficiency. The sooner you learn to act "automatically" without thought, the quicker you become efficient with a shotgun!

The human brain is a self-compensating mechanism. If, for instance, the first hit is three inches to the right, the brain may over-compensate and place the next shot one inch to the left of the target. Then it adjusts this sequence and with the new data places the third shot a half-inch to the right. Learning from these mistakes, the brain makes the next adjustment right on target. The same for vertical placement of the hit. It never forgets that the task is to hit the target and automatically compensates when the results are not satisfactory. Once it is satisfactory a set of "success patterns" is established and, if all things are equal, it performs them over and over without deviation for the success pattern has been established for all times. You see this in a professional skeet or trap shooter as he breaks his targets over and over without a miss. The only problem is when the shooter adds some outside habit that overrides that success pattern and then starts to miss.

This success pattern is often referred to as "the groove" and is used in all sports in one method or another. Golfers often refer to the groove, so does a baseball batter or bowler. All refer to their success as being "in the groove"

In assuming the proper position for handling a shotgun, the feet start at roughly a ninety-degree angle to the position stake, facing the target. Walker insists that a gunsmith must shoot properly to evaluate any firearm.

when their mental and physical efforts result in a projectile being dispatched toward a target. A successful shotgun shooter employs the same coordination of abilities.

While the human brain can give the correct orders, it is totally dependent upon muscle activity to carry out the set of orders. Together they perform the task with success, but are equally dependent on the other. Like the brain, the muscles will form a pattern of success and, given the chance, will repeat the success pattern over and over.

The human eye serves as the method of relaying the visual data to both the brain and the muscles. Without this input the brain is operating totally in the dark as are the muscles involved. It is this "team" working in complete coordination that makes a successful shotgun shooter. Thus if the gun itself performs with peak efficiency, and this "team" performs equally well, then the shooter will enjoy success with a shotgun.

This mind/muscle coordination is so efficient that although the shooter places them in an awkward position, they will still perform remarkably well. This is the reason why so many shooters, breaking every rule in the book, can hit with a shotgun; they hit in spite of this hinderance.

Therefore, if they can give this degree of success under adverse conditions, it only stands to reason that under correct conditions the results will be much better. By correct conditions I am referring to placing the body and the shotgun in the most favorable position so the gun can work

in perfect cooperation with the eye, brain and muscles.

This relationship of shotgun to body cannot be over-emphasized. No golfer, bowler or similar person ever achieved any notable success until he learned the correct body relationship with the item being used. The same is true with the shotgun shooter. The body position may seem awkward at first, as it does in any sport, but slowly the position will begin to feel normal and perfectly at ease. With practice, the body will assume the correct position automatically without thought or effort.

The following is a body position and method of shotgun shooting that I have used to teach many people, both beginner and old hand. It is not by any means the only method nor would I go so far as to say that it is the best. I can only say that it works!

First, place the butt of the shotgun stock in the correct location on your shoulder. Fully eighty percent of all shotgun shooters fail in this step. The butt plate ends up anywhere and everywhere almost from collar bone to elbow. This is the reason why so many shooters' shoulders and arms become sore or black and blue with bruises after only a little shotgun shooting.

Regardless of gauge, power of shells or weight of shot, a person who knows the correct spot to place the butt of a shotgun can shoot all day without acute discomfort. Those black and blue bruises hurt and are the major cause of flinching! Even a rank beginner knows that flinching in

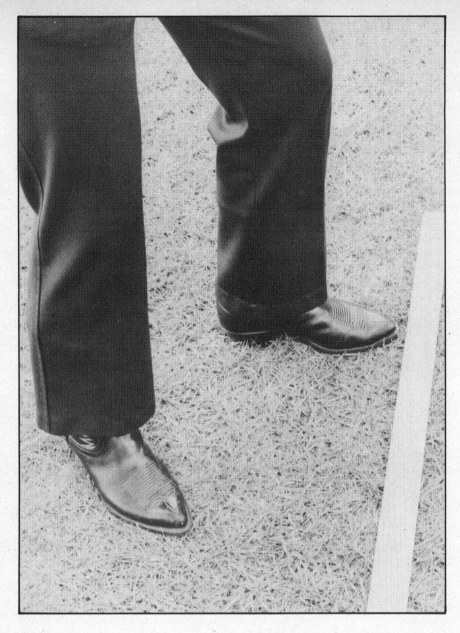

With the left foot still in place, the right foot is moved to a 45-degree angle, with weight forward.

anticipation of punishing recoil prevents accurate shooting.

Place your left hand on your shoulder, fingertips upward, between your collar bone and where your right arm joins the shoulder. Now slowly lift your right elbow until it is horizontal. As you lift your elbow, you will feel a hollow place or pocket form under your left hand. The butt of the shotgun stock fits into this pocket. This is the only correct place for the shotgun butt to fit when shooting. If nothing else is learned but this fact, your shotgunning will improve.

No matter what type of shotgun or shotshell is used, every shot should be with that butt stock firmly implanted in this pocket. Even in a fast, awkward field shoot, the number one rule is this pocket. This cannot be over-emphasized.

Why? First of all, by placing the butt of the stock in the pocket, the gun will be mounted to the shoulder in the same spot and in the same way shot after shot. Consistent plac-ing of the shotgun stock in the same position will eliminate many errors in aiming. This will halt the habit of placing the butt plate anywhere from collar bone to elbow. It goes a long way in eliminating misses due to vertical misalignment. The best comparison is with the rear sight of the rifle. And remember that the shooter's eye is in reality the rear sight in reference to a shotgun. With the pocket, it is the same as leaving a rifle's rear sight in the same position shot after shot as compared to running the sight elevator up and down between each shot.

Second is that the pocket occurs between the collar bone and the deltoid muscle. Of all the places on the human body, this exact spot is better able to give with and absorb recoil energy than any other place. In fact every shotgun stock is specifically designed for this pocket position. To place the butt plate elsewhere is wrong.

Being a true pocket, the butt plate or recoil pad is held inside and avoids slipping between shots. If not in the pocket, the recoil tends to push the butt plate out onto the arm muscles and thus the black and blue bruises occur.

Equally important is the shot that follows up. If in the pocket, the next shot — and the next — will be with the shotgun in the same position as the first shot. In rapid field shooting this is important, but it is also important that the shotgun is in the same position as related to the body and eye for each and every shot.

If the elbow is lowered even a small amount between shots, the pocket will tend to disappear and the butt plate slips onto the muscle of the arm. Thus it is important to hold the elbow as high as possible in shooting. This may be against some shotgun shooters' opinions, but one has only to place the left hand in the initial position on his shoulder, then slowly lower the elbow of the right arm. In the beginning, a specific effort should be made to keep the right elbow high. After you become used to the correct position and the pocket, you can lower the elbow if desired, but the pocket disappears in direct relationship. With the elbow ten degrees below the horizontal position, the pocket no longer is formed in the shoulder.

There also are correct and incorrect ways of getting the butt plate into the pocket. The average person brings the gun straight up and into the pocket. In doing so, the heel or top of the butt stock catches on the clothing almost every time. A common problem also is encountered with this method in that the height of placing the butt plate into the pocket varies from a low to extremely high position. This plays hob with an established pattern or sequence of mounting the gun in the same position on the shoulder for each shot.

The correct way is to first push the gun slightly out from the body on its way up to the shoulder pocket. Then bring the gun back toward the body and position the butt plate into the pocket seating it firmly. With a little practice this out-and-back sequence rapidly becomes an established habit and the shooter will mount the gun to his shoulder the identical way for every shot. This habit is especially important when wearing loose-fitting hunting clothes, which increases the possibility of the stock catching in the clothing on its way up to the shoulder.

Now we come to a correct body position and there are several schools of thought on exactly which is the best method. The following is the method I have used for many years to teach literally hundreds of beginners in the shotgun game. Perhaps some will disagree, but I can only state that I have yet to have a failure when this method is used correctly. Another interesting point is that a good many older shooters have tried it and found a vast improvement in their shooting.

Basically it consists of two separate phases. First, the

By lifting the right elbow — if you shoot right-handed — a pocket is formed into which the shotgun butt will fit.

Walker insists that the proper gun angle is 45 degrees, meaning that the shoulders are 45 degrees from gun line.

shooter assumes a rigid position that is artificial in many ways. By practicing this artificial position in the home and dry-firing for about a week, the shooter establishes a pattern that stays with him forever. The second phase is simply to relax from the rigid position into a more natural and comfortable stance while not losing the basics. It is extremely important to begin with the rigid position until a pattern is established, then switch to the second, relaxed position.

Begin by placing a round black target about three inches in diameter on a wall at eye level about ten feet away. Check religiously each time to be absolutely sure the gun is not loaded and use a snap cap in the chamber — or chambers — to protect the firing pin as the trigger is pulled during the practice session.

Stand facing the target about ten feet from the wall. Shoulders should be parallel with the wall, feet evenly spaced with toes pointed toward the wall and the target. The gun is held in the low position — using both hands to hold it — the muzzle pointed in the general direction of the wall.

With the left foot take one normal step toward the wall, but keep the big toe of the left foot pointed toward the wall. Now rotate your right foot until your toe is about forty-five

degrees away from its original pointed toward the wall position. The left toe now points toward the wall and target, the right toe points forty-five degrees from the wall.

Lightly bend your left leg slightly at the knee, but keep the right leg straight. Now shift about one-fourth or one-third of your body weight onto your left leg. The upper body weight should be balanced evenly at the waist and not leaning toward one side. The reason for this is that when the gun is fired you absorb the recoil energy by allowing the gun to push your weight rearward. With magnum shells or a hard-kicking gun simply shift more weight forward. It is the identical system used by boxers to absorb an opponent's blow. Allow your body weight, not the muscles, to absorb the gun's recoil energy.

Simple as it may sound, by shifting your weight forward and allowing your body weight to absorb recoil, you can fire any gun without excess punishment. The more the recoil, the more body weight forward. Never stand upright and firm and fight the recoil, flow with the recoil rearward allowing it to firmly push you back. You can practice this by dry-firing and rocking with each trigger pull slightly backward. It will become a habit.

Now back to the basic position: Move your right shoulder back a bit until a line — if drawn from the right shoulder

In holding the shotgun in the shoulder pocket, note that the right elbow is high — just below parallel — the position relaxed.

to the left — would be roughly forty-five degrees from the wall. Learn this shoulder position thoroughly, for even in the relaxed stance it is an absolute necessity. The shoulders are always forty-five degrees from the target, left shoulder more toward the target than the right.

One of the most common habits — and one of the hardest to break — is to position the right shoulder too far to the rear. In doing so you allow the butt of the shotgun to slip out of the pocket on the outside edge and back onto the arm muscle. Most shotgun shooters who never were taught the correct body position will invariably move that right shoulder back too far. If the stock has been customized by a gunsmith for a perfect fit, all is lost if the shooter moves that right shoulder back too far as the stock then automatically becomes too short. Forty-five degrees and no more!

Now remember to push that shotgun out to clear the clothes, then bring it up and back into the pocket. That right elbow must be horizontal. The left elbow is brought as far inward as possible and directly under the barrel. This is not always possible to achieve with everyone, so the basic rule is to bring that left elbow as far under the barrel as humanly possible, until it becomes uncomfortable. Most shooters will point the left elbow off to one side and a few bring it up almost horizontal to match the right one. Nothing could be more wrong; the left elbow should be under the barrel.

Next is the position of neck and head. If you have assumed the correct body position and if the gun fits you, there will be no need to drop the head or bend the neck in order to see down the barrel. A good shooter keeps the neck straight, head up. If you cannot see down the barrel, the stock does not fit you and you will never learn to shoot that specific gun with any proficiency. Dropping the head or bending one's neck indicates poor gun fit.

Some of the best shotgun instructors in the business specifically teach a student to bend his neck or drop his head onto the stock to see down the barrel. I disagree one hundred percent. If the stock fits right, it is not necessary.

In my opinion, the shooter should adjust the stock to fit his body not adjust his body to fit the stock.

If you lower your head or bend the neck, the question is how much? Each time you lower your head to bend your neck the amount will vary. It is exactly like moving the rear sight elevator up or down between each shot and then using the sight to try to align with the target. Consistency is impossible.

The shotgun must be mounted as near the same spot and as nearly identical as humanly possible for each shot. This consistent mounting means that the shotgun is in the same place in relation to the body for every shot. The head must be in the same position in relation to the shotgun, for it must be remembered that the human eye is the rear sight for a shotgun. Even placing the face down onto the stock is nowhere near as accurate as holding the head and neck erect, which is a natural position for same.

Some shooters, especially those who have shot a great deal, say they cannot get the gun into position this way. As anyone knows, old habits are hard to break and there is a tendency to resist change. I never have had a beginner make this statement. They quickly learn to hold the head erect and make the gun fit them instead of themselves to the gun.

As previously stated, if the head cannot be maintained in an erect position while shooting, then the stock is at fault and not the position. As a general rule, the basic problem is that the stock length is too much for that particular shooter. This invokes a natural tendency to move the right shoulder more rearward and force the shooter to move his head too far forward to compensate. Depending on the physical makeup of the shooter, the drop at the heel may be wrong, but the most common problem is the drop at the comb, that part of the stock that comes into contact with the face. Long necks require a higher comb, short necks require less comb height.

When going through the position procedure it is essential to combine it all into one flowing motion: One step forward with the left foot, shift the right foot to that forty-five degrees, bend the left leg slightly, shift weight onto the left leg, push the gun out, then bring it up and back into the pocket, raise the right elbow to horizontal position while the left elbow goes as far as possible under the barrel. With a bit of practice in a room at home, it all seems to go together in a flowing motion that soon becomes automatic and comfortable. It gets to be one smooth motion. As the sights align on the target, pull the trigger. Now go back to the original stance and repeat this over and over.

With about one week of practice (about thirty minutes per day) the position no longer will seem artificial. Try to concentrate on one smooth continuous sequence, pulling the trigger to complete the sequence.

When the week is up, you can go to the more relaxed position. The left toe is in the general direction of the target while the right foot is still about forty-five degrees from the wall. This places the feet in what will become a normal position for actual shooting, but do not get too far from the original artificial stance. The weight is still on the left leg and it is still slightly bent, the degree of bend depending on the individual. But remember that it is this weight forward that absorbs that recoil.

The step forward with the left foot at the beginning of the sequence is important. It is referred to as "stepping into the shot" and is the best way to get one's body to get into the desired shooting stance. While stepping into the shot is not always possible while field hunting, this learned sequence quickly becomes second nature to a good shooter. It will automatically place that body weight forward to absorb the recoil energy.

The left elbow can be about forty-five degrees from horizontal and still afford good control. I personally prefer to bring it under the barrels. Some fast wingshooters feel that bringing the elbow out a bit gives more leverage to "push" the gun around, but I tend to doubt this. I never have had any problem pushing the gun about as needed even on fast game.

Keeping both eyes open when shooting a shotgun is a habit some people never seem to acquire, yet it is a requisite for good shotgun shooting. Any time you close one eye, you immediately lose depth perception. Distance to game is very important in shotgun shooting as the gun has limited range and the choke has a narrow minimum and maximum bracket. For example, if the gun is choked tightly it is necessary to allow the game to get downrange a bit to allow the shot pattern of a thirty-inch circle to open up fully. At close range you are attempting to place the game in a fifteen to twenty-inch pattern, doubling the chances of a miss. Therefore depth perception is most important in this regard. It is equally important in the lead of the flying game or, as the British term it, "forward allowance."

The whole reason for the correct shooting stance and getting the gun mounted the same each time is for one reason: You look at the game and bring the shotgun up until it is aligned on the game. Most shooters mount the gun,

Walker is a believer that the gun should fit naturally into the shoulder, with rework of the stock to make it fit right.

then move the gun until it is on target. This is wrong.

Unlike rifle or handgun shooting, the shotgunner's target invariably is moving. You must keep your eye locked on that target. The gun comes onto the target and you concentrate on the target, not being side-tracked by trying to juggle the gun onto the target. You invariably lose concentration each time you do this. This is the reason why the shotgunner's correct stance is so important.

Robert Churchill, the well known English gunmaker and shooting instructor, made a habit of repeating to his students: "Forget the gun. Concentrate only on the target." Churchill automatically assumed his student's body was positioned correctly and the gun mounted correctly. Thus truer words were never spoken and this more than any other factor is the key to good shotgun shooting.

This is only possible if bringing the gun to bear on the target becomes a well established habit that is automatically assumed without thought. That strained, artificial position first explained is the best teacher. The relaxed position comes after the habit is formed, not before.

Canting the top of the receiver to one side is most likely when the gun is mounted to the shoulder incorrectly. If the top of the receiver leans to the right, the shot charge will strike low and to the left of the target. If canted to the left, the shot charge goes high and to the right. While this may not seem important when one considers that a shot pattern covers thirty inches of diameter, the center of that pattern diameter shifts considerably at this distance when a gun is canted.

Quite often a gunsmith is informed by a customer that his shotgun is shooting to one side or the other and either high or low. This may be true, but fully seventy-five percent of the time the culprit is the shooter canting the gun! A wise gunsmith asks the owner to shoulder the gun several times, paying particular attention to possible canting. No gunsmith can make adjustments on a shotgun unless the owner can properly mount the gun and hold it in something resembling vertical alignment. I have seen numerous attempts to correct this by actually bending the gun barrel to change point of impact for a canting gun shooter. A bit of explanation and recommended practice generally solve the shooter's problem.

If you shoot directly at a moving target, it will have moved by the time the shot charge reaches the spot. The only answer is to shoot where the target will be, not where it is. This is called lead or forward allowance and reams of words have been written on the subject. There are three schools of thought as to which method is correct to hit a moving target.

The first method is called snap-shooting. A spot ahead of the moving target is determined and the gun is brought up and fired the moment the butt plate hits the shoulder This system is at its peak efficiency when a target is close; as distance increases, the chance of error increases in direct ratio. I prefer this system when quail hunting in the Deep South. The birds rise fast and are quickly lost among the many pine trees or tangled growth. You have to shoot fast or forget it, hence snap-shooting is a must and no other

Below: When the gun is brought into the pocket, weight is forward to absorb the gun's recoil. (Right) Gunner is seen from front, making it obvious that his head is not lowered. Lowering the head to gun is a poor habit.

This over-the-shoulder photo is meant to show proper position of the shotgun in relationship to shooter's head. Note that head is held level, not bent downward.

system will suffice. I look at the bird and pick a spot directly above its head where it will rise in its upward climb. The gun is fired the instant it hits that shoulder pocket.

A friend of mine who is also a skeet-shooting machine was one of the best snap-shooters I have ever seen. For years he had hunted quail all over the South and used the same snap-shooting technique on skeet. Normally he could run one hundred targets straight without a stutter. A wager developed one day and, although I was at a disadvantage, I made the bet and volunteered to fill the hopper with claybirds prior to the shoot. Unknown to my friend, I took a couple of healthy turns on the trap machine's tension spring. The claybirds were almost smoking when they came out of the house. Said friend's snap-shooting at the extra-fast birds resulted in his shooting behind most of the time. He finally caught on to the trick and compensated his point of aiming, but it proves this system does have its limitations.

The second method involves sustained lead or sustained forward allowance. In this you determine the amount of necessary lead, then swing through the target until in front of it the correct pre-selected amount, then maintain this distance until the gun is fired. Sustained lead is the opposite of snap-shooting. It is at its best when the target or bird is at a great distance and the amount of lead is critical and hard to predetermine. It is also probably the hardest of the three to learn.

The third and best method is to swing through. Imagine a large paint brush stuck in the end of your barrel. Start behind the target or bird and "paint" through the bird pulling the trigger when the game is covered and continue this swing or painting past the bird or target. You paint the target out but keep the rate of swing faster than the flight of the bird. It is the simplest of all three methods to learn.

The swing-through method can be used at any range and will give excellent results. It must be a slow, steady increasing-speed swing in a flowing motion and devoid of starts or stops. Whether the game is passing right or left, coming toward you or departing the scene, the swing-through paint-brush method will deliver hits. The trick is always to start behind, watch the target, and as you pass pull the trigger and keep on swinging!

Fully eighty percent of the misses with a shotgun are due to two reasons. By constantly trying to eliminate them you will improve your game.

The first and most common fault is stopping the gun. Most start the swing-through fine, pull the trigger at the right time, then foul up by stopping the swing. You must follow through once past the point of pulling the trigger. It is no different than a golfer or ball player continuing his swing past the point where he contacts the ball, which is much the same as pulling the gun's trigger. If you stand behind most shooters and watch them in action, you will see them stop the swing the moment they pull the trigger. It is a hard habit to break, but necessary if any degree of skill is to be achieved.

The second reason for missing is failure to give enough lead to moving game. The shot charge passes behind the target. Some shooters persistently believe that game flies slower than it actually does and they just as persistently shoot behind the game. The solution is to lead more than the first impression suggests. Pattern performance is on the side of the shooter when this is done. Depending on the choke, the shot pattern will be from about a foot up to two feet in length. Hence while the shooter may miss with the forward edge of the pattern, the trailing tail edge catches the game.

For example, a skeet target and most game birds fly at about thirty miles per hour. If the target is passing directly in front at around twenty-five yards, the correct lead is about four feet. At the forty-yard range lead would be seven to eight feet ahead of the speeding target or bird. To get an idea of this, place two spotting points forty yards out, then walk back to the firing line and make a guess at what a seven-foot lead looks like. Chances are you would place the second spotting point only about three or four feet from the initial point. Placing spotting targets the correct distance apart, then backing up to a shooting point is sobering. Range estimation can be done the same way and is good practice.

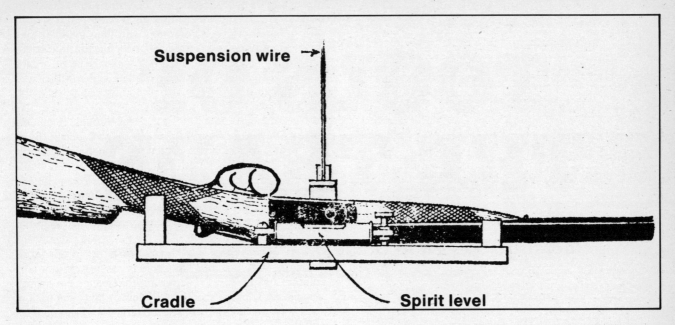

Suspension wire

Cradle — **Spirit level**

Although rather basic in design, this rig is an excellent means of determining the shotgun's proper balance point.

Once you have learned correct body stance, have practiced at home and have some idea of necessary lead, it is time to put all of this into practical experience. As in any endeavor, practice makes perfect and the most thorough training is for naught without it.

It amazes me at how many people buy a good shotgun, have it perfectly fitted to them, buy a case of shells, then wait around for the beginning of the hunting season. They go out to dove shoot which usually starts the season, and fully expect to take their limit within a few hours without missing a shot. If they miss, it is always the fault of the gun or the ammunition. Never is it lack of practice. Many think of having the choke altered or buying a case of magnum shells or some similar solution. In short, they want to buy proficiency.

In its original concept skeet was a clay-pigeon game intended to sharpen field-shooting skill. The gun was held in the low position and when the shooter called for his bird, there was often a delay in releasing it. When it left the skeet house the shooter mounted his gun and fired. Unfortunately skeet has degenerated to a game that has little in common with field shooting. It now is a game of endurance. Shooters are allowed to mount their guns prior to calling for their bird which is thrown instantly at command. It becomes so automated that one looks for the wind-up key in the skilled shooter's back! Only in International skeet is some semblance of the original game observed.

Trap shooting, even doubles, always has the target going away from the shooter. This has some, but not much, field similarity. The new game of Hunters Clays that is advocated by the NRA and several gun companies gets back to field-type shooting, but I will lay odds that this is soon "gamed up" by someone trying to get an edge. Every type of shooting we have has started for hunters and been "im-

proved on" until it resembles the original game in name only.

This does not mean the hunter desiring to sharpen his skill has to follow the rules. I shot skeet for many years and quite a bit of trap and never went in for the "game." I shot for skill improvement and changed the rules to fit the needs.

Along the way I have taken a lot of kidding about holding the gun low and "stepping into the shot" from those who play the standard rule game. The only consolation is that on the game field the roles are reversed and I have the last laugh.

Skeet fields offer the game shooter the best place to practice as the birds cross from each of the houses and one can change the rules by shooting doubles from midway or start at the low or high house and walk toward the house from which birds exit. If no other shooters are on the field and it is permitted, one can increase the distance of shooting by simply backing up past the regular point. Trap fields can be used also and the so-called game rules forgotten for an hour or so while you do some field shooting.

The main advantage of shooting at claybirds is that a missed shot can be repeated. You can shoot the same target flying an identical path until you have it down right. An inexpensive trap such as Trius or Outers can be mounted on the ground with some form of tie down. Then cock the trap, insert a clay and pull from any distance via a long string. Even an inexpensive hand trap can be put to good practical use taking turns with a friend.

The finest shotgun ever built is worthless unless the person doing the shooting can do his part. Unlike firearms of other types, the human becomes a part of the gun with the two working together as a team.

Chapter 6

TOOLS OF THE TRADE

Shotgun Tools Hold Some Special Requirements, Even If You Make Them Yourself!

AS WITH gunsmithing requirements for handguns and rifles, there are some special tools, jigs and fixtures that will be needed if any amount of gunsmithing is done on shotguns. Common tools, such as screwdrivers, punches, hammers and files can be used on all three firearms types and it is assumed that the reader will have these at hand, as well as a place to work.

A good bench vise is an absolute necessity for any gun work and there are several available that will offer good service in shotgun work. However, the best vise for shotgun work, in my opinion is the Versa-Vise, which is available from Brownell's. This particular vise is capable of being

The Versa-Vise, available from Brownell's, swivels vertically or horizontally and locks in position when jaws are tightened, offering exceptional convenience.

pivoted in any number of directions and angles for which I have found a need in shotgun gunsmithing.

The one feature I dislike is that the vise must be tightened to an extreme in order to keep the vise head from rotating. This problem can be rectified by simply drilling and tapping the rear of the head where it mounts on the vertical round base. A 5/16-18 threads-per-inch (tpi) Allen-head screw, easily obtained from any hardware store, is the right size to prevent the vise head from rotating. It can be loosened for positioning, then locked firmly in a few seconds. Needless to say, wood vise jaws cut from one-quarter-inch plywood always should be in place when holding a shotgun. Additional vise jaws can be made from any material, but one set should be included that utilizes ordinary carpeting material glued to the faces to prevent marring of barrels and parts.

This inexpensive, small bench vise has been fitted with brass angles, available from Brownell's, to prevent damage to steel workpieces when in use.

Automatic center punch, from Brownell's, is used to establish a small punch mark for drilling. The handle is pulled against spring tension and released.

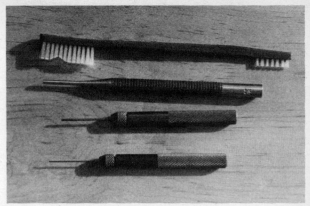

An assortment of pin punches, showing but a few of the many types and sizes available as solid types or with replaceable pins. Brush is handy for cleaning.

I prefer to have some form of bench covering to avoid marring a stock or metal surface. Masonite nailed to a bench is good, while relatively inexpensive. The better solution is to purchase remnants of common floor carpeting and place this loose on the bench top. It can be removed and shaken periodically or even vacuumed to remove any metal particles that might become imbedded in the fabric. Most carpet installers have odd ends left from any job that can be purchased at give-away prices. You can even choose your color, if you have a preference!

As a rule, shotguns have more pins that require removal for rework than is the case with handguns or rifles. I think everybody that ever designed a shotgun had to include some oddball-size pin as an expression of individuality! There is no such thing as having too many pin punches of every conceivable length and diameter for shotgun smithing. The standard one-piece set offered by Brownell's will start your collection. I also recommend their replaceable head punch set. Roll pins are found more and more in recent designs such as the Remington M3200, so a set of punches for them is invaluable.

Stock repair pin kit from Brownell's is used with Acraglas and supplied drill bits to reinforce repairs in split or broken stocks per furnished directions.

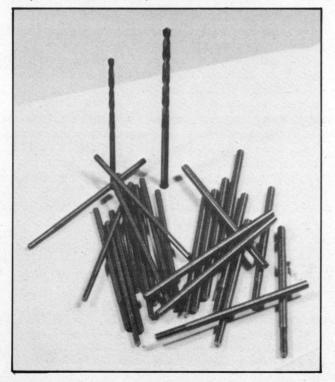

After you have assembled every pin punch set or individual punch you can find, start collecting every diameter rod or pin that you can lay your hands on. Regular drill rod, which is available in an abundance of diameters, makes good pin punches. Simply heat one end until it turns light yellow, then plunge the end into oil to harden this end. Leave the other end at normal temperatures for future use. Such punches made from drill rod should be about four inches long to allow a pin to be driven from one side of a receiver to the other.

Drill some holes in a common piece of scrap 2x4 wood. Tack a piece of masonite or any one-eighth-inch paneling on the back side. With the punches placed in the holes point up, this simple fixture will keep the punches available for instant selection.

Most semiauto and pump shotguns of modern design utilize one or two cross pins to secure the fire control trigger group to the receiver. The pins are designed for simple removal and the common practice is to use regular pin punches and a hammer for same. This is not necessary and a more simple tool can be made from the right diameter drill rod, about six inches in length. Drill a slightly undersize hole in the end of a common wood file handle and push one end up into the hole. It looks like a four-inch screwdriver without the end ground. This can be used to remove

A spring-loaded nylon insert in the center of the shotgun snap cap protects vulnerable firing pins during dry firing, as when checking out repairs.

Above, an assortment of roll pins in various lengths and diameters, from Brownell's, handy when such items need replacing. Below, firing pin spring repair kit from same source can be a lifesaver.

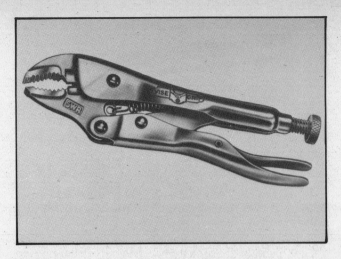

Above, miniature Vise-Grip pliers are five inches long with easy-release lever. Below, firing tester set includes chamber adapters to hold a shotshell primer for testing reliability of repaired actions.

these pins quickly and you soon will wonder how you worked without this and other simple homemade pin removal tools.

The best two screwdriver sets on the market are Brownell's Magna-Tip and the Chapman set. These two use interchangeable bits, which cuts cost to a minimum as the bits can be purchased separately. Order the full set to begin operations, then, as necessity dictates, grind the bits to fit odd-size screw slots. The Chapman set has a small ratchet that fits onto the octagonal handle and will allow you to exert about two hundred pounds of pressure.

Another useful rig for stubborn screws is the impact driver. The bit is fitted via an adapter to the driver and, with the bit firmly in the slot, the back of the driver is given a healthy whack with a mallet. A simple angled cam inside the driver converts the whack to a rotary motion to loosen a stuck screw.

Somewhere along the line, you will start to make your own screwdrivers with the blades ground for a precision fit in a screw slot. There are several so-called one-piece

gunsmith screwdrivers on the market, but from my experience and money wasted buying these, forget them. They do not live up to the advertised claims!

One final word on screwdrivers for shotgun work. Virtually every modern pump or semiauto uses a one-piece stock secured by a large screw from the butt plate to the receiver. It is a good design and quite a few double- and single-barrel shotguns have stocks secured to the receiver in the same fashion. Most use a large slot-head screw that can be removed with a large screwdriver. Others use hex heads of every imaginable size which will drive you to frustration as you try to see down the length of the stock bolt hole and guess at the diameter.

Some years ago I designed a simple set of take-down

Impact driver couples to ⅜-inch wrench sockets or special screwdriver bits to loosen the toughest screws. it's reversible for use with LH threads, too.

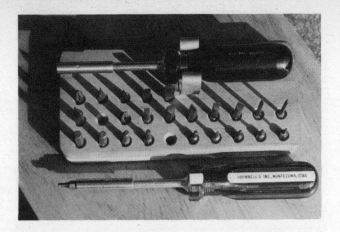

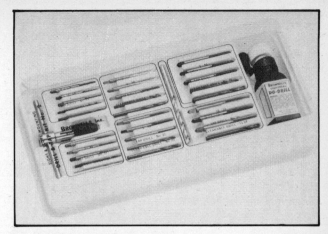

Above, two of Brownell's magnetic screwdrivers with an assortment of the bits they handle. Below, a sampling of the many types and sizes of files, including a Surform wood rasp for rough forming.

Brownell's drill and tap kit #2 for mounting sights and scopes has carbon steel taps that can be broken with a punch if the tap snaps off in the hole, as they sometimes do.

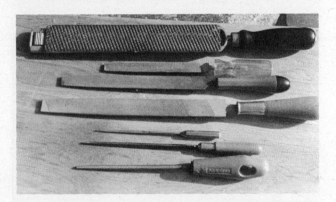

Tap Magic for aluminum is a must when working with that metal. Below, Brownell's tap/die kit #1 includes all common sizes except 6-48 which usually is purchased in quantity.

tools for Bob Brownell. This set consists of an extension of adequate length to reach down into a butt stock. An assortment of blades and sockets snap on the business end, while a T-handle snaps on the other. That impact driver mentioned earlier can be substituted for the T-handle to remove stubborn stock bolts. Such stubbornness occurs about half the time, the stock wood expands over a period of time, hence tightening the stock bolt or screw.

I am firmly convinced that a dastardly plot exists among European shotgun makers to frustrate the gunsmiths of the

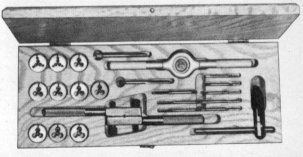

world. This is evident in the ultra-thin screw slots that one encounters on European-made guns. It appears someone sharpened a safety razor blade and used same to cut European screw slots! The most common occurrence that is encountered is on Browning shotguns made by FN, although other makers also are in the plot. There is only one out for a shotgun smith. Just take the time to grind special screwdrivers or the bits for a Magna-Tip or Chapman to fit the critters. Do not use these on other screws. I use a small plastic box to keep these handy, but separate from other screwdrivers.

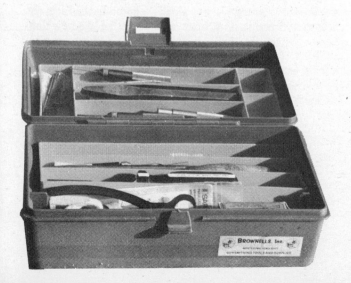

Brownell's has this handy little tool kit to aid in keeping track of the myriad small tools the gunsmith needs in day-to-day operations; finding's half the fight.

A small jeweler's saw is handy for performing fine cutoff chores and its narrow cut or kerf is likewise a valuable asset in certain operations. Top right, pliers, side-cutters and a small scribe are indispensible. Lower right, the Tru-Tapper from B-Square goes in drill press chuck to tap threads that are absolutely square with workpiece held in a vise.

The drill press is one of the hardest-working tools in any shop and examples range from this simple and inexpensive unit to vastly more elaborate ones.

All true shotgun smiths collect metal files simply because a lot of parts and components for older shotguns are not available from any source. You have to make the part or build up the old one with weld and recut the part to fit. Files are an absolute must in such an effort. The most common files are a four-inch mill bastard single-cut and the Brownell pillar files. Screw-slot files and a clockmaker's file will prove invaluable in reconditioning those thin European screw slots. I have about three dozen in my own collection — which does not include a set of needle files of standard and micro size.

An assortment of good flat tool steel in various thicknesses will prove invaluable for parts-making tasks. This work is not as hard as most think, provided you have the patience to make a part from scratch. If you have the old part, the task is made easier and it is a smart idea to retain every old broken part you can find for such ventures. Use Dykem layout fluid or a felt-tip pen to darken one side of the raw steel. Then use a scribe to lay out the basic lines. Hacksaw or rough file away the excess metal, then switch to precision files to finish the task. A good set of gunsmith-grade hard Arkansas stones of various shapes will quickly pay for themselves.

Keep in mind, though, that it is less than brilliant to make

This small drill press stand converts the super-handy Dremel Moto-Tool into a convenient setup for precise drilling. Press bed moves up and down via knob.

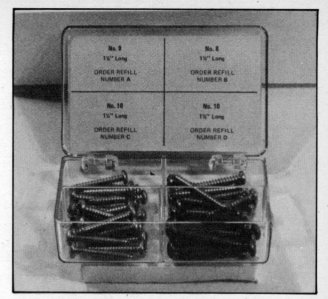

This is the professional pad mounting screw kit from Brownell's, with forty-eight screws in #10 and #12 size. Refills are available from source.

a part when you can buy a replacement! Chances are the one you make will not be as equal in strength and fit as well as a replacement part. If a customer will not wait until you order the part, then often he is doing you a favor to take his business elsewhere. Making a part takes time and time is money. Even at ditch-digger wages, a hand-made part can quickly climb to exorbitant price. Yet, if you ask ten bucks for a firing pin that required three hours of your time, a gunowner often hits the ceiling. Advise him of the expected cost involved and if a part can be obtained, give him a

A 10x24 Jet metal lathe from Corbin Supply of Phoenix, Oregon. Such tools are the vital essence of the gunsmith's equipage for countless operations.

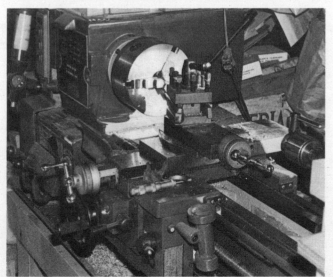

choice between waiting a few weeks or paying through the nose for the hand-made version. Gunsmiths who survive quickly learn to offer this choice.

The most important item you can possess is a collection of every conceivable shotgun diagram you can beg, borrow or steal. If the drawing has a parts list with part numbers, even better. Squirrel these away in some filing order. When you need a part, give the gun make, model, type, gauge and serial number. Give the part number from your library, even if out of date, and the source from which you obtained the number. (DBI Books' *The Gun Digest of Exploded Firearms Drawings, 3rd Ed.* contains drawings of over ninety shotguns.) If all else fails, make a photocopy of the part and give a full description.

Knowing where to buy parts is equally important. Hoard every parts catalog you can locate. Keep clippings from the *Shotgun News* which has a wide selection of such sources. Even if out of date, write the company for they may have one or two available. The two main sources for parts are Numrich Arms in West Hurley, New York, and Walker Arms R2 B-73, Selma, AL 36701. Both sources publish parts catalogs that will be invaluable.

As suggested, the rule of the game is to make a gun part only when there is no other alternative. The second rule is that, if you do not know how to make the part, farm out the work to someone who does. For some unfathomable reason many people think a part for a shotgun can be made from any metal handy. It is amazing how many firing pins are made from common nails! I know of one case wherein this was done and upon firing said nail-made firing pin exited the gun and imbedded itself in the shooter's skull, killing him on the spot!

Many of the screws on shotguns — specifically the older models that seem never to wear out totally — are oddball sizes and replacement is a major problem. Many were made before the standardization of screw thread sizes and you often find something like 9/64-19 tpi. If you should find some of the old taps and dies in these non-standard dimensions, buy them on the spot, for they will quickly

A kit of filister-head screws from Brownell's with several diameters, furnished blank so they can be threaded to the pitch required for the job at hand.

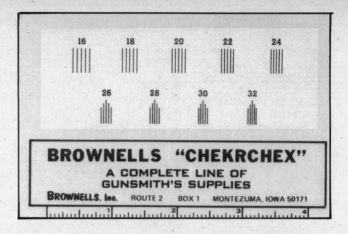

Brownell's Chekrchex offers a quick means for verifying the number of lines per inch. Below, a homemade trammel, handy for precise hole spacing.

earn the funds expended. Using a good metal lathe capable of reproducing odd diameter and irregular threads is another solution. Keep every old screw you find in some locatable container, as they are worth their weight in gold when needed. Another source is to cannibalize every old and unserviceable shotgun you can purchase, regardless of condition. The same advice goes for flat and coil springs of every description; squirrel them away. Blank screws and spring stock are available from Brownell's, incidentally.

Contrary to popular belief, a lathe is not an absolute must in a small gun shop. The drill press is much more important and simply by using a file while the metal stock is being rotated, you can fabricate an amazing number of pins, screws, et al. Your first lathe perhaps should be the versatile little Unimat which is capable of turning out just about any part that can be made on any lathe or a milling machine. This unit is capable of more precise use than the user is capable of putting in it! The six-inch Atlas, no longer available except in used condition, is the next step up the ladder, as it allows eighteen inches between centers and will machine a wide range of threads. Barrel work will require thirty-six inches between centers and the low priced

choice is a twelve-inch Atlas, which is usually purchased used, although a few new ones are found in some lathe supply houses. It is tragic that no American company today offers a small lathe; the only choice is an import, which usually is more lathe than necessary.

The drill press and a good set of numbered, fractional and letter drills should be the first choice of large power equipment for shotgun work. A good three-eighths-inch electric hand drill should be purchased first, as it will do a lot of work not possible with a drill press. Bench grinders of about six inches and a few buffers and a scratch wheel will soon find their way into a gun shop growing in requirements.

The single most important hand power tool is the Dremel Moto-Tool, for its use is non-ending. I recommend the ball-bearing model with variable speed. You never will regret the choice, for it lasts almost indefinitely, and should the need arise, the Dremel company will rebuild it at nominal cost. Like files, there is no such thing as having too many Dremel tool accessories. I cannot think of a single accessory I have not used at one time or another in shotgun work.

If you do much shotgun smithing, you will find an unexpected amount of soldering required. Three solders will fulfill most requirements. Silver solder is the strongest and should be rightfully termed silver-brazing, for it is the next

Dremel's #3701 variable-speed Moto-Tool kit, with case and accessory heads, bits and burrs.

Dem-Bart offers this starter's special with three basic stock-checkering tools.

Most soft solders simply are not adequate for shotgun requirements. The best is Force-44, which is a silver-bearing solder that acts like lead solder but has about five times the strength. One must use the matching flux, but take proper precautions for this flux removes bluing faster than you can say, "Jack Daniels Bourbon Whiskey..."

Some years ago I ran across another solder that I found amazing. I promptly advised Bob Brownell who now offers it under the name Gunsmiths Solder. What makes it unusual is that it melts at a low temperature and will *blend* with all other solders. For instance, if you have a rib loose on a double barrel that was originally bonded with common solder, it is not necessary to remove all of the old

Hydraulic dent-raising kit from Brownell's can save what might seem like a hopelessly damaged shotgun.

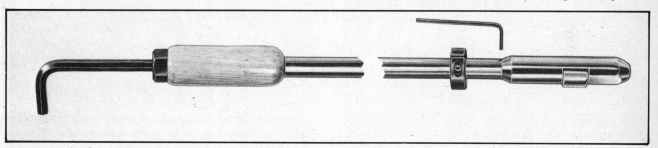

thing to welding in regard to strength; a lot of shotgun components are joined with it. If you try the local hardware, you will find more types of solder than a dog has fleas and most are totally useless for gun work. Bob Brownell sells the right type for gunsmithing under the trade name Silvaloy. The flat strip type is the one most used although the round will occasionally be needed. Also buy the matching flux.

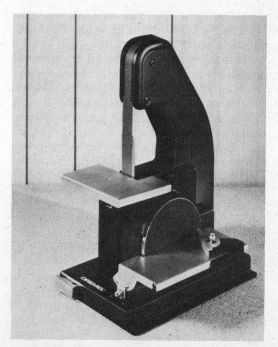

B-Square recoil pad jig takes the sweat and worry out of installing pads for shotguns or rifles. Above, Dremel's compact and moderately priced disk/belt sander, Model #730, has its own driving motor.

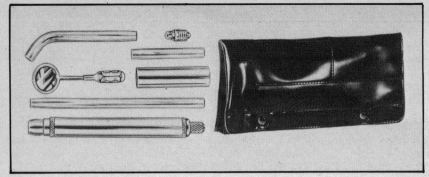

solder. Gunsmiths Solder can be applied and will blend with the original. Use it for one rib replacement job and you never will be without this solder again!

For soldering, a heat source is a necessity and the regular oxygen-acetylene torch is handy, but not an absolute requirement. A good propane torch will cover more uses in shotgun work, but buy the best you can find. Recently Bernz-O-Matic marketed a new rig that adds a bottle of oxygen to the unit. This is fed via a hose to a mixing valve somewhat like an oxy-acetelyne torch and doubles the uses of a regular propane torch due to the available extra heat. The same torch can be used for heat treating of gun parts, for example.

The secret to all soldering is proper surface preparation. You cannot solder a rusty or contaminated surface. Scrape it clean, use the right matching flux and the job becomes simple. The second secret is to use the absolute minimum amount of solder, for the solder alloys with the metal and really is the key that provides strength and bonding. Excess solder always means a weak joint!

One of the common tasks in shotgun smithing is installation or replacement of sight beads. Someone is always knocking one off or loosening it in some fashion. The most common sight consists of a round bead on the front and possibly a smaller bead midway down the rib. Normally they are size 3-56 with a few 4-40 and the larger size, 6-48, which means that taps of these sizes are a necessity. It is best to have both a taper and a bottoming tap in each size and keep these in some special place as their shapes are important. The taper is used to tap a hole through a barrel,

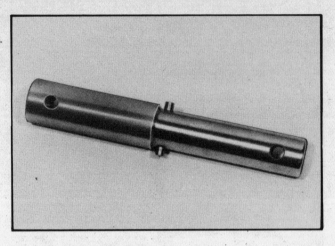

the bottom tap, properly used, keeps the sight shank from going through the barrel and into the bore.

Sight beads themselves are made in a variety of sizes and materials, but the most common are the silver (aluminum) or gold (brass) beads. Brownell's offers an inexpensive sight bead kit that contains both types. The beads in the kit are in three sizes to allow a correct match and each size is available in aluminum or brass with different pre-threaded shank sizes. The choices in this kit match about seventy-five percent of bead requirements.

Somewhere along the line, Brownell also started marketing a gadget for installing these beads. The tool consists of a twist-lock miniature vise with the jaws preground exactly to match the three bead diameters. With one of these it takes little time to screw a bead sight in place

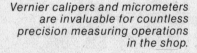

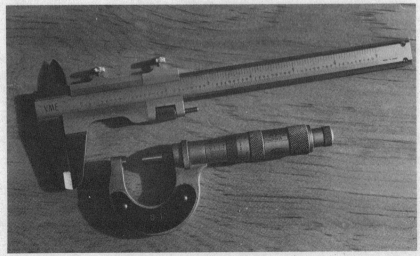

Vernier calipers and micrometers are invaluable for countless precision measuring operations in the shop.

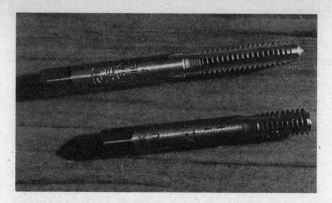

Above, a broken taper tap was reground into a bottoming tap from original shape. Below, flannel cleaning patches from Brownell's hold oil and take off fouling better than most other materials.

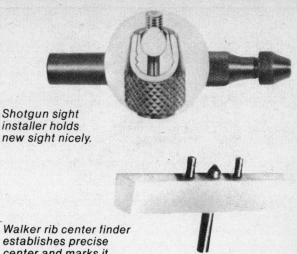

Shotgun sight installer holds new sight nicely.

Walker rib center finder establishes precise center and marks it for easy drilling.

Shotgun sight kit includes all sizes and threads in normal use, each type available in ten-packs.

without a single blemish on the bead. Twist counterclockwise and the vise releases the installed bead.

Some shotgunners prefer a red glowing plastic sight such as the Raybar or the Simmons Glow Worm. The plastic tends to gather the light and presents a red or orange dot for aiming. These sights screw in the same way as the beads and the only real task is to get the bead parallel with the barrel. A bit of careful filing on the bottom usually will allow correct installation. Poly-Choke offers a sight somewhat the same called the Sunspot and another available in various colors is the Bradley. These require a special .146x48 tap which is available from Poly-Choke or Brownell's.

Acraglas is a fiber-reinforced epoxy from Brownell's with many uses in the gunsmith shop for repairing breaks and filling gaps as well as bedding actions.

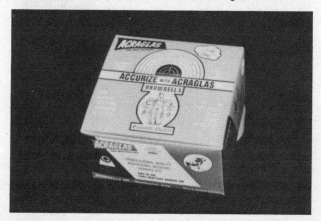

The Poly Bev-l-Blok sight is the one normally found on a Poly-Choke and its best use, other than replacing one lost from a Poly-Choke, is when the barrel of a Browning or Remington Model 11 has been cut off or the sight damaged. These sights, being on a block, elevate the bead to the right height.

I designed a handy jig for Brownell's some years ago that makes installation of a sight bead on the exact center of a ventilated rib quite easy. This job is often necessary when someone wants to add a middle small bead or the rib is damaged in some way. All that is necessary with the jig is to allow both of the extended legs to cross the rib, twist lightly to put the legs against the sides of the rib. Then tap the center punch which is self-contained on the jig. The resulting mark is dead center of the rib and ready for drilling and tapping to receive the sight. It's called the Walker Rib Center-finder.

There are several other sights for shotguns such as the Marble and Lyman drive-in beads, but their use is limited strictly to replacement of an existing sight. Rifle sights are common for slug barrels and generally soldered into position. A Remington Model 700 rifle sight makes a good choice for this slug work and is easy to attach.

As stated in other chapters, barrel cleaning is of extreme

Ithaca Raybar shotgun sight picks up ambient light to give a .160-inch-diameter glowing pink dot.

tached to a rod for powered use for bore and chamber work.

Another common gunsmithing chore is recoil pad installation, for more of these are used with shotguns than rifles. Having tried virtually every recoil pad available, I am convinced that one style will suffice for fully ninety percent of the gunsmith's requirements. The Pachmayr Model 325 field pad is one inch thick and comes in small, medium and large sizes. The large size will fulfill requirements for even the widest butt stock and allows ample excess for grinding away for a hairline fit with the stock. The pads come in red, brown and black. Most shooters prefer the red or black, so I stock only the 325 large in red or black. This cuts inventory needs and avoids a customer waiting for pad delivery from a supplier.

A disc sander is an absolute necessity if you install pads and do not wish to spend a mountain of time at the job. The six-inch-diameter disc is the absolute minimum size, while twelve inches is maximum with a nine-incher just right. Pads that are self-gluing to the disc can save a lot of unnecessary time.

A disc grinder simplifies the whole process, but has one bad facet: ground rubber ends up on everything, including the one doing the installation. Most disc sanders have a means of hooking a vacuum cleaner to the side, so this can eliminate most of the problem. I would advise a face mask

importance to assure continuous trouble-free function and performance with a shotgun. The standard shotgun cleaning rod such as that made by Outers will do nicely for all needs. I'd suggest you purchase two of them. One is used in the normal way as designed. Remove the handle of the other rod and toss it in the trash can. A three-eighths-inch electric hand drill, preferably with variable power, is attached to the rod in lieu of the handle to give the gunsmith a rotating powered head to remove stubborn foreign residue from the chamber and bore. The common brass bore brush will do most work, but the trick of wrapping 0000 steel wool around the bore brush will remove the caked-in crud. A 20mm cannon bore brush will scrub a rusty chamber, but the brush should be soldered to a rod for insertion in the electric hand drill. The Brownell's hone also can be at-

Tru-Oil stock finish is a blend of linseed and natural oils that dries in sixty to ninety minutes. RIG 2 is a lubricant/protector, RIG 3 is a degreaser, both quite useful as is Break Free for cleaning, lubing, protecting or loosening stubborn threads.

High-speed orbital sander from Brownell's operates at 12,000 cycles/minute.

Brownell's d'Solve is a cleaning concentrate that's non-hazardous, non-flammable, odor-free and biodegradable. Their 1,1,1, trichloroethane pre-cleaner cuts greases, leaves no residue.

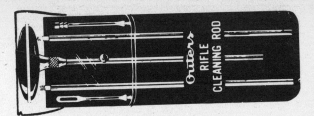

Outers cleaning rod is of strong aluminum alloy, has palm-rest handle and extra-long joints.

Optiloupe is easily attached to any visor, gives 6X magnification.

will custom turn one for you provided you supply the old broken stock or the gun itself. Their stocks are available raw, fitted to an action without finish or checkering or they will supply one fully ready to deliver to your customer.

Another little jig that Brownell's markets is used in test firing to check firing pin function. In essence, it is a solid shotshell that requires only a standard primer which is replaced each time the jig is used. It saves considerable dough on shotshells for initial testing, although a final func-

to keep rubber dust out of your lungs and thus add a little to your life expectancy. Safety glasses are also recommended.

Some years ago Dan Betchel of B-Square simplified recoil pad installation with a special jig. Having done it every possible way, I've found nothing compares with his jig for precision and fast installation time. The current price tag will be refunded in time saved with the first couple of pads. I will not go into the method of using this item, for detailed instructions are packed with the jig.

The same tools and accessories used for stock work on rifles lend themselves to all required work on shotguns and no special tools are necessary except a drop-pull gauge. In checkering, most shotgun stocks have fewer lines per inch than normally is found on rifles. While factory replacement stocks suffice for most requirements, the best source for out-of-production stocks is Reinhart Fajen of Warsaw, Missouri. If the stock you need is not in their catalog, they

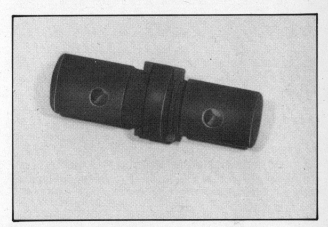

Above, forend wrench for Remington 870. Left, universal forend spanner.

Savage-Stevens forend wrench installs tube collars on those guns without marring; fits all gauges.

Tornado shotgun brushes are of looped wire that's non-corrosive; stiff enough to remove fouling, but won't damage the finest, most delicate shotgun bore.

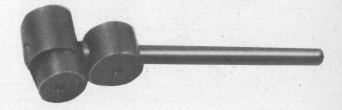

Available individually or as sets in the four gauges (12 to 28), the Critchley-Six adjustable reamer is for work on shotgun chokes.

Tube nut wrench for removing the stock of Remington's Model 1100 has recessed tool steel blade.

tion test always should be done with factory shells at both rapid and slow rates of fire.

Speaking of firing pins, Brownell's and Walker Arms stock and sell about all that you will require except oddballs. The Brownell's firing pin protrusion gauge is well worth the cost, incidentally.

Other tools such as chamber depth gauges, choke reamers, long forcing cone reamers have been covered in other chapters. Even if you do not buy the tools, the instruction books for each contains a wealth of shotgun knowledge and

Wrench at right is for removal of the forend on the Winchester Model 12 shotgun. Below, adjustable wrenches come in many sizes, here in four-inch and twelve-inch to handle nuts and bolts as needed.

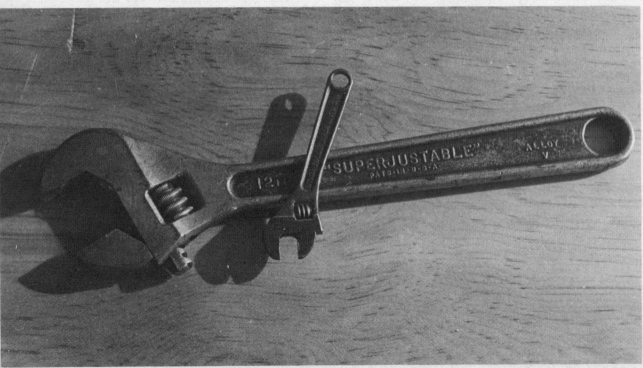

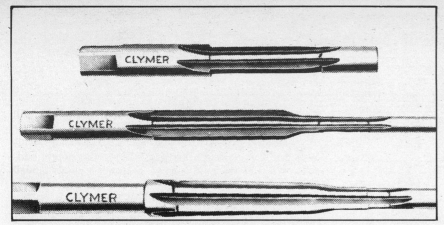

The Clymer reamer at the top, left, is for use in chambering shotgun barrels, others are for rifle chambers. All are to be had from the Brownell's catalog.

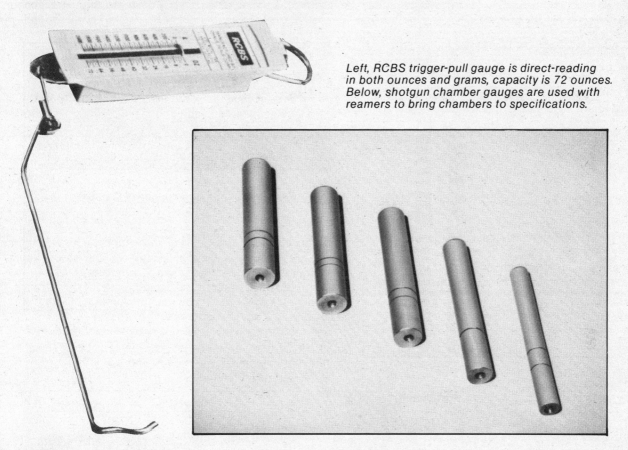

Left, RCBS trigger-pull gauge is direct-reading in both ounces and grams, capacity is 72 ounces. Below, shotgun chamber gauges are used with reamers to bring chambers to specifications.

one should have a working knowledge of such aspects of shotgun smithing. I am a fanatic on gathering information. I have every gunsmithing book and a rather extensive library of gun books, plus a couple of filing cabinets running over with scraps of information. I cannot over-emphasize the absolute need for continuing reference sources.

Brownell's also carries a full line of Menck shotgun tools which are top quality. Included are such items as forend wrenches for the Winchester Model 12. A useful item is the universal wrench used to remove lock nuts on pump shotgun forends, which can be a task. Until quite recently there simply were no special shotgun tools or jigs available. Everything I have designed in this respect is available to others either through Brownell's or Walker Arms.

Some may question the necessity of these tools. You have only to face the problem arising from need and the time-consuming task of trying to solve the problem with some homemade jerry-rig to learn that these jigs eliminate the problem. If you have nothing but time that's fine, but a jerry-rigged tool usually will not be as good in design nor in fabrication. I buy every new jig or tool I see and have had rare regrets.

I have known Bob Brownell for well over thirty years. His company, more than any other, has advanced the gunsmithing profession to where it is today with top-quality tools and other needs. Gunsmiths from all over the country

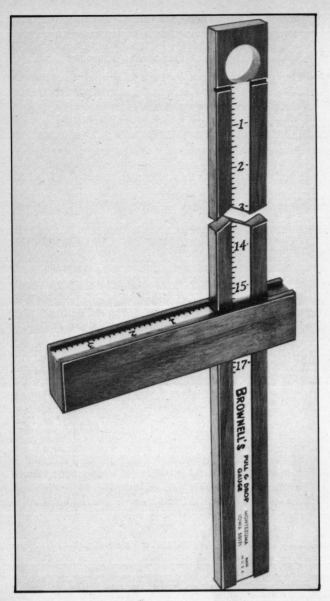

Brownell's pull and drop gauge makes easy work of checking these important dimensions of stocks.

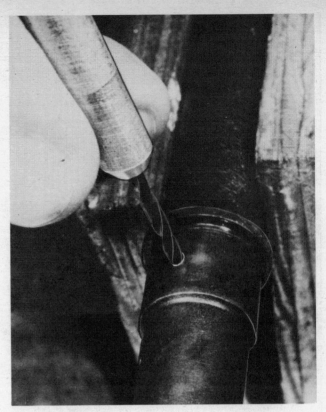

Using a gas-port reamer to remove caked residue so as to restore full working capability to autos.

use his company as a clearing house for tools and ideas. You are fooling yourself if you think you can go it alone without the tools and ideas from these professionals.

Bob Brownell prints an information sheet several times a year and gives it to anyone who asks besides his regular customers. You will find a virtual gold mine of ideas and how-tos in every issue. I keep every issue in a ring binder. I have used ideas from other professionals and made a large number of the special jigs and fixtures that are listed with full details and dimensions.

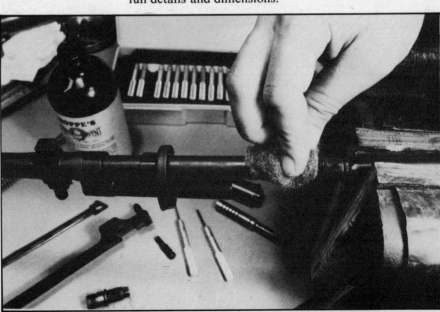

Use Hoppe's #9 bore cleaner on fine steel wool to clean the area around the gas port.

Arrows indicate locations of gas-port holes on the Remington Model 58 autoloader.

Several years ago Brownell incorporated many of these ideas, drawings, et al., into a book called *Gunsmith Kinks*. I know of no other single source that offers as many usable tools, jigs and ideas on shotgun smithing.

The latest item I have designed for Brownell's is the new gas port reamer kit. Gas ports are the key to the correct function of any semiautomatic gas-operated shotgun. Powder residue, shot protector residue and plain rust and dirt clog them and ultimately the gun stops working.

Before this kit was offered, neither the tools nor the correct data concerning gas port sizes per the manufacturer was available. I used up a lot of IOUs with various manufacturers' engineering departments to acquire port size data which is included in the detailed instructions. The reamers are made to remove all accumulated foreign substances without removing metal, returning the port size back to proper specifications. The unit is hand-operated and so easy to use in solving this constant problem.

Few realize that port size can be critical in proportion to barrel length; with many guns, any reduction in barrel length necessitates gas port dimension adjustment. This includes the installation of a Poly-Choke, Cutts or similar choke adapter. The gas-operated shotgun may or may not work without port modification. If in doubt about the need for these, buy the book and you will be quickly convinced. It is rather extensive in explanation and available from Brownell's without purchase of the kit.

Each time you buy a jig, special tool or fixture, or even if you whomp up a brainchild of your own, do yourself a favor and use a Dremel engraving tool to inscribe on the tool its exact use and the gun model for which it is meant. I learned this the hard way when I made up a special tool and simply tossed it in a drawer without any marking. In need of some tool steel one day, I whacked it up to make another tool I needed.

About a month later — you guessed it — I needed the original tool and had to make it all over when I realized the mistake I had made.

I learned from this and now take a few minutes to scribe on the tool its name and use.

Photo at left shows the magazine cap of the Model 58 Remington set for light loads while the other two photos show the cap of the same shotgun as adjusted for best performance with heavier shotshells.

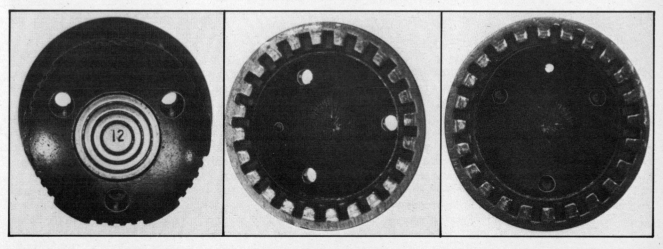

Ill-Fitting Screwdrivers Create More Problems Than Cures!

Assurance that all of the screws are tight in your top shotgun can add confidence in the field or on range. Loose screws can lead to problems as well as missed shots.

REMOVING THE FOURTH GUN from its case, the Air Force major laid it beside the others on the counter and said, "I usually do my own cleaning, but I just reported in to the local base and I don't have time to get them cleaned before the season starts." After giving instructions to disassemble, clean and adjust his guns, the major left.

The four guns on the counter — two rifles and two shotguns — were worth over $2000 in the era when a grand bought a lot. The metal-to-wood fit was so close that it was difficult to see where one stopped and the other began. Good figured wood with a soft glow, nice engraving and an overall clean appearance verified that the major had taken good care of the guns.

Lifting one of the guns to more closely examine the engraving, my admiration was suddenly turned to a sick feeling. Quickly examining the other guns I saw that they also had been defaced badly, not through intent, but through lack of knowledge. Not one single screw, even the engraved ones, had escaped the marring use of the wrong type screwdriver. Screw slots were burred in every conceivable way with some wallowed out at the ends of the slots.

The major was obviously a gun fancier and had spent untold hours cleaning and otherwise caring for his collection. His only fault was in his selection of a simple tool — the screwdriver. He is by no means the only one to fail at this point in gun care, for fully fifty percent of the guns my customers bring in exhibit the same mauling. I have even seen guns with bluggered screws where gunsmiths were responsible.

Some years ago a gunowner at least had an excuse, for almost all available commercial screwdrivers were of the common wedge blade. For the life of me I could never understand why screwdriver manufacturers persisted in the wedge blade. Perhaps the only excuse is that they expect one blade to fit everything from a Swiss watch to a locomotive. An inspection of screw slots around a home or automobile will reveal that, almost without exception, they have parallel side slots instead of the wedge-shaped slots. Some wood-screw slots have the wedge shape, but most manufacturers are switching to the more efficient parallel-sided slot. It's about time, as any freshman engineer knows that twist pressure applied to a wedge-shaped blade in a wedge-shaped slot will result in said blade coming out

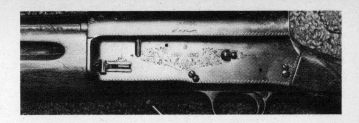

There is a screwdriver for every use as with three-prong unit at left. The screws on Browning (right) have been treated badly with tools that don't fit.

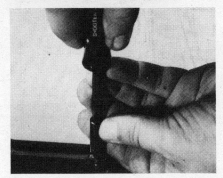

Choosing the right attachment can be an aid to speed, making a faster, profitable job.

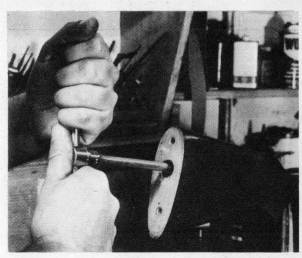

Author has found it necessary to make his own screwdriver blades for some special jobs such as the removal or installation of screw holding on the stock.

of the slot and gouging holes in whatever is outside of the slot, be it wood, metal or a finger.

The only alternative until a few years ago was to make your own screwdrivers with correct hollow-ground blades to match the vertical-sided gun screw slots. Even this presented a problem, as the right steel usually was hard to find. The average sportsman without tool-making equipment was simply up the proverbial creek without a screwdriver.

Fortunately in the last few years several companies have placed quality screwdrivers with the correct blade shape on the market at prices any sportsman can afford. There seems to be two basic approaches. One utilizes the common wedge blade, but with the tip reground to parallel sides in order to match the vertical walls of the screw slot. The other system uses blades that are hollow ground with the sides of the blade arcing inward in a convex shape and the blade tip flaring out to form the necessary parallel sides. The principle behind the hollow-ground type is the same as that of a tapering flat gun spring. The pressure exerted by the torque is dispersed upward into the thicker section of the blade like a spring, thus preventing the blade from breaking. One thing is certain: Either system is a one-hundred-percent improvement over the wedge-shaped blade.

It seems that once there was a crack in the wedge blade screwdriver dam, a flood of good tools flowed out and we now have not only good parallel blades but several special-made gun screwdrivers. There are currently a half-dozen different brands of correct screwdrivers on the market providing both the sportsman and the gunsmith a wide choice.

Grace Metal Products, Box 67, Elk Rapids, MI 49626, utilizes the first method whereby regular wedge-bladed screwdrivers are reground to form a section of blade with parallel sides. Only a short forward section of the blade is reground with the rest of the blade left unaltered for strength. The square-shanked screwdrivers come in different lengths with blade widths and thicknesses to match the most com-

mon gun screws. The handles are of wood with four flats on the sides to provide a good grip and taper at the front into a metal ferrule. A set of eight (No. HG-8) is available from gunsmith supply houses and many sporting goods stores. There are also sixteen special-ground blades for specific gun screws. An unusual feature is the guarantee to regrind broken or twisted tips at no charge.

Bonanza Sports of 412 Western Avenue, Faribault, MN 55021, also markets a parallel-sided blade screwdriver that differs slightly from the Grace screwdriver. The Bonanza shank is round with a grooved and hand-filling plastic handle that is cast on the shank. The blade itself is unique in its shortness. A seven-screwdriver set includes the most-used blade widths and thicknesses. Bonanza also offers individual blades ground for specific gun screws.

Christy Gun Works, 875 Fifty-seventh Street, Sacramento, CA 95819, markets blades for gun screwdrivers at approximately forty cents each. These are small parallel-sided blades ground from flat tool steel and with a flat shank. Due to their small size they are best used for close work.

The second system consists almost predominantly of a single basic handle with a chuck or receptacle on the front end of the shank to receive and hold short replaceable bits. The idea obviously originated to utilize the short and well made parallel hollow-ground bits used in impact and power screwdrivers so common in manufacturing industries. These bits are of top-grade steel carefully ground and tempered to withstand the extreme high torque of these power tools. By eliminating long shanks and a multitude of handles, the price can be kept quite low.

Brownell's, Incorporated, of Montezuma, Iowa, offered for some years a prime example of this system under the brand name of Magna-Tip. As the name implies, the tips (or bits) are held in the shaft chuck by a permanent magnet. This allows the bits to be changed rapidly from one size to another by simply pulling the bits free of the magnetic force. The magnet offers another advantage, as the magnetism is passed through the bit to the screw and will hold the screw firmly to the bit. This trick really comes in handy when you are faced with the task of trying to hold two gun parts together with one hand, a screwdriver in the other hand while positioning and starting the screw.

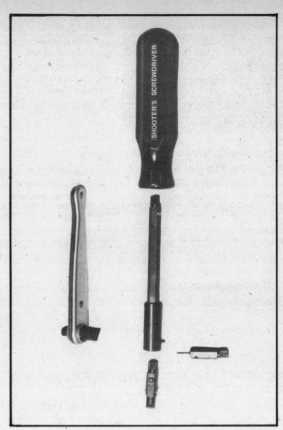

This screwdriver set, designed specifically for work on firearms, allows one to approach problem from a number of angles simply by installing the correct attachment.

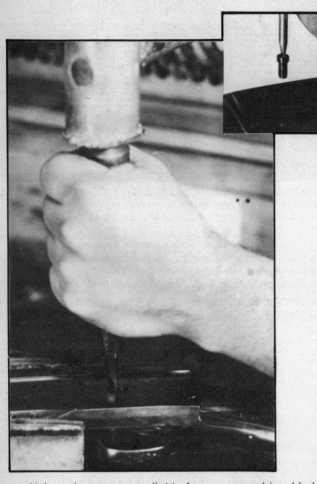

Using a hammer or mallet to force a screwdriver blade into the screw slot damages the screw, marks an amateur. (Inset) Screwdriver should be selected to fit the slot.

Brownell's offers one version that consists of a hollow handle to hold the bits plus four of the most commonly needed bits. The best buy is their assortment of twenty-four bits. The bits go into the block butt-first, which places the bits up for easy view and selection. The assortment of twenty-four includes hollow-ground parallel bits specifically selected to match gun screws, three Phillips type bits and a set of hex or Allen screw bits.

A recent and well thought out addition is the Shooters Screwdriver Kit by N&J Sales, Lime Kiln Road, North-

ford, CT 06472. This also uses interchangeable short bits but with a different system. The handle is of moulded plastic with a built-in quarter-inch chuck. A 3⅜-inch extension shaft is pressed into the handle chuck and is retained by a snap ball bearing and spring. On the opposite end of the extension shaft is another quarter-inch chuck to receive the individual bits each of which are equipped with the snap ball bearing and spring to hold them in place. An extra is a set screw in both the handle and the shaft chuck that, when tightened, locks the components together and eliminates wiggle. If a short shank screwdriver is desired, the bits can be placed directly into the handle chuck.

A Chapman midget ratchet also is available that will snap on the shank in lieu of the handle or directly on a bit. Reversing sides of the ratchet provides tightening or loosening direction. Normal torque with any hand-held screwdriver is around fifty inch-pounds. The Chapman ratchet provides over three hundred inch-pounds of torque which allows removal of screws that would be impossible to budge with a regular handle.

N&J offers three different kits. The field kit consists of the handle, the extension, nine bits and a carrying case. The deluxe kit has eleven hollow-ground bits, one Phillips bit, eleven hex or Allen bits, a quarter adapter for use with nut driving sockets, the handle, extension, Chapman ratchet and a plastic fitted case. There are thirty-two different bits available.

There is one screw in some guns that can give a mountain of trouble. I am referring to the stock screw or stock bolt used to hold the butt stocks to the receiver on guns with two-piece stocks. Constant recoil or a Strong-Wrist Charlie at the factory can get these so tight that it becomes a major task to get them loose. Too often, gun owners attempt to use a standard large long-handle screwdriver for the job. In many cases the blade slips out of the screw slot and the twist is exerted against the inside of the stock. The result is a screwdriver blade sticking out the side of a split stock.

As gunsmithing is my primary method of feeding a devoted wife, three daughters and three bird dogs, plus assisting on the national debt, I encounter the problem almost daily. The screwdriver obviously necessary is one thick enough to fill the stock hole and prevent the bit from sliding out of the slot. Washers were one solution, but I improved on this by making a screwdriver shank out of three-quarter-inch electrical conduit with another piece brazed across one end for a T handle and a bit soldered into the open opposite end. I used this for quite a few years.

I finally worked out a better system by using a regular three-eighths-inch drive socket assembly with a twelve-inch extension for the shank of the screwdriver, a sliding snap-in T handle and a three-quarter-inch-diameter modified drag link hollow-ground bit on the opposite end. The thinned drag link bit is used for regular slotted stock bolts and twelve-point sockets for the bolts with square, hexagon, and octagon heads. Bob Brownell of Brownell's became interested in the assembly and, at my urging, offered it in his catalog. The handle assembly, extension, drag link bit and four different size twelve-point sockets is a set.

Everyone working on guns, especially used ones, eventually will encounter a screw that absolutely refuses to budge even a thousandth of an inch. A short rap on the butt

Blade shapes (from top) are: Brownell Magna-Tip, short Christy flat blade, a reground blade from Grace and the wedge-shaped blade found in most hardware stores.

This blade is too thin for the screw slot. Outer edge of blade is only partially in contact with the slot. This causes edges of the blade to break and distorts the slot.

of the screwdriver, penetrating oil and heat are common remedies that often get things moving. Working with a difficult screw always creates the risk of the screwdriver bit breaking or slipping out of the socket and damaging the surrounding metal. Heat, if improperly used, can discolor the finish, plus there is always that extra-stubborn screw that resists even these efforts.

A gadget recently made available to gunsmiths and sportsmen is the equal of the most stubborn of screws. This is the impact driver, or rotary driver as it's sometimes listed. Several models are available from the gunsmith supply houses and sporting goods stores at various prices, but the best set I have found for gun use is marketed by Richland Arms Company, 321 West Adrian Street, Blissfield, MI 49228.

The set consists of the impact driver, six Apex hollow-ground bits, of which three have been ground for those narrow European screws, and an adapter to connect the bits to the impact driver. Two special plug drivers are designed to fit firing-pin bushings countersunk into the face of the breech of many double-barrel shotguns. One of the plug drivers is for the two-hole type bushing and the other matches the three-hole. An adapter to fit the plug drivers to the impact wrench plus extra plug pins are included in the set.

The impact driver can be used as a regular screwdriver, but its main job is to get those stubborn screws moving. In use, the bit is placed in the screw slot, the impact handle twisted in the correct direction and the back of the driver given a sharp rap with a hammer. The blow jars the screw which aids in loosening. But most important, it forces the outer shell of the driver down over the inner section. A cross pin and a cam connect the two sections and the downward movement causes the cam to exert snap torque to the bit. The combination of the jar and the snap torque will move screws when all other methods fail.

The amount of torque is in direct proportion to the force of the hammer blow. Therefore, the impact driver also can be used to tighten screws by simply rotating the handle in the correct direction before the rap with the hammer. This tightening action is useful when screws such as those on scope bases must be as tight as possible. The impact driver when used with the Brownell stock screwdriver will loosen those jammed butt stock screws in seconds.

With the wide selection of parallel-sided screwdrivers, special blades and inexpensive kits, no gun owner or gunsmith need use wedge-shaped screwdrivers. For those who desire to make their own hollow-ground screwdrivers, the correct tool steel is available from Brownell's. This is

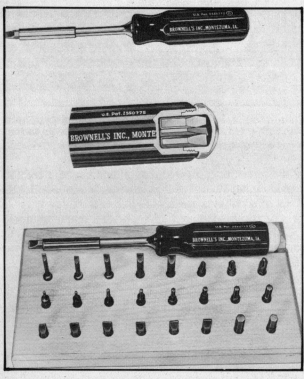

This handy combination set for which several blades fit the same handle, with internal storage, has been a top-selling item among gunsmiths for Iowa-based Brownell's.

Solar Hex Rod in ¼-, 5/16- and ⅜-inch across-the-flat thicknesses.

Solar Hex Rod is an alloy tool steel. Composed of carbon manganese, silicon and molybdenum, it is manufactured by the Carpenter Tool Steel Company of Reading, Pennsylvania. When hardened and drawn to C-59 Rockwell, it is the strongest and toughest too steel known with a tensile strength of 323,000 pounds per square inch. Screwdrivers correctly made and hardened from this steel will last for years without damage.

After hollow grinding the blade to the desired thickness

and cutting to length, heat the steel with a torch to a bright cherry red color or, if you have a furnace, to 1550 degrees Fahrenheit. The steel can be quenched in water or five-percent brine, but I personally prefer to use light oil. The quenching, whatever the solution, should be made with the blade tip entering the solution straight down, rapidly followed by the rest of the shank. This method prevents warping and uneven hardening. You can use the screwdriver just as it comes out of the quenching solution but, if you will place it in a regular kitchen oven at 300 Fahrenheit for one hour, the stress in the metal will be relieved and your

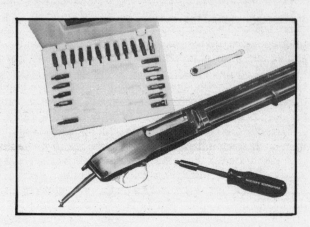

The N&J Deluxe Shooter's Screwdriver Kit, with fitted case, is shown (above) with a Model 42 Winchester .410 shotgun. The midget ratchet is offered by Chapman. (Below) The N&J Kit has bits, a handle, extension and a ratchet that will offer a high degree of flexibility.

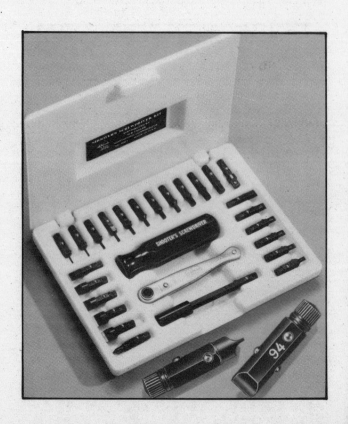

screwdriver will give better service. Handles can be turned on a wood or metal lathe, if you prefer your own design to commercial handles.

Correct selection of the screwdriver for the job is equally important as owning the right type. The blade tip should enter the screw slot without pressure, but with a firm snugness that eliminates wobble. A blade that is too thin will have all of the torque exerted against its outer edges with a potential burring of the screw slot or breaking of the blade. Dirty screw slots can give a false impression, so check and clean if necessary before using a screwdriver.

The width of the blade should just equal or be a fraction of an inch less than the width of the screw slot. Too little blade width will damage the slots or overtax the blade, while too much blade width will result in scratches in the metal surface around the screw.

With the gun held firmly in a padded vise or pressed against a clean workbench, guide the blade tip into the screw slot with the thumb and forefinger of your left hand. I keep these two fingers in this position all the time the screwdriver is being used to prevent the blade from accidentally slipping out of the screw slot.

The butt of the screwdriver handle should be pressed against the back of the palm of your right hand with your fingers curled around the handle and pointing to the blade. When ready, give the screwdriver a quick snap turn and the screw should start to move. Continue guiding the blade with the fingers of your left hand, as you reposition your right hand for another grip. Keep constant, downward pressure until the screw is removed.

If your gun has burred screws as a result of yur handiwork or that of others, the damage still can be corrected in many cases. Usually only the top section of the slot will be burred with the metal puckered up into an edge. The remedy is to get the metal back into its original position.

Select a one-eighth-inch punch with a short shank and polish the point with the edges lightly rounded. Incidentally, this is a good use for broken punches. Place the punch on one edge of the screw slot and hold it lightly between the thumb and forefinger of your left hand. Tap the butt of the punch lightly with your hammer and allow the punch to strike and bounce.

Keep repeating this while moving the punch back and forth across the length of the screw slot edge. Your rapid tapping may sound like a mad woodpecker, but the burred edge can be ironed neatly back in place. Repeat the same procedure on the other side of the slot. When finished use a thin clockmaker's file to touch up the insides of the screw slots and smooth the top edge. These files are available from Frank Mittermeier, Incorporated, 3577 E. Tremont Avenue, Bronx, NY 10465, or from Brownell's.

A set of screwdrivers that is well worth mentioning is marketed by Belco, Box 91501, Wordway Center, Los Angeles, CA 90009. This includes five screwdrivers with carbon steel blades and square, non-slip wood handles. The blades measure ⅛x2, 3/16x2, 3/16x4, ¼x2 and 5/16x2, all five coming in a plastic carrying case.

On a final note, if possible always align the screw slots parallel with the length of the gun or, in the case of butt plates, parallel with the length of the butt plate. Most fine guns have the screws aligned this way initially. Your parallel alignment of screw slots, repair of bluggered screws and the use of correct screwdrivers says to the world, "Here is a man who appreciates craftsmanship."

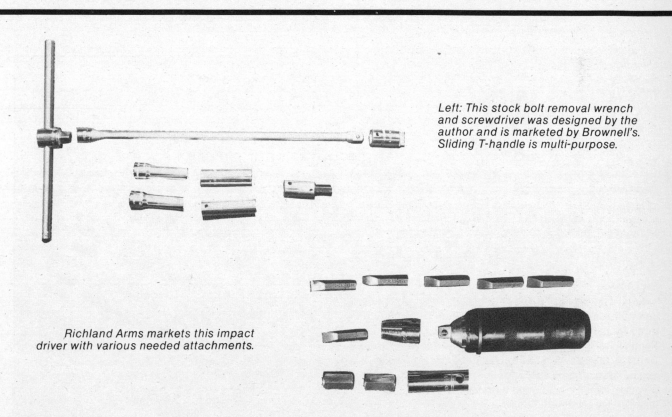

Left: This stock bolt removal wrench and screwdriver was designed by the author and is marketed by Brownell's. Sliding T-handle is multi-purpose.

Richland Arms markets this impact driver with various needed attachments.

Chapter 7

CHECK YOUR PATTERN

The Do's And Don'ts Of Determining Your Shotgun's Real Capabilities

Your ultimate success in the game field scan depend to a great degree upon how well your shotgun patterns.

These deformed shot pellets, enlarged for inspection, are somewhat misshapen. Damage of this type will affect pattern.

THE BEST indication of what each shot size, shot load, powder type and load, various chokes and gauges will or will not do at different ranges is the pattern board. You can read everything in print about shotgun patterns, spend hours sitting and theorizing, and yet learn more in ten minutes about actual performance of a shotgun with a given load by simply shooting patterns. And in smithing a shotgun, you have to know how it shoots if you ever want to make it shoot better.

If you ask one hundred shotgun shooters whether they have ever patterned their shotguns, seventy-five will answer a flat "no." Of the remaining twenty-five, about twenty-four, if questioned closely, will admit that their idea of patterning is to set a beer can on a post. If the can is perforated several times or dented severely, the gun is considered a "hard shooter." If the can goes sailing off the post, the gun is a "close patterning shotgun." Only one out of that hundred have actually shot at paper.

About half of those who have done some patterning have limited their experience to hanging a newspaper on a barbed wire fence, stepping off a distance and banging away. The newspaper is retrieved and given a quick glance at the number of holes in same. If there is an abundance of holes, the gun is pronounced as "chunking a right good pattern" to use a Southern expression.

From my own experience with shotguns and their owners, I have found that the person who has taken the time to carefully pattern his shotgun is a rare bid! Those who have, know what a shotgun will or will not do at various ranges. Invariably they are among the finest shooters, be the target made of clay or feathers.

Dove shooting here in my native Alabama is not a sport, but approaches a disease that affects both men and boys and quite a few ladies. More shots are fired at doves in one season than our ancestors fired in the four years they tried to establish the Confederacy. Drive down any road and it sounds like a war zone. Most shooters carry four boxes of shells (one hundred rounds) afield for every shoot and

Shot pattern can be controlled to a degree by selection of the one-piece wad used. At left is Windjammer wad with eight petals to catch air resistance, cause wad to separate from shot rapidly; other wads are ranked by petal stiffness. Stiff petals stay with wad longer and thus result in tighter pattern. All are 12-gauge for 1⅛-ounce loads of shot.

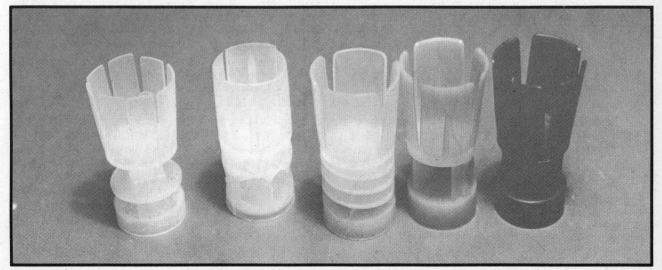

One can change the choke of his shotgun simply by cutting off the shot protector petals. A full choke gun would shoot modified with shot protectors so altered. With soft shot, spread is even greater, but shot will deform more.

most average about five or six doves total. Anyone who collects his limit of twelve doves is a real hot shot. The reason for such poor showing is a lack of knowledge.

For example, last year I was in a sporting goods store when three local hunters asked for my recommendations for a good dove load. As all were shooting 12 gauges, I recommended buying regular trap loads of 3 drams, with 1⅛-ounce #7½ shot. They thanked me courteously and walked away. Later when I was standing in the checkout line, the three hunters were ahead of me. Two were buying a case of game loads — 3¼ dram with one ounce of #8 soft shot; the other had several boxes of short magnum shells. So much for advice.

Let a lone dove come zipping across the field a full sixty yards high and everybody has to take a crack at him. Even if the lead was right, the range is out of the question, yet I have counted up to thirty shots fired at such a bird. Few hunters have any great practical knowledge of what their guns will do and what is the best load for a given set of hunting conditions.

What few realize is that with the exception of waterfowl, most shotgun game is taken at a realistic twenty to thirty yards with the hits out at forty yards a rare exception. The choke most often sold is full. Switch to a more open choke such as improved cylinder or modified and the score goes up with the same shooting conditions. I remember one instance when a shooter broke the ejector on his old Remington Model 11 with a full-choke barrel. Another shooter loaned him the only available barrel, one cut off to twenty inches for quail hunting and with a straight cylinder bore, no choke. That guy started busting doves like crazy and ended up having his own full-choke barrel bobbed off later.

Over the years I have asked literally hundreds of shotgun shooters why they do not take the time to pattern their guns Most don't know how and those who have some idea are thoroughly confused by the multitude of instructions and variations of patterning.

Shooting shotgun patterns begins with setting up a sheet of paper exactly four feet square at a measured forty yards from the firing point. Right off the bat a problem arises at just finding such paper. Most such paper in my neck of the woods is three feet wide. No sweat with the missing twelve-inch width — I use the thirty-six-inch paper with no problems; however you can tape two pieces together, although little is gained.

Now we go back to the forty-yard line with our improved cylinder choke and fire a shot at the supposed center of the paper. Retrieving same, we place it on a table and select the most dense part and draw a thirty-inch circle around this section. Count each of the holes and put a check mark on each to keep score. You consult the chart and find out how many pellets were in your shell before firing and you use this number to divide your count by and thus arrive at a percent of the pattern.

An improved-cylinder choke should give a fifty percent pattern. Were we shooting a full choke, the percent would be seventy, modified would be sixty, while straight cylinder gives us forty percent. If we follow the Oberfell and Thompson system we draw an inner circle of twenty-inch diameter and count the pellets both within this inner circle and outer circle. Now we count the pellets in the thirty-inch circle and divide by the number of pellets in the twenty-inch circle. This in turn is multiplied by one hundred to give the pellet distribution factor. Still with me?

Not so, says the National Rifle Association. According

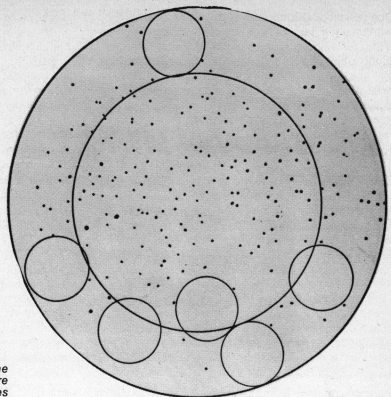

By drawing five-inch circles on the sections of patterning target where there are no pellets, one determines where holes are in a gun's pattern.

to the NRA, the inner circle should be exactly 21.21 inches in diameter. They reason that this figure gives the exact same area total as that of the outer circle which is that space between the 21.21-inch circle and the outer thirty-inch circle. Next step is to draw a line from north to south on the paper, then from east to west. We now have a total of eight sections, supposedly to give a more accurate count in case you get lost along the way. So the total of the inner four pieces of the pie-like pattern divided by the total of the outer four pieces gives us what is known as center thickening.

According to Oberfell and Thompson, we have one more step to go. We must count the number of patches in the pattern. To do this we make a plastic disc five inches in diameter and move it about over the holes. Each time we can place that disc without covering a shot hole, we draw a circle. When finished we count all of these circles and thus have our "patch factor."

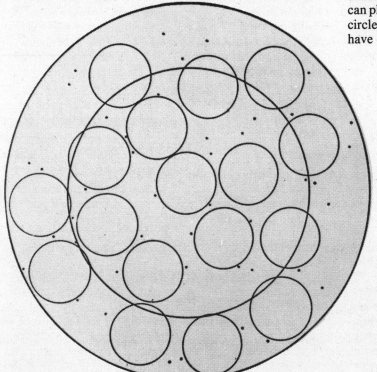

As shown by the five-inch circles drawn on the patterning target to indicate open areas, hitting game with this particular gun had to be considered more luck than talent!

Don't count on the thorough Germans for help, as they divide that outer ring into twelve sections and the inner ring into four for a sixteen-section pattern drawing episode.

If you are not thoroughly confused or tired of drawing circles and lines by now, you are one in a million. One can only imagine doing this the suggested ten or twelve times to arrive at the "pattern average" which so many gun writers recommend. Confidentially, I think most of this is done on a typewriter, for anyone would be hard pressed to go through all of this over and over and still stay out of the nut house.

Our British cousins, who are supposed to be shotgun specialists, make a great production of shooting at a steel plate with the thirty-inch circle pre-drawn and the center serving as an aiming point. A non-drying paint made from white lead and oil is used to wipe out the previous shot.

Some people carry this a bit far. I read not long ago that someone figured out that all British percentages should be reduced by two percent as they fired with the muzzle past the forty-yard point, hence they were just a few inches closer to the target than the American pattern shooter!

What has all of this to do with practical answers to shotgun patterns? Before I am struck from the rolls of life membership in the NRA let me explain. The NRA staff is stuck with the problem of evaluating one shotgun against another, using a common yardstick for both. As everyone expects that organization to be the epitome of truth, they do count all of those little holes. Whether it makes one tad of difference between the Oberfell & Thompson's twenty-inch circle and the NRA's 21.21 inches is open to doubt, but technically the NRA is correct. That north to south and east to west line on the pattern is also of doubtful use, but I suppose they are trying to make it all as technical as possible. The O&T five-inch patch counter has its merits, but I suppose the NRA felt the subject was confusing enough without this addition.

Now that I have bad-mouthed everyone else's method of patterning a shotgun, the question remains as to whether I can offer a better and simpler system. Time and knowledge are the only things a gunsmith has to sell, so I do not waste either on patterning, yet have arrived at a satisfactory method.

First let's forget the matter of firing from a fixed position that is forty yards away from the target. Forty yards is about the maximum for a shotgun and is correct for full-choke guns. But who in his right mind shoots an improved-cylinder-choked gun at forty yards? This is absurd and so is the matter of counting fifty percent of the pattern at this range for this choke. Like a broken watch, the time is only correct every twelve hours, hence the forty-yard range is only correct for a full-choked shotgun barrel.

Why this forty-yard technique for all patterning of all chokes has persisted for so many years is a mystery to me. Perhaps it is chiseled in stone somewhere and followed religiously as the last word on the subject. It is definitely not practical for field shooting.

However, the figure of seventy percent of the pellets striking within the designated thirty-inch circle is as good a yardstick as any. It could just as well be eighty percent at less yardage or some other figure. For the sake of clarity, let's stay with that seventy percent in the thirty-inch-diameter circle. We change only the distance from the fir-ing point to the target and remain within reason.

If we move the firing line forward until we are thirty-five yards from the target, we now have the correct distance for a modified choke. We still use the seventy percent pattern percentage figure as the goal within that thirty-inch circle. Move forward five more yards until the distance from firing line to target is thirty yards and we have the correct range for an improved-cylinder-choked barrel, still maintaining that seventy percent pattern within the circle. Move forward to twenty-five yards from target and we have the range for a straight cylinder barrel.

This, in my mind, is a more practical approach to patterning shotguns and duplicates the conditions found in the field and on a skeet range. The pattern results will be more practical. Said another way, shot pattern will change approximately ten percent for each change of five yards distance. Note that I say approximately; there are always variables, but this system is realistic.

If this more practical approach is used by gunsmiths and field shooters they can instantly see the potential of any given choke, shot size or weight and the load of the shell variations. It gives a good picture of what the pattern will look like as it is on its way to the target, be it clay or feathered. The inner circle of twenty (or 21.21) inches is totally eliminated in this system. I also do not use the five-inch-diameter plastic disc that Oberfell and Thompson advocate. My hand is approximately the same size as a clay target or a bird. I simply place my hand over any "weak" spot in the pattern and quickly have an idea of any section of the pattern that would not have sufficient pellets for a good pattern. I mark an X over these spots. Now we can look at our pattern and concentrate on a good even distribution of the pellets which is what takes game. It is quick and clear.

What if the forty-yard full choke delivers more than seventy percent? Well, we simply have an unusually tight choke. Make the distance forty-five yards and shoot another pattern. If this is seventy percent you have an extra-full-choke gun. This is not so uncommon, as many shotguns will deliver such a pattern, including trap guns designed for the maximum twenty-seven-yard position. Some guns are custom choked for long-range shooting, which our British cousins term "over choke." The thing to remember is that that shot patterned at forty yards or less range is no longer thirty inches in diameter but much less.

How about sixty-five percent at forty yards or seventy-five percent at the thirty-five-yard range? There is a standard choke between full and modified known as an improved-modified choke that will deliver about this pattern percentage at these ranges. Improved-modified could be termed as a weak full or tight modified choke. It was quite common in early America and the British system would designate it as three-quarter choke. Some screw-in choke tubes such as the WinChoke offer such a choke, although it has to be special ordered. It is best used in a double-barrel gun with one barrel bored extra-full and the other improved-modified, but it has limited practical use.

There is also a choke designation that falls between the regular modified choke and the improved-cylinder choke. This is Skeet-2, but is not common on guns of modern manufacture. It was used on skeet guns of the double-barrel type for outgoing clay targets. It makes a fine choice for some upland game shooting. Its partner is Skeet-1 which falls between an improved cylinder choke and a true cylinder bore used in the past for incoming clay targets. If you use an over/under or side-by-side, a choke of Skeet-1 in the bottom barrel and Skeet-2 in the top barrel makes about as perfect an upland game shotgun as you will find. I have a Beretta over/under that was custom-made at the factory for me some years ago. One of the two-barrel sets is choked Skeet-1 and Skeet-2 and it is my pride and joy.

Straight cylinder or true cylinder is simply no choke at all. This is hard to beat for quick-rising game such as quail. It puts that thirty-inch circle of shot up at about twenty-five yards and is quite deadly in the hands of someone who normally shoots fast when a target is in view. Modern shotguns, built after introduction of the plastic shot protector and marked *Skeet*, are straight cylinder with no choke. From a practical point there is no difference in modern guns marked cylinder or skeet. Straight cylinder is quite popular in my neck of the woods and many guns that are purchased of necessity with a more tighter choke undergo what is commonly called here as a "hacksaw choke." Meaning that the choke section of the barrel has been cut off and the gun is now straight cylinder or no choke. I have often advocated that the best choke for a beginner is straight cylinder and teach him what twenty- or thirty-yard range looks like in the field. The end result is that he makes a lot more hits and thus gains confidence in his ability.

With the advent of the modern plastic shot protector and other improvements in shotshells in general, the old choke constrictions were simply too tight. For example, if you shoot handloads with the shot protector in a straight cylinder barrel, then cut away the shot protector petals with all

other conditions the same, the results are surprising. The unprotected shot load will give the same pattern percent that the protected shot load gives at an increased five-yard range. This five-yard advantage held true with all of the old chokes. Full became extra-full, modified choke then was improved-modified and so on, which resulted in the amount of constriction of chokes in modern guns being less than in the older guns manufactured prior to the advent of the shot protector.

This is the reason one no longer sees the old Skeet-1 and 2 designations, for these were made for the unprotected shot load. As previously stated, the need was for less choke for skeet ranges, hence the straight cylinder bore in so-called skeet guns. Skeet range is close and some advocate a wider pattern than even a non-choked gun will deliver. The Tula choke that the Russians use is really just an old idea. The old Cutts spreader tube did the same thing as did the Lyman system with the spreader tube; the Poly Choke has a reverse choke. All result in identical results. This is the thirty-inch-diameter circle at twenty yards or, in other words, a spread.

If you use unprotected shot you also will get the spread effect. You can use straight soft shot and gain that desired spread. If you handload, French square shot or British disc shot will give the same results. They simply take advantage of air flow around a shot that is not spherical in shape and the air flow spreads the shot. All of this is really ancient history, but one would think that the Russians had invented something new. If you want the same as a Tula choke, install a Lyman choke with the recoil chamber attached prior to the choke tube.

The foregoing system of drawing that thirty-inch circle around the most dense section of the pattern is correct, if

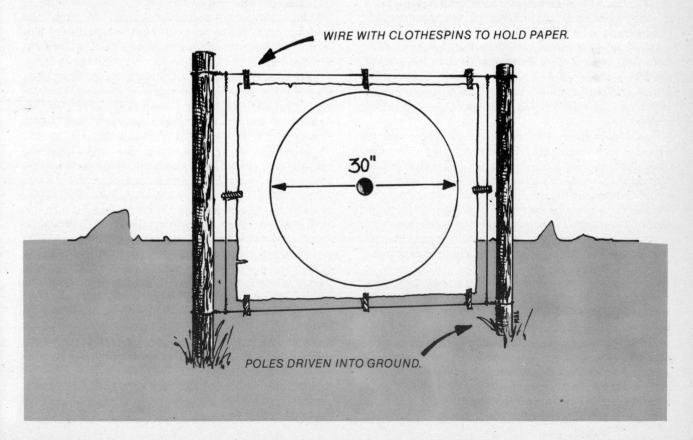

WIRE WITH CLOTHESPINS TO HOLD PAPER.

30"

POLES DRIVEN INTO GROUND.

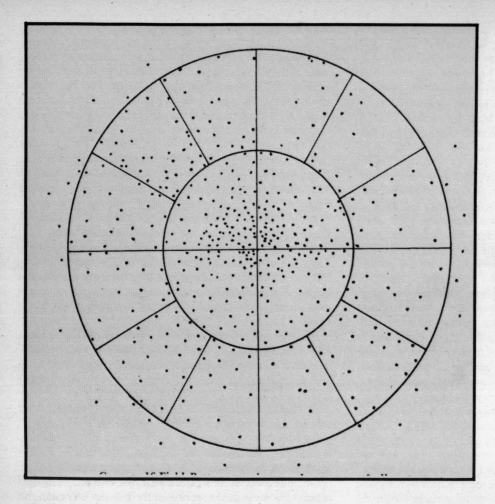

German shooters often favor this patterning target which features sixteen different areas for determining the spread of shot from barrel.

the only aim is to determine the maximum potential of a barrel. You also can draw that inner circle and use the five-inch plastic disc. All depends on how technical you want to get. The firing of more than one pattern to arrive at an "average" is useful only if you want to carry things to the final decimal point. But remember that this data and information provides only the hypothetical maximum potential of one specific barrel shooting one specific shell. It does nothing else.

There are variables. For instance, you can use a chart to work out how many pellets of any shot size are in one ounce or fraction thereof. The chart is an average. American shotshells of standard load will vary from a plus-three percent to a minus-five percent, which is an eight percent variable. This is a good load of the target class or premium class. The so-called field loads run from a plus-four percent to a minus-seven percent for an eleven percent variable factor. This must be taken into consideration when counting pellet holes.

Now we must consider the Random Factor, which is a fancy way of saying that no two shot patterns will have the identical number of holes in the identical place on the paper. Each will differ. The weak section of a pattern will shift from one location for one pattern shot to an entirely different sector on the next pattern. To get that "average," you must shoot more than one pattern, total all patterns, then divide by the number of patterns shot. There is no other way to be absolutely technically correct.

For field shooting this can all be forgotten. You cannot

pre-select the shotshell nor would you know where to look for this shell. From a practical point of view, "shoot the shell and take your chances." The only reason for bringing up the fact that actual pellet count will vary in shotshells and that the random factor does occur is to get things down to a practical view for the gunsmith or shooter who wants to learn what the gun will do. Simply said, shoot a pattern and view the results, but bear in mind that there are some factors over which you have no control — and don't worry about that last decimal point when evaluating a pattern.

There is one more fly in the punch bowl in that one specific load will not shoot identically to the same specific load made by another manufacturer. For instance, if you take a quality shell such as a trap load of 3-1⅛ #7½ shot made by Winchester and shoot some patterns, an identical shell made by Remington or Federal will not give the same results; nor would an initial pattern with Remington loads give the same results as that of the same shell load made by Winchester or Federal shot in the same gun. If you change barrels, even made by the same manufacturer for the same gun, results will also vary.

In effect, with one specific barrel you may get best results with the Winchester shell, second best with Federal and last with Remington. Change barrels and the results may be just the opposite. You cannot predetermine the results of a manufacturer's shell performance. The key thing this teaches is that any given barrel will give the best possible results only if you shoot patterns and learn from the results. This fact should be a red flag waving to those who buy any shell handy, even if it is top quality. Each barrel must be treated as an individual.

Now let's go one step further in discussing variables. The powder charge of a shotshell is extremely important as far as velocity is concerned and it is equally important for propelling each pellet. The slightest variation in the powder charge will produce variables in pattern performance. Thus change from one power load to another, in even the same brand of shell, and results change drastically in the same barrel. There is no way to anticipate what a variation in powder will mean on the pattern board. You must test each powder charge to learn the results. Each shell will pattern differently and you simply settle on one that offers the best performance.

If you handload, switching from one brand of primer to another also can result in wide variations. Federal primers for instance, are hotter than Winchester and Winchester hotter than Remington. Industry sources also say that swapping of primers can be dangerous! The hot primer simply ignites powder faster and the burn rate is changed. Stay with the same primer and don't switch.

Shot size is probably the most misunderstood thing about shotshells. Most shooters feel that if a barrel is stamped full choke, they will get the same pattern with all sizes of shot. Not so. Each shot size will give different results through any choke. Usually the tighter the choke, the smaller the shot size it will handle efficiently, but this is not an irrevocable law.

For example, I shot a Browning Auto-5 for quite a few years with a modified choke. With 7½ shot it would deliver almost a full-choke percentage. Drop to size 8 shot and the percent went even higher. Increasing shot size to #6 and I had the modified pattern that was stamped on the barrel. Number 5 shot gave about the same results, but shot any larger and I was shooting an improved-cylinder choke for all practical results. I finally put a Poly choke on the gun so I could make different settings to achieve the modified choke with various shot sizes.

I have seen other Brownings give similar and also different results. A cardinal rule is to use the choke designation as a guide only. Actual results may or may not coincide and only the pattern board can tell for sure.

Therefore if you decide on a certain pellet size as the one you want to shoot, my advice would be to buy a full choke and find a top-notch gunsmith who understands chokes. By removing a bit of choke at a time he can arrive at the exact specification that will give the exact pattern you want with this shot size. Don't forget that powder charge and all other factors must be consistent or the game is off. I have custom-choked barrels for my customers many times and it is not cheap. The customer has to decide exactly what shell he will shoot, the manufacturer and the exact powder charge. Then he must decide on the pellet size.

The custom-choking task is not easy; it is a matter of cutting one-thousandth-inch, shooting patterns, repeating the process over and again until the desired pattern is achieved. I always warn customers that I do not guarantee anything else and any change, no matter how small, voids my guarantee. Provided you start with a full choke, which gives adequate metal to work with, you can decrease the amount of choke constriction about one-thousandth-inch

in diameter each time with a reamer. While most knowledgeable gunsmiths know about the dimension needed for a certain shot size, no one can be specific and the only way is to cut and shoot, cut and shoot. One-thousandth-inch in diameter can make a lot of difference in pattern percentage. Switch to even another pellet size and you are back to square one as far as knowing what the results will be.

The entire purpose of shooting patterns is to determine the maximum capability of the barrel with different shot sizes, loads and manufacturers. You can only determine maximum barrel potential, nothing else. The patterns could be shot equally well using a machine to hold the barrel as the point of impact is not important, the thirty-inch circle being drawn around the most dense part of the achieved pattern.

If you shoot many patterns you will quickly learn that the more balanced the load you use, the more evenly distributed the pellet hits. Move up to the short magnum shells and the pellets start to clump in one area, leaving another relatively untouched. This is misleading to the hunter. Should he by chance down game at a long range, he automatically thinks that all of his shots will be equally proficient. What he does not consider is the large number of misses when game passes through the open spaces of the pattern. A balanced load on the other hand will give more equal pellet distribution throughout the entire thirty-inch circle.

All of the foregoing is fine in determining the maximum capabilities of any given barrel, load and shot size. But no game bird will back up and apologize for not placing itself in the thickest part of your pattern. What is required is to place the center of that thirty-inch circle directly onto the target and take advantage of the pattern spread to compensate for any failure to exactly center the pattern. Think of the extra spread as a form of insurance that allows hits that otherwise would be misses.

Getting that pattern on target is a different problem that is not given much airing. There seems to be endless words on pattern percentages, but little on placing the pattern where the target is.

The British use a pattern plate with the thirty-inch circle pre-drawn. The shooter shoulders the shotgun and tries to place the pattern within that circle. With the results of several such shots a knowledgeable gunsmith can determine the root cause of any miss and herein lies a lot of know-how that is not easily taught. This, of course, assumes that the shooter knows how to mount the gun properly and is reasonably proficient with it. If not, the fault can be with either the gun or the shooter.

If the gunsmith has learned how to shoot and can compensate for any individual customizing of the gun, the problem is cut in half. This was the reason for the lengthy explanation of proper stance in another chapter. A gunsmith must learn this lesson thoroughly to eliminate the human factor as much as possible. The shooter may be short or tall, but the difference in gun length, et cetera, can be compensated for in most cases. Good shooting cannot be taught out of a book, but the correct stance and lessons can speed the gunsmith along this road.

Once it has been determined that the fault in not placing the pattern properly is that of the gun and not the shooter, certain steps can be taken. It is wise to make final adjustments using the customer to do the final shooting. The gunsmith only works on what is obvious in corrective measures on the gun.

One of the most common complaints is that a gun is shooting left or right and above or below the target consistently. It is surprising how many times the cause is a bent barrel. Shotgun barrels being relatively thin are bent quite easily. Even a simple fall can bend the barrel, so such a complaint should be taken seriously.

The best way of checking this is to remove the barrel from the receiver if possible. Pick a lighted doorway and use the edge of this door to cast a shadow line down the outside of the barrel. If the line stays constantly straight, the barrel is straight. If you see a bend in the line, the barrel is bent at this point. The second check utilizes the same system in looking down the bore itself, as on a rare occasion the bend will not show up on the exterior of the barrel.

Straightening a bent barrel is a tough job and I never have found a simple explanation of the process. It is best learned by following the instructions of someone who knows how to do the job. Basically you apply pressure at the point of the bend, but this takes a lot of practical experience as it is easy to bend too much or in the wrong place and make the job impossible afterward. For those who would learn the technique, I would suggest practice on old, junk barrels until you learn how. The first thing to learn is to bend the barrel back a small amount at a time in a springing action rather than by sheer force.

Choke adapters installed on the muzzle constitute another prime course of the shot charge striking off-center. Simply look down the bore at the adapter carefully and you can usually see that the adapter is off-center. Correction can best be accomplished by loosening the solder joint and letting the adapter settle in the centerline of the bore. If this is not possible, a short length of rod turned to bore size is clamped in a vise and the turned end placed in the bore. Springing action will center the adapter, but do it a bit at a time, instead of with one big application of pressure.

Double-barrel shotguns — side-by-sides and over/unders — with bent barrels are a major problem. It takes an unusually skilled gunsmith to correct the problem and even his ability is somewhat limited. Should this occur, turn the gun over to a gunsmith you are convinced is capable of doing the job. On some guns it is necessary to cut the choke to an oval shape to achieve centering of the pattern. This should be left to a skilled gunsmith.

One cause of shooting off-center can be a replaced front sight or even the original in a few limited cases. It may not be apparent at first, but I have seen it happen numerous times. Correction consists of locking the gun in a vise and leveling it left or right. Generally the off-center sight can be observed quite easily, then adjusted as necessary.

The butt stock can affect the shotgun's point of impact more than is commonly realized. The stock must be fitted to the person doing the shooting or altered to fit him. The common factory stock is a compromise to fit the average person. Normally the owner tries to adapt to the stock rather than altering the stock to fit his needs. What is surprising is how easily this can be corrected by minor adjustment.

Generally a stock that is too long will cause a right-handed shooter to fire to the left of the target, reverse for a left-handed shooter. The reason is that the butt plate is too far out; in the case of the right-handed shooter, at the moment of firing the recoil pushes the gun quickly to the right, resulting in a hit to the left of the target. Correction is simply cutting the stock to the correct length to fit the shooter, which eliminates the "too far out on the arm" tendency of the shooter.

A stock that is too short can result in the reverse effect, hitting to the right in fast shooting. A short stock can cause the impact to go slightly low, but this depends on individual physical build. One thing is sure: such stocks will kick the living daylights out of the person doing the shooting. A recoil pad normally will solve this problem.

A straight stock — one with little drop — invariably shoots high and above the target. On rising birds this is desirable, but not for general shooting. A recoil pad installed to give more pitch makes the gun shoot lower. (Pitch is the distance from a wall to the barrel when the gun is set firmly on its butt plate on the floor next to the wall. Stated another way, the toe of the stock is closer to the muzzle than original while the heel or top of the stock remains unchanged. You simply change the angle of the butt plate.)

A stock with a lot of drop, such as those found on old side-by-side doubles, will shoot low for most people. Sometimes an imported gun will have excessive drop and result in lower hits when fired. Correct by reversing the foregoing; the toe of the stock remains unchanged while you cut the upper portion or heel of the butt stock forward a little more. The result is a gun with less pitch than before. This makes the muzzle point upward more than normal which is the reverse of the stock that is too straight and shooting too high.

A trial set-up can be done prior to shooting that will give some idea of what is being done. Just unscrew the butt plate screws a couple of turns. Now place a common washer under the lower screw which gives the impression of the toe coming back and the heel going forward; this is for a stock with too much drop. If you like, fire a few shots at paper

Author uses 3x5-inch file cards, approximately the size of a game bird's body, in working on chokes. Each of the cards was shot from 30 yards with shells from the same box, as progressive adjustments were made in choke.

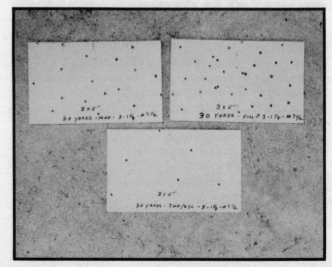

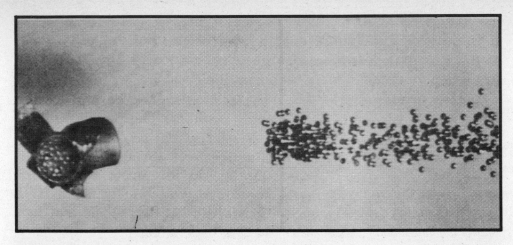

Full choke offers a stringing effect as shot is held closer on leaving muzzle.

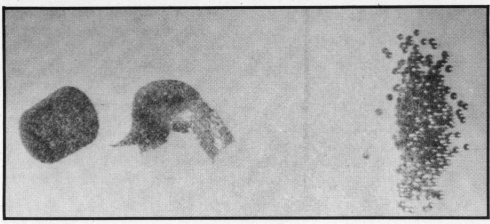

Cylinder choke, shot with plastic wad protector, is pancake-like in appearance.

and, if necessary, put in another washer on the bottom screw. Once you have the correct angle established, measure it and duplicate it when you cut the stock to install a recoil pad.

For the straight stock that is firing too high, simply reverse the procedure. Place the washer under the top screw, between butt plate and stock, then shoot the gun. Add another washer if desired. This trick puts the toe of the butt plate at the original angle while the upper heel is farther back.

This may sound confusing, but it is quite simple to understand when you start changing that angle of the butt plate. Test it and you will understand quickly that it is necessary only to remove a small section of wood and that the actual angle change is small. If you want to temporarily lengthen the pull prior to putting on a recoil pad to permanently change length, then just install a washer or washers under both of the butt plate screws. A one-eighth or quarter-inch change in length will amaze the beginner. If you want the stock temporarily shorter remove the butt plate completely and shoot the gun without it. Most butt plates are about one-quarter-inch thick, a lot when you are shortening a stock.

Where does the average person or regular gunsmith do this shooting? I doubt that the average shooter wants to make up a steel pattern plate and the same can be said for the regular gunsmith. These are expensive and require a permanent location as the weight is a problem. There is a simpler system that works just as well.

Remember that thirty-six-inch-wide common wrapping paper? Tear off two sections about three feet long. Tape the edges of these two sections together. If you shoot enough patterns the taping can be eliminated as you end up with a thirty-six-inch square to shoot at. It all depends on how much paper you want to print the results.

Cut a board three feet in length and drill two holes in the ends. The holes are for cords to hang the board in a nearby tree. Use thumb tacks to hold the top of the paper to your board. Cut a similar board for the bottom of your paper which will pull the paper down and keep it taut. If you want to get fancy, you can put the large clipboard-type retainers on the boards and eliminate the thumb tacks. I never have made one this fancy.

With a black felt pen put an aiming spot about three inches in diameter in the center of the paper. If you wish, draw the thirty-inch circle around the aiming point, but as the paper is thirty-six inches wide anyway, you will have three inches outside the circle on each side left. Who says that the pattern must be exactly thirty inches and must be round?

What is important is that you shoot several patterns, make it as simple an operation as possible and the paper changing easy. When you make the business of shooting patterns complicated you may gain accuracy, but keep the job easy and more shooting is done. Pattern shooting is the teacher, but the results do the talking. The more patterns shot the better, as you quickly learn to evaluate the results by vision only. The test facilities must be set up easily, taken down easily or the shooter will go back to that beer can on a fence post!

Chapter 8

What To Do About HEADSPACE

Here's An Age-Old Problem That Can Blow Your Patterns If Not Properly Controlled

THE AVERAGE shooter thinks that all shotgun chambers require is to stick the appropriate gauge shell into the hole, close the breech and bang away. Nothing could be farther from the truth as the chamber of any shotgun plays an important role in the gun's overall performance

There are actually three sections to any shotgun chamber, the headspace recess, the chamber walls and the forcing cone that leads from the chamber into the bore. Each is important and therefore should be considered individually.

A recess is cut at the rear of every chamber to accept the rim of the shotshell. The thickness of the shotshell rim and the depth of the recess cut for it play an important part in the recoil of the shotgun. A few years ago I was on an assignment to a manufacturer in Brazil who was exporting a shotgun to the United States. My job was to solve some problems and to arrive at a set of specifications on the chamber. A sample gun was built at the research and development department of the factory and I thoroughly tested it on the company range. The sample gun performed flawlessly with excellent shooting results. As all testing was done with shotshells manufactured in Brazil, the final step was to bring the gun back to the States for the same tests with American shotshells.

The action of this shotgun has been tightened by peening the bottom of the lugs that exit at the bottom of the frame. The author considers this the ultimate in sloppy workmanship and states that, at best, it is a temporary measure.

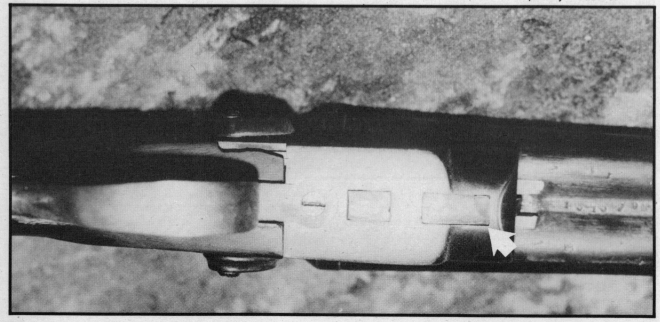

Another poor method for taking up the slack in an action is to peen the front of the lug with a hammer, as shown.

Pattern performance was good, but the gun offered far more recoil than I had experienced in Brazil. I asked for the shotshell data from the manufacturer and went over this thoroughly comparing it to known pressures and velocities of American shells. There was little difference that would account for the difference in recoil. I then asked for specifications of the chamber which was, of course, in metric. There was the culprit!

The Brazilian shells were manufactured with a thicker rim and the chamber recess for that rim was cut deeper to match the shell. By SAAMI specifications, the recess was so deep that it did not meet the maximum allowed tolerance. To make a long story short, another R&D gun was manufactured to American specifications and shipped to me for testing. With the same shell that was used in the first test, the excess recoil disappeared. The production model of the gun then was made with a new set of specifications to match the American shell and this part of the problem was solved.

Why should the depth of the rim recess make such a difference? This requires explanation that is not commonly considered when a shotgun is repaired by a gunsmith.

Said one way, headspace is the distance between the rear of a fully chambered shotshell and the face of the fully closed breech or breech bolt. Another definition is the distance from the face of the fully closed breech and the for-

ward section of the recess cut in the chamber. It all depends on how you are measuring this space. Personally I prefer the latter definition, as it is a bit easier to work with.

Headspace gauges manufactured in the United States consist of two solid metal plug-type gauges. The only difference is the thickness of the rim of the gauge. One is marked *minimum*, the other *maximum* and the gun's gauge is designated. They are available through Brownell's Incorporated.

The minimum gauge simply means that when the gauge is inserted into the chamber and the gun fully closed, it should close without difficulty. If it does not close, the recess cut for the shotshell rim is not deep enough to accept a standard American shotshell. With this gauge removed and the maximum gauge inserted into the chamber, an attempt is made to fully close the breech. It should not close. If it does close, the rim recess is cut too deeply and the chamber has excess headspace.

Excess headspace in a shotgun chamber is not as critical as in a rifle chamber, but it still should not be taken lightly. There is a danger point in this situation for excess headspace means that the rim of the shotshell is not fully supported by the surrounding chamber. In a rifle the cartridge is quite thick at this point and will forgive a multitude of sins. The shotshell rim usually is made of folded metal and is considerably weaker. In extreme cases the rim will split

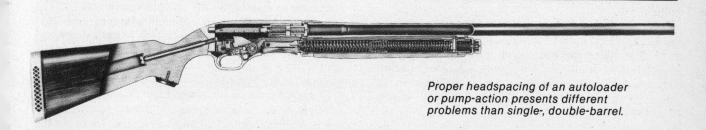

Proper headspacing of an autoloader or pump-action presents different problems than single-, double-barrel.

or rupture and release gas from the shell. I have seen this happen and it is not a pleasant feeling to have gas spewing that close to your face. Under these conditions a fired shotshell may have a split rim or the rear of the shell may be blown off to leave nothing to contain gas pressure; in a shotgun chamber, such pressure is in the neighborhood of 10,000 pounds per square inch (psi).

Even if this pressure is not reached, the rear of the shotshell can be bulged, making the case useless for reloading, but more important, the gun will not properly extract or eject the fired case. On some pumps and semiautos, the brass rear of the shotshell is torn loose and the forward section of the shell is left in the chamber. This can create considerable safety problems, but at the least another shell will not chamber and thus you have a feed condition that could be mistaken as to source of probable cause. In short, headspace can affect three things on a shotgun: failure to correctly extract, eject or feed the next shell. Every shotgun chamber should be checked with headspace gauges before any conclusions as to root cause of a problem is decided by the gunsmith. Yet this is often either overlooked or ignored in shotgun repair.

It is good practice to check every gun not manufactured in the United States with the gauges, as foreign shotshells are not made to the specifications of the American shotshell. Incidentally, this can be considered a point of national pride, as no other country produces a shotshell even close to the quality and precision of American shotshells. I have fired a lot of foreign-made shells and can testify as to the truth of the foregoing. So, if the gun is made overseas, hold it in suspect until the chamber is checked with the minimum and maximum headspace gauges.

What actually happens when a shotshell is fired in a chamber in which the rim recess is excessively deep? The striker or firing pin drives the shell forward until it is halted by the front shoulder of the cut recess. The primer is ignited and in turn ignites the powder charge. The resulting gases expand the walls of the shotshell until they obturate or seal to the inner ways of the chamber under normal conditions.

When excess headspace is present, before obturation can occur the gas pushes the shotshell to the rear and slams it against the face of the breech. This slam force creates a rearward thrust on the complete gun. Added to the force of the shotshell in its rearward thrust of the gun, which we call recoil, you have a combined thrust and excessive recoil is felt on the shoulder of the shooter.

Degree of extra recoil depends on the depth of the recess cut in the chamber rear and the rim of the shotshell. The more space created, the more the slam force. If the barrel is corrected to give zero space, my own experience suggests reduction of between ten and twenty percent. There is a definite difference before and after the headspace is corrected.

The only shotgun that completely solves this problem is the French Darne side-by-side. This gun has a breech block that slides forward on the frame and closes the breech instead of utilizing the normal break-open design. The forward closing of the breech block compresses the rim of the shotshell, which means that headspace is zero when the shell is fired. The Darne is lightweight, but the recoil is amazingly soft. This has been tested several times using a regular-designed shotgun of identical weight, firing the same shotshell in both guns. The Darne always has less recoil as measured on a scale. The only logical explanation is compression of the shotshell rim to zero headspace. I understand that the gun was designed deliberately to eliminate the problem of varying shotshell rim thickness.

To correct a chamber that has the rim recess cut to a depth that allows closure on the maximum headspace gauge is not simple. It depends to a great extent on both the type of shotgun and the barrel itself. There is no pat answer.

For starters, assume the problem involves a shotgun barrel with a barrel extension, the most common. The barrel screws into the barrel extension which, in turn, has a recess cut to accept the locking block of the breech bolt. The Mossberg 500 series pump shotgun uses this design facet, as does the Remington 1100 and 870 as well as many others. The inserted maximum gauge and the closed breech block indicate excess headspace. Incidentally this is best checked with the barrel and barrel extension removed from the gun and the breech block also removed from the receiver. They are held together by hand for inspection.

Check the locking lug recess for excess wear and the face of the locking lug for wear; the face is the rear of the lug that comes into contact with the recess in the barrel extension. On some guns such as a Mossberg 500 this recess extends fully through the barrel extension. If there is excess wear and the consequent excess play there are two ways to solve the problem. First is to try a new locking block. With this installed, recheck with the maximum gauge. Sometimes this is all that is required to close the excess headspace gap. If not, the locking lug recess cut in the barrel extension must be rebuilt as barrel extensions usually cannot be purchased separately from the manufacturer.

Push the breech bolt fully foward and also push the locking block upward. Now use a thickness gauge to measure the distance between the rear of the upward locking block and the face of the cut in the barrel extension. Done another way, the breech block is pushed rearward until the locking block is in contact with the cut in the barrel extension, then the thickness gauge is inserted between the face of the breech block and the face of the minimum headspace gauge. Once this measurement is obtained, you know how much wear has occurred.

With a Dremel cutter and carbide tool — or with files and stones — cut the recess for the locking block farther rearward to enlarge the gap between it and the rear of the locking block. The reason for this is that a small piece of tool steel must be silver-soldered to the face of the barrel extension recess cut. One needs to have additional room as the attached piece of tool steel is then cut back until the locking block will enter correctly with the minimum headspace gauge inserted in the chamber of the barrel. The silver-soldered tool steel is sufficiently thick to replace the worn face of the locking recess of the barrel extension. I have used this method numerous times with excellent results, but it takes time to measure accurately and care is essential in soldering the bit of tool steel in place.

Some gunsmiths solve this problem by using the welding rod to build up the worn surface, but this requires expensive equipment. The silver-soldered tool steel does equally well if the workmanship is good. Use silver solder, not soft solder, as breech pressure when the shell is fired hits 10,-000 psi.

Breech blocks themselves occasionally wear. Usually it is the worn locking block or its recess cut in the barrel extension that are the source of the headspace problem. The recess should be cleaned of all residue before dimensions are taken. This area tends to wear simply because few shooters take the time to clean the breech block, locking block and that recess cut in the barrel extension. If cleaned properly wear seldom occurs, but with mixed residue and oil you have the equivalent of valve grinding compound, wearing away at the surfaces.

Another corrective method is basically the same as used to correct headspace in a rifle barrel. One sets the barrel back one or more turns and rechambers. On a shotgun one must take into consideration whether setting the barrel back one or more turns will affect the forward lug on the barrel into which screws the magazine plug. On a semi-auto shotgun the setback may be too much for the gas ports to still function.

Clean the locking bolt, its recess and the chamber. Again insert the minimum gauge into the chamber, then lock the breech bolt fully. Push it to the rear by hand until its locking lug is pressing fully against the recess cut in the barrel extension. Insert a thickness gauge leaf between the face of the breech bolt and the minimum gauge. Naturally you have to check with different leaves of the thickness gauge until one finally will just slide between the two surfaces. Write down the gauge thickness. If it is the five-thousandths leaf this is expressed as .005 inch in decimal.

Next remove the barrel from the barrel extension. This usually is done with the aid of a barrel vise and barrel wrench, as the technique is similar to removing the barrel from a rifle. Clean the threads on the barrel thoroughly, then use a thread gauge to determine how many threads per inch are involved. For the sake of mathematics let's say that there are twenty threads per inch. Check the pitch and lead of such threads in a machinist handbook and you will find that each complete revolution of the barrel will ad-

vance exactly 0.050 inch. This means that if we move the barrel backward one full turn we will have moved it this amount, which is more than adequate for the purpose of correcting the excess headspace of 0.005 inch!

Next, clamp the barrel in the lathe using a four-jaw chuck and a dial indicator to be sure everything is lined up. The compound is set to ninety degrees and the cross-feed of the lathe is locked to the bed with the lock screw on the side of the cross-feed assembly. The lathe bit should be just touching the face of the barrel at the chamber end. Turn on the lathe and, feeding the tool bit in slowly, watch the compound dial until you have removed exactly 0.050 inch of metal. In gunsmithing terms you have "faced the breech." Now move the tool until it just contacts the shoulder of the barrel where threading begins. This also is faced back exactly 0.050 inch. To avoid the trouble of cutting additional threads, you simply machine the section of the barrel behind the threads down until the diameter matches the bottom diameter of the threads. This will allow the barrel to screw in farther and the threads will pass over the recess you have cut behind the barrel threads.

Remove the barrel from the lathe and reinstall it in the barrel extension. The rim recess of the chamber now should be too shallow for even the minimum headspace gauge. All that remains is to cut another rim recess in the chamber that will just accept the minimum headspace gauge when the locking block is engaged in its recess cut in the barrel extension. If a full chamber reamer is used for this purpose it will cut the chamber and the rim recess. Partial chamber reamers may not have a rim cutter. In such cases cut the recess for the rim with a separate cutter, then deepen the chamber to compensate for the 0.050-inch shortening. In this method the rim recess is cut to correct depth by hand. You cut and gauge, cut and gauge until the dimension is achieved, removing only a minute amount of metal each time.

To save time, before the barrel is removed from the lathe the rim cutter is inserted into the tailstock of the lathe or in a floating reamer holder. The tailstock is advanced until the rim cutter has removed almost all of the required metal, then is finished up by hand as described previously. It is a

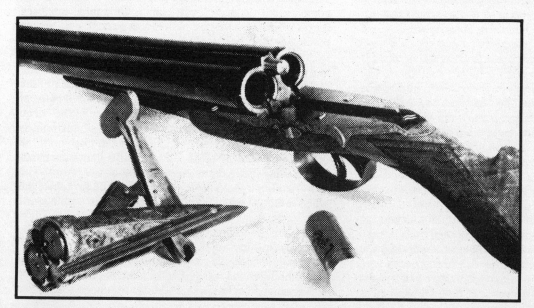

Headspacing of French-made Darne double gun is discussed in text.

Another wrong way to take up headspace in a sloppy action is to center punch the half-moon area; temporary at best.

good idea to use the lathe to remove only part of the required metal, say 0.030 inch, which will leave exactly 0.015 inch to be removed by hand to take up the 0.005-inch excess headspace. If you are really good with a lathe all of the dimensions can be final, but if you doubt your ability, play it safe and make the final cut by the cut-and-gauge, cut-and-gauge trial system. This is not as difficult as it may sound. Any real good gunsmith uses the same system on a rifle barrel that has excess headspace.

I have suggested the use of the minimum headspace gauge for correcting excess headspace; however, remember this is minimum and some difficulty may occur with pump or semiauto shotguns in feeding, extraction and ejection. The best advice is to keep that rim recess depth as close to minimum as possible. If problems occur, the rim recess must be made a bit deeper, but before taking this step, be sure the walls of the chamber are clean, that the extractor is biting into the rim of the shell and that the ejector is working correctly. It is a good idea to cycle unfired shotshells through the action by hand to check all conditions before cutting the rim recess to a depth between minimum and maximum gauges. I would change shotshells before taking this final step, as occasionally you will find some shells, especially the cheapies, that are not to SAAMI specifications.

One item I should mention: Always remove the extractor or extractors from the breech bolt and also the shell holder, which appears to be an extractor but simply holds the shell against the extractor. The reason is that the extractor may hold the gauge against the face of the breech bolt and result in a false reading. The forward edge of the gauge must rest firmly against the deepest edge of the recess cut for the rim in the chamber. The breech bolt must be fully rearward, pressing against the recess cut in the barrel extension via its locking block. Only then can a fully correct reading be taken between the gauge and breech block face with the thickness gauge leaf. All must be clean to prevent any foreign residue from causing a false reading.

This technique of setting a barrel back can also be used when a chamber is damaged for some reason such as a shooter trying to remove a forward blown-off section of a shotshell with a pocket knife or nail and damaging the walls of the chamber. If a chamber is deeply pitted with rust, it can be corrected by setting the barrel back and recutting the chamber with a reamer. If the extractor cut in a barrel is damaged for some reason, resulting in a bulged shotshell when fired, the same technique can be utilized for correction. A cardinal rule is to measure, then measure again before any cutting is done. Think your way through the problem carefully.

Although I consider bolt-action models as the armpit of shotguns, they occasionally develop excess headspace and must be corrected. On these the bolt handle body fits into a recess in the receiver and acts as the locking lug for the bolt. Remove the extractor and press the breech bolt fully forward onto the headspace gauge. Any gap between the recess cut in the receiver and the body of the bolt handle is excess headspace.

The simple method of correction is to carefully weld the front of the cut in the receiver. This build-up then is cut back until the breech bolt will close with the minimum headspace gauge. If desired, the recess cut can be cut more to make a gap larger than the reading, then silver solder a piece of tool steel in place to take up more of the gap than necessary. Cut this back until the bolt handle will just close, thus taking up the excess headspace. If necessary the barrel can be removed from the receiver and set back one exact turn to correct the problem.

The cut in the barrel side to accept the extractor will line up the same if the barrel is set back one exact turn of the threads. If necessary remove sufficient metal to allow the extrator to take a firm bite on the rim of the shotshell.

This takes care of pump, semiauto shotguns and the bolt-actions. What about the swing-open or drop barrel system found on most single-barrels, side-by-side and over/under shotguns? These also develop excess headspace and must be corrected, but the problem is a bit different and requires more measuring.

First take into consideration whether the rear of the barrel presses firmly against the face of the breech. Next, determine whether the rim recess cut is too deep, resulting in excess headspace. Two things are involved and consequently both require correction. The rear of the barrel must

fit snugly to the face of the receiver and this must take priority in all cases.

While some gunsmiths contend a one-thousandth-inch tolerance between the rear of the barrel and the face of the breech is acceptable, I feel that this should be zero. If you want to check this quickly, take a cellophane wrapper from a cigarette package, placing it between the rear of the barrel and face of the breech. Try to close the action. That cellophane wrapper is one-thousandth-inch (0.001) thick and serves as a simple gauge. If the action will close you have a problem. You can fold and refold the cellophane wrapper if desired or use the leaf of a thickness gauge, but regardless of the method, determine how much excess space exists between the rear of the barrel and the face of the breech. Write this down, for the figure will be needed in the final solution.

Remove the barrel from the frame and insert the minimum headspace gauge into the cleaned chamber. Now use a depth micrometer with the legs of the micrometer resting on the sides of the barrel past the rim recess cut. Turn the barrel of the micrometer until the measurement rod touches the face of the gauge. The reading will show how much the outer walls of the barrel outside of the rim recess are in excess of the minimum gauge. If the maximum gauge is used the same way, the reading will indicate the amount of excess headspace past the maximum. If there is none, the face of the gauge will hold the depth micrometer back and not allow the legs to touch the edge of the barrel outside of the rim recess cut. This measurement will determine whether the rim recess cut is too deep and, in itself, is causing excess headspace in addition to the space between a fully closed barrel and the face of the breech.

If you do have excess headspace the problem is doubled as two elements are involved. This is extremely important for it will determine the method of correction, so take your time and measure several times, writing the figures down. Next think your way through the final solution carefully. Be certain of the steps before you take action. I cannot emphasize this too much, for once committed it is hard to change directions.

Let's assume that no headspace was involved with a rim recess cut too deep and we have only the problem of moving that barrel back until it fits snugly against the face of the breech. There is one common method that never should be used. Unfortunately, some gunsmiths take the easy road and complicate the task of correctly solving the problem later. This is by using a center-punch to extrude metal around the half-moon recess under the barrels. The idea is that the extruded metal will press against the hinge pin of the receiver and thus press the barrel backward until it contacts the face of the breech. It works for a time, but constant use of the gun will wear the extruded metal quickly and the problem reverts to the original gap, but now the punch marks must be removed to accomplish the correct solution.

The basic idea of adding more metal to that half-moon

Leaf or thickness gauge inserted between the barrel and breech face shows side-by-side has dangerous headspace.

recess to push against the hinge pin of the receiver is correct. The proper method is to cut the half-moon recess back even more, then shape a piece of tool steel to match the half-moon and solder it in place. This shim usually is too large, so you cut the new piece back, maintaining the lines of the original half-moon cut. The recut half-moon shim will move the barrel back as it has taken up the gap between hinge pin and barrel.

A similar method is to cut the half-moon original back to a square shape, then solder a matching square of tool steel in place. Cut the half-moon in the piece of tool steel to compensate for the gap created by wear. I personally prefer the first method, machining the tool steel shim. I usually use a piece of hollow rod that is cut in half lengthwise. By machining it on the lathe, I can match the diameter of the hinge pin for a close fit and the outside of the piece is cut back prior to soldering.

As this section of the shotgun barrel may be soft soldered onto the barrel, check the joint closely. If it is to be soldered to the barrel, it may or may not stay in position during the sidering process. To play it safe, use gunsmith soft solder, a variation of common soft solder but with about five times the shear strength of common solder. Brownell's is the source of supply. Silver solder can be used to join the shim with the original later, if care is taken to prevent melting the original solder.

The second method of correction is to leave the half-moon recess in place and make the correction on the hinge pin. Quite often, if you simply push the hinge pin out of the receiver or frame, then turn it ninety degrees and push it back in place, you will solve the problem. The face of the hinge pin has been worn in its contact with the half-moon. So, by turning it ninety degrees, you place a fresh hinge pin surface in contact with the half-moon. This will not work every time but is worth a try.

Hinge pins normally are installed in the receiver by simply pressing them into place with tolerance held to a minimum for a tight fit. Removal always should be done with care after first checking to be sure no retaining pin or screw is used to hold the hinge pin in place. Care must also be taken not to spring the receiver when removing a hinge pin. Pounding on it with a hammer and punch can cause such problems. It is best to press the pin out slowly. If not possible, take the precaution of putting a matching block of metal between the sides of the receiver to prevent springing.

Measure the removed hinge pin with a micrometer to check wear and also its original diameter. A new hinge pin can be machined to compensate for the wear on the half-moon. Normally this will be only a slight increase in dimensions.

When completed, the diameter of the new hinge pin is used as a guide for enlarging the hinge pin hole in the receiver. A milling cutter is the best tool, but a common drill can be utilized if dimensions are compatible. With the hole in both sides of the shotgun receiver sufficiently enlarged, the new hinge pin is pressed in place. The barrel half-moon will mate properly with the pin, if dimensions are correct, and thus move the barrel back until it touches the face of the breech correctly.

If desired the new hinge pin can be made oversize in diameter. The barrel is installed on the receiver and pressed rearward mechanically until it is in firm contact with the face of the breech. Now — and only now — is the hole in the receiver drilled to the new diameter to match that of the hinge pin. By holding the barrel firmly against the face of the breech, the half-moon can be cut at the same time. When the new hinge pin is installed the fit of the half-moon against the hinge pin surface should assure that the barrel is pressed rearward the precise amount.

Incidentally, when installing a new set of barrels to a receiver, normally the half-moon is left oversize. By removing the hinge pin, then using a reamer or drill of identical diameter as the hinge pin hole, the half-moon can be cut provided the barrel is pressed against the face of the breech. This is a quick, easy method of mating a new set of barrels to an old receiver that provides correct fit when the hinge pin is reinstalled. This method is quite often used at a factory to fit a set of replacement barrels to a customer's old receiver. The method also can be used when fitting an extra barrel set to a receiver without altering the fit of the older barrel set.

If the rear of the barrel is fitted properly to the face of the breech, but the rim recess cut is too deep resulting in excess headspace, how is this corrected?

There is a simple way of correcting excess rim recess depth that, in my opinion, is the best of several methods employed by gunsmiths. The excess rim recess is cut deeper by about 0.125 inch with the normal rim cutter or the rim cutter on the chamber tool if they are joined. The excess chamber depth that results with the last type reamer will not adversely affect shooting. I prefer the separate rim recess cutter-type reamer for this job. In addition, a good milling reamer of correct diameter can be utilized provided it is aligned correctly. The regular rim cutter has a guide built in that eliminates this need.

With the recess cut deeper than originally we must now plug this gap. A washer-type replacement is machined on the lathe with a width that will make up the extra 0.125 cut and eliminate the headspace measurement excess. You also can make the washer-type replacement oversize. Either way, the outside diameter is machined to a close fit with the recess cut while the inside hole diameter is less than that of the chamber by a few thousandths of an inch. Be sure that the front edge of the machined washer closely matches the forward edge of the rim recess cut.

The machined washer is tinned with solder on its outer edge. The rim recess that has been cut deeper also is tinned with gunsmith's solder. The two are pressed together with a bit of solder flux between. A propane torch is used to melt the solder on both pieces while the washer is being pressed firmly into place. When cooled, the tinned joint will be very close. This incidentally is known as sweat soldering and the trick is to keep the solder joint as thin as possible, for the less solder involved, the tighter the joining of the two pieces of metal.

When cool, the inside of the machined washer is cut to correct dimensions with the appropriate shotgun chamber reamer. The juncture of the machined washer and the original chamber will be almost invisible if the job is done correctly. All that remains is to cut the new rim recess depth correctly by using the rim cutter and the minimum gauge to guide the process.

When sweat soldering the machined washer into place, care must be taken not to melt the solder joint holding the barrels in place. Wet rags can be placed on the outside of the barrel to retard the heat. If working on a double barrel, a wet rag can be inserted in the other barrel to aid in retarding heat. A propane torch is the best method to heat the solder and only enough heat to do the job is applied.

The machined washer can be made from any good steel. One simple source is a section of the rear of an old shotgun barrel as this is of sufficient thickness and the hole for the chamber reamer is already there, but be sure the hole is concentric with the outer diameter or the chamber reamer will be angled and might hit the sides of the rest of the chamber.

The newly installed machined washer will withstand chamber pressure, for the shotshell rim is supported correctly and the actual pressure occurs farther forward when the shotshell is fired. The Wichester Model 12 pump shotgun uses a similar washer in the chamber for correcting headspace; the installed machined washer is farther back than the Model 12 ring.

Someone probably will get the bright idea that he can ream out a swollen or worn chamber and machine a replacement to be installed the same way as the machined washer. This I do not recommend as the remaining wall thickness of the original barrel over the chamber area is normally too thin for safety even if you do a very close job of machining and reaming. The actual pressure is too great for such an arrangement at this point of the barrel. In short,

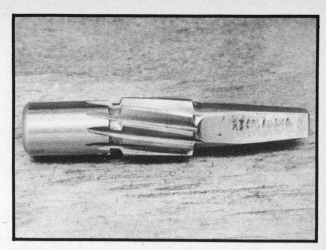

This chamber rim recess reamer from author's collection was made in Italy. It is useful in headspacing work.

you are on thin ice and the repair job may or may not hold for shot after shot with someone using the short magnum shells that create maximum breech pressure. Many barrels are made of soft steel, particularly in older guns. Play it safe and pass up such jobs.

Few gunsmiths would do any type of work on a centerfire rifle chamber without checking with headspace gauges. Yet these same gunsmiths often take shotgun headspace for granted. Headpsace on any firearm is important for both safety and correct gun function.

On old hammer guns, one should check first to be certain the barrels are not of Damascus steel. The headspace should be checked, as some are fired with magnum shells for which they were not designed, creating a danger.

Chapter 9

THE CHAMBER BODY

Accepted Lengths Have Changed Over The Years To Match Ammo Developments; You Have To Know The Difference!

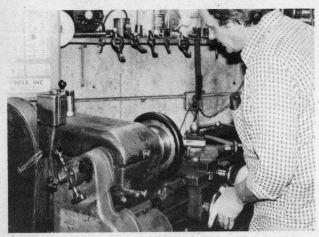

Jerry Stevens is considered a top gunsmith who makes a specialty of shotgun work. He knows the importance of the shotgun chamber and its being of proper dimensions.

THE SECOND SECTION of the shotgun chamber starts at the forward shoulder of the rim recess cut and extends forward to the point where the chamber forcing cone begins. This normally is referred to as the chamber body. As previously stated, the three sections of the chamber are the rim recess cut, the chamber body and the forcing cone.

However, in measuring the shotgun chamber, this length extends from the rear of the rim recess cut forward to the beginning of the forcing cone section. In other words, chamber length consists of both the rim recess cut and the chamber body. It does not include the chamber forcing cone.

When we speak of a chamber being 2¾ or 3 inches we are referring to the measurement from the rear of rim recess cut forward to the point where the chamber body stops and the forcing cone begins. This length is important as it plays an important role in shotgun performance.

Over the years chamber lengths have been changed many times. For instance, the common 12-gauge was made with a chamber length of 2⅝ inches for many years; in fact, until 1930 when the length was standardized at 2¾ inches. All shotguns after that date were made with the standardized 2¾-inch length. Prior to 1930 every manu-

facturer had his own personal ideas and some were in between the dimensions stated. Any gunsmith working on a gun made prior to 1930 should consider the chamber length suspect until he measures it with a chamber length gauge, which eliminates any doubt.

The SAAMI specifications for both the chamber length and shell length of the common 2¾-inch 12-gauge always are listed as the recommended maximum. The old unfired rolled-crimp length of the shell was 2.530 inches, but when the star crimp was introduced the unfired shell length was reduced to 2.410 inches. However, when fired, the length was set at 2.760 inches, which is 0.010 inch past the chamber length. This specification was changed to allow for the stretch factor in modern plastic-bodied shells; thus the overall fired length of modern shells is around 2.720 inches. This, however, varies from shell to shell as the plastic does not always stretch the same amount when the shell is fired.

Chamber length for the 2¾-inch shell is listed by SAAMI as 2.750 inches, which is the decimal equivalent of 2¾ inches. SAAMI always lists chamber specifications as the minimum allowance, therefore we have the shell length maximum and chamber length minimum. A shell manufacturer may manufacture the shotshell to less than the specifications, but not exceed them; to do so would make the fired length longer than the chamber minimum. By the same token, the gun manufacturer may make his chambers slightly in excess of minimum, but not less than this specification.

The reason for all of this concern is simple. Remember that the chamber body ends where the chamber forcing cone begins. If a fired shell was in excess length of the minimum of 2.750-inch chamber, then the front end of the shotshell when fired would pass the forward end of the

When fired shell case enters forcing cone (left) that is not of correct length, squeezing can deform the shot, raise pressures. Proper length (right) does not allow case to enter cone. Dotted lines mark beginning of the bore.

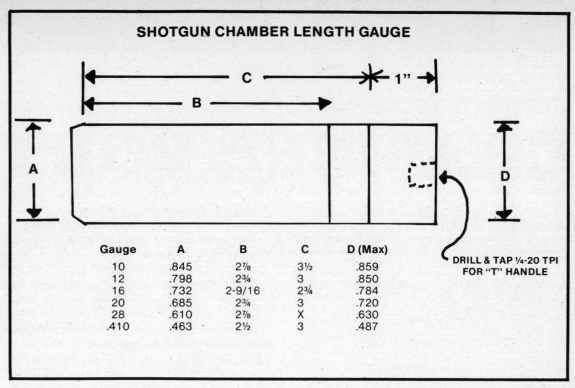

SHOTGUN CHAMBER LENGTH GAUGE

DRILL & TAP 1/4-20 TPI FOR "T" HANDLE

Gauge	A	B	C	D (Max)
10	.845	2⅞	3½	.859
12	.798	2¾	3	.850
16	.732	2-9/16	2¾	.784
20	.685	2¾	3	.720
28	.610	2⅞	X	.630
.410	.463	2½	3	.487

This chamber length gauge can be made in the gunsmith's shop of cold-rolled steel; no hardening is required, the author states. The gauge is purposely smaller at the rear than SAAMI chamber specs for ease in measuring.

chamber body and extend itself up into the chamber forcing cone. This increases chamber pressure!

A modern shotshell is carefully engineered. The speed of burn or burning rate of the powder is regulated to provide an exact amount of gas pressure in a specific time frame. The *ejecta* — everything in front of the powder — is regulated as to weight. The pie crimp fold on the end of the shotshell also is regulated as to the amount of resistance it offers to the moving ejecta before it unfolds and allows it to

pass. Everything works as a controlled unit for maximum efficiency and minimum variation from shotshell to shotshell. Were this not so, results would vary widely.

Anything that offers added resistance to this unit tends to change the whole circumstance. If the forward end of the shotshell unfolds into the chamber forcing cone it restricts the forward movement of the ejecta; this restriction makes the burning rate of the powder faster to increase the chamber pressure. If the forward end of the shotshell is not

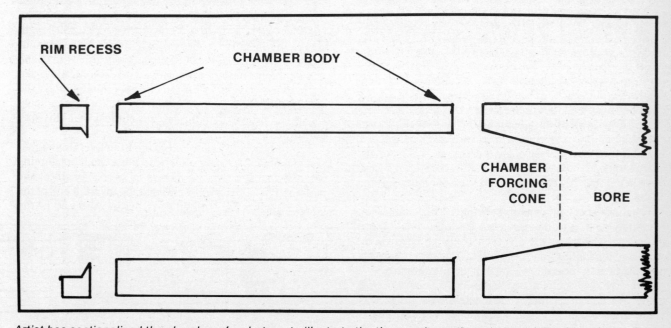

RIM RECESS

CHAMBER BODY

CHAMBER FORCING CONE

BORE

Artist has sectionalized the chamber of a shotgun to illustrate the three main sections that need consideration.

EUROPEAN CHAMBER LENGTHS

European chamber lengths are normally stamped on the bottom of the barrel under the chamber. Example: 12-70 indicates 12-gauge 70-millimeter chamber length. Conversion to American chamber lengths are:

European (mm)	American (inches)
50	2
63 or 64	2½
65	2-9/16
70	2¾
73	2⅞
76	3
89	3½

NOTE: Metric chambers are not an exact duplicate of American chambers as the European system is carried to the nearest millimeter. For example: 2¾ inches is exactly 69.8 millimeters, yet the European equivalent chamber is 70mm which is actually .2mm longer. This can be ignored for all practical purposes, but may be the cause of sticking American shells in European chambers if the nearest millimeter chosen results in a chamber shorter in length than the American Standard Chamber length.

allowed to unfold into the forcing cone, no resistance is added and the shotshell and its components function according to plan.

From a practical point of view, if the chamber pressure is increased, then the recoil of the gun is increased in direct ratio. Lower chamber pressure and you lower recoil in direct ratio. On the same note, if chamber pressure is increased, pressure against the shotgun breech and all of its components also is increased. Each such shell fired is a blow to the mechanism, and although the gun is built with a safety factor for such an occurrence, each blow will definitely increase wear in the gun. Keep it up and the gun mechanism will slowly be pounded to the point that excess

headspace occurs in addition to damaged parts and components.

Let's return to the gun made before 1930 with its chamber length of 2⅝-inch. If we fire a modern 2¾-inch shotshell in the gun, the forward end of the fired case will extend up into the chamber forcing cone one-eighth-inch or, in decimal equivalent, .1250 inch. As described this adds resistance to the ejecta to raise the chamber pressure. The excess chamber pressure, in turn, produces more recoil to the shooter's shoulder. As an added negative, the gun is subjected to a pressure that it was not built to contain, resulting in a definite blow to the complete mechanism. It is just a matter of time before the gun shoots "loose," causing all sorts of problems with the mechanism. If, however, the chamber is cut to the length of 2¾ inches (2.750 inches), the problem is resolved and everything goes back to normal pressure.

Several years ago I brought this to the attention of Bob Brownell and discussed the potential hazard involved to both gun and shooter. I designed a set of simple chamber depth gauges for the Brownell company and turned over all rights to them. Since then they have turned up in virtually every gunshop that is involved in shotgun repair to receive nothing but favorable comments. I also wrote a booklet on

CURRENT U.S. SHOTGUN CHAMBER LENGTHS

Gauge	Chamber Lengths (inches)
10	3½
12	2¾, 3
16	2¾
20	2¾, 3
28	2⅞
.410	3

FIGURE NO. 1: STANDARD BORE, CHAMBER & CHOKE DIMENSIONS

GAUGE	BORE	CHAMBER						CHOKE									
								FULL		IMP MOD		MOD		IMP CYL		CYL	
	A	B	C	D	E	F	G	J	K	J	K	J	K	J	K	J	K
10	.775	.841	.933	.8854	2.875	.074	.026	.739		.748		.757		.766		.775	
10 MAG		.8379			3.500				2-1/2		1 7/8		1-1/4		5/8		0
12	.729	.798	.886	.8118	2.750	.072	.026	.693		.702		.711		.720		.729	
12 MAG		.7968			3.000												
16	.662	.732	.820	.7458	2.750	.065	.026	.636		.6425		.649		.6555		.662	
20	.615	.685	.766	.6988	2.750	.060	.024	.589		.5955		.602		.6085		.615	
28	.550	.614	.688	.6284	2.875	.060	.022	.530		.535		.540		.545		.550	
410	.410	.463	.537	.478	3.000	.060	.020	.390		.395		.400		.405		.410	

This drawing and the specification information was released by Ithaca prior to advent of plastic shot protector.

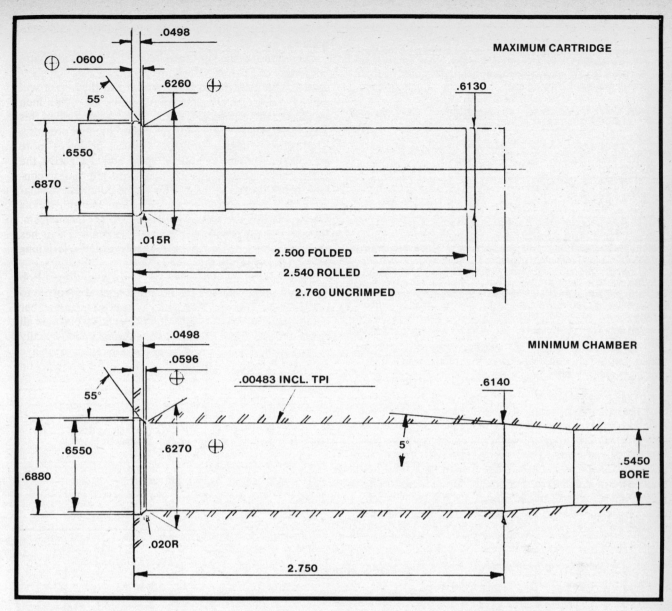

The drawing shows the approved specifications of the Sporting Arms and Ammunition Manufacturers Institute for the 28-gauge 2¾-inch shotshell and recommended chambering to handle the shell. It was issued in 1968.

how to use the set of chamber-depth gauges. For those interested, both the set of gauges for all shotgun gauges — .410 to the 10 — and the booklet are available from Brownell's, Incorporated, Montezuma, Iowa.

These gauges are simple to use and will provide a specific depth indication of any chamber length within seconds. Once the chamber depth is known, steps can be taken with a reamer to increase the length to modern specifications should the length be too short. I make it a practice to check every shotgun chamber with the gauges and the results have been surprising over the years.

As suggested earlier, the 12-gauge has been made in an astounding array of chamber lengths. The British made some guns with a chamber length of only two inches in an attempt to provide a 20-gauge load in a barrel with a larger diameter and thus increase the pattern of the 20 load while not increasing gun weight. The standard British chamber

length is 2½ inches and guns that find their way into the United States other than via the established commercial route will possible still have this 2½-inch chamber length. Obviously if an American shotshell is fired in the chamber, you have one-quarter inch of the shell unfolding up into that forcing cone to create a bottleneck for the ejecta with the resulting rapid powder burn rate increase, et cetera.

Until 1930, guns made in the United States by various manufacturers also had various chamber lengths in 12-gauge, while other gauges have an even broader selection of chamber lengths.

Until the post World War II period few shotguns were imported into the United States. American servicemen in the European theater seldom passed up a war trophy when it was of the shotgun persuasion, so zillions found their way back, some being put up for sale when beer money ran short. The military forces, to protect the public from itself,

U.S. CHAMBER LENGTHS 1900 TO DATE

Gauge	Chamber Length (inches)
10	2⅞, 3½
12	2, 2½, 2⅝, 2¾, 3
16	2-9/16, 2¾
20	2½, 2¾, 3
28	2¾, 2⅞
.410	2, 2½, 3

NOTE: American chamber length prior to 1900 varied considerably from manufacturer to manufacturer, often resulting in odd fractions.

began to confiscate anything that fired, from cap gun to cannon. After the war some smart money boys promptly bought up the warehouses and dumped the contents onto the American market. This included shotguns of every form and description. Almost without exception they were of pre-war manufacture to European specifications.

As American manufactures did not settle on a set of specifications until 1930, neither did the Europeans. Each country had its own specs, all of which added up to a shotgun chamber length nightmare. Needless to say, every one of these European guns must be checked with chamber

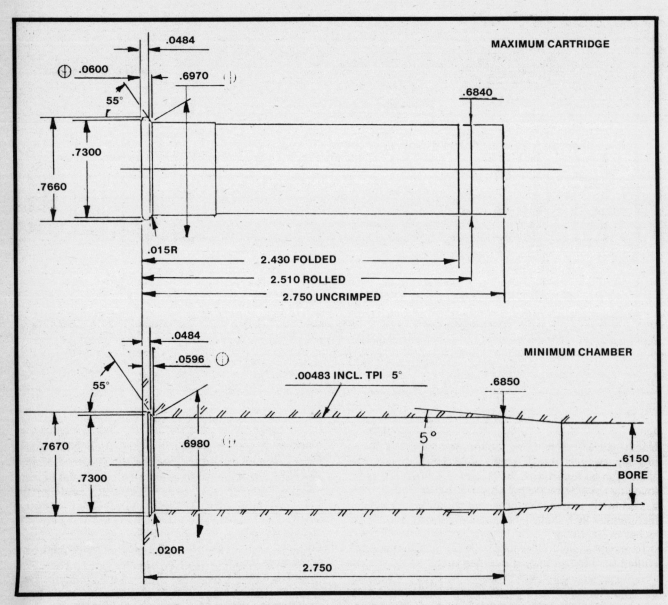

These specifications for shotshell and chamber of the 20-gauge 2¾-incher were issued by the technical committee of SAAMI in 1968. While chamber lengths had been lengthened, they considered former dimensions safe.

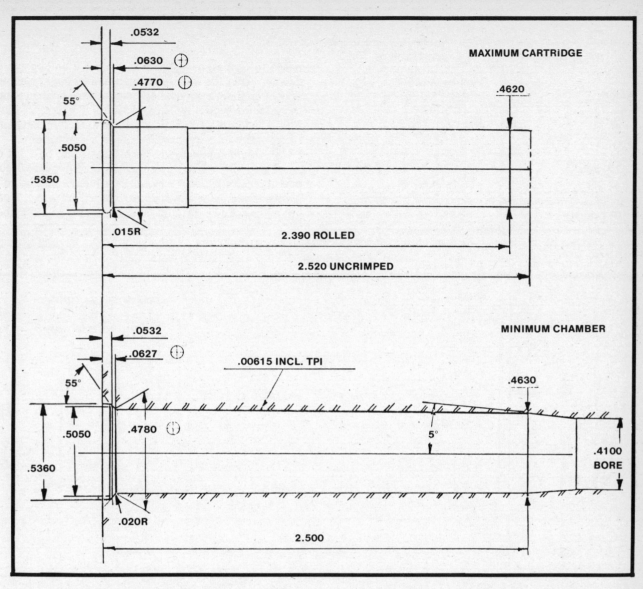

A good deal of research went into the changes of 1968 for specs of the .410 bore, 2½-inch shotshell, chamber. Although fifteen years old, these specifications still are used today throughout the American firearms industry.

length gauges before firing. Many have not, the owner blasting away in total ignorance of the consequences. Many can be found with the rear of the barrel not quite touching the face of the breech: excess headspace. This has occurred because the owner has fired currently manufactured 2¾-inch shells in a chamber that is less than 2¾ inches in length.

Even when new European guns were imported into the United States soon after the war, many were made with 69mm chamber lengths. This converts to 2.7165 inches which is short of the desired 2.75-inch length. This length later was changed to 69.9mm and finally to the current 70mm length which converts to 2.7559 inches, allowing a little room to spare for fired shotshells even if they stretch past that magic number of 2.75 inches.

What happens if a 2¾-inch shell is fired in a chamber that is designated as three-inch length? The front crimp of the shell unfolds to maintain the desired amount of resistance. Chamber pressure is neither increased nor decreased. The ejecta — which includes the shot — must of course jump the extra quarter-inch to the forcing cone. In doing this, the shot and its wrapper expand to the inside diameter of the chamber, then are rapidly pushed back down in diameter to enter the smaller forcing cone. Any time you expand, then constrict a shot charge you automatically deform some of the shot pellets. These deformed pellets meet increased air resistance on their way to the target and are spun off to one side of the main shot charge. Because of these spin-off pellets the pattern percentage is decreased.

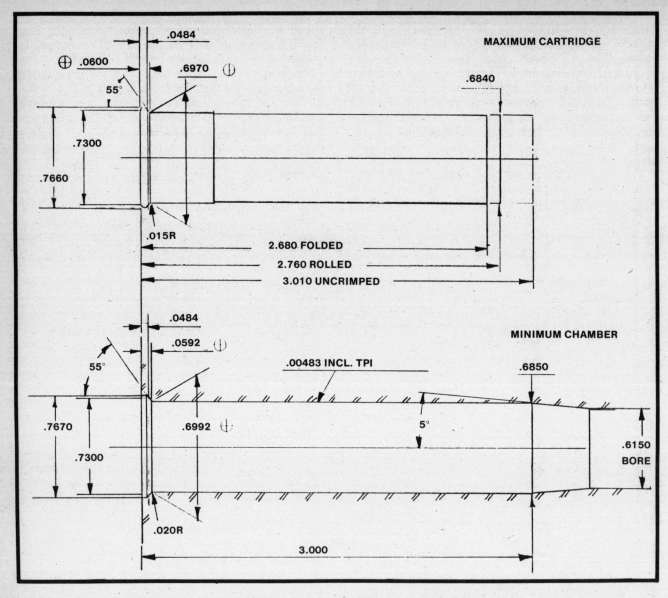

.0484
.0600
55°
.6970
.7300
.7660
.015R
.6840

2.680 FOLDED
2.760 ROLLED
3.010 UNCRIMPED

.0484
.0592
55°
.00483 INCL. TPI
.6850
.7670
.7300
.6992
5°
.6150 BORE
.020R
3.000

The manual for the SAAMI Technical Committee offers the specifications shown for the 20-gauge 3-inch shotshell.

So, while there is no change in the chamber pressure when a 2¾-inch shell is fired in a three-inch chamber, there is a pellet percentage decrease.

Were the same shell fired in a 2¾-inch chamber, the pellet deformation would not occur and consequently the pellets in question would remain round and stay with the main shot charge to register more efficient pattern percentage. The 2¾-inch shell can be fired in the three-inch chamber safely, but those who state performance would be the same are incorrect!

Two more specifications must be considered in discussing the body of the chamber; three, if you want to read it another way. This is the internal diameter of the chamber just in front of the rim recess cut which can be considered the rear of the chamber body. The next dimension is the internal measurement of the chamber body where this section ends and the forcing cone begins, or the front of the chamber. These specifications are important, for when you combine these two specifications with the chamber length, the resulting calculation is the inclined taper per inch.

Stated another way, the chamber is slightly smaller in internal dimension at the front end. This taper allows shotshells to enter the chamber easily and to be extracted easily after firing. The taper is slight — in a 12-gauge it is exactly .00448 per inch — yet it is sufficient to do the job required.

The problem again arises with chambers on early U.S. guns and those of some European models even of current manufacture. While the rear internal dimension is extremely close, the front internal dimension is usually tighter in some European-made chambers. In a few cases an unfired shotshell's front dimension is greater than that of the front of the chamber. The results is that the shotshell is forced forward and slightly compressed when fully seated. This can cause feeding problems in European guns, specifically pumps. Add a bit of powder residue at the front of the chamber and the problem is amplified as the available diameter is further reduced. The only corrective measure is to rechamber the gun using an American reamer that will bring it to SAAMI's forward chamber body diameter. Several foreign countries have become aware of the problem and changed to the U.S. specifications, but guns imported prior to this change still have the smaller-diameter chamber.

This brings us to a subject that involves every shotgun chamber, especially the chamber body: the formation of rust or, to use the technical term, ferrous oxide. Specifically ferrous oxide is the changing of steel into another state by the introduction of oxygen into the metal.

All iron absorbs oxygen whenever it is exposed; steel, simply an alloy of iron and other metals, meets the same fate. If a non-oxidizing metal such as chrome is added the amount of oxide formed is decreased in proportion to the alloying of this metal to the iron. What we call stainless steel is iron with a high chrome alloy content. If regular iron or a steel alloy with little non-oxidizing metal is covered with a protective agent that prevents it coming into contact with oxygen, then oxidation is prevented. Plating is a perfect example and so is common oil. Both prevent contact with oxygen.

Adding heat to iron or steel increases the rate of oxygen absorption and thus the oxide forming on the surface. The more heat, the faster the rate of oxidation. As an example, a common oxygen acetylene torch set up for burning simply heats the metal until it reaches its liquid state, then adds

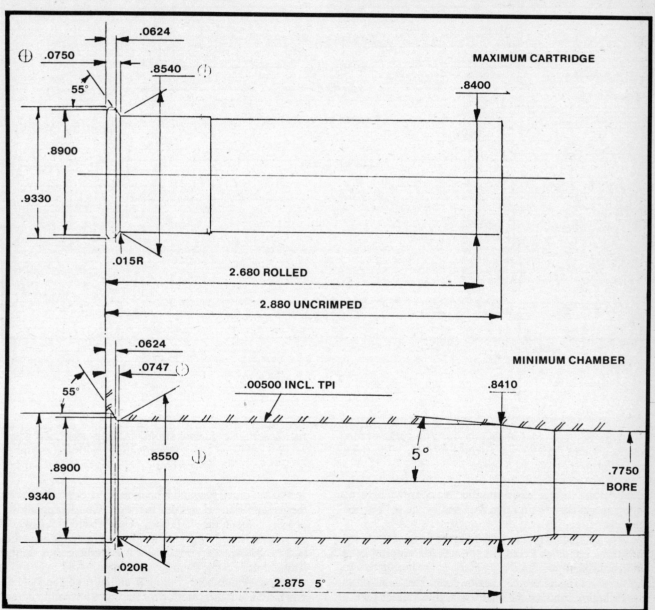

Compared to some of the smaller gauges, SAAMI specifications for the 10-gauge 2⅞-inch chamber appear mammoth.

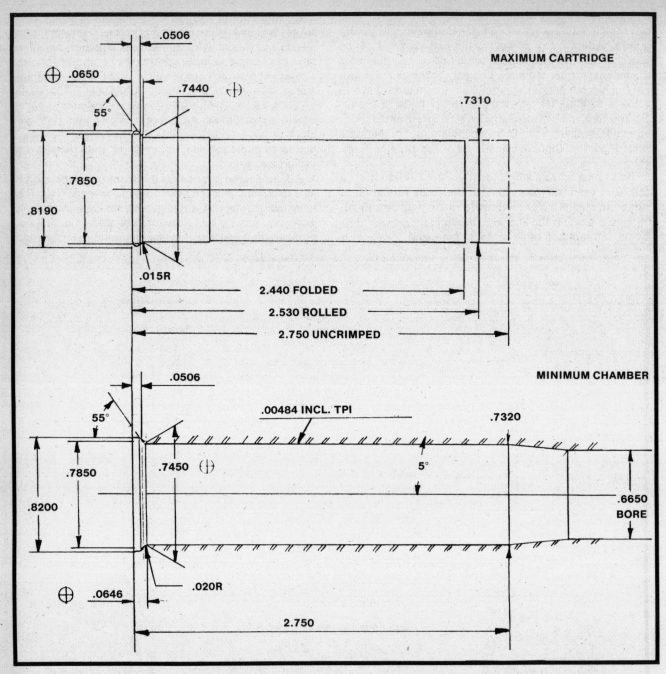

The specifications for the shotshell and chamber of the venerable Sweet Sixteen were standardized in 1968 at the same time as those of other gauges were brought to a common denominator by the technical staff of SAAMI.

compressed oxygen to the liquified metal which is turned into ferrous oxide at a rapid rate and hence is "burned" through.

When shotshell bodies were made of paper, in previous days, the paper was coated with wax for waterproofing. When the shell was fired in a chamber, the heat generated by the resulting burning of the powder melted some of this wax coating, and as the shell obturated (sealed) to the walls of the chamber some of the wax was transferred. This deposited wax formed a protective coat on the chamber walls to prevent contact with oxygen. As long as this type shell was used, chambers showed little rust formation.

With the era of the plastic-body shotshell, chambers seemed to breed rust and it became a major problem. One theory was that rust was due to the ink used to print various designations on the shell body. Others said that it was in the plastic itself. My conclusion was that the shotshell bodies no longer deposited the wax coating on the chamber walls, thus leaving them as bare metal. Add heat to the equation — said heat coming from the fired shells —and you have a perfect situation for the rapid formation of rust. Any light, protective coat of oil was quickly burned away by the heat of the fired shells, baring the inner chamber wall surface.

If you close the breech, you seal one end of the shotgun barrel trapping heat and moisture in the bore to add to the formation of oxide. Open the breech and the oxidation is less. I proved this to be a non-believer some years ago by using two barrels, one left open after firing, the other closed. Both formed rust, but the closed bore had a full fifty percent more at the end of a specified period.

If oxidation is allowed to form in the chamber body, several things take place that directly affect the function of the complete gun mechanism. First, the rust decreases the internal dimensions of the chamber body. This will add to any difficulty in fully chambering an unfired shotshell. In the case of the self-loading semiauto, these decreased internal dimensions fight the pressure of the spring that is trying to load the next shotshell to result in feeding problems. Unless the chamber is checked for this condition, it will lead to a false direction as far as correcting the problem of feeding.

When a shell is chambered and fired the walls of the shell expand and obturate to the walls of the chamber body. When pressure drops from the internal fired shell the shell body should partially return to its original state, but the accumulated rust will hold the fired shell and prevent or retard its extraction from the chamber. On a semiauto, which depends on self function, the extractor cannot overcome the resistance and will tear through the rim of the fired shell or simply ride over the rim and leave the shell in place. When the self-loader attempts to load another shell, the fired shell blocks the way and you have a jam. The same thing can happen with a pump-action.

On a side-by-side or over/under, you feel stiff resistance in opening the action, since the act of opening is mechanically tied to the extractor mechanism or ejector mechanism. In rare cases, when additional pressure is exerted the mechanism can be broken. With automatic ejectors, which depend on spring action to toss the fired shell from the chamber, the spring is not strong enough to overcome

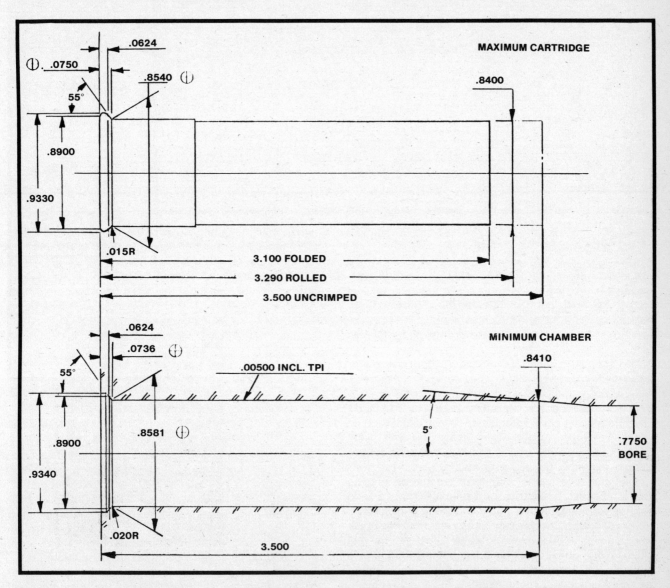

With the 10-gauge 3½-inch shotshell, specific measurements are listed for folded length, when rolled and uncrimped. The same measurements are listed by SAAMI for all of the other gauges as well in a continuing effort for standardization.

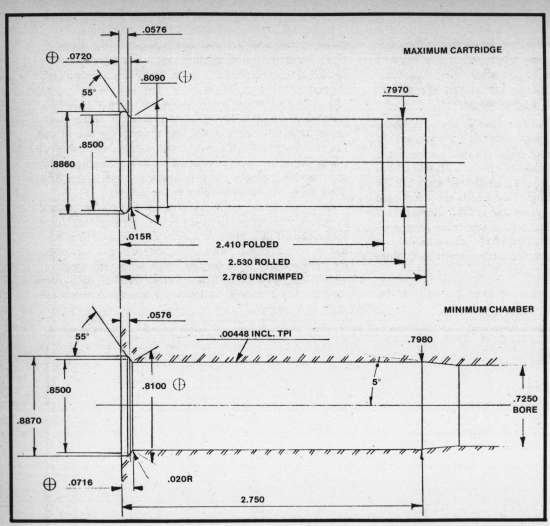

.0576
.0720
55°
.8090
.8500
.8860
.7970
.015R
2.410 FOLDED
2.530 ROLLED
2.760 UNCRIMPED

Differences in SAAMI specs for 12-gauge 2¾-inch shell and .410 3-inch shell (on opposite page) become obvious with some study.

MINIMUM CHAMBER

55°
.0576
.00448 INCL. TPI
.7980
.8500
.8870
.8100
5°
.7250 BORE
.0716
.020R
2.750

the rust holding the shell in the chamber and the gun will simply fail to eject.

All of this can be prevented simply by cleaning the chamber — especially the body of the chamber — thoroughly after firing and depositing a light coat of protective oil to the inner walls of the chamber. If rust starts to form, this can be removed with a regular shotgun bore brush or the special chamber cleaning brush marketed by Brownell's.

Unfortunately many shotgunners, too lazy to care for the chambers properly, allow a thick coat of rust to form. They only take notice when the gun fails to feed, extract or eject due to the rust. If rust is allowed to form and increase in such a chamber, it's a problem to correct and return the chamber to its proper state of smoothness from rim recess to the beginning of the bore. Corrective measures depend to some extent on the degree of rust.

The goal is to use the minimum amount of force to remove the rust. In some cases this involves only a good soaking with rust remover or common nitro bore solvent. Follow this with the chamber wire brush or a bore brush wrapped with 0000 steel wool. If luck is with you the rust will be removed to expose bare metal. It is a good idea to make at least three hard tries using this method before moving to something more severe.

If so much rust has formed that it is necessary to hone it from the walls of the chamber body, the Brownell choke hone can be used. If oil is applied to the hone, the end result

will be much smoother although the use without oil will be more rapid. Pitting of the inner wall surfaces also must be eliminated as the pits will allow the fired shotshell body to expand into them and thus prevent ease of extracting. The problem is that each time you hone a chamber you remove

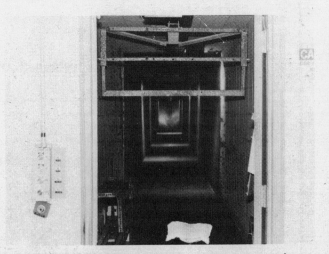

Every gunsmithing shop should have a test range of some sort so that functioning of every shotgun — or other type of arm — can be tested prior to return to customer.

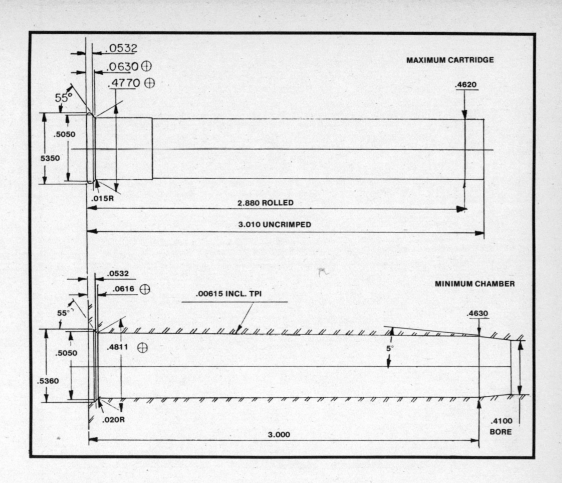

MAXIMUM CARTRIDGE

.0532
.0630 ⊕
.4770 ⊕
55°
.5050
5350
.015R
.4620
2.880 ROLLED
3.010 UNCRIMPED

MINIMUM CHAMBER

.0532
.0616 ⊕
55°
.5050
.4811 ⊕
.5360
.020R
.00615 INCL. TPI
5°
.4630
.4100
BORE
3.000

metal and there is a limit to how much metal can be removed without enlarging the chamber to the point that it is no longer safe or the obturated shell presents an added difficulty. In short, hone as little as possible and only when

Browning's repair facility in Arnold, Missouri, has the ultimate in modern equipment for checking chamber specs and other facets dealing with safety of shotguns.

there is no other alternative to smoothing the walls of the chamber.

A strong light can be shined up into the chamber of the shotgun barrel to inspect for rust. This step should be automatic for a gunsmith every time a shotgun barrel comes to his work bench.

Even if no rust is apparent, modern plastic body shotshells can add another problem for a chamber body. If you examine an unfired shotshell's inner body as well as the exterior, you will note that the plastic is smooth. Now examine a fired shotshell body for a slightly rough surface due to the plastic coming under intense heat when the shell was fired. Any time you rub plastic against metal, some of the plastic is rubbed off onto the metal. The same thing occurs on the walls of the shotgun chamber. Some of the plastic rubs onto the metal. Normally this will not create a problem, but an accumulation of this transferred plastic eventually will make extraction difficult as does formation of rust. The plastic prevents easy extraction of the fired shotshell as it grabs the outer walls and adds resistance to the pressure exerted by the extractor. Again, the use of a chamber brush or a bore brush with 0000 steel wool will quickly remove the accumulation.

Any form of foreign residue will restrict the inner dimensions of the chamber body to some degree and prevent easy entrance of an unfired shotshell or extraction of a fired case. This puts a strain on the other components of the gun's action. The result is a shotgun that does not function correctly.

In the days of black powder hunting and shooting, forcing cones were not a problem, as they were not used in the muzzleloading arms of the era. The black powder went down the bore, then a series of wads was followed by the shot.

ALL ABOUT CHAMBER FORCING CONES

THIS THIRD section of the shotgun chamber is its most forward part. It begins where the chamber body ends and extends to the point where the barrel bore begins. As the name implies, it is shaped as a cone with a larger diameter at the rear where it joins the chamber body and a smaller diameter where it joins the barrel bore. Its purpose is to force the shot charge down from its diameter while in the shotshell to a size that will match that of the bore diameter, thus allowing the shot charge to travel the length of the barrel.

In the days of the muzzleloader there was no forcing cone nor for that matter even a chamber as such. The pow-

der went down the bore to rest at the bottom, then a bore-diameter wad, or series of wads, was followed by the shot to be capped by an over-shot wad. When the powder was ignited, it expanded into a gas that forced the wads and the shot back up the bore to the muzzle.

The all-important key is two words: pellet deformation. When a shot pellet in good condition exits the shotgun muzzle it is immediately acted upon by the surrounding air. As it passes through the air — assuming it still is completely round — the air flows around the sphere equally on all sides. This allows the spherical pellet to pass through the air and not be spun off to one side. If a pellet is deformed

out of round in its passage through the shotgun bore, as it passes through the air on the way to the target the air flows irregularly around it. If one side has been dented or pushed out of shape, air pressure builds up to push the pellet toward the side where there is less resistance. Hence the shot pellet leaves its initial path and deviates to one side.

An old baseball that is no longer round is hard to throw with any accuracy because of the difference in the flow of air around its shape. In terms of shooting a shotgun, the more pellets that are deformed, the less that continue with the main pack on their way to the desired target. Deform enough pellets and it becomes a problem to place a high percentage within a circle in patterning. The deformed or stray shot hit outside of the circle and are lost for all practical purposes.

When you push shot pellets through any type of cone it reduces the original diameter of the combined shot to a smaller combined shot diameter. The spherical shot load is somewhat like a load or group of common marbles. The walls of the cone push them inward toward a common center. As the center is made up of pellets also, it is nonyielding. Thus the only direction left is either forward or backward. If you try this with marbles you will see some move forward while others move rearward until they all pass through the smallest of diameters. The key ingredient is the time frame in which they are allowed to move to a new position. If the time is sufficient, nothing damaging happens. Compress the time frame and the pellets, or marbles, will press upon each other and be deformed in shape during the process. Now it is important to realize that a

forcing cone exists in front of the modern chamber and also in front of the choke section, thus subjecting shot to two rearrangements of position.

The old muzzleloader did not have a chamber forcing cone. Later, as the choke was added, it had one forcing cone to pass through. This is the reason many of the old records of pattern percentages with early choked muzzleloaders could not be surpassed or even duplicated with the breechloader and its shotshell. The shot passed through one forcing cone in the muzzleloader, but was subjected to passage through two with the breechloader. Less shot were deformed with the choked muzzleloader and thus delivered more round pellets to strike the circle on the target.

So, why is the forcing cone necessary in a chamber that accepts a shotshell? The bore cannot be made the same diameter as the outside of the shotshell itself. To do so would mean that the wads inside of the shotshell would be less in diameter than the bore. This also would mean that the gas from the burning powder would flow past the wads and thus not exert any pressure on the wads. As the wads are behind the shot, the shot would not be pushed forward and everything would stay in place with little if any movement.

They don't make the bore and the wads the same diameter for the same reason. The gas would not seal and would not exert any pressure behind the wad. In turn, there would be no pressure to push the shot forward toward the target. The only solution is to make the bore smaller in diameter than the wads, so we need a type of cone to accomplish this, as an abrupt shoulder would present a host of problems to overcome.

The wad directly upon the powder was relatively thin in comparison to the filler wad in front of it which was made of a soft material that would compress easily in passage through the forcing cone. As it passed through the cone, the thin over-powder or nitro wad folded backward due to decreasing diameter of the cone to form a seal for the expanding gas. This provided the push from the gas necessary to propel the shot charge up the bore at a rapid velocity.

Now we come to the time frame in which those round pellets were forced to find a new position to pass through the forcing cone. The common length of such forcing cones was around a half-inch, which meant that little time was allotted for this passage and, as the time frame was short, a lot of pellets were deformed in the process. This was a necessary evil as that thin over-powder wad had to seal rapidly or the gas would pass around it and get up into the

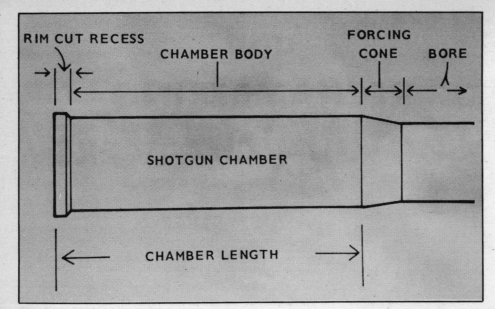

RIM CUT RECESS

CHAMBER BODY

FORCING CONE

BORE

SHOTGUN CHAMBER

CHAMBER LENGTH

The function of the forcing cone is to funnel ejecta into the bore. The more smooth this transition, the less chance there is for pellet deformation.

shot, resulting in even more pellets being deformed in addition to thrust being lost behind the pellets.

So the short forcing cone was standard throughout the period of the flat nitro or over-powder wad. The need for this length ended when Winchester introduced the first cupped paper nitro wad in the late 1940s. The cup shape held the powder in the shell, but when it turned to gas, the sides of the cup were forced outward from the gas pressure to form a more perfect seal than ever was accomplished with the old flat wad. When the cupped plastic wad over powder came into being, sealing efficiency became almost perfect.

I began to question the reason for leaving the chamber forcing cone the same old half-inch length, as it was no longer necessary to form a quick seal. If the forcing cone was made longer, the time frame would be increased and allow a longer period for the pellets to find a new position as necessitated by the smaller bore diameter. Hence fewer pellets would be deformed in shape as they made the trip through the forcing cone. Would it work?

I started with a forcing cone length double the original: one inch. A half reamer was made on the lathe and used to lengthen the standard forcing cone of a Savage Model 94 single-barrel 12-gauge. I had shot a few patterns with the gun prior to rechambering for before and after results. The percentage went up around five percent increase with no apparent change in velocity or penetration. Next I tripled the original length of the forcing cone in a similar barrel and repeated the test. The 1½-inch forcing cone pushed the gain up to an average of ten percent with the same brand of shotshell. I made other reamers and tried the test on different barrels until the forcing cone was six inches in length. My thought was that the time frame for pellet repositioning would be increased and less pellets would be deformed.

It didn't work out according to theory. Beyond 2½ inches there was simply no pattern gain. I do not know why, for the theory of an increased time frame for pellets to reorganize themselves and thus result in fewer pellets being deformed seems correct.

The plastic cupped wad came on the market during these tests and was tried in the increased-length forcing cone barrels. Pattern gain was a bit more, around three percent average over the cupped Winchester paper over-powder wad. The maximum achieved was fifteen percent and only with handloads. All testing was done sans the shot protector as this would change results to a greater percentage of gain, the plastic shot protector decreasing the number of deformed shot pellets.

I used the old reamer to cut a few barrel chambers for friends and made another discovery. Bore diameter varies considerably among manufacturers. The Browning bore and most European 12-gauge bores are around .715-inch in diameter while American bore diameters range around .730 and to .735 inch. The 2½-inch forcing cone is not necessary in the larger diameter bores; in fact the 1½-inch produced identical results with no variation that I could see. With the smaller diameter of .725 inch the short forcing cone length of 1½ inches gave less percentage of gain than if the length was increased to 2½ inches. The middleground .730 inch bore seemed to give best results with a two-inch forcing cone length.

If you think about it a while, it becomes obvious that the shot pellets do not require the same length of time in the larger bore diameter as in the smaller bore diameter. The latter, with the longer forcing cone, provides this time gain and will deliver the relatively same percentage of pattern gain. Why this does not work with an even longer forcing cone is something that I often wonder about.

I used the same technique on other gauges and found about the same pattern percentage gain due to fewer pellets being deformed in the longer forcing cone. The actual percentage gain is less in the smaller gauges than in the 12-gauge, but by only a few points. It seems to work all the way down to the tiny .410 bore with each drop in bore diameter per gauge resulting in a drop in the percentage gain figure. On the opposite end of the gauge list, the 10-gauge will deliver about the same gain as that of the smaller 12-gauge. This is another mystery that I have not resolved, the only guess being that the big 10 normally uses a larger pellet size than the 12-gauge and the larger the pellet, the slighter the drop in pattern percentage gain.

My old friend Bob Brownell became interested in my tests and the pattern gains. I had worked out a design for a straight-fluted reamer that would work on any bore diameter from .724 to .740 in a 12-gauge and Bob asked if I could do the same with the other gauges. Brownell's, Incorporated, ultimately purchased all design rights and placed the reamers on the market along with an instruction manual for cutting the long forcing cone in existing short forcing cone barrels. To my knowledge there previously was no such thing as a long forcing cone reamer on the market, nor do I know of any published tests prior to this introduction. Suddenly everybody and his brother was cutting the long forcing cone and Brownell sold a lot of reamers and instruction books. Since then other reamers have been introduced, but all are of the spiral-fluted design.

I prefer the straight-fluted reamer as it depends on pressure on the rear of the reamer to push the reamer forward and the feed of cutting depends entirely upon the pressure exerted. A spiral-fluted reamer has a tendency to be self-feeding and unless handled with great care will bind and gouge the metal. There is an old rule that mechanically-turned reamers should be straight fluted while all hand reamers should be spiral fluted. Not so. The straight-fluted rifle reamer is always used for the final cut in a precision chamber.

No matter what one does in design, someone will misuse the tool. The long forcing cone reamer with straight flutes is hand turned for maximum precision. If stoned correctly, they will cut smoothly and maintain alignment with the original chamber. All of this assumes that reasonable intelligence exists on the other end of the reamer. If chips build up in front of a particular flute of the reamer, this flute is too high and is cutting the most as evident by the accumulated metal chips. Stone this flute down until it is of equal height with the other flutes. The reamer then will cut smoothly and produce a clean forcing cone. Adequate cutting oil is another point that many overlook. I literally flood the reamer to float away the accumulating metal chips — this causes the reamer to cut without binding.

While the Brownell reamer will cut most barrels, the forward end is designed for the most common small diameter of bore in each gauge. Occasionally you will find a vastly undersized bore that will not allow the reamer front to enter. When this happens it is necessary to grind the small pilot flutes down a wee bit to make the front end smaller in diameter. Continue the angle of grinding all the way back to the body of the reamer and the problem is solved. I have found this necessary only for the 16-gauge and then only in pre-war European barrels that always were undersize in bore.

When a barrel is fired a considerable number of times, the original forcing cone comes under a lot of pressure and stress as the shot passes over the surface. Ultimately the metal becomes slightly work-hardened on the surface. This can result in the reamer having difficulty starting the cut. The trick in these cases is to break through that hard surface; once this is done the reamer will have no problem in getting a bite. The hone marketed by Brownell's to finish smoothing the reamed surface will get the job done. Naturally all accumulated foreign material in the original forcing cone must be removed prior to any work.

When the cut is finished correctly for the forcing cone, all traces of the old cone should have been removed. Any metal that is left may or may not influence pattern gain, so use the Brownell expanding hone to finish polishing the surfaces you have cut. Use the hone dry initially for fast cutting, then add oil for the final turns. A lap using fine aluminum oxide cloth backed with expanding foam rubber on a rod also can be used for final polishing. The end result should leave the newly cut surfaces as smooth as possible.

Chrome-lined barrels present a major problem in cutting a new long forcing cone. Chrome is extremely hard and can dull or otherwise damage the cutting edges of the reamer.

GAUGE	BORE	CHAMBER							CHOKE									
									FULL		IMP MOD		MODIFIED		IMP CYL'R SKEET		CYLINDER	
		A	B (in)	C	D	E	F	G	J	K	J	K	J	K	J	K	J	K
10 / 10 MAG	.775	.841 / .8379		.933	.8554	2.875 / 3.500	.074	.026	.739		.748		.757		.766		.775	
12 / 12 MAG	.729	.798 / .7968		.886	.8118	2.750 / 3.000	.072	.026	.693		.702		.711		.720		.729	
16	.662	.732		.820	.7458	2.750	.065	.026	.636	2½	.6425	1⅛	.649	1¼	.6555	⅜	.662	0
20	.615	.685		.766	.6988	2.750	.060	.024	.589		.5955		.602		.6085		.615	
28	.550	.614		.688	.6284	2.875	.060	.022	.530		.535		.540		.545		.550	
410	.410	.463		.537	.478	3.000	.060	.020	.390		.395		.400		.405		.410	

The chamber dimensions for the old Ithaca were made up prior to introduction of the long forcing cone.

INCLUDED TAPER .005 PER INCH

MINIMUM CHAMBER

ITHACA GUN Co, Inc.
ITHACA, N.Y.

STANDARD
BORE CHAMBER & CHOKE
FOR SHOT GUNS

T-113

A	8379 WAS 835, 7968 WAS 797	7-2-2	1-6-45	7-2-2 3-10-39					1=1
REV	REVISION	BY	DATE	DRAWN BY	CHECKED BY	TRACED BY	LIMITS OK	MATERIAL	SCALE

There is only one way to cut such barrels, a stop-gap measure I do not like and use only if a customer insists and fully understands what is involved.

As with the work-hardened surface of a barrel that has been shot a lot, the extra-hard surface first must be removed before the long forcing cone can be cut. I use the Brownell hone to cut past the chrome-lined surface and down to regular barrel metal. This requires time. The only way to know you have accomplished the surface removal is to try the reamer lightly. If it starts picking up chips of cut metal, all is fine and you can finish the job. If not, more honing is required. When finished, the barrel still will have a chrome-lined chamber and a chrome-lined bore, but in between is a section of barrel without the chrome which must be maintained as an usual barrel.

I personally do not care for chrome-lined barrels. Any time metal is deposited on a surface through plating by an electrical process, the deposit depends on the electrical circuit; as electricity follows the path of least resistance, one has an irregular deposit on the plated material. It cannot be seen with the naked eye but nevertheless the deposit is not the same thickness on all surfaces. Thus that you cannot obtain an exact same amount of deposited nickel or chrome the full length of the barrel from rear of chamber to muzzle. Any deviation of dimensions will change the ultimate pattern results.

I have seen a lot of shotgun barrels with chrome-lined inner surfaces. Every one examined always has more residue build-up in the chamber, forcing cone, bore and choke section. I am not certain why, but the chrome lining seems to hold more of the residue to the surface and in doing so changes the dimensions, however slight, of the barrel inner surfaces. This results in a change in performance.

The long forcing cone is not a miracle worker and does have limitations as to length and efficiency. It accomplishes one thing only: prevention of deformation of the shot pellets from shell to bore. Every barrel must be treated as an individual. No two barrels, even if they were side-by-side on the manufacturing line, will give the exact same results with the exact same shotshell!

When you change the hardness of the shot pellet, you change the percentage gain by the long forcing cone. If you use soft shot with little antimony, the long forcing cone will be at its best in preventing these pellets from being deformed during the passage from shotshell into bore.

If you use chilled shot, which is found in most quality shells, the antimony content of the pellets is greater and resists deformation. With deformation less than with soft shot, percentage of pattern gain will be slightly less than that of the soft shot when the long forcing cone is utilized for both. There is a gain, but not as great.

When magnum shot such as made by Lawrence is used, the antimony content is around five percent and the individual shot pellets are much harder than even chilled shot. The long forcing cone will give slightly lower pattern percentage gain as compared to a short forcing cone with this type shot. In other words, the harder individual shot pellets resist deformation themselves, the long forcing cone simply aids their resistance.

Plated shot — nickel or copper — adds little to deformation resistance through pellet hardness, but manufacturers

Prior to alteration described in chapter, this Browning chamber was too short to accept indicated machined ring.

are in the business to give the shooting public what it wants; they want plated shot, they get plated shot! If you handload both, all other components being equal, there is no measurable difference between magnum hard shot and plated shot.

As for the new steel shot, I have not conducted any tests with this shot in a short and a long forcing cone. Don Zutz — who needs little introduction as to his qualifications — did conduct some tests and his results are outlined later in this chapter. Any time steel shot is used, you have a completely new set of problems.

What difference is there in muzzle velocity between a standard-length forcing cone and the long forcing cone? Earl Larson, until his retirement, was in charge of customer service for Remington Arms. I discussed this with him during a hunting trip in New Mexico and he offered to conduct the needed tests. Consequently a standard Remington barrel was test fired and very carefully checked for velocity using premium Remington shotshells. The barrel was shipped to Walker Arms at Selma where a long forcing cone was cut in it and carefully polished. The barrel then was returned to Larson for the final stage of the testing.

Using the same shotshells, the identical shooting was done as with the original-length forcing cone. I discussed this thoroughly with Larson a few weeks later. The bottom line was that the before-and-after velocity tests revealed absolutely no change in shot velocity. As velocity has great influence on patterns and consequently on range results as well as penetration of the pellets, there is no loss and no gain in this respect. Differences in soft, chilled, and magnum hard shot as well as plated shot were not checked thoroughly as it would have involved considerably more expense and time. I can only fall back on my own tests and that of others in stating that the biggest percentage gain is with the soft shot, next with chilled shot and finally with the hard magnum or plated shot showing the least gain of all due to their resistance to deformation.

Over years of cutting this long forcing cone into various customers' barrels and listening to their opinions, as well as privately conducted tests, there is less recoil of the gun with the long forcing cone. I have never heard anyone voice an opinion to the contrary.

Recoil is directly dependent on resistance to the ejecta; if less resistance is offered with the more gradual taper of the long forcing cone, it stands to reason that the powder burning time would be lengthened, thus a prompt quick climb in chamber pressure will not result. This would in turn mean the powder burned at its correct rate which would translate to a more gradual and uniform climb of chamber pressure as there would be less resistance to the ejecta mass of shot and wads. A 2¾-inch shell fired in a 2-9/16 16-gauge chamber results in added resistance to the ejecta, thus a rapid climb to higher pressure in the chamber. Cut a 2¾-inch chamber length, even with the old-style short forcing cone, and recoil is decreased noticeably. If a long forcing cone is cut in the same chamber, there will be even less recoil.

I realize there is a difference between "felt recoil" and "measured recoil" and I have never tested the long forcing cone against the short forcing cone in a mechanical device that would measure the exact amount of actual recoil. However, the long forcing cone results in less felt recoil which is improtant to a shooter who has his shoulder against the butt plate as the shotgun is fired.

Over the years many manufacturers have changed to the long forcing cone — but they have been foreign manufacturers! Under my direction two shotgun manufacturers in Brazil conducted tests with the regular short and long forcing cone in the same barrel of their guns. The resulting patterns caused both to change to the long forcing cone immediately: one company in Sao Paulo, CBC, and the other a thousand miles to the south in Veranopolis, E.R. Amantino. Half-way around the world, in Manila, I supervised identical tests at the Arms Corporation of the Philippines with a pump shotgun. Results were the same in pattern percentage gain with the long forcing cone and again a factory changed reamers for their chambers.

Several manufacturers in Italy have switched, other Spanish shotgun makers have also switched and all use the long forcing cone as part of their advertising programs. One Japanese manufacturer has also switched. An English gun manufacturer conducted tests and as a result order a complete set of long forcing cone reamers from Brownell's.

"Why isn't the long forcing cone used in American shotguns?" was the question I put to one of the engineers of a well known manufacturer. The only answer he could think of was the NDH equation. Translated, this means "Not Developed Here." Personally I think it is simply a

matter of time before U.S. makers start using the long forcing cone. Until then the results can be accomplished by any of the many gunsmiths who offer the service. If anyone wants to do his own work, the necessary reamer can be ordered from Brownell's, Incorporated, with the detailed introduction booklet I wrote many years ago.

There have been numerous tests of the long forcing cone, but one of the best was conducted by Don Zutz, who has an inquiring mind.

"Every modern shotgun bore has a segment known as the forcing cone. It is a taper that runs from the larger-diameter, cylinder-like chamber to the smaller-diameter bore. Its purpose is to funnel the shot and wads into the bore," says Zutz.

The word *cone* is not misused. For if one were to visualize this segment of the barrel geometrically, it would indeed represent a truncated cone situated between the chamber mouth and the start of the gauge-sized bore. Practically any shotgunner can understand the need for such a feature that enhances the fluidity of ejecta flow from case to bore.

"However, the forcing cone's taper isn't standardized. They can range from short, abrupt ones to long, gradual ones. The forcing cone's length and taper can influence both recoil and pattern. On a theoretical basis, a short, abrupt forcing cone will invariably give greater recoil and lower pattern percentages than a longer, less abrupt forcing cone when all other factors are equal. When a shot charge or rifled slug emerges from a case mouth only to slam directly into a short, sharply angled forcing cone, its forward movement is impeded enough to let additional pressures rise in the chamber. The pressures rise because just a minor delay in ejecta movement lets more powder burn in the chamber's limited combustion space. In turn, the heightened gas pressures generate a more violent action-reaction situation, which translates into heavier recoil."

The short, abrupt forcing cone contributes to patterning problems by deforming pellets. This occurs when the pellets jam and mash against each other upon encountering a short, sharply tapered cone after emerging from the shotshell's mouth. If the leading pellets are slowed, even briefly, the mounting gas pressures and accelerating wad will

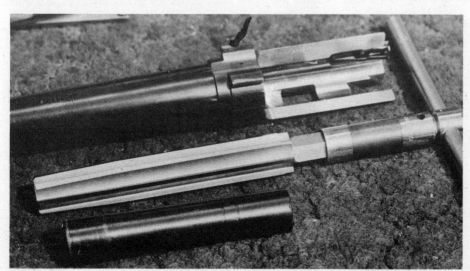

Special tools needed for the modification include chamber gauge, T-handled wrench and a cone reamer. The Browning A-5 had short chamber, while the forcing cone was only ½-inch.

pinch the pellets between the cone an themselves to compress the shot charge and place deforming pressures on the lower half of the payload. Impact with the abrupt cone can also cause additional deformation to some leading pellets before they find relief in the bore. Deformed pellets flare from and/or trail the main mass after muzzle exit; consequently, deformation from any cause will affect downrange performance. Obviously pellet hardness will be a factor: the harder the pellet, the less likely it will be deformed during setback, during case-to-bore transition, and during the remainder of its bore travel. Current brands of chilled shot are relatively soft, deforming at 2500 to 3000 pounds per square inch (psi), which is easily reached in modern shotshells which run chamber pressures of 7000 to 11,000 psi. High-antimony shot, such as Lawrence brand magnum and Remington RXP, can withstand more pressure, deforming at around 5000 psi. Copper- and nickel-plated pellets are even more resistant to chamber/bore pressures. Although pellet hardness can overcome some of the potential deformation caused by short, abrupt forcing cones, theory still indicates that there is an additional way of doing things; using a longer, less abrupt forcing cone.

A longer cone expedites payload passage. The ejecta moves from case to bore more smoothly because the funnel effect is more gradual. Too, a long forcing cone may not reduce recoil entirely, but it does seem to lessen it somewhat by opening the way for easy ejecta passage.

Theoretically, a long forcing cone is more desirable than a short one. But how does this work out in practice? Assuming the shooter starts out with a good barrel, does the longer cone — which is normally a custom feature — justify its expense?

"I chose a pair of 12-gauge guns for my own work," Zutz reports. "One is a Browning Belgian-made A-5 with thirty-two-inch full-choke barrel chambered for the three-inch shell; the other a standard-chambered 2¾-inch 12-gauge Remington Model 1100 with a twenty-eight-inch full-choke barrel. My testing method was simple enough: I fired a series of patterning tests with each barrel using a mixture of factory loads and reloads through the original short forcing cones, after which I sent the barrels to Ralph Walker for reaming. After he had cut the longer cones, I shot an identical series of tests using identical ammunition to determine what effect the longer cones had."

The Remington 1100 barrel had an original forcing cone length of just 0.625-inch ahead of a chamber length of 2.750 inches. Walker recut the forcing cone for a new length of 2.00 inches. Other dimensions in the 1100 barrel included a basic bore diameter of 0.728-inch and a choke parallel diameter of 0.688-inch for a rather standard 0.040-inch choke constriction.

The three-inch Browning A-5 had a bore diameter of 0.727-inch, two inches ahead of the forcing cone, but that tapered to 0.725 inch, two inches from the start of the choke taper. This Browning had an original forcing cone length of only 0.50-inch, and its chamber was undersize at 2.952 inches. Magnum shotshells obviously opened into the forcing cone, creating a bottleneck condition that served as an obstruction to the ejecta, and higher pressure/recoil factors resulted as the wad and shot charge had to squeeze down and ram their way out of the case mouth. Walker recut the chamber for a proper three-inch length, then increased the forcing cone to 2.00 inches. The Browning's choke diameter was 0.688-inch, giving a constriction of 0.038-inch which, like the Remington's 0.040-inch constriction, is nominal for full-choked 12s.

"The results of my patterning are interesting and appear helpful to shooters and hunters. The patterns were shot over the standard forty-yard range. Following accepted practices, the thirty-inch-diameter circle was drawn after the shot had been fired into a blank sheet; the overlay was then centered on the area of maximum pellet density. The resulting statistics open the way for some rule-of-thumb observations:

"First, long forcing cones apparently do lead to pattern improvement with most hunting loads using bulky shot. The generous cone space and length provide the gradual taper which lets coarse pellets flow into the bore with minimal jamming and deformation. For example, the three-inch Browning averaged seventy-one percent using 1⅛-ounce reloads of hard (Lawrence magnum) #2s with its original short chamber/cone dimensions; however, once the chamber and cone had been lengthened, the same reload averaged eighty percent. The difference figures out to fourteen to fifteen pellets per pattern, which can be meaningful in long-range wing-gunning.

"The standard-chambered M1100 also put on an almost amazing display when fed a reload using 1½ ounces of hard 2s over 35.0/HS-7 in an AA case. It averaged seventy-seven percent from the original short cone, which is already an excellent performance from a baby magnum in the stan-

Using the long reamer on the T-handle wrench, gunsmith lengthens the chamber and forcing cone of Browning A-5.

The shotgun barrel hone is used to polish out the new chamber and cone after they are reamed to new dimensions.

dard 12; with the long forcing come it averaged a whopping ninety percent. That is the best performance I've ever seen from a standard 12 pushing 1½-ounce loads through an unaltered choke! The difference again could mean anywhere from twelve to fifteen more pellets per pattern, which is a sizable increase in downrange energy when we're talking about hard 2s."

In general, long forcing cones are an asset when using chilled shot, which is rather soft today and inclined toward easy deformation. The term chilled makes it sound good, but it really isn't. Chilled shot readily deforms under pressures of 2500 psi, while it takes about 5000 psi to start deforming high-antimony hard shot such as Lawrence magnum grade. Some of the cheaper factory loads, known as promotion loads, also have soft shot to hold down manufacturing costs. The shooter is only fooling himself if he thinks he's getting something for nothing when he buys cheap ammo. The Remington Mohawk load tested in the M1100 is a good example: hosting soft shot, it averaged only fifty-seven percent from the original forcing cone because of pellet deformation. The lengthened cone gave some relief to shot charge flow, and the pattern increased to sixty-two percent. That's still only a strong modified-choke performance, of course, but it is better than fifty-seven percent, which is close to improved cylinder.

When the three-inch A-5 was originally fed a 1⅝-ounce reload of chilled 4s, it produced only fifty-seven percent. That, too, is nearly improved cylinder and is hardly a long-range pattern. With the lengthened chamber and forcing cone, the A-5 threw loads from the same batch into a sixty-eight percent average. Obviously, there was less pellet deformation after the forcing cone had been lengthened. In these tests, and in certain other cursory patterning, the long forcing cone tends to enhance patterning with soft chilled shot by five to twelve percentage points. Thus, the hunter who wants utmost performance from inexpensive chilled shot would do well to investigate the long forcing cone.

"I did a certain amount of testing with steel shot and came up with a puzzling situation. The three-inch Browning responded like a champion. Firing three-inch Federal loads with 1⅜ ounces of steel 1s, it averaged eighty-four percent with the original chamber/cone condition. After lengthening the chamber and cone taper, I got a ninety-one percent average, and it held most of the pellets inside a twenty-five-inch-diameter area at forty yards for a rifle-like effort. That, again, puts maximum energy into the distant pattern.

"But the M1100 did an about-face! It originally threw 83.5 percent for five patterns with Federal, 2¾-inch 1¼-ounce loads of steel 2s. After the cone had been lengthened, though, it fell to just seventy-one percent for five shots with shells from the same box. Why this reversal of form occurred is beyond me. I'll have to think on that one for a while! Fortunately, seventy-one percent is still a bona fide full-choke average. Cursory shooting with other brands of steel loads produced the same basic average after the long cone had been reamed.

"Does the long forcing cone produce lower velocities? I have run some over the chronograph and I find no deterioration. Using control loads, instrumental velocities from the original cones and the lengthened ones overlapped.

"Throughout the tests I noticed that patterns shot after the cones had been lengthened gave better shot-to-shot uniformity. A variation of only three percentage points was noted in most loads fired through the lengthened cones, whereas five percent variation was common for the shorter original cones. Loads with ordinary chilled shot could vary as much as seven percent from the original short cones. Obviously, there is room here for gun/load variations and my patterning serves only as a rule-of-thumb indication, not a universal truism."

A few other points of interest developed. Shooting with 1⅞-ounce loads in the A-5 was a bit uncomfortable when it still had the original short chamber/cone tandem, but after reaming the sting of recoil was lessened, thanks to the elimination of the bottleneck condition. Too, center density improved after the forcing cones had been lengthened, which is important in long-range wing-gunning; for it is the central pellets that remain in the basic thirty-inch circle beyond forty yards, the fringe pellets flaring into space.

"Loads with copper-plated pellets also tightened when fed through a long cone. I did not run the five-target string with copper-plated shot, but 2¾-inch handloads with 1⅜ ounces of Lawrence copper-plated 4s did eighty-four percent through the M1100's original forcing cone while going up to an honest ninety percent for two shots from the lengthened cone. Several patterns with Federal's three-inch Premium loads of plastic-bedded, copper-plated BBs (1⅞ ounces) did eighty-three percent from the A-5's original chamber and cone while moving to ninety-one percent from the lengthened dimensions.

"Finally, not all loads showed the same amount of improvement. There is still a certain amount of individuality in the guns, as we know. A reloader will still have to experiment if he wants the optimum load for his long-coned gun. Factory loads must also be patterned, because they are made with varying qualities of shot.

"In general, a lengthened forcing cone will tend to improve pattern density by five to ten percent, the final figure depending on the myriad variables. And hunters who need all the downrange energy they can get would do well to consider this alteration for their specialized long-range smoothbores."

Chapter 11

THE SHOTGUN BORE

This Section Of The Barrel Receives The Least Amount Of Attention Despite Its Importance

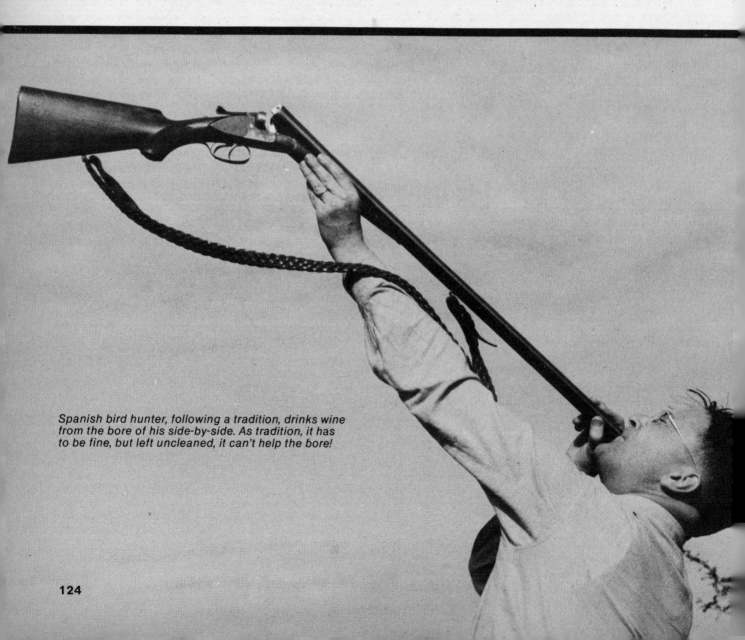

Spanish bird hunter, following a tradition, drinks wine from the bore of his side-by-side. As tradition, it has to be fine, but left uncleaned, it can't help the bore!

In England's Westley Richards gunshop, craftsmen used the time-tried traditional methods of boring shotgun barrels.

THAT SECTION of the shotgun barrel that begins at the point where the chamber forcing cone ends and extends forward to where the choke forcing cone begins is commonly referred to as the bore. In some texts it is called simply the shotgun bore or barrel bore, but all three terms are identical. Few people realize it plays an extremely important part in overall gun performance in addition to the ultimate pattern performance.

Unfortunately, it is the section of the shotgun barrel accorded the least amount of attention. This probably is due to the fact that it is extremely difficult to inspect and also to properly gauge. It should be remembered, however, that during its passage from the shotshell to its exit at the muzzle, the shot charge stays in constant contact with the barrel the greatest length of time in the bore section. A lot of things can occur during this passage to add to or detract from overall performance.

The absolutely perfect bore would include all of several equally important factors. The problem in obtaining this perfect bore is not overcome easily during the production of a shotgun barrel. Added to this original built-in imperfection is the deterioration of the bore due to neglect and abuse over a given time period. Oddly enough, if the deterioration is eliminated, there is no detrimental change in the bore regardless of how many times the gun is fired. If anything, the passage of the shot will actually smooth the bore by removing small imperfections!

As previously explained, the designated bore diameter is determined by the gauge and this was drawn up in a series of charts many years ago in England. Later it became the recommended standard for the entire world, although few manufacturers stick to the exact established standard!

The variation in bore diameters for any gauge is astounding! Over the years I have used a precision bore micrometer to gauge barrels and have recorded the results in a series of notebooks. For instance, lets take the 12-gauge. Bore diameters for this gauge are as small as .720-inch and as large as .744-inch in my records. Poly Choke, which makes chokes to match the bore diameter for best results, offers an even wider range in 12-gauge; the smallest diameter being .716 inch and the larger diameter at .746 inch, and I would take their figures as being more precise than my own as they have checked this for quite a few years. The same range is found in the other gauges also.

If we take the 12-gauge for comparison sake, what is the correct recommended bore diameter? The answer is .729 inch, but currently manufactured 12-gauge bores run from .725 inch to .735 inch diameter.

Regardless of the chosen bore diameter, that perfect

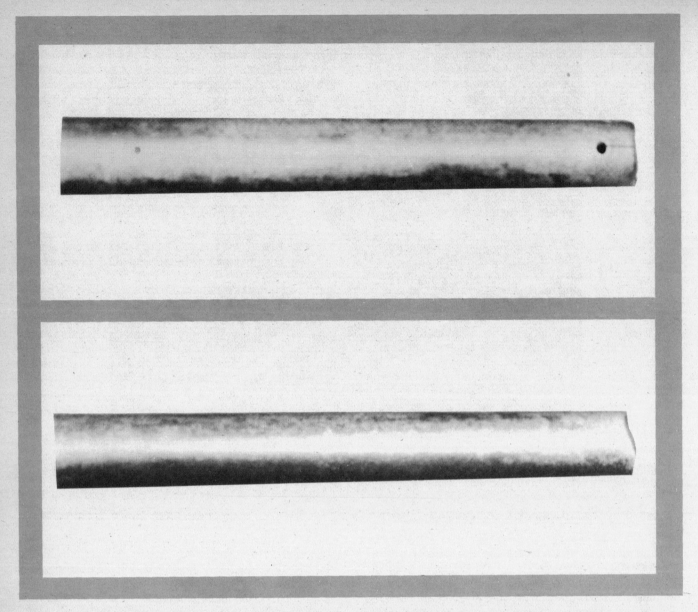

In the upper photo, the front sight bead extended down into the bore. Fired shot hit this resistance. It split the end of the barrel, blew out the sight bead. This is dangerous. (Lower photo) This is the wrong way to cut off a barrel. Angle cut causes shot charge to hit too high. Numerous tools can be of help in making proper cut.

bore would have one important factor: consistent diameter from one end to the other. In other words, the measurement just in front of the chamber forcing cone would be the same at any point of the bore up to the beginning of the choke forcing cone without the slightest variation. If not consistent, the shot column is subjected to restriction and expansion to match the diameters at various points in the bore. This always results in deformed shot pellets with the end result being a decrease is pattern percentage. It does not take much to deform pellets; in fact, you can easily test variations as little as .0005 inch simply by checking pattern percentage.

Correction of such a bore with varying diameters requires sophisticated equipment and even then the task is not accomplished easily. What is required is that the minimum diameter be increased to match the maximum diameter. Basically the tooling requires an expandable hone that is first locked to a diameter that will just pass through the bore without taking a cut. The hone diameter is set to a slightly larger diameter and the first cutting pass is made through the length of the bore at this setting, removing a small amount of metal. Then the hone is set to a larger diameter and the sequence repeated until the bore's diameter is consistent and matches that of the maximum original dimension. This is the most accurate method of correcting the problem.

Another less accurate but workable system is to lap the bore. This can take several forms, but one utilizes a round brass rod closely matching that of the bore in diameter. Aluminum-oxide cloth is inserted in a slot cut in the round brass rod and wound around its exterior. The brass rod is attached to a smaller rod which is power driven. The aluminum-oxide cloth will lap the bore as it is passed through and is rotated. When this dimension is achieved, foam rubber is placed under the aluminum-oxide cloth and between it and the brass rod, thus increasing the overall diameter. Another pass is made through the bore to remove more of the minimum diameter section. This is repeated with even more foam rubber added to further increase overall diameter of the lap.

Efficiency depends to a large extent on the lap operator's prior experience as he must depend on "feel." When the lap reaches a hard spot, which is a minimum-diameter section, the rig must be given more time to cut by decreasing hand feed through the bore. When a soft spot is hit — the maximum-diameter section — the hand feed speed is increased to give less cutting effect. This system is slow and not easily learned, but it serves for most shops not equipped with expensive honing equipment.

Instead of the round brass rod and the aluminum-oxide cloth, a lap can be made by casting it in an old barrel section from pure lead. If necessary, the lead casting can be decreased in diameter by turning in a lathe. The cutting effect is achieved by coating the exterior of the lead lap with common valve-grinding compound of fine grit. The only problem with this system is that as the diameter of the bore is increased, the lead lap no longer is of sufficient diameter and another lap must be cast and machined to a slightly larger diameter. Only .001 inch can be removed from the bore with each lead lap, but in some cases this is sufficient to achieve desired results.

The Brownell expanding choke hone can be modified for this task by soldering a long extension to the rear of the hone drive section. As the expansion of the hone body is achieved through constant action spring, you cannot control its diameter at any given point. When used for this purpose, it must be passed through the bore rapidly without hesitation at any point. Its correct use depends upon familiarity of the gunsmith with its cutting action. The cutting action is faster if the hone is dry and slower if oil is added to the cutting surface.

Whichever of these three methods is used, the drive rod must be kept from vibrating and striking the inside surface of the chamber and bore. A simple solution involves a fired shotgun shell of the same gauge as the barrel. Cut off the body section in front of the brass section and punch out the primer. Next, drill a hole through the primer hole of a diameter that will match that of the drive rod.

The modified rear of the shotshell is slipped over the drive rod and is between the front cutting component and the electric power source. The modified rear section of the shell is pressed forward until it seats in the chamber of the barrel and is held in place with the operator's finger. A few drops of oil are added at its contact point with the drive rod. The rod rotates, the shotshell does not, thus serving as a stabilizing bushing for the drive rod. Vibration is almost nonexistent and I have not found a need for a bushing in the bore when such a shotshell guide bushing is in place at the chamber.

An old system still used in Europe to lap and burnish a barrel is within the reach of anyone who wants to take the time to make the tool. To make the tool for a 12-gauge bore, select a long rod one-half inch in diameter; this can be of common cold rolled steel. Machine a section about six inches long on one end to a diameter of around one-quarter inch. The shoulder produced by the two diameters serves as a stop. The same thing can be accomplished without machining by simply soldering or brazing a half-inch washer to a quarter-inch rod. The forward end of the quarter-inch section is threaded to receive both a washer and a nut. Washers are cut from leather to be slightly larger than bore diameter on the outside diameter; an inner hole is cut to match the quarter-inch rod diameter. The series of leather washers then are installed onto the quarter-inch-diameter rod section. These are loose. Next, the half-inch metal washer is installed, then the nut which is pulled up loosely, not compressing the leather washers.

Some form of handle is attached on the other end of the rod. A light compound then is sprinkled on the surfaces of the combined leather washers. The unit is inserted into the bore and the leather washers compress to match the bore diameter. The tool is pushed — without rotation — from one end of the bore to the other and allowed to exit. As it is pulled back through the bore, the leather washers again compress to match the bore diameter. This is repeated over and over until the bore is mirror bright. If less compression of the leather washers is desired, just tighten the nut. This in turn decreases the amount of room for compression of the leather washers, thus increasing the permissible outer diameter of the working end of the tool.

By varying the type of cutting compound on the leather washers — and the addition or subtraction of oil — the amount of cutting of the bore is decreased and more burnishing takes place.

There is a more modern method of accomplishing the same results faster. While this method burnishes more than it polishes, the end result is the same: a bright mirror-like bore. Burnishing is not new and has been used for hundreds of years by skilled craftsmen who also use it to finish the exterior of fine guns prior to bluing. The technique hardens the surface and actually closes the pores of the metal in the process. This is a desired effect as there is less breeding ground for rust to form on a surface. When done inside a shotgun barrel, the bore becomes slick and in turn does not offer added resistance to the passage of the shot column.

Four-aught (0000) steel wool is the burnishing tool working surface. It can be used in several ways, but a simple and efficient tool can be made from a common bore brush, a shotgun cleaning rod with the handle removed and a power source such as an electric hand drill.

Steel wool actually is small steel wire woven together to form a length of the material. A section of the material then is folded back upon itself to form the common steel wool pad. The diameter of the wire determines the cutting effect of the pad and the numbers of same run from the finest (0000) to the more coarse single-aught (0), then to a series of numbers. For bore use, only the four-ought (0000) is used, as anything coarser (fewer zeros) may damage the bore. This size will not damage the bore regardless of how many times it is utilized.

To make the burnishing tool, insert the bore brush into its recepticle in the shotgun cleaning rod and place the other end of the cleaning rod in the chuck of the electric

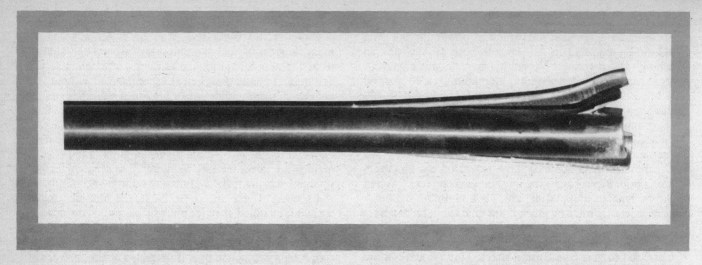

The choke area of this barrel was ruined because muzzle was plugged. Barrel can be cut off and the bore rechoked.

hand drill. Unwind the folds of a section of 0000 steel wool and place it on a table or similar flat surface. Touch the drill trigger lightly and allow the unfolded steel wool to "climb" up on the shotgun bore brush until it covers its outer surface. If you hold the brush to the left side of the unfolded steel wool pad, the action is quick and simple as the drill starts to rotate the brush. It may be necessary to add or remove thicknesses of the steel wool, depending on both bore and brush diameters. You want only a snug fit.

Again the chamber bushing made from a fired shotshell will stop any rod vibration. The assembled burnishing bob is inserted into the bore — preferably from the chamber end — to take advantage of the shotshell modified bushing. The drill is turned on and the bob begins to rotate. I prefer to push the burnishing bob at a steady pace through the length of the bore and allow a forward portion to exit the muzzle. Without stopping the drill, pull it back through the bore until it touches the shotshell bushing in the chamber. The sequence is repeated over and over until the bore is mirror bright. Oil added to the bore will result in a slight improvement in the burnished surface, but is not absolutely necessary.

I used a similar burnishing tool as a method to clean a personal shotgun bore that had seen a lot of use. The bore was miked at the beginning and at the end when the gun was sold five years later. The reading was absolutely the same and the only change was that the bore was bright from the burnishing/cleaning it had received. I still use the tool on all of my shotguns, including a prized custom-built Beretta over/under.

Assuming the shotgun bore is perfect in diameter from one point to the other either through original manufacture or by rework, what is the next requirement for a perfect bore?

Some shotgun bores are not perfectly round! This can be the result of a manufacturing defect when the bore was cut or from some accident somewhere in the barrel's existence. Another possibility is when the top rib — or in the case of two barrels — the side ribs were added. The addition of a rib or ribs to a barrel generally requires some form of heat. This may be when the ribs are attached with solder,

or in many modern instances by induction brazing or even welding. Heat always expands metal, and when it cools, the metal may — or may not — return to its original specification. The end result may be a bore that is not consistent in roundness. Pump and semiauto shotgun barrels have ribs added and usually some method of attaching a lug to engage the magazine assembly end to stabilize it. Again heat is applied with expansion and contraction of the barrel metal, resulting in an out-of-round bore.

Shotgun barrels, being relatively thin walled, are subjected to any number of dents from outside sources. It does not require much pressure and the dent often is quite shallow, but the bore still is out-of-round. The non-round bore compresses, then expands the shot column and deforms pellets as they pass this point in the bore.

Dents constrict the bore and in essence consist of metal moved from point A to point B, which is corrected by moving the metal back to point A, its original position. The best way to accomplish this is with a dent remover tool. B-Square produces an efficient tool for this work and is hydraulic in action. A small anvil on a stem is pushed outward as a screw is turned in the handle of the tool. In turn this exerts pressure against the hydraulic fluid. If used with care, a dent can be removed, little if any trace remaining. The only potential hazard of using the tool is in the application of too much pressure in which case the anvil of the tool continues to press against the bore wall and this can result in a bulge! You have only to apply a small amount of pressure via the screw at a time to move the dent back to its original position and check the work periodically.

If the dent is of great dimension or if a length of the barrel has been compressed inward, the only solution is a machined ironer. This is a length of hard steel of four to five inches turned to within .001 inch of the bore diameter. A slight taper is turned on one end that will be less than the minimum diameter of the affected bore section. The bore is scrubbed clean to remove all residue, then coated lightly with oil. The oil prevents the ironer from sticking and also will increase its overall diameter slightly. Considerable force is required to push it through the bore from the chamber end, always stopping before the choke forcing cone area of the barrel is encountered. In most cases this can be done with the barrel cold, but if severe dimensions are involved, the barrel can be heated to a dull red color. This allows the metal to be moved more easily by the ironer as it passes the smaller diameters. The barrel never should be heated to a yellow color, for this may result in more problems of the barrel being out of round.

The only other solution is to rebore the barrel with a reamer, but this has limitations. The metal removal will result in one wall of the bore being thinner than its opposite side and could result in unsafe barrel dimensions when subjected to normal pressures. Before resorting to the reamer, a lot of measuring with precision tools is required. Practicality of this solution depends on how much the barrel walls are pushed inward and the resulting thickness after reaming. Safety always must be the final consideration. If the section is close to the chamber, more pressure is involved when a shotshell is fired. If close to the muzzle end, pressure will be less.

A bulge increases the bore diameter. This normally occurs when the barrel is fired with some form of obstruction in the bore. The ejecta strikes the obstruction and pressure is exerted against the bore walls building up quickly as the obstruction slows its forward movement. An owner may swear by all that is holy there was no obstruction, but even an obstruction of one or two thousandths inch can result in a bulge. To correct the problem, there is a limit to what can be accomplished.

Bulged metal is somewhat like a toy balloon that has been blown up, then the air released; it never will return to its original dimensions, as the material has been stretched past its point of elasticity. In a shotgun barrel, the metal is thin where the bulge begins and even thinner at its major diameter. You cannot compress metal without leaving traces of damage. It is possible to machine a close-tolerance plug that matches the bore diameter, insert it directly under the bulge, then push the metal down until it is stopped by the plug. Usually there is a slight wrinkle of metal where the correction occurred. To partially remove this requires that the bore be honed, then lapped and burnished — but it will still remain visible.

Heating a barrel, as in installation of a rib, often results in the barrel metal expanding, then not returning to its original diameter. Little can be done in such cases except precision honing to bring the bore to proper diameter.

The perfect bore is smooth from beginning to end. Anything less can decrease the efficiency of the shot column as it passes on its way to the muzzle. Prior to firing, each pellet must be assumed to be perfectly round and the idea is to let it exit the muzzle without even minute deterioration in its spherical shape. The shot must make its way from the shotshell and into the bore past the forcing cone. The plastic shot protector does its best to prevent deformation during the passage through the bore, but this is tough to accomplish for many reasons.

Every irregularity in bore wall smoothness will result in some pellets being deformed. If the irregularity is in the form of a depression, the pellets under pressure from the gas will be forced first into the depression, then as it leaves this depression, must push against other pellets to obtain another position in the shot column. Should the irregularity be the opposite, a bump of some description, the pellet must compress the shot column to obtain a position in the mass, then is pushed outward again when past the bump. When pellets are moved back and forth in this manner they are always deformed in the process, and also deform other pellets that are bearing against them.

The original manufacturing process can leave these irregularities in the bore, although if a strong light is directed through the bore, it will appear smooth. Diffused light affords a much more accurate view. A ray of light behind wax paper will provide the necessary diffusion as will a white wall with the light falling upon it. Quite often when a barrel is viewed from one end, the bore will appear smooth, viewed from the opposite end, a defect will stand out like Mount Everest!

There is a device marketed that contains a tube with optics inside and a small bulb on the end. Inserted into the bore it affords a clear view of the bore walls at any point it is placed. The only fault is the price tag. With training and patience, a gunsmith can learn to use diffused light to show most bore imperfections.

Removal of these faults is not easy, but most can be improved drastically. In most bores, the "bumps" are a result of build-up from the plastic wads or rust and can be removed easily. (This is covered in another chapter.) Rust pits in the bore are a different matter best compared to a tooth cavity. The only final solution is to increase the diameter of the bore to equal that of the deepest pit, thus removing the pit. There is a limit to this for safety reasons, but, except in extreme cases, rust pits can be eliminated.

The bore hone, as previously explained, is used to increase the bore diameter and produce a new bore surface. It all depends on the depth of the pits.

The cardinal rule of gunsmithing work is to use the minimum pressure or force possible to accomplish the goal. Start with a good cleaning job, then use the steel wool burnishing bob. If this fails, use a lap. If this also fails then go to the hone to remove metal.

Should all of these efforts fail, the only solution is the

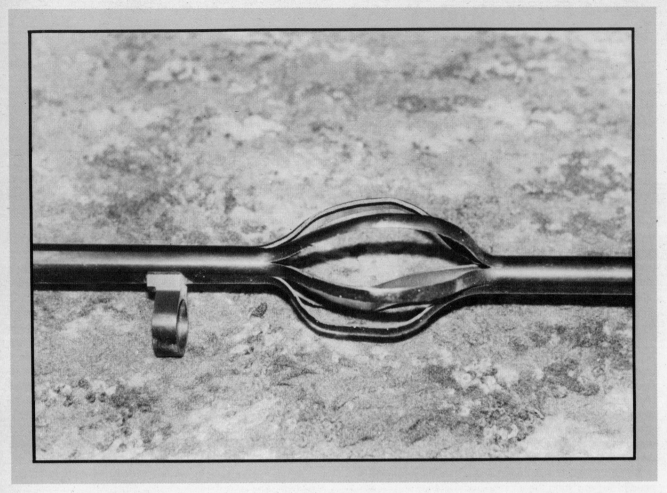

The birdcage effect in this barrel was caused when gun's owner fired with mud in the bore. It destroyed forend, too.

boring reamer to remove considerable metal from the walls. There are several reamers that will do the job, but the problem involves the skill and the tooling necessary to hold the barrel secure while the boring or reaming is in process; this requires a lot of know-how and skill. It is a wise gunsmith who knows the limitations of his skill and his equipment, so let someone who knows how tackle this job if it is the only way to solve the problem.

A recent technique is known as "porting the barrel," which translates to a series of holes drilled in the bore from the outside of the barrel just behind the choke forcing cone. The theory in favor of porting contends that the holes on the upper portion of the barrel act as a muzzle brake to push the muzzle of the gun down. This keeps the muzzle closer to the target and assists in aiming and in follow-through. At the same time, the gas acting against the sides of the holes pulls the muzzle forward to counteract the force pushing the gun rearward, thus decreasing recoil.

The second phase of the argument is that the holes rapidly lower the gas pressure by exhausting it to the outside of the bore; this decreases the amount of pressure bearing against the shot column before it enters the choke forcing cone. This pressure decrease from the rear allows the shot to rearrange itself for its passage through the cone and choke with minimum pellet deformation.

The anti-porting crowd calls this latter argument so

much hot air and points out that shot pellets enter the holes. This deforms more pellets than could possibly be rescued from the rear gas pressure exerted on the base of the shot column. They also contend that, with the modern one-piece plastic wad, any pellet deformation takes place when the initial surge is made as the shot column starts to move; the rear pellets are forced to absorb the weight of the forward pellets before they start to move. They also point out the fact that the current one-piece wad will absorb the energy of the gas pressure. Opponents also point out that the gas exerted sideward carries much of the muzzle blast with it. This becomes irritating to anyone standing at the side of such a ported barrel.

I have mixed feelings about the whole matter. For a claybird shooter shooting trap singles, any help in keeping that muzzle down is welcome as is any reduction of gun recoil. The reduction in muzzle whip and recoil is an accomplished fact, but here I switch sides.

I believe that anything that adds irregularities to that glass-smooth bore is a step in the wrong direction! The holes in the bore will shear particles of plastic from the one-piece wad in addition to shearing particles of lead from the pellets themselves. Any serious shooter who has a ported barrel engages himself in cleaning out those little holes between rounds. As for the decrease in pressure prior to the shot entering the choke forcing cone, were it possible to achieve this without the ports, it could possibly be a pellet saver, but the whole matter is questionable.

Another current 12-gauge fad involves "back boring" a shotgun barrel. In essence, the normal bore diameter is increased by boring behind the forcing cone of the choke with a reamer, maintaining this enlarged diameter all the way back to the chamber forcing cone end. Supposedly this is to increase the pattern percentage.

The normal 12-gauge bore diameter of barrels manufactured in the United States will be close to the SAAMI-recommended specification of .729 inch, although some are as large as .735-inch. The European bore of the same gauge is smaller, running .724- to .726-inch average. Thus we have two schools of thought.

Every gunsmith engaged in back boring has his own ideas of dimensions. Some advocate enlarging the bore all the way up to .750-inch diameter and use a fixed-diameter reamer to achieve this. Others use the older but accurate armorer's reamer which can be expanded to any desired diameter of cut.

If you measure the hard part of a plastic shot protector — just behind the petal section and before the compression section — virtually every one-piece wad will measure .690 to .700 inch in diameter. This hard section supports the forward shot protector section and its petal-like protectors. When the shell is fired, the shot pellets tend to move backward, resisting the effort to get them moving. This follows the well-known law that mass at rest tends to remain at rest until acted upon by an outside force; in this case, the gas pressure energy furnishes that force. This rearward movement of the shot pushes the shot outward to expand the diameter of the shot protecting plastic petals of the wad. The hard section just behind the petal remains unchanged. The rear cup section of the wad expands to seal the gas while the center section of one-piece wad compresses upon itself to serve as a shock protector. There is initial expansion due to these pressures, and following the rules, we do not want to expand and compress any more than absolutely necessary, thus minimizing deformation of the pellets.

The expansion is contained by the inner walls of the forward section of the chamber body, then it must pass through the chamber forcing cone and into the bore. If the forward section of the forcing cone is less in diameter, then there is less compression of the shot and hence fewer pellets are deformed. At least, this is according to those who advocate back boring.

Now let's go back to that .700-inch wad diameter at the hard section just behind the shot protector section. The shot column expands very little if you examine the dimensions of a good chamber and consider that these measurements do not take into consideration the wall thickness of the shotshell. This will run around .025 inch, which is one side of the shotshell, and we have to double this figure to get the inner shotshell diameter which surrounds the plastic wad. So we have .050 inch combined thickness of the shotshell. Subtract this from the chamber wall diameter at the forward end of the chamber and you get a surprising figure. It is all a close fit in the chamber and reduces the diameter in question. The plastic wad does not expand to the inner chamber forward diameter. It expands to the inner diameter of the shotshell and thence into the bore diameter via the forcing cone. So why expand the forward end of the shotshell out to .750-inch diameter when its nonfired diameter is .700 inch? You are expanding the shot column far in excess of the design of the plastic shot protector diameter!

Gunsmith fires into test chamber following work on shotgun to ascertain that the gun is functioning properly overall.

The tight European bores shoot tight patterns at extreme ranges. If choke constriction is the same for both a large bore diameter and a small bore diameter, the shot column of the small diameter is constricted only when it passes through the forcing cone section of the choke and the choke itself. The larger bore diameter first expands the shot column, then constricts it, subjecting the shot pellets to two changes in dimension.

In my opinion, back boring has only one place in a shotgun barrel bore: when you must enlarge the bore diameter while the choke diameter remains unchanged, thus increasing constriction ratio. If the bore is .730-inch and you enlarge it to .750-inch diameter, and the choke constriction remains at .710 inch, as an example, you have increased the constriction ratio from .020 to .040 inch. This changes a modified choke to an extra-full choke. (This is explained in greater detail in the chapter on chokes.) The bottom line is that back boring's only practical use is to increase the choke constriction ratio when the choke is of the fixed built-in type.

There also is a danger in back boring: As the bore diameter is increased, the wall thickness of the barrel is decreased. In barrels made from barely adequate metal that will just contain pressure in its original state, back bor-

ing can create dangers if carried to extreme. When barely adequate metal is used for barrel construction, the wall is thick. Top-quality barrel metal normally results in a barrel with less wall thickness as there is no need for the extra metal to provide barrel strength to contain pressure.

To this must be added the fact that quite a few shotgun barrels have bores not concentric with the outside, thus some parts of the barrel have a wall thickness that is less on one side than on the other. If back boring is carried to the extreme, the thin wall thickness is reduced even more in the process and the safety factor is greatly reduced.

We also find barrels that bend up or down or to one side for one reason or another. While this may not affect the inner bore except in extreme examples, it is a subject that should be covered and this is as good a place as any.

Shotgun barrels manufactured without a top rib depend upon the shooter to "see" the forward one-third of the barrel. The reason for this is that the center of a shot pattern will drop about one foot in fifty yards, hence a hold over is necessary. This is achieved by "seeing" that forward third of the barrel. Other manufacturers bend the muzzle slightly upward to compensate for the shot pattern drop and thus eliminate that forward view of the top of the barrel. When a rib is added, this eliminates this require-

In rebluing shotgun barrels, care is taken that the bore is properly plugged, protecting it against bluing solution.

ment by its height and taper at the muzzle. Thus, when the rib is installed, there suddenly is double compensation for the drop and the barrel will shoot high.

This is simple to check by holding the barrel between centers on a lathe that is indexed correctly. If the center section is not in line when the barrel is rotated, the barrel muzzle is bent upward. Before installing the rib the barrel must be straightened. This can be done in the lathe by placing the cross feed of the lathe half-way on the barrel. Reverse the tool holder and use it as a point to exert pressure against the barrel. The side where the barrel is bent outward is rotated until it is on the side of the reversed tool holder. By turning the tool holder inward, the barrel is sprung inward. Pressure is applied until the barrel will be in line when freely rotated.

There is an even simpler way to straighten a barrel when it has been bent or has suffered a damaging blow. The key is determining the point where the bend begins. Select a door face where there is a strong light behind it and hold the barrel up parallel. The light and the door face will create a straight-line shadow which is used in the process. Look down the bore of the barrel. If straight, the shadow line will also be straight and without deviation.

However, if the barrel is bent, the shadow line in the bore will dogleg to one side, then continue. Where this interruption of the straight shadow line occurs is the point where the barrel is bent. If the dogleg is to the right, the bend is to the right and vice versa. If the first view is a straight line, it means only that the barrel is not bent in this direction. Slowly rotate the barrel through 360 degrees and watch the shadow line for a telltale dogleg which indicates a bend.

Some use the shadow line technique on the exterior sur-face of the barrel. This is a mistake, as the polishing of the barrel surface prior to bluing could be the source of the line deviation. If used as an indicator, an otherwise straight bore is thought to be bent due to incorrect data. Always use the bore as the indicator.

Straightening the barrel requires placing it on two blocks about eighteen inches apart. A pressure point then is applied on the other side of the barrel directly between the two blocks. The straightening action is one of a series of slow springing motions onto the barrel instead of one big push. The bent barrel will slowly be sprung until straight with this simple action.

There is an old adage that a bent barrel can be straightened by catching it in a door frame and applying pressure. In every case where I know this action to have been tried the end results have always been the same. The bend becomes worse or the barrel is bent past the center point to a sort of Z shape, which renders it virtually impossible to straighten. A similar incorrect method is whacking the end of the barrel against a tree stump or the floor. This may work for some skilled in the process, or with rifle barrels. Shotgun barrels, being of a thinner wall construction, simply cannot be straightened with this crude process. The barrel may be dented and thus compound the problem.

B-Square manufactures a barrel straightener that is both easy to use and inexpensive, but the actual job of straightening a bent barrel requires a lot of skill. I would recommend this be tried first on a junk barrel bending in and straightening it over and over until the knack is acquired.

The bore never should be taken for granted and assumed to be perfect. It must be as uniform in diameter as possible, as round as possible and devoid of any irregularity in its surface if maximum efficiency is expected.

Chapter 12

A MATTER OF THEORY

Early Barrel Choking Was More Luck Than Knowledge, But All That Has Changed!

"**I** WANT to cut my thirty-two-inch shotgun barrel back to twenty-six inches, so how much choke will I have left?"

"I'd like to have a twenty-six-inch barrel as my twenty-eight-inch is too long, how far can I cut it without losing the choke?"

"Can you put the full choke back in my barrels that were cut to eighteen inches because I blew the ends off?"

These and associated questions are put to the average gunsmith at least once a week. I think I get more than my share, as I specialize in shotguns.

If there is one mystery regarding firearms of any type, my vote would go to the matter of choke in the shotgun. Many people not only do not know where the choke is in a barrel, but I doubt that one in a hundred has even a foggy notion of what it does. All the average shooter knows is

English gunsmith William Pape has been credited with design of the first shotgun choke. (Left) These shotguns at author's gunshop are awaiting various types of work, but greatest call is for choking.

Left: Stars on Italian-made Beretta indicate choke: one star is full, two designates improved modified. (Lower left) Browning choke markings utilize asterisks and dashes. In this case, the code identifies the modified choke of this shotgun.

own barrels, which were predominantly of large bore single-shot muzzleloading persuasion. The story goes that he goofed during one such job and decided to rebore the barrel to a larger size. Inadvertently he left some of the original smaller bore diameter at the muzzle. Test firing revealed an unusually tight shot pattern at extreme distance; being inquisitive, Kimble gauged the bore and discovered the accidental constriction at the barrel muzzle. He purposely bored other barrels with various constrictions at the muzzle and did a lot of test shooting. This happened "around 1870," but Kimble never patented the process.

In England, W.R. Pape patented a choke-boring process on May 29, 1866. His patent #1501 states, "The invention further relates to an improvement in the manufacture and construction of the bore of barrels of breechloading and other shotguns. Instead of making the bore cylindrical throughout, I propose firstly to bore the barrel or barrels through and through one size or number smaller than the true bore to be formed; I then rebore the barrel with one full size or number larger than the former, begin-

that his barrel is choked — it says so right on the barrel — and it keeps the shot together somehow to hit a target at a long distance. Beyond this, choke is a dim, vague subject.

Two individuals have been credited with initial choke development for shotgun barrels. Fred Kimble was a professional market hunter of Peoria, Illinois, whose skill with the shotgun was legend. He personally bored many of his

The Baker barrel micrometer is packaged in a box that features printed instructions on how to use it properly.

Stan Baker Shotgun Barrel Micrometer
INSTRUCTIONS
This is a precision instrument and should be properly handled in order to insure that it will maintain its accuracy.

Do not put the probe into a dirty bore. You will not get a proper reading and the bore fouling will find its way into the probe and spoil its accuracy.

The standard included in your kit measures .700" inside diameter. Slip it over the probe and turn the outer ring of the dial to put the needle on '0'. This will be .700" and the dial will read in a logical manner. When the needle is on 30, it will be read as .730". When the needle is on 90, it will be read as .690".

To determine the constriction of the choke, in relation to your barrel, just subtract the choke diameter from the bore diameter.

If the probe becomes sticky or sluggish, squirt some WD-40 into it through the ball holes.

Choke Diameter Chart

CHOKE DIAMETER	CHOKE DESIGNATION	CHOKE CONSTRICTION
.680" .685" .690"* .695" .700"	Full Choke	.030" to .040"
.705"* .710"	Imp. Mod.	.020" to .030"
.710"* .715" .720"	Modified	.010" to .020"
.720"* .725" .730"	Imp. Cyl.	.005" to .010"
	Skeet	.000" to .005"

*These are approximate standards for barrels with a .729" bore diam

Stan Baker Bore Reader is similar to the Poly Choke micrometer for bore, except it has a dial indicator head. (Below) Front end of gauge uses three ball bearings for measuring.

ning at the breech or open end, but continuing only to within one inch or thereabouts of the muzzle end; I then finish the bore by a taper from the conclusion of the larger bore direct to the very extremity of the muzzle. By this improved constriction of the bore, stronger and closer shooting will be acquired besides other advantages.''

Pape's description is of a conical choke in the truest sense and the description unquestionably is the beginning of the term, "choke boring." His is the conical choke still in use today. The London Field Trials were held on May 22 and 23, 1866, one week prior to Pape's patent date and there is a known record that "soft shot was used at the trials and choke boring was not known to England gunmakers," in reference to a description of the gun used in the trials by one William Rochester Pape, a well known gunmaker of the period.

To add to the confusion there is ample evidence that one Jeramiah Smith, a gunmaker in Smithfield, Rhode Island, discovered the merits of choke boring in 1827. He bored quite a few guns using the system and also taught another gunsmith, N. Whitmore of Mansfield, Massachusetts. Whitmore in turn bored guns for many sportsmen of the area using the choke principle.

The one man who introduced choke boring and chokes to the average shooter was W.W. Greener of England. Fred Kimble publicized the system with his skill in matches and in hunting. Greener imported one of his barrels in 1870 and conducted numerous tests of the principle. Wide

recognition was all that choke boring needed to bring it to the fore among sportsmen.

Greener described his boring by saying, "Barrels intended for choking are left two sizes smaller than the cartridge (shell) they are intended for — that is to say, the 12 bores are left 14 bore, the 16 is left 18 bore — and the barrels are bored up within three inches of the muzzle with a fine boring bit, using a spill and liners as described.'' This description is of the conical parallel type of choke, which will be explained later in this chapter.

So take your pick: Pape has the patent, Kimble publicized the advantages and Greener put choke-bored shotgun barrels into the hands of the shooting public. Regardless of who gets the credit, by 1880 choke boring was a well established practice, which others have been trying to improve for the past hundred years!

Simply stated, there are no magic answers as far as choke is concerned nor are there any dark secrets in choke boring known but to a few old gray-haired gunsmiths who refuse to share the knowledge. Many people think there is a magic answer and one hears stories about such and such a choke that "shoots like a rifle" out to amazing distances. There ain't no such critter!

One rumor persists that a barrel with one or more chokes placed in its length of bore would deliver that magic pattern. The fact is that the bore must be absolutely the same diameter from its beginning to the choke at the muzzle to be efficient. Any constrictions within its entire length decreases the proficiency, not the opposite. As previously explained, shot pellets are deformed any time they pass through a constriction. Therefore one or more constrictions in the bore would result in the pellets being deformed with resulting loss of pellet percentage within the target.

Another fallacy is that some form of tapered bore can produce a magic pattern. Detail of this particular dream is that the bore diameter must be formed as a cone or taper extending from the beginning of the bore at the chamber to the muzzle or up to the beginning of the choke section itself. This does not work either.

Some years ago a well known American shotgun was so constructed and ballyhooed to the public as the final answer to tight choke shooting. It did taper gradually from the beginning of the bore to the muzzle extreme. I test pat-

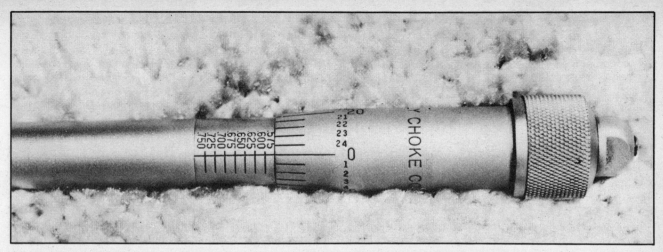

Head of the Poly Choke bore micrometer shows the range of instrument's capabilities. It is simple to use in that it is read the same as a common micrometer. The author feels this is the best available for determining bore specs.

terned one of these shotguns, shooting just about every shotshell on the market, including a one-piece-wad skeet and target precision load. To say that the pattern results were discouraging is an understatement. It shot with less efficiency than the cheapest single-barrel shotgun with a crude choke system.

In an attempt for a fair test, I loaded some shells using the old nitro card or over-powder wad and felt filler or cushion wads. Results were even worse! Since that time I have seen others attempt "something new in choking."

Results were always the same: a less efficient pattern than those shot through a regular choke.

Nothing is totally impossible in this old world and perhaps someone out there does have a taper-bored shotgun barrel that is the hottest thing around in delivering tight patterns, but I have never seen such a critter in all my years of gunsmithing. Nor do I know of anyone else who has seen such a gun barrel or the patterns produced.

There are only three basic types of chokes with all other variations of these three. Without exception, all are some

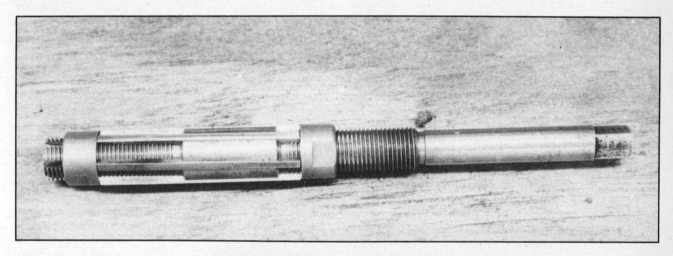

Author designed Brownell choke reamer; it is angled, tapered, adjustable. (Right) The three ball bearings on Poly Choke's bore micrometer move outward as dial is turned on the head. A tapered rod makes them move until they contact walls of bore. The bearings move inward when measuring lesser diameters.

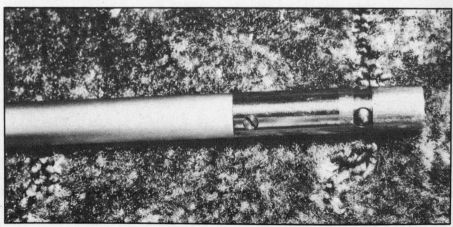

form of constriction that reduces the diameter of the bore just before the choke starts, to a smaller diameter at the muzzle. It is this constriction of the inside diameter from large to small that produces the choke effect on the shot leaving the muzzle of a shotgun barrel. The definition of choke is positive: *Choke of a shotgun barrel is a constriction of the bore diameter inside to a smaller diameter inside taking place within the last few inches of the barrel near the muzzle.*

Even the three basic types of chokes follow this established definition. It is the method of achieving the reduced constriction and the dimensions resulting that give the varying amount or degrees of choke effect on the exiting shot column. This has never changed since the days of Pape and Kimbel. Improvements, yes; basic principle change, no.

The earliest choke — the one described by Pape in the patent he obtained — is known as a *conical* choke. The reduction of bore diameter is achieved through a continuous angle from large to small with the small end of the taper exactly at the muzzle where the barrel ends. The large end of the taper being at the bore diameter section before the start of the taper. The taper also is referred to quite often as the choke forcing cone. To avoid confusion taper is a mechanical dimension; choke forcing cone describes an effect in that the shot column is forced via a cone shape to a smaller diameter.

The second form of choke is a variation of the first. The term *conical parallel* aptly describes the shape. The conical reference is to the first type of choke in that it is a taper inside of the shotgun barrel that reduces the bore to a smaller diameter through a taper or cone. Unlike the first type of choke, the taper or cone begins at the bore diameter, but has its smaller end a specified distance from the muzzle of the barrel. Where the smaller end of the taper takes place, a section of the bore with a dimension smaller than the bore behind the taper runs *parallel* out to the muzzle. In other words, the taper reduces the diameter of the bore, then there is a parallel section where the diameter is smaller but continuous in dimension until it ends at the muzzle. Thus a combining of the two words, *conical parallel,* for a clear description of the second type of choke.

The third choke type takes the combination of the first two, then one more aspect is added. Result is that there are two taper sections and two parallel sections inside the barrel. The first taper begins where the bore ends, but the small end of the taper is toward the chamber end of the barrel, the large end of the taper toward the muzzle. Then where the large end of the taper ends, there is a parallel diameter section of the bore, but the diameter of this section is larger than the diameter of the bore before the choke section begins. Toward the muzzle, where this large-diameter parallel section ends, another taper begins with the large end of the taper where the enlarged bore diameter ends. This in turn tapers down exactly like a conical choke toward the muzzle. The second parallel section is exactly the same as the parallel section of a conical-parallel choke, but the dimension of the parallel section is the same as the diameter of the bore prior to the choke section. This type of choke is a recess choke.

The first use of the recess choke came about through a method wherein straight cylinder-bored muzzleloading shotguns could be given the choke effect by cutting a larger "recess" behind the muzzle an inch or so. This recess, or enlarged bore diameter section, allowed the shot to expand to the greater diameter, then be "choked" down to smaller diameter, although this smaller diameter consisted actually of the original, unaltered bore diameter. This type of choke was used in newly produced barrels in less expensive shotguns as it did not require retooling of bore reamers. The original reamer simply cut the bore the same diameter from chamber to muzzle. A small but less expensive reamer was used then to cut a recess into the bore a little way back from the muzzle and produce the recess choke type with resulting choke effect.

Today, the recess choke is not used on shotgun barrels currently manufactured. Its primary use is to put choke back into barrels where the choke section has been cut off for one reason or another. By enlarging the bore diameter of a cut-off barrel, then letting the column of shot be reduced in diameter, some degree of "choking" can be attained. The amount is strictly limited by the wall thickness of the barrel where the recess is to be cut. In most shotgun barrels only a minor amount of choke is possible because of this limitation. One of the new hot-shot chokes is nothing but a variation of the basic recess choke.

Even though one knows what the three basic choke types look like, the questions remain: What do they do and how do they work? These questions are not easily answered. To be totally honest, no one can offer answers with full understanding or accuracy. Exactly how chokes work is still a partial mystery. There is an abundance of theory, not all proved completely. What choke does from a practical standpoint can be explained in most respects. There are portions of even this phase, however, that cannot be explained fully.

A crude and not totally accurate explanation of choke function is as follows: Assume we have a two-inch-diameter pipe through which water is being pushed under ten pounds of pressure. Now we take a large-diameter bucket and place it facing the water exit end at a distance of five feet. The pressure pushes the water over the five-foot distance and we catch it all in our large-diameter bucket. If we double the distance to ten feet, then we can no longer catch the water as some of it goes outside of the diameter of the bucket. We could enlarge the bucket diameter, of course, but this does not fit our needs, so let's say we do not have the larger bucket.

So we reduce the size of the water pipe via a taper to one half its diameter, which would be one inch, maintaining the same water pressure. The catch bucket, same diameter, is then at ten feet from the end of the pipe "muzzle." As the stream of water is half the diameter of that with the two-inch pipe, it travels farther before it starts to break away from its exiting diameter. Hence we can capture the water in the original-diameter bucket.

As I stated, this is a crude, not totally accurate example. The tapering section of pipe that reduces its diameter from two inches to one inch is somewhat like the taper or forcing cone portion of a shotgun choke. The reduced section of our water pipe to one inch is the parallel section of the choke. The pressure behind the water, as the pressure in a shotgun barrel from the gas, is in essence the same. The water bucket is the shot pattern diameter. Catching the

Brownell choke calipers were designed by the author. The end of one side goes into the barrel or choke and a common dial caliper or micrometer is used to read the other opened end to determine measurement; an inexpensive instrument.

water is the same as the impact of shot pellets onto the pattern. Shot, of course, is not the same as water, but if we substituted sand for the water, the effect would be roughly the same.

Virtually the same effect can be seen with a common lawn water hose. When turned to the open setting we have a wide stream that does not go very far. When we turn the nozzle to a smaller diameter setting, the smaller stream extends farther. But this can be slightly misleading when compared to shot in relation to the distance. Shot pellets exiting the muzzle of a true no-choke cylinder bore and that of shot exiting from a fully choked bore will travel the same distance and at the same rate of speed or, to use the correct term, velocity. Comparisons are fine for purposes of explanation, but must not be construed to have the same mechanical effect.

The only thing that can be stated with total accuracy is that a restriction of the diameter will result in the *impact* diameter being less at the same distance or the same at a greater distance. The amount of diameter constriction will determine the diameter of the impact. There is, of course, a limitation to the amount of diameter constriction for which this effect takes place. Exactly what takes place in the constricting system inside a shotgun barrel is not completely known.

Having studied theory upon theory over the years, I have formed my own opinions of what occurs in the choke section. This is based on a lot of experience in altering or changing choke, building choke, reaming barrels and the thousand and one things that a gunsmith who specializes in shotguns does throughout a lengthy career. In addition I have shot my share of shotgun patterns, then carefully examined and recut barrels to improve same. So I hasten to state that what follows here is opinion only.

Recognized laws of physics state that a mass at rest tends to remain at rest until acted upon by an outside force; a mass in motion tends to remain in motion until acted upon by an outside force.

So in this instance mass would be the column of shot as it travels up the bore toward the muzzle. For purposes of explanation, assume that we have a hypothetical centerline drawn lengthwise through the mass.

When the mass strikes the taper edge of the choke forcing cone, the individual pellets are acted upon by the walls of the tapering bore. The outside pellets touching the taper to a greater degree than those on the inside of the mass. The pellets, being solid, cannot be compressed as a liquid would be. However they must rearrange their positions in order to pass through the taper. In doing so, the shot are pushed inward toward the mass centerline to become mass in motion. As the centerline cannot be compressed, there is a limit to this rearrangement of pellet position, but pellets from the outside inward are definitely in motion toward that centerline.

The mass, having passed through the taper and parallel section of the choke, are freed by their exit from the restricting walls. The thing to remember is that, although freed, there still is the principle that the mass remains in mass centerline even though the mass has left the muzzle. The force toward the centerline lasts for only milliseconds, but it does exist.

The key to performance lies in velocity of the mass exiting the bore with the velocity imparted by the gas pressure behind the mass of shot. A standard 12-gauge shotshell will impart a velocity of around 1200 fps. Change this to yards and we have four hundred yards per second velocity. As the target is forty yards away, the shot would take roughly one-tenth-second to cover that distance. Naturally velocity drops off, but this is only a rough explanation.

With the laws of physics demanding that the mass in motion toward its centerline remain in motion, there is a millisecond of inward "push" toward the center of the mass. As this happens, forward velocity is still pushing the mass toward the forty-yard target. Let's consider two things: (1) the shot mass is being pushed toward its centerline; (2) the shot mass is pushed toward the target by its powder charge gas pressure. Both time frames indicate that the mass would tend to stay together to some degree as the mass covers the distance to the target.

A steel ball bearing dropped on a solid surface will bounce, the reason being that part of its velocity energy is not absorbed and is redirected backward from whence it came. A shot pellet will do exactly the same thing.

So when the instant of time occurs that the shot pellets cannot be compressed farther toward that mass centerline, the "bounce" effect takes place and the energy of the shot is redirected in the direction from which it came, in this case directly away from the centerline. From a practical point of view, the choke effect is no longer is effect and the reverse is occurring in that the shot is "scattered." Air resistance to the shot passing through it enhances the scatter direction.

It is an established fact that shot as it leaves the muzzle is not in the shape of a large ice cream cone or an ever-expanding taper toward the target. Shot will stay together to a large degree and then start to expand to a greater diameter of coverage rapidly. If you wanted a comparison, then the shot would not appear as a cone but rather somewhat like a trumpet or bugle shape with a flaring at the end. This is the "bounce" and air resistance coming ito form the flare.

If constriction of the choke is extreme, the desirable choke effect does not take place. Just the opposite occurs and the shot is scattered as it leaves the muzzle. In effect, the "bounce" effect occurs too quickly and the air resistance force must be added. Decrease the amount of constriction and the "bounce" will decrease in exact ratio.

The more choke constriction, the more the shot column

Brownell dial choke calipers are designed for the dial to give the reading of opening of the arms as choke is being measured. For best accuracy, dial is set on zero with a ring-type gauge, then dial is read plus or minus.

In custom choking, Brownell's choke hone is being used to open up a choke a little at a time. An electric hand drill powers the hone. The ring at rear of the visible spring is used to increase the tension of honing stones.

is strung out in length in its trip toward that distant target. Wing shooters take advantage of this known effect when shooting at distant game. The portion of the shot pellets at the rear of the "string" hit the target. With less constriction, there is less stringing of the shot mass and the charge of the shot from front to rear is much less in measurement. With a full-choked gun the shot string can be as great as eighteen inches in length. This is simply because there is not enough room for all of the shot to find a new position toward that centerline, hence it passes through the choke constriction a millisecond or more behind the forward end, but that motion of mass toward the centerline does not change.

So ends my opinion except for one small item: The shot striking the taper walls transfers that motion to the shot closer to the centerline. But the outer shot is restricted in movement toward the centerline by the shot blocking its path. The outer shot, in turn, hesitate a split millisecond and allow the shot toward the centerline to pass forward first. Then finding space the outer shot "fall in" behind the centerline inner shot. This is somewhat the principle of an explosive shape charge effect. This "falling in" behind the centerline shot would account for the lengthy shot string on the way to the target.

Amazing about choke is that so little dimension change will produce such varying effects of shot pellet impact dimension. The cellophane on a common pack of cigarettes is about one-thousandth-inch in thickness. If you change bore or choke dimension this much overall — or a one-half of one-thousandth-inch increase in one wall specification — you change the entire performance of the shot

pellet impact diameter! By the same token, change the angle of the taper or forcing cone one-half degree and the whole pellet diameter impact area will change.

Change the diameter of the shot one size up or down to the next size and the efficiency of the choke will change in its effect on the shot pellets which, in turn, changes pattern percentage at the same range. Change the velocity of the shot as it exits the bore, with other specifications identical, and again the shot pattern will change.

Therefore any change, no matter how small, from a given position will always result in a change in pattern percentage or — stated another way — in shot impact diameter. Knowing this can be an advantage to both gunsmith and shooter as a dimensional change in bore and choke diameter can give a desired difference. From the shooter's standpoint it can give an undesired difference. For example, if a barrel is fired a lot without cleaning, plastic from the shell body will slowly build up in the choke area. This build-up changes choke dimensions and results in a change in shot impact diameter area. Remove the plastic build-up and you go back to consistent results. This can mean the difference between a hit or miss on game.

An increase or decrease in shot velocity will result in a change that the shooter can place to his advantage. Shot size change in relation to a given choke dimension also can result in an advantage.

By maintaining consistency as far as chokes go, you can maintain consistency of the choke effect results. By doing so and knowing the effect, you can make shot after shot give the same result and thus increase your odds of hitting a desired target.

Chapter 13

WHAT TO DO ABOUT CHOKE FORCING CONE LENGTH

Here's A Subject That Never Enters The Mind Of The Average Shotgunner!

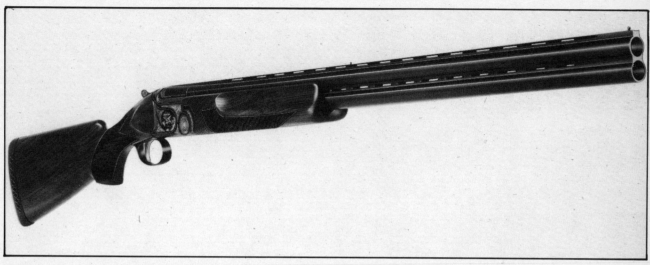

As long as his shotgun hits in the general area at which it is pointed, the average scattergunner gives little thought to such technicalities as forcing cone length. Such knowledge could do much to improve overall effectiveness.

THE CONICAL parallel choke, the most common type found in shotgun barrels, has been the subject of continuing discussion and considerable experimentation. Obviously both the conical and the parallel facets play an important part in overall performance of the choke itself.

Geometrically speaking, if we assume a set angle for a taper such as that found in the choke forcing cone, then its length would be determined by the bore diameter and the parallel section of the choke's diameter. If we increase bore diameter while the choke's parallel diameter remains the same, we lengthen the taper. Combine both and the taper section is further lengthened. Reverse the procedure, independent or combined, and we decrease the taper length. So we see that forcing cone length or taper length depends to some extent on the diameters.

Obviously, by changing the taper angle plus or minus a degree or less, we could compensate for this change in length. All of this leads to an interesting and highly techni-

cal set of specifications, but what is the practical application if we leave geometry to the school books? Here you will find some disagreements between knowledgeable gunsmiths and shooting students. I can only base my opinion on years at a bench and at the pattern range.

As with the length of the chamber forcing cone, there is a practical limit to the length of the choke forcing cone — with one exception. Where the added length of the chamber forcing cone did not increase pattern percentage it did not detract from its efficiency. Not so with the choke forcing cone. The added length past a practical limit will without question decrease the pattern percentage efficiency!

To the best of my personal knowledge, a choke forcing cone length should not exceed two inches from end of the bore to beginning of the choke parallel section. In every instance wherein I have test patterned a shotgun with a longer forcing cone length, the results have been poor. One instance sticks in my mind. A customer brought in an European double with an extremely tight choke that would

The avid claybird shooter usually is familiar with all aspects of his favorite competition shotgun, including function of the forcing cone. The less experienced, however, often wonders why his goose gun isn't that good on skeet range.

not shoot anything resembling a good pattern. The choke itself seemed all right, but careful measurement revealed a forcing cone three inches long. As all else was normal the poor results seemed to be in this length, but changing the angle of the forcing cone taper was impossible without damaging the bore. A short section of steel was fashioned into an insert-type choke. The original choke, including the forcing cone taper and the parallel section, was removed from the barrel by deep boring. A recess was cut into the barrel at the muzzle to accept the insert choke tube. This was machined with the exact same amount of constriction, but with a forcing cone two inches in length. With the insert

installed the gun was test patterned and the results were amazing. With only the forcing cone length changed pattern percentage jumped a full twenty percent throughout the tests!

As for a short forcing cone, I never have seen any difference in pattern percentages between a two-inch length and a shorter length with a steeper angle of taper. A short, abrupt taper with a length of .750 inch seems to be the shortest practical. So, anything between .750-inch length and out to 2.00-inch length seems to give the same practical results, with one exception.

That exception is found in some European-made barrels

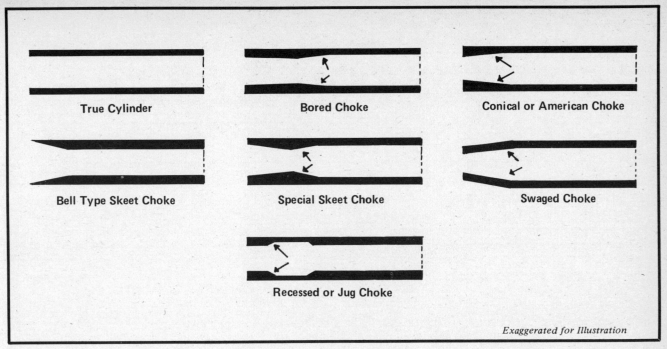

True Cylinder	Bored Choke	Conical or American Choke
Bell Type Skeet Choke	Special Skeet Choke	Swaged Choke
	Recessed or Jug Choke	

Exaggerated for Illustration

Arrows on the exaggerated drawings indicate the choke forcing cone; true cylinder, bell type chokes have none.

wherein bore diameter is at a minimum, such as .725 inch for a 12-gauge and choke diameter is extremely tight. In these cases a forcing cone length of 1½ inches out to two inches gives better pattern percentage. If bore diameter is up to the standard — .729 to .730 inch — the shorter forcing cone seems fully adequate.

Short forcing cones must be cleaned more often. I presume this to be due to the fact that they receive more thrust from the shot charge in the effort of the taper to reduce the diameter of the shot. There is a slight buildup of lead or plastic on the taper walls. If taper length is less than .750 inch, you stand a chance of pressure buildup behind the shot the same as would be the case with an obstruction in the bore. This possibly could result in damage to the shotgun bore through pressure buildup at the forcing cone point.

Exactly why the extra-length forcing cone offers poor results is something of a mystery. I believe it is due to the

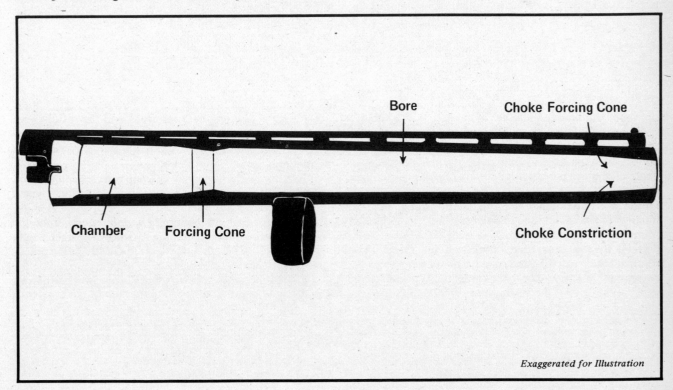

Exaggerated for Illustration

145

Contours of currently made RXP wad from Remington (left), with thinner walls, tend to follow contours of the older type with thicker wad.

The flexibility of the Remington RXP plastic wad is illustrated, showing how the petals will bend in the bore.

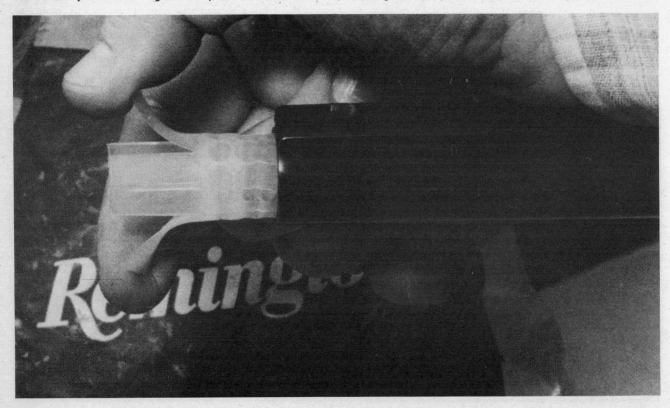

effect of the mass of shot being forced toward its centerline as previously explained. A long taper or long forcing cone would stretch the time frame and thus foul up the works in allowing the mass in motion and "bounce" effect to function properly. This is one of the intrigues about chokes. No one can be sure any statement is one-hundred-percent correct in every respect. Nonetheless, I have never seen a long, gradual taper forcing cone offer consistent results.

The parallel section of the conical-parallel choke also has become subject to a wide variety of opinions. The closer you put the tapering forcing cone to the point of the muzzle or end of the barrel, the less the length of the parallel section.

Some years ago George Oberfell and Charles Thompson wrote a book entitled, *The Mysteries of Shotgun Patterns*. Probably the most quoted book on the subject, it was the result of a long, drawn-out series of various tests. Written prior to introduction of the one-piece wad and the plastic shot protector, this fact must be kept in mind when reading the test results. Unfortunately it is out of print and copies of the book bring a premium price. The two experimenters started with a fixed length for the taper section, forcing cone and a parallel choke length of 2½ inches.

They shot patterns, then proceeded to cut off the parallel section in increments of one-half inch and shot more patterns. This sequence continued until the parallel section was eliminated. The test results showed the parallel section with a two-inch length produced the best pattern, but percentage was small between one-half-inch and the two-inch length variations. Incidentally they conducted the same tests with a conical-type choke, but maintaining the same exit diameter, changing angle and cone length. Best results were with the conical choke length at two inches.

Again I emphasize that these tests were carried out prior to introduction of the one-piece plastic wad and the shot protector. Change anything and you change the end results with a shotgun barrel!

For instance, it became a known fact in the days of the nitro or over-powder wad with filler-type wads that a rough parallel section of a choke shot better than a smooth parallel section. Many gunsmiths purposely roughed up the surface of the parallel section of the choke. Reason was that one of the problems with the old-style wad occured as the shot left the muzzle. Under pressure from the gas, and being lighter than the shot, it accelerated once it had left the muzzle. The wad ran into the rear of the shot column to

The older style Flite Max manufactured by Alcan featured a fiber base and had fewer petals than current RXP wads.

Even with the amount of equipment available, not every gunshop is equipped with tools for barrel machining work.

scatter the shot. If the parallel section of the bore was rough on its surface, this abrasion held the edges of the wad to retard forward motion. This slowing of the wads prevented them from running into the rear of the shot.

This is not the case with the current one-piece plastic wad which encompasses the cupped wad over the powder, the center cushioning section and the forward shot protector. These wads require the surface of the choke parallel section be as smooth as possible. I have seen shooters follow the old system of roughening the surface of the parallel section in a new gun in an attempt to improve pattern percentage. The results are just the opposite, as the pattern deteriorates. They get the parallel section as slick as glass once again and the percentage picks up!

Based on my own experience, that of gunsmiths at my company, Walker Arms, and various friends versed in the technical aspects of choke, there is a minimum parallel choke length for the modern one-piece-wad shells. This minimum length from the end of the forcing cone to the muzzle is five-eighths-inch or, expressed in decimals, 0.625. You simply do not get as good a pattern at a shorter length.

As for longer length, those knowledgeable on the subject agree that length of the parallel section of the choke should equal or slightly exceed the length of the shot column. In inches, this would be from 0.75 to 1.25 maximum. Personally I have never found an advantage past the one-inch length, but others recommend slight differences to handle

148

heavier shot charges which would, of course, lengthen the shot column.

There is a side note regarding the current trend toward the one-ounce shot load in 12-gauge trap guns. The one-ounce load is about equal in distance from front to back as it is in diameter, which means a shorter column than with the standard 1⅛-ounce shot load. This load gives excellent results in just about every trap gun. This would bear out statements regarding dimensions of the parallel section of the choke as most modern guns have around a one-inch length for this section!

The one-piece plastic wad has brought about a host of variations in pattern regulating aspects in addition to its main job of preventing shot pellets from being deformed on the inner walls of the bore and choke. Few people realize additional control can be gained with the plastic shot protector and wad once it has left the muzzle.

Prior to advent of the one-piece plastic wad and its shot protector, a lot of experimentation was done with what were known as shot restrictors or constrictors, with several other names for the same thing. The principle stated that if you wrapped the shot column in some form of protective cover, the shot would be held together longer during its trip to the target. In principle these devices worked. The need was for a method of regulating the time element that would allow the protective cover to drop away and allow the shot to start expanding and form the wide shot pattern. Otherwise the unit continued on its way as one unit, somewhat like a shotgun slug. Several patented contraptions found their way to the market with varying degrees of success.

The modern one-piece plastic wad stays with the shot column past the muzzle of the barrel to form a restrictor that would prevent the shot from scattering immediately upon leaving the muzzle. Some brands seem to stay with the shot longer than others. You can see this by firing several brands and types of shells on a range and noting the

This type of choke forcing cone reamer is available from Bob Brownell as well as other gunsmith equipment dealers.

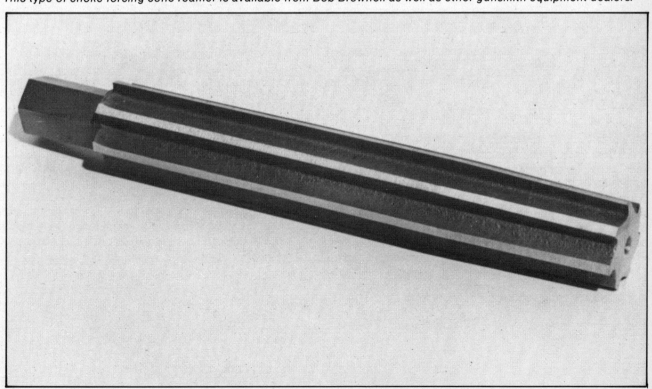

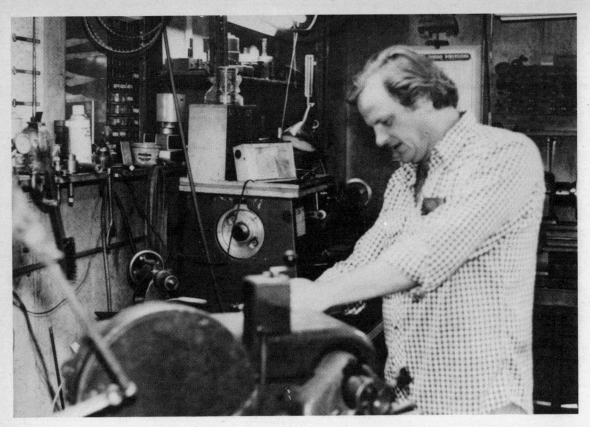

Author considers Jerry Stevens, who operates the Nu Line Gunshop, as being one of the better shotgun mechanics today.

An ideal installation for use in shotgun work is this machine designed specifically for shotgun bore honing.

Jerry Stevens works on barrels in his shop. He wears safety glasses when working with machinery, a must for safety.

distance from the point of firing to where the used wad is found on the ground.

Many who reload shotshells have noted that various types of one-piece plastic wads have varying degrees of strength. While the plastic shot protector section normally is divided into four increments called petals, this division is not always the same. Some wads have thin petals and light plastic that offers little resistance to pressure. Others have thick petals that offer stiff resistance.

The purpose of the petals is to "catch" the air pressure as the combination of shot and wad exit the muzzle. The air pressure peels the wad and protector from contact with the shot somewhat like the effect of a parachute opening. A standard 1200-foot-per-second (fps) shotshell will push

the shot from muzzle to the forty-yard target in one-tenth-second. If the wad stays with the shot part of this distance, the shot will start to spread later to result in a tighter pattern. Consequently, if the protector separates from the shot column earlier, the shot spreads more quickly.

Ballistic Products markets a special one-piece plastic wad made from tough plastic; there are no petals. Instead, the shot protector is a single unit without cuts. The reloader cuts the petals as he desires and the depth of the cut and number of cuts will regulate the time frame in which the shot protector stays with the shot column! It works well and allows a shotshell reloader to put together a really efficient long-range load for waterfowl shooting. When used in conjunction with hard Lawrence magnum shot or plated

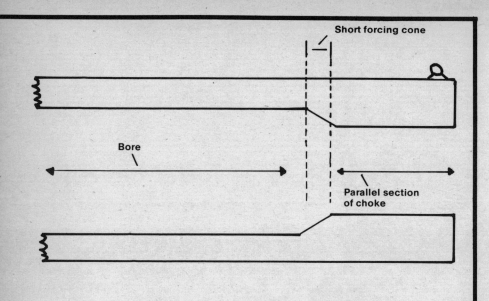

Short forcing cone

Bore

Parallel section
of choke

This chart illustrates the differences in the short and long forcing cones, showing how and where cuts must be made to accomplish latter.

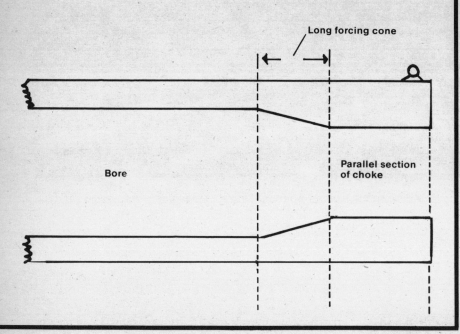

Long forcing cone

Bore

Parallel section
of choke

shot and the addition of plastic "graf" sprinkled around the shot to prevent pellet deformation in the bore, the combination results in maximum pattern tightness.

On the other end of the stick, Windjammer wads are made with eight petals instead of the normal four. The plastic is soft and offers little resistance to pressure. When fired, the eight petals and thin sides catch the air resistance quickly and the protective plastic departs from contact with the shot. They are at their best when a skeet-type load is desired for close shooting, maintaining the protection for the shot pellets while the unit is still in the bore.

I do not think that experimentation with the one-piece plastic wad and its shot protector section has been completed. It offers a shotgunner a wide range of possibilities in the future. Some companies are experimenting with variations that include a post in the center of the forward unit, air cushioning of the shot, cupped rear of the forward unit, ad infinitum.

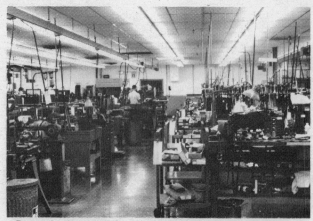

Browning's repair facility in Arnold, Missouri, has been fully equipped to handle all facets of shotgun repair and rebuilding for the firm's customers.

The shotgun gunsmith must be able to test patterns as he reworks the choke forcing cone. (Below) This precision shotgun bore and choke honing machine can take a lot of drudgery out of handwork often required in choke work.

Chapter 14

THE IN-BUILT CHOKE

Every Shotgunner Knows About It, But Few Know How Or Why It Does Its Thing!

IN-BUILT CHOKE — choke that is an integral part of the shotgun barrel — is the most common use of the choke principle and the most misunderstood.

Regardless of type, choke should be understood easily if you will remember one simple rule: Measure the diameter of the choke section at its smallest point, then measure the bore diameter before the choke section begins. Subtract the choke diameter measurement from the bore diameter measurement. The result is the amount of barrel bore constriction, or, in simple language, the amount of choke. This sometimes is referred to as the "choke constriction."

Putting this to practical use, suppose we have a barrel and our measurement shows that the bore diameter before the choke section begins is 0.730 inch. We measure the tightest diameter in the choke area and come up with the figure of 0.700 inch. Subtracting 0.700 inch from 0.730 inch leaves 0.030 inch. Therefore our barrel has a choke that constricts the diameter 0.030 inch from the bore diameter. The common usage of this is simply thirty-thousandths constriction (0.030 inch) or thirty-thousandths choke.

If we were using the most common set of figures, this would be a full-choke barrel in a 12-gauge gun, but only in a 12-gauge, as the other gauges use a different set of figures. More about this later.

What confuses most people is not the method of determining the constriction, but the fact that they stick by the measurement figures instead of the constriction figures. For example, suppose we had a gun of European origin with a bore diameter that measured 0.725 inch (and this is not uncommon). If we used measurement figures of the choke being 0.700 inch as in the first sample then did the subtraction bit we would end up with a difference of 0.025 inch or 0.005 inch short of that required thirty-thousandths constriction (0.030 inch). The result would be a tight modified choke! This is like trying to subtract oranges from apples. As the little boy said, "It ain't possible."

Subtract the choke diameter from the bore diameter of each and every barrel separately. One barrel has absolutely nothing to do with the other and only adds confusion. Each barrel must stand or fall on its own measurements.

One of the supposedly sure-fire methods you will run across is to drop a dime coin down the bore of a 12-gauge barrel. Supposedly if the dime sticks in the bore, you have a full-choke barrel; if the dime passes through, it is a cylinder bore barrel. You will see this practice at gun shows and I have seen it in some of the best gun shops. However, the best description of this I have ever heard was from another gunsmith: "What you have is a dime on one side, a barrel on the other and an idiot in the middle."

First of all, few dimes are round. Check it with a micrometer! Most important of all, no round disk or even a plug gauge will work for measuring choke, although there are several on the market. One of the most common is a tapered piece of brass with the various chokes inscribed thereon. It is as useless as the dime gizmo. If you machined a plug gauge somewhat like a rod and it was 0.700 inch in its diameter, then tried it in the full-choke barrel with a bore diameter of 0.730 inch, it would slide right in as the choke diameter would match that of the gauge. Now try it in a barrel with a bore diameter of 0.725 with thirty-thousandths constriction or full choke. Thirty-thousandths constriction (0.030) in this particular barrel would place the choke diameter at 0.695 inch. Naturally the gauge with its 0.700 diameter would not go in, yet both barrels would have thirty-thousandths constriction.

The most accurate choke measuring instrument available is marketed by Poly Choke. While expensive, I have one that has been in use for thirty years and it is still going strong. It was designed specifically for the job of measuring bore diameters and choke diameters and the differences between the two in 20-, 16- and 12-gauge barrels. It will not work on the 28-gauge nor the .410 and will not extend up to 10-gauge. This tool resembles a common micrometer

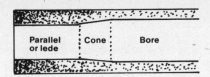

Standard or English choke boasts a parallel section at end of barrel.

The cone choke is of American origin and also is known as the taper choke.

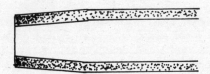

Swaged choke has been found on less expensive models. It is achieved by merely tapering muzzle of the gun.

The so-called jug choke is made by hand with a rod, emery cloth. This is popular with Russian shooters.

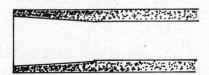

The reverse or bell choke design is meant for throwing a broad pattern.

in its barrel or reading section which is connected through a long shaft to a precision tapered end of the shaft. The shaft bears against three ball bearings located at the end of the instrument. As the taper is pushed forward by turning the barrel, it exerts pressure on the ball bearings forcing them outward to contact the walls of a shotgun bore. Naturally the walls halt this movement and the measurement is read on the barrel section of the instrument just as you would read a common micrometer. As the taper shaft moves backward it exerts less pressure on the ball bearings and they retreat into the end unit for a smaller diameter reading.

Stan Baker, one of the nation's finest shotgun smiths, designed a variation of the bore micrometer that uses a dial indicator for its reading. A ring gauge of exactly 0.700-inch dimension is used to set the dial indicator at zero. With the ring gauge removed from the ball bearings, the instrument then is placed in the bore and the diameter is read directly on the dial indicator. This tool is quick and accurate for bore readings and choke readings. Its only drawback is that it is limited to 12-gauge.

An advantage of the Poly Choke bore micrometer and the Baker Barrel Reader is that either can measure the bore diameter to a distance of twenty-three inches. Thus if you measure from the muzzle, then remove the instrument and

measure from the chamber end of the barrel, you have a forty-six-inch measurement range, which will cover virtually any shotgun barrel. Both also can be used to measure chamber forcing cones.

Brownell's also markets a dial-indicated choke caliper. This also must be set by turning the dial while the ends are in a ring gauge. Once set, it will give a readout quickly. Being short, it will measure only the choke section and the bore diameter directly behind the choke. Its other use is in measuring the dimensions of a chamber from rim to bore.

All of these instruments are costly. If you do a lot of shotgun barrel work or choke work, the price is justified. Some years back I designed a simple, inexpensive choke comparison caliper that is marketed exclusively by Brownell's. One end is inserted into the bore section, held open, then locked. A common micrometer or dial caliper is used on the opposite end of the calipers to take a reading. It then is unlocked and moved up into the choke section of the barrel and relocked. Again a reading is taken via a micrometer or caliper. Thus you have the bore diameter just behind the choke area and the diameter of the choke. Subtract choke from bore and you have the amount of constriction or difference between the two diameters. It is a simple instrument to use and also can be utilized for chamber and chamber forcing cone dimensional reading.

Both the inexpensive choke comparison calipers and Brownell's dial caliper offer a range from the .410 up to and including the 10-gauge. Any of these four instruments will give the necessary precision reading of bore and choke diameters that are absolutely essential for accurate choke designation and gunsmithing requirements.

Many years ago the British came up with the definition of choke and how to measure it. They gave only five specifications: *Choke* was what we would currently term as full choke and consisted of a difference of forty-thousandths inch between bore and choke diameter. *Three-quarter choke* was thirty-thousandths inch between bore and choke diameter; *half choke* was twenty-thousandths inch between the two dimensions. *Quarter choke* was a difference of ten-thousandths-inch. *Cylinder* had no constriction.

The British called every one-thousandth-inch constriction a "point". Hence forty points of choke was forty-thousandths inch (0.040 inch), thirty points of choke being thirty-thousandths inch (0.030 inch), and so on. They still stick by their original system and it is simple to use.

On the European continent everything was metric, which can be confusing to us. To convert millimeters to inches simply multiply by the figure of 0.03937 or if you want to chop off a few figures, 0.04 to round out the multiplication process. I am too old a dog to change and use the metric system only if there is no alternative!

Every manufacturer in the United States had his own idea as to how to mark the amount of choke on their barrels, causing no end of confusion. Some figured it was none of the shooter's business and you will find many of the old double-barrel guns sans any designation!

Those makers that did mark their barrels for choke generally used only one single number for the purpose: #4 for full; #3 for improved modified; #2 for modified; and #1 for improved cylinder, with #0 being no-choke/cylinder. This was the system used on most Ithaca double-barrel guns and with their Model 37 pump. Several others adopted the system and used it to great extent.

There have been dots, dashes, stars and whatnot used as a code for choke markings. The Italians use one star for full, two stars for improved modified, three for modified, and four for improved cylinder. Straight cylinder is generally marked only CL or CIL. The Browning shotguns use a variation with asterisks and dashes: * is full; *- marks improved modified; ** is modified; **- improved cylinder; **S marks skeet and *** is cylinder. Another variation is the metric points of choke. For instance, the numeral 7 would indicate .7mm points of choke or .7 millimeters of constriction, which if converted would be roughly twenty-eight-thousandths inch constriction. Perazzi used a form of this with 7/10 being the same figure of .7 millimeters of constriction (0.028 inch).

Somewhere along the line it became evident shooters did not carry a code book of various numbers, dots, dashes, stars and asterisks to figure what chokes they had in the guns they were carrying over hill and dale. So the current system is to stamp the choke designation in plain English on the barrel near the gauge designation. Full was simple enough to stamp, although a few use the letter *F* as some sort of saving of time or stamp I guess. Improved modified comes out, *Imp-Mod* usually or again the abbreviation *I-M*. Modified choke is *Mod* or *M*. Improved cylinder is *Imp-Cyl* or *I-C* on most barrels. No choke is *Cylinder, Cyl* or simply *C*.

The joker is those designated as skeet barrels. In past years there were two skeet chokes which had to do with whether the claybird was going away from you or coming toward you. *Skeet Out* and *Skeet In* were the terms in use. Choke designation was *Skeet-2* or *Skeet-1* with abbreviations of *S-2* and *S-1* respectively. Skeet-1 was a choke constriction half-way between improved cylinder and straight cylinder. Today a barrel marked as *Skeet* has zero constriction and is identical with cylinder in every way. Bar-

This microflash photo was taken by White Laboratories in 1971 to show pattern from a full choke 30-inch barrel. The distance was four feet from the end of the muzzle.

rels marked *Slug* are intended for shotgun slugs. If marked *Buck* they are simply no-choke cylinder barrels. This marking is a sales gimmick; hence, if you cut off a thirty-four-inch barrel and mount open sights, you have the same thing as the Buck barrel sans the stamp on the barrel. Quite recently some barrels have had *Riot* stamped on them. It's the same thing: zero constriction, no choke.

There has been one choke, if you wanted to call it a choke, that reversed the procedure. It spread the pellets rather rapidly and was used to some extent in skeet and in some upland bird hunting. It bore a host of names such as reverse choke, spreader, et al. It also was bored into one high-quality gun as a "Reversed Conical Parallel." Whatever it is called the basic principle has been to enlarge the end of the muzzle to a diameter in excess of the bore diameter; in doing so the gas behind the old-style nitro wad rushed around the wad and mingled with the shot thereby scattering the pellets to quickly produce a wide pattern.

A slight variation came about a few years ago when the Russians "discovered" the principle and quickly named it the Tula Choke, Tula being the name of the arsenal at which the barrels were made. It worked fine in International Skeet competition and one American firm currently markets a version, the Smith & Wesson Super Skeet. All is well as long as the old-style wads are used in the shotshells, but the modern one-piece plastic wad with the shot protector plays hob with the principle as it does not allow gas to enter the shot column. Soft shot also works best in conjunction with the old-style multi-piece wads for this system.

Occasionally another oddball choke idea is rediscovered. By cutting the choke section larger on each side, the existing shot forms a somewhat rectangular pattern. A variation is simply to push the barrel toward the center from top and bottom to form an elliptic-shaped barrel end. Again the shot is supposed to exit in this shape and add to the chance of hitting game to each side of the normal pattern. Not too long ago a firm marketed a similar arrangement for riot purposes calling it the Street Sweeper.

The degree of constriction that constitutes choke is most confusing and it is virtually impossible to get a straight answer from any source and impossible to secure exactly the same set of dimensions from any two sources!

For matters of comparison, let's stick to the 12-gauge, for each gauge has its own set of requirements regarding amount of constriction. Let's also back off the standards established by the British, as they were set with the old shotshells that consisted of the nitro wads, filler wads, no shot protector and a roll-type closure with the over-shot wad. With the advent of the star-type crimp and the elimination of the over-shot wads, the same gun would shoot a slightly tighter pattern with the same constriction, but not enough to constitute a radical change.

The one-piece plastic wad with the shot protector changed the rules. Constriction of 0.040 inch now delivered a pattern too tight for the full-choke designation and commonly accepted pattern. To compensate for this and return to the accepted standard of seventy percent of the shot hitting in a thirty-inch circle at forty yards, the amount of constriction was opened up to around 0.030 inch. This amount of constriction was the old improved modified standard that now delivered the same pellet count that the old 0.040 constriction did with the old shell. As a choke designation the term *improved modified* went the way of the carrier pigeon and is seldom used.

The modified choke remained at around 0.020 inch with some barrels having a few thousandths inch less constriction for this choke designation. Improved cylinder remained in the neighborhood of 0.010 constriction, again with some a few thousandths less constriction. On the other end of the stick, a choke with 0.035 constriction usually was termed extra-full or over-full. A constriction of 0.040 constituted a trap choke and was referred to as the maximum choke that should be used in a 12-gauge bore.

In recent years there has been a movement toward even tighter chokes. This is what the public demands and gunmakers always produce the gun and the choke that the public is willing to buy; that rule overrides everything else, I've learned.

As I have stated previously, the correct method for determining degree of choke is not to test every choke at the forty-yard limit, then compute the pattern percentage, as the information is totally useless from a practical point of view. No one shoots an improved cylinder or cylinder choke at forty yards! The seventy percent pattern is a good standard, I only advocate retaining it and changing yardage.

SEVENTY PERCENT DESIRED PATTERN PER CHOKE DESIGNATION

CHOKE	YARDAGE OF RANGE
Full	40
Modified	35
Improved-Cylinder	30
Cylinder	25

As you can see, each degree of choke designation is equal to approximately a five-yard increase or decrease. So, what is the pattern percentage for other yardage? Perhaps the following will shed some light on the subject:

PATTERN PERCENTAGE PER CHOKE PER YARD

Yards	10	15	20	25	30	35	40	45	50	55	60
Full				100	90	80	70	60	50	40	30
Modified			100	90	80	70	60	50	40	30	20
Imp-Cyl		100	90	80	70	60	50	40	30	20	10
Cylinder	100	90	80	70	60	50	40	30	20	10	

I hasten to add that the above figures are only approximate to what will be achieved with most 12-gauge shotguns with the 2¾-inch chamber

Bore diameters vary from manufacturer to manufacturer, but the Small Arms & Ammunition Manufacturers Institute (SAAMI) does issue a recommended standard dimension for each gauge. These and the amount of choke constriction per designation is as follows: The chart below covers internal diameters.

Gauge	Bore	Full Choke	Modified Choke	Imp-Cyl Choke
	(inch)	(inch)	(inch)	(inch)
12	.729	.694	.710	.720
16	.667	.639	.652	.660
20	.617	.592	.603	.510
28	.550	.528	.538	.545
.410	.410	.393	.402	.406

Cylinder choke would of course be exactly the same as the bore diameter per gauge.

This particular chart covers each of the chokes in the amount of constriction maximum.

Gauge	Bore	Full Choke	Modified Choke	Imp-Cyl Choke
	(inch)	(inch)	(inch)	(inch)
12	.729	.035	.019	.009
16	.667	.028	.015	.007
20	.617	.025	.014	.007
28	.550	.022	.012	.005
.410	.410	.017	.008	.004

Cylinder choke has no constriction and is the same as the bore in diameter.

There is no recommendation for improved modified choke nor for Skeet-1 and Skeet-2 chokes, but I have found the following figures very close, altered as necessary to give correct percentage with the modern one-piece plastic wad and the shot protector.

Gauge	Bore	Improved Modified	Skeet-2	Skeet-1
	(inch)	(inch)	(inch)	(inch)
12	.729	.025	.012	.005
16	.667	.020	.010	.004
20	.617	.019	.009	.004
28	.550	.016	.007	.003

These constriction specifications were determined by checking numerous custom chokes in a wide variety of barrels.

While cylinder choke is supposed to have zero constriction, with the diameter the same as that of the bore, I have found that a constriction of about two points (.002 inch) will result in a slightly improved pattern. The small amount of constriction seems to result in a more evenly distributed pellet pattern while the straight cylinder will show holes in some areas in pattern tests.

157

It is important to take these specifications as average, for they will not be exact for every barrel. Whenever the bore diameter is changed, even one-thousandth inch plus or minus, from the recommended standard, you change the choke constriction for any designated choke! Nothing can be taken as exact when it comes to chokes, any gauge, any designation. This is the first thing to learn in working with custom choking.

Normally, as the bore diameter is increased, the amount of constriction required to produce a desired pattern percentage will be less. In other words, less constriction will be required for full choke results if the bore is .735 inch in diameter as compared with a bore diameter of .725 inch. This works in reverse in that a tighter than normal bore diameter will require more constriction than a standard bore diameter.

Pattern performance is the final deciding factor for any constriction of choke, regardless of designation of type of choke. This cannot be over-emphasized as too many shooters and gunsmiths are seemingly awe-struck by a set of constriction figures. Pellets break targets or kill game, not statistics! One of the problems is that so few shooters or gunsmiths have a clear mental picture of the expanding shot charge pattern diameter at various ranges both before and past the target. The following should help clarify this:

TOTAL SPREAD OF PATTERN DIAMETER PER CHOKE AND PER YARD

YARDS OF RANGE

Choke	10	15	20	25	30	35	40	45	50
Full	10"	15"	20"	25"	30"	35"	40"	45"	50"
Modified	15"	20"	25"	30"	35"	40"	45"	50"	
Imp-Cyl	20"	25"	30"	35"	40"	45"	50"		
Cylinder	25"	30"	35"	40"	45"	50"			

When the diameter of the pattern exceeds fifty inches, it is of little practical advantage. If it is remembered that a pattern considered "good" is one of seventy percent of the pellets within a thirty-inch circle, then a fifty-inch-diameter pattern would mean that there was a pellet in almost twice the area and would result in a lot of open spaces within the fifty-inch circle.

Most people are of the opinion that the shot charge diameter opens up somewhat like a large cone with the small end in the barrel muzzle. The cone continues in diameter in proportion to distance from the muzzle. This is not quite correct. The cone shape exists for a distance as the chart above shows. Then the pellets tend to flare out somewhat like the end of a trumpet with the diameter increasing rapidly. Past the fifty-inch diameter the spread widens at a much more rapid rate as the distance increases.

This can be proved to anyone's satisfaction by placing a series of six-foot-square sheets of paper at five-yard intervals. Now fire the shotshell at the center of the first sheet of paper. The diameter of the pattern will increase on each sheet about the same as shown on the chart up to fifty inches, then it will flare rapidly.

If the chart is examined closely and studied per choke, per range, you will have a good picture of what the exiting shot charge looks like as far as diameter is concerned. It must be remembered that the shot charge is three-dimensional, some of the pellets ahead, some trailing behind to resemble a tear drop with the tail at the rear.

To prevent that trumpet-shaped flare from taking place at fifty yards with a full choke it is possible to increase the constriction past full choke for an extra-full choke and thus extend the thirty-inch diameter circle about five yards to a maximum of ten yards, but this is about tops. The diameter of the pattern circle then would increase for a few yards as shown on the chart. A hard shot protection wad will help as will increasing the number of pellets in the shot charge to some degree. This is the thinking behind the magnum-type shotshell loads. However there is a limit to all of this.

Simply stated, most shotguns have a maximum efficient pattern at forty to forty-five yards. By increasing bore diameter, as a 10-gauge, and increasing the choke constriction, the maximum efficient range can be increased out to sixty yards, but beyond this forget it if you are thinking of shot-after-shot pattern efficiency.

Nonetheless there seems to be an unending quest to obtain a proficient pattern at the longest possible range. Someone always is trying to get just a hair more distance with a shotgun by any means possible. Little practical advantage is gained by such yard stretching except for some waterfowl shooting and turkey hunting; this is a limited need in proportion to the time and energy spent in this quest.

Most game taken with the shotgun is within the twenty-five- to thirty-five-yard range. With a full choke you are trying to hit game with a pattern much smaller than the thirty-inch desired pattern diameter. If successful, all you have is a big red mist in the air and a few feathers floating down! With a smaller pattern diameter of fifteen to twenty inches, you also have increased the probability of a miss by one hundred percent; it is difficult enough to score with a thirty-inch-diameter pattern.

Game does not position itself at any exact yardage. Range varies with every shot. Therefore there must always be a minimum and a maximum pattern diameter to work with. Anything below twenty-five-inch diameter is simply too much shot, both in size of the pattern and the number of pellets striking the game, rendering it useless for food. If we thin the pattern much more than a forty-five-inch diameter, it becomes too skimpy. So a workable minimum would be twenty-five inches and a maximum diameter would be forty-five inches. With any choke this gives a working range of twenty yards inside of which we can be reasonably sure of success, provided the pattern is placed on the target.

Again looking at the chart and being realistic, we find that most game could be taken with the improved-cylinder choke which would give that working pattern a kill range of from fifteen to thirty-five yards. This is adequate to compensate for poor range estimation and within the need for more than seventy-five percent of hunting needs for the shotgun.

During World War II a common saying in England was that the trouble with American troops was, "over-sexed, over-paid, and over here." If we apply this adage to shotguns, it could say, "over-choked, over-shot content and over-powered." This would not be far wrong from a practical view of most American shotgun hunters. Anyone who doubts this can satisfy himself with a simple experiment. Most game bird's bodies are not more than a three-by-five-inch rectangle, the size of a large index card. Simply cut a few of these rectangles from a piece of cardboard and nail them to a stick. Place the sticks with the cards at the ranges as shown on the chart. Back up to the firing line, bring the shotgun to your shoulder and fire. Don't rifle shoot the gun, but bring it up and fire as you would normally. One shotshell per card. Take a close look at the results and it will be an eye opener.

All of the shot within that thirty-inch desired pattern diameter will not be used under actual game conditions. Only the shot pellets that strike the card are of practical use, with the rest of the shot only stirring the surrounding air. Unless the bird is sitting on a limb or a power line, you will not have the same shot. A moving bird, feathered or clay, will be struck only by the shot within the space where it is at the moment of impact. Taken in respect to miscalculated speed of the target or lead, the wider diameter of circle of pellets assures that the shooter's error will be compensated for by its diameter. Thus what is desired is as wide a pattern as possible with enough pellets striking the game to score a kill. This means that we must have as efficient a pattern as possible with even pellet distribution.

No two shotgun barrels made — even those side-by-side on the manufacturing line — will shoot exactly alike on the pattern board. Even if you shoot shells from the same box, the results never will be identical. I do not know why and neither does anyone else. It is simply a fact that must be accepted. I have bored shotgun barrels, same model, within less than one-thousandth-inch variation and have never obtained the same identical results. You can use dimensions as a guide, but only as a guide. The final dimension is obtained only by trial shooting.

Few shooters realize that no barrel, no choke, will give the same results with different size shot! In other words, a full-choke barrel on a specific gun will give full-choke patterns with size 8 shot, but if you switch shot size, same load, to size 9 or 7½ shot, the percentage will go up or down to extra-full choke or improved-modified. Change to a larger shot such as #6 and you may or may not get modified pattern results. In other words, a barrel marked *Full* may deliver full with one size shot. Switch shot load, same size shot, and the results will not be identical. Change the power of the shotshell and again you change pattern results. You will obtain consistent pattern results only with a consistent shotshell. Change any factor and you have another set of results on the pattern board. Why this occurs is unknown, but anyone who has spent any amount of time shooting patterns will agree that it does occur.

The only solution is to shoot different shot sizes, shot loads, different powered shotshells, all by different manufacturers. You will learn which gives the perfect patterns, which show a variation — which may be small but still a variation.

Proficiency with a shotgun depends to a large degree on consistency. This is in the shooter mounting the gun the same, the same power of shotshell and of course the same consistent pattern diameter at the same range every time. Then and then only will the percentage of hits on a target increase!

There was a time when hunters might take more than one gun into a blind, but today's interchangeable choke tube concept has changed this habit.

Reducing Your Gauge By Tubing Can Give Added Versatility To Your Favorite Shotgun!

Outfitter Alberto Lleras illustrates the effectiveness of tubed barrels with an afternoon's take of doves in his homeland, Colombia, where there is no limit and the birds are considered a hazard to nation's agriculture.

OUTDOOR EDITOR of the *Pittsburgh Press,* Roger Latham, has been hunting almost exclusively with a .410 for several decades. I thought he was a little tetched for using a scattergun so puny, but in recent years I've come to see his point. He doesn't use the .410 because he bags more birds, because he doesn't, or because he considers it more sporting. Latham uses the .410 because it's more fun!

In the Cauca Valley of Colombia there are tremendous numbers of non-migratory doves. Two close shooting friends, Alberto Lleras and Bill Farfan, started a Colombian safari company that caters to American wingshooters. Farfan is perhaps the world's finest wingshot. That's not only my opinion, but that of most anyone who has seen him shoot. From the time he was 8 years old he's enjoyed

no-limit shooting. In some years he has fired 50,000 rounds at live birds! His partner, Alberto Lleras, isn't far behind him in wingshooting skills. Both were avid and champion International Skeet shooters prior to starting their safari company.

There never were two more ardent 12-gauge nuts than this duo. They accused visiting sportsmen of being sissies if they dropped down to so much as a 20-gauge, smiled disapproval, whispered to one another in Spanish, then laughed heartily. On one of Roger Latham's trips to Colombia they tried his .410 as a lark. They laughed and joked, weren't too impressed the first try, but a year later they tried the .410 a second time. A year after that they each bought a 28 and a .410. They never pick up a 12-gauge anymore.

In Colombia it's not unusual to fire up to five hundred

shells a day at doves. This can be brutal punishment after a while. The big 12s cause strawberries on the cheeks, black and blue shoulders, and who knows how bad the subconscious can be affected by such harsh, repetitive punishment. The point is, Lleras and Farfan are still sacking plenty of doves, but now the experience is totally enjoyable, never a chore.

With dove limits around twelve birds a day in the U.S., it's easy to get a sore shoulder around here, too. Most scattergunners will fire three or four shells to put one dove in their coat. Nearly two boxes of 12-gauge shells will be fired in a day if a guy or gal is in a good spot. This much shooting might be experienced several days in a row. This is the ideal hunt for a 28, maybe even a .410.

"The town where I live is blessed, or plagued, depending upon your point of view, with a blue jillion pigeons. I gun them often around surrounding farms. While I once used nothing but a 12 for such forays, I've dropped back to smaller and smaller gauges, all in the name of fun," reports Nick Sisley, who researched this section for us.

Skeet shooters almost invariably start this game with a 12-gauge gun. A few children or women will start with a 20, on the advice of a close relative who is an avid skeeter. But any shooter who takes up this clay target game seriously

The barrel-insert tubes made by Jess Briley fit snugly into the existing barrel and lock properly in place.

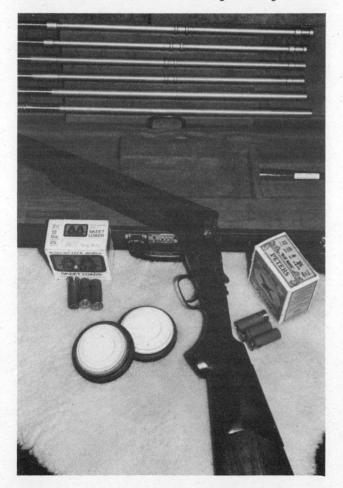

The array of small-gauge tubes shown with Nick Sisley's favorite 12-gauge over/under do much to increase his fun afield and can even aid in reducing shooting costs.

turns to the smaller gauges, both from a competition standpoint and from an enjoyment standpoint. Once he has a couple of years under his belt he looks forward to shooting the big gun with less and less enthusiasm; mostly because it hurts too much and the little .410 and beautiful 28 are pure pleasure!

Although they're not new to skeet, small-gauge tubes that fit 12-gauge over/under skeet guns are becoming the rage in this highly competitive game. As you might guess, they're becoming the rage because they're winning so many events: the only reason any gun becomes the rage in competition.

These tubes, made of a lightweight metal, are carefully machined to fit individual skeet guns. They are not interchangeable. A complete set comprises two tubes each in .410, 28- and 20-gauge. The tubes are not interchangeable between top and bottom barrels, so each tube must be marked accordingly. The guy who has provided considerable information about tubes for skeet shooting has been Jess Briley, Briley Manufacturing, 1035 Gessner, Suite C, Houston, TX 77055, maker of these scientifically sophisticated tubes.

"I have a Remington 3200 skeet gun fitted with tubes and this fairly recent acquisition has increased my scores tremendously, especially in the little .410. I also hunt with

161

The Ruger over/under, made originally in 20 gauge and now in 12 gauge, does a good job with insert tubes.

this 3200 and often I'm inserting either the 28 or .410 tubes in that over/under," Sisley says.

"I've long championed ultralight guns for upland hunting, where long tramps are the order and pulling the trigger occurs only a few times a day. I'm just as convinced that in some types of hunting, and especially in skeet shooting, a heavier gun is of definite benefit."

Don't jump to the conclusion that skeet chokes are too open for most hunting. Most of the game we encounter will be at ranges that are encountered on a skeet field, twenty to twenty-five yards. There are exceptions, and with that type of game it'll pay to have a big 12 belting your shoulder. But before getting into why small gauge skeet guns with tubes can be effective in the hunting field as well as on the skeet field, let me digress a bit.

Jess Briley took up skeet more than a decade ago. This is not an inexpensive game. In addition to travel costs to distant shoots, entry fees, tons of practice, case upon case of shotgun shells, hour after hour at the reloading bench, there are the costs of the guns themselves. This is because skeet is a game of 12, 20, 28 and .410. No serious competitor shoots less than all four gauges.

A skeet gun must be totally dependable. Not only is a shooter penalized after two gun malfunctions, anything that doesn't go exactly as expected on the skeet field breaks the shooter's concentration, and losing concentration on one target is enough to keep a competitor out of the winner's circle. A dependable skeet gun is often an expensive one. While the Remington 1100 put skeet within economic range of more skeet buffs than ever before, one sees the over/under type more often on skeet fields these days, except maybe in 12-gauge, where recoil-conscious skeet shooters will opt for a gas-operated autoloader. The purchase of even three over/unders, instead of four, can be taxing to most anyone's pocketbook.

Such a purchase was too taxing for Jess Briley's pocketbook when he started shooting, but he was a machinist. He experimented, making barrel sets in 28 and .410 for one of his over/unders. Krieghoff, Remington and Browning are three current skeet gun manufacturers who make four-barrel sets: skeet over/under barrels in all four gauges that fit one receiver and one forend. The retail price on one of

the four barrel sets may be in the $7000 range.

When Jess Briley found his special-made barrel sets weren't what he was looking for, he decided to try tubes. They weren't totally new, for another machine shop had turned out the first tubes: Purbaugh in California. A constant experimenter, Briley tried different metals, different techniques, different ways to have tube extractors match up with the ejectors on the 12-gauge gun.

After years of experimentation he's settled on 17-4PH precipitating stainless steel for the chambers of his tubes and sulfuric-acid-hard-coated anodized aluminum for the barrels of the tubes. The barrel surface of these tubes is hard, resisting wear and scratches, and it also takes a high polish, important because less friction and resistance results as the shot charge is racing down the barrel. The stainless steel is extremely tough, tensile strength in the 170,000 psi range, twelve percent elongation and with excellent ductility. A tube weighs approximately seven ounces, more in .410 bore. If the shooter wants the tubes of all three gauges to weigh the same, he can purchase .410 chambers made of extra-light titanium. These are more expensive.

How does this extra weight affect the skeet gun? To put the answer as succinctly as possible, *it makes it better!* Those few extra ounces in a tubed gun are between the breech and the front end of the barrels. This weight addition keeps the muzzle moving, even if the shooter tends to slow or stop his swing. The best competitors invariably utilize the sustained-lead method in skeet. Their gun barrels track ahead of the target, maintaining a specified lead, varying with each station, with the barrels moving at the same speed as the target. Any roughness or unevenness of the swing results in a missed target. Added muzzle weight tends to smooth out the swing, as well as keep the barrels moving.

In 1978 Sisley's National Skeet Shooting Association .410 average for the year was just under 80. "I did not use tubes that season. When I switched to tubes for the 1979 season, my averages shot up dramatically, to more than 90. I attribute some of my increased scores to more practice, but there's absolutely no question that my Briley tubes improved my abilities. Why? Smoother swings, less tendency to go slow or stop the swing, and better patterns.

"On this latter point readers are urged to scrutinize what I say with extreme care. Jess Briley has gone to the trouble and expense of using computers to examine shotgun patterns. The skeet shooter's target area will measure about four square inches, the side view of a clay bird. It takes three or four #9 pellets to break a clay. Briley asked the computer how tight his patterns had to be at twenty-one yards and still insure that any clay bird within the typical pattern would be hit by three or four pellets. The results are important."

What some shooters once assumed as ideal chokes for the little .410 aren't tight enough to break targets consistently. In other words, even if they hold perfectly on one hundred targets with their little .410s, shooters have a statistical chance of breaking ninety-four to ninety-seven percent of them. Obviously tighter chokes, perhaps only in the .410, were called for. Just as obvious, extremely even

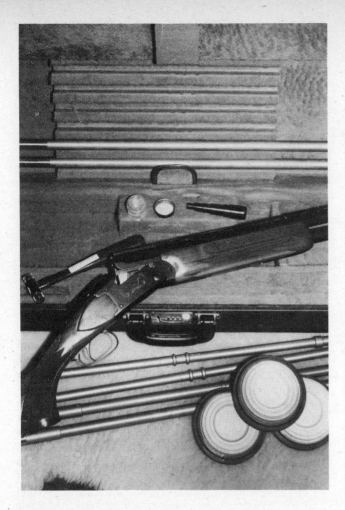

Jess Briley offers a complete kit with his insert tube package that allows for quick, efficient gauge changes.

shooters will swing to them in the future. They are less expensive than the four-barrel sets previously mentioned. It's possible to purchase one of several fine over/unders with tubes in the three smaller gauges for $1400 to $2000. That's still a heck of a ticket, but reasonable compared to most four-barrel sets.

Many skeet shooters fire a 12-gauge gas-operated auto-loader such as a Remington 1100 in the big-gun event. This shotgun, and others of similar design, suck up a tremendous amount of recoil. For skeeters who prefer this type of shotgun it would be well to consider a reasonably heavy 20-gauge over/under, then have Jess Briley tube it in 28 and .410. Such a 20 would also make a dandy hunting gun in all three gauges. The problem is the minute difference between a 20 and a 28. A 28-gauge tube must be very thin to fit a 20-gauge barrel. Jess Briley is working on solving that problem.

The main reason tubes are not interchangeable with other guns is the close tolerances in the chamber area. The fit of the tubes into the over/under's chamber must be almost perfect. If not, the chambers of the tubes would be taking the multiple 12,000 psi punishment doled out with every shell. The over/under's mono block was built to take these pressures, so tubes must fit into the chambers of each individual over/under with exacting tolerances. The walls of the .410 tubes are reasonably thick, so perhaps they're capable of taking more pressure. The walls of the 20-gauge tubes for a 12-gauge over/under are thinner. I assume they would not hold up to a high pressure load quite as well. The point is, even if these tubes fit into another gun, it would be unsafe — and could cause the tube's chamber to split — at the least!

The tubes fit easily into the barrel of the over/under, except for the last one-half or one-quarter inch. A mallet and plastic drive rod are included to tap the tube the last little bit into the barrel. The same plastic rod is used to tap the tubes out of the barrel.

It's possible to purchase a tubed set direct if you already have an over/under. The most common 12-gauge over/unders seen on the skeet field with tubes are the Remington 3200, the Perazzi, the Krieghoff, Browning Superposed, etc. However, any over/under can be fitted with tubes. This could be done with a good side-by-side shotgun, too, but side-by-sides aren't seen on skeet fields anymore.

Knowledgeable skeet competitors are well aware of these relatively new, scientifically designed tubes. They know how these tools can help them break better scores, but the average hunter may not be aware that they exist. In my opinion these tubes are an excellent way to take up the pursuit of hunting with the 28-gauge and .410 such as when plenty of shots are to be encountered and when a heavier gun pays off with smoother swings. A heavy skeet gun with tubes is not recommended for game like grouse or quail or woodcock — where long tramps through thick covers are the rule, when the gun must be carried at port arms continually, and when super-fast gun handling and ultra-quick shots are called for. But for ducks over decoys in the early season, doves in reasonable ranges, pigeons that might plague the outskirts of the town where you live, and other game encountered regularly at ranges of twenty-five yards and less, these tubed skeet guns, especially in 28 and .410, make beautiful hunting arms.

patterns are essential. This is where the Briley scientific choking comes into play.

Tighter chokes mean smaller pattern diameters, so the shooter who continually pulls the trigger at the wrong time may shoot worse scores with these scientifically choked tubes. Serious skeet shooters, those who are aiming for the top of the class, want to be able to statistically break 100. At the top shoots these days, 100-straight with the tiny .410 is not unusual.

These slightly tighter and more evenly choked .410 tubes also result in better hunting guns. Carefully choked tubes throw magnificent patterns, even patterns that devastate doves and pigeons at close ranges, up to twenty-five yards.

Jess Briley's skeet averages have been increasing steadily since he started using his scientifically designed and choked tubes. In 1978 he made the Sub-Senior All American team with a 97.1 average. Wayne Mayes of Hixson, Tennessee, led all skeet shooters in 1978 with a 98.94 average, firing an all-time high 11,250 targets. Mayes uses a tubed over/under. Wayne Mayes, Jess Briley and yours truly are only three examples of the thousands who are using tubes in competitive skeet. It is likely that even more

Chapter 15

A LOOK AT CUSTOM CHOKES

With The Proper Work, You Can Get Anything Out Of A Choke That You Desire!

I F A SHOTGUN barrel is delivering the desired thirty-inch-diameter shot pattern with a shot size and shot load selected by the shooter at a range other than the one desired by the shooter, then something must be changed. As previously explained, results can be changed somewhat by switching shotshell manufacturer, pellet size, shot load and shotshell power. In many cases the available change will not give the exact results desired. For instance, if a shooter wants the thirty-inch-diameter pattern at thirty-five yards with shot size 7½ and all of the possibilities have been exhausted, then the only answer is to change the internal dimensions of the choke in his barrel. Should a shooter want a pattern at thirty yards, then no amount of available choice will give this to him if the barrel he is using is a full or extra-full choke.

The only way to arrive at the desired results is to increase constriction of the choke if more range is needed or, if less range is needed, decrease the amount of choke constriction. Stated another way, a properly custom-choked barrel should deliver a pre-selected shot pellet size and shot load with a pre-selected shotshell power at a desired distance. This is not so hard to achieve and does not require a fully equipped machine shop with exotic tooling. By the same token, it is not a job that can be accomplished in one evening while sitting in front of the television set with a can of suds!

Four things are required: a method of securing the barrel, such as a vise on a good bench; the correct but inexpensive tools; a thorough understanding of what is to be done; and patience. I emphasize patience, for each slight change in the barrel's balanced dimensions will result in a change in the pattern results.

The finest shotguns have barrels that have been "regulated" to shoot one shot size, one shot load and one shotshell power perfectly at one distance. The custom choke is a duplicate of the regulated barrel except that a modern mass-produced barrel is altered to achieve a specific result. The surprising thing about fine shotgun barrels is that a double-barrel with the same choke designation for each barrel will vary both in bore and choke diameters. This reemphasizes the fact that each barrel must stand on its own and have its individual bore and choke dimensions to offer identical results on the pattern board.

Patience and persistance are the ingredients for a regulated barrel or a custom choke. Each minute change in dimensions will cause a change in results. This requires a willingness to shoot patterns each time the dimensions of bore or choke are changed. The task is not so much in the cutting as in the shooting. Time is what you pay for if the work is done by a gunsmith. It is a matter of cut and shoot, cut and shoot, over and over until the pattern is perfected.

Some type of a tool capable of measuring the amount of choke constriction is a prime requirement. This requires

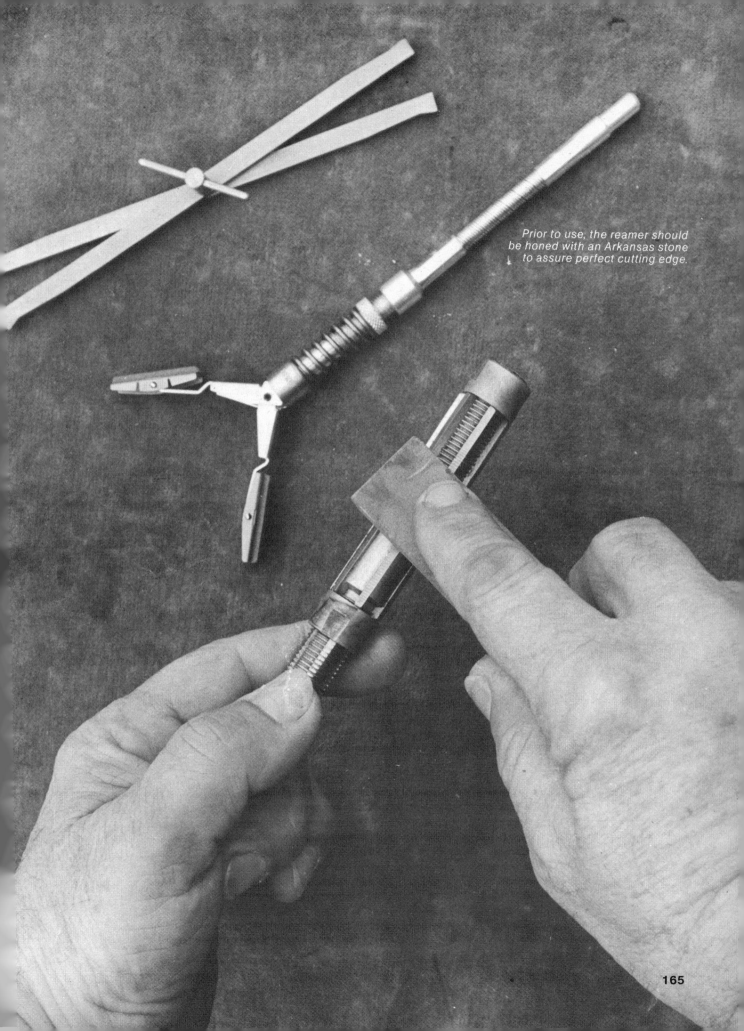

Prior to use, the reamer should be honed with an Arkansas stone to assure perfect cutting edge.

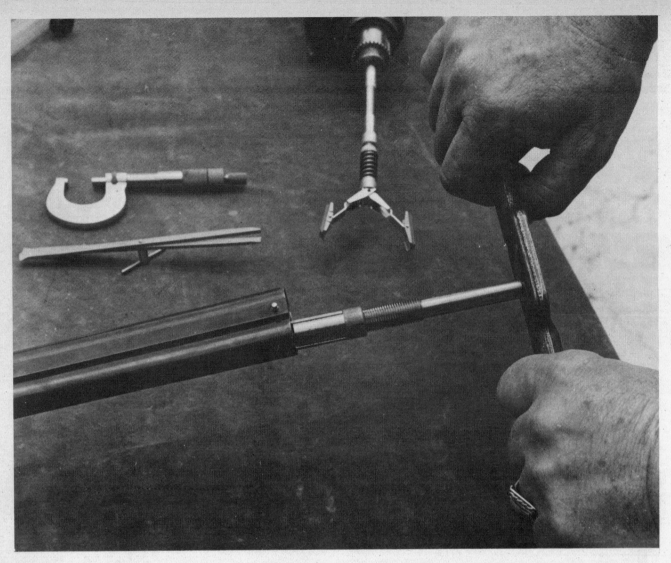

If necessary, the reamers can be used with the shotgun barrel held in the horizontal position, but care must be taken to be certain that the reamer is held at a correct angle. Final honing is done with the barrel in a vise.

two sets of figures. One is the bore diameter, the other the choke diameter, as constriction is the difference between the two. The least expensive tools for this are Brownell's choke dial calipers and Brownell's choke comparison calipers. The first has movable arms to engage the inside diameters with the results read on the dial. Some method of setting the dial is required, but this is accomplished easily with either calipers or a micrometer. It is fast and will give a visual reading; as the arms are moved from the tip of the muzzle back to the bore and the reading will be continuous.

The second tool, I designed for Brownell's about ten years ago. It consists of two long arms joined in the center. When spread, with one set of arms engaging the inside diameter, the other set of arms extends outside and the measurement across the outside arms is identical to those on the inside set of arms. Thus if a micrometer or caliper is used to measure the outside arms, you have a reading identical to that of the arms touching the inner walls of bore or choke. The choke comparison calipers' main advantage is low cost.

The first step is to carefully measure the existing choke, choke forcing cone length and the bore diameter. Take several measurements to be sure. It helps if you draw a sketch of the bore, forcing cone and choke with the dimensions showing both diameter and length noting your measurements on this sketch. The entire job can be accomplished more easily if the shotgun barrel is detached from the receiver. Naturally the bore and choke should have been cleaned to remove any leading or build-up which would give false measurements.

The tool with which the metal is removed is both inexpensive and simple to use; most important, is that it does not remove a lot of metal in a short time. This is the choke hone marketed by Brownell's. Some years ago I ran across the tool and Bob Brownell decided to offer it to the trade. It looks like a common brake cylinder hone and is used for that purpose. However, it provides constant pressure to the detachable stones and is of sufficient size to work in any bore from 20- to 10-gauge. A flexible shaft is utilized between the stone support section and the end that receives the power. Said power is provided by a common one-quarter- or three-eighths-inch electric hand drill. A common egg-beater drill can be used, but it is slow and tiring.

Chuck the hone tool in the drill. Hold the shotgun barrel horizontal on a bench, or better yet, in a padded bench vise. The drill chuck should be parallel with the bore, although the flexible shaft will compensate for minor misalignment. You can keep it straight by vision. A friend seated to one side can keep you straight up or down or if a friend is not available, a common mirror can be used for this purpose.

With the stones in the choke area, turn on the drill and allow it to run for thirty seconds, then stop the drill and remove the stones from the bore. Never start the drill before the stones are in the bore and always let their motion come to a complete halt before removal, otherwise the stones may be broken. Wipe the bore clean and measure the choke diameter. Compare this with the original measurement. Note the difference. It is important to realize that different steels will cut at a different rate and that each hand drill will turn at varying revolutions per minute so you set a metal removal rate and time per job. This is the reason for the timed thirty seconds followed by measurement.

Photos by T.L. Bish

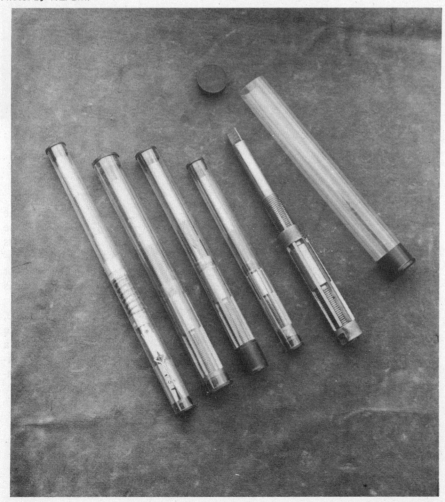

A good method for storing all of your reamers is to place each in a plastic tube after it has been given a coating of preservative.

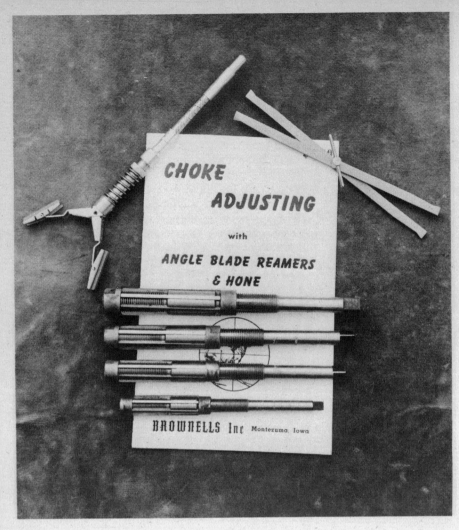

Angle blade reamers are made in four gauges — 28, 16, 20, 12 — but a hone and calipers also are necessary for the work.

Some tough steels or slow drills may require a cutting period of one or two minutes before any difference can be noted in measurement. Once the time period is known you can regulate the amount of metal being removed. Also remember that the stones cut faster if dry, slower if oil is present in the bore.

In removing metal from the choke constriction section you are decreasing the amount of constriction and the amount of choke. It is a good idea to test fire each time you remove a half-thousandth of diameter — 0.0005 inch — as this small amount will vary the pattern results. After each test firing clean the bore and choke of all leading and foreign residue to prevent incorrect measurement. Try not to hurry the process. Shoot test patterns over and over with the selected shotshell. You will see the pattern change slowly as you remove metal from the choke area. If you have preselected the distance, initially you will see too tight a pattern diameter. As you remove metal the pattern diameter will increase and you should see even distribution of the pellets within the pattern. Each pattern will be slightly different from its predecessor, as there is a factor of random pellet distribution from shot to shot.

Removing metal is easy, replacing it difficult, so go slow. If you keep the drill parallel with the cutting stones it is possible to hone the choke constriction all the way from extra-full to cylinder. It just requires time and patience, which explains the high cost of gunsmithing on this project.

By removing choke constriction we can move the thirty-inch-diameter pattern back toward the firing line bit by bit as we have less choke. Do not overdo the honing. When the thirty-inch pattern is achieved at the desired distance squirt a little oil in the choke area and run the hone for fifteen to thirty seconds to obtain the smoothest surface possible in the area and the job is complete.

With the selected shotshell the pattern will be consistent and with hits more frequent the shooter will gain confidence to help his overall score. Switch any component of the shell and you will change the pattern results to some degree. To get the best out of your choke switch only the shot size, keeping shot weight and shell power constant. Generally this will give the least variation in the pattern.

I have a Beretta over/under that was regulated at the factory for me with #7½ shot at 1200 feet per second (fps). One set of barrels is Skeet 1 and Skeet 2 choke, the other barrels are extra-full and full choke. I can switch to #9 shot with the skeet barrels but not with the other set. The tight barrels will accept #8 shot and 6s only if I handload the shells. Factory shells in this barrel go haywire!

Calipers designed by the author are used to check the choke of the shotgun before work is begun.

In the foregoing we were decreasing the amount of constriction by decreasing the diameter of the choke section. Result was that the range at which the thirty-inch pattern was shot also was decreased. To increase the range would require increasing the amount of constriction. This is impossible as we cannot add metal to the choke section's diameter, but we can increase the diameter of the bore section behind the choke section, thus increasing the amount of constriction. In other words, we add choke. This technique sometimes is called back boring as the boring takes place behind the choke section. I prefer the term *overbore*, as the bore of the barrel is bored over normal diameter size. Both terms mean the same thing.

To overbore we must increase bore diameter from the beginning of the choke section back to the chamber area where the chamber forcing cone ends. The problem is that the bore diameter must be consistent the whole length, a rather difficult task.

There is a simple answer, however, that allows the bore diameter to be increased as required without encountering the problem if boring the full length. This is accomplished using only the choke hone tool as previously described.

A technique as old as shotgun chokes is simply a recess choke; a recess cut behind the existing choke. It also is referred to as "jug choking." A section of the bore is cut to a larger diameter with the hone for a length of four to six inches, terminating where the original choke forcing cone begins. The larger-diameter recess section increases choke constriction for its diameter is greater than original. There is a safety limit to the increased diameter, for you also are decreasing barrel wall thickness at this point. No more than five-thousandths-inch- (0.005) diameter increase should be attempted. This means wall thickness is reduced by half this amount (0.0025) as there is a wall on each side. This would place a maximum choke constriction increase of the same total (0.005) or about one degree of choke.

It is essential to know the exact distance from the muzzle that the choke forcing cone begins and the barrel bore ends. Mark this on a sketch of the bore and choke. A suitable recess would be about three inches minimum and six inches maximum. I use a half-way choice of four inches. Remember that you have to cut a tapering cone that starts in the bore near the chamber end, gradually increasing to the full dimension of the recess cut. One inch is about right. At the same time, we must have a similar cone on the other end of the recess toward the choke. So we have a one-inch cone tapering from the regular bore diameter to the recess diameter, which is four inches in length, then another cone — also one inch in length — that tapers from the recess to the original choke forcing cone.

We then cut a new section in the bore that is a combined six inches in length (one-inch taper, plus four inches of recess, plus the other one-inch taper). Compress the stones of the choke hone tool to the diameter of the bore, then use a thin piece of black plastic electrician's tape to lay out the one-inch beginning taper, the four-inch recess and the one-

The most foolproof method of reworking a choke is to place the shotgun barrel in a bench vise in the perpendicular position, then run the reamer straight down the bore. Be sure the vise is padded.

Once the barrel has been reamed, the hone is placed in a drill, then spring-loaded stones are inserted in the bore and the opened choke is polished. Use of a good lubricant can be an aid in speeding this part of the process.

inch ending taper. Place the thin-width tape around the hone's body section so you will have a visible mark on the tool when it is cutting.

Operate the choke hone exactly as before, timing the cut so you will know how much metal per minute you are removing. Most important is to cut the recess section first. Remember to skip past the one-inch taper and cut the recess first. Thus when the taper is cut on both ends of the recess, the tool will angle as needed between the two diameters involved and cut on a taper. As you will remove less metal in these two operations, you simply decrease the cutting time of the tool.

After the first cut, including the two tapered ends, thoroughly test fire. If needed, go back and cut the recess deeper, then the two tapers. Then test fire again for pattern results. Just as the watch words with decreasing constriction were cut-and-shoot, the same applies when increasing constriction. If you cut the recess too much and end up with too much constriction, you can always decrease the choke diameter with the same tool.

The Brownell choke hone is the correct tool to use, as it was developed especially to fulfill this requirement. I would recommend that the beginner try his first job on a junk barrel. Most gunsmiths have scrap ends of barrels around their shops; these ends are perfect practice material. Being short, they can be checked for progress by holding one end up to the light.

If you are only beginning to work on chokes, I would recommend that you use only the Brownell choke hone until thoroughly aware of what is involved in this process. You also must learn that a seemingly minute change in constriction dimensions, bore or choke will create change in shot pattern. Only then should you try the other forms of bore and choke change.

When the choke is being changed say from full to modified, this entails about a ten-thousandths-inch decrease in constriction. This is a small measurement, but a lot of metal when you are trying to remove it with just a hone! So the need is to remove the greatest portion of the metal rapidly, then finish up with the hone for the last half-thousandth.

The quickest way to do this is with some form of reamer or boring tool. The old way was with an armory reamer, which basically is a square section of tool steel that is just shy of being bore filling if placed in the bore or in the choke section. To move it up to contact with the walls of the barrel, bore or choke, a piece of wood is placed on the bottom opposite the cutting edge. To increase cutting a shim of common paper is placed between the cutting tool's bottom and the wood. This increases dimensions so the amount of metal removed will be equal to the thickness of the paper shim. For more cuts you just add additional paper shims. This is repeated until the desired diameter is obtained.

The hone is worked slowly back and forth in the shotgun's bore to ensure that the entire reamed section is polished.

The armory reamer was used to bore the barrel bore section, the forcing cone of the choke and the choke itself decades ago and is still in use by some firms. Most good English shotgun barrels were made using the armory reamer tool. An advantage was that by varying the type of paper shim and its thickness, the amount of metal removed could be closely regulated. Most reamers of this type were extremely long, ranging from twelve to eighteen inches. They were powered in a variety of ways, but always at a slow speed and always with plenty of oil. Only the forward edge of the square tool did the cutting; the trailing edge was radiused for a burnishing action which smoothed the cut surfaces.

Generally the choke was cut to the initial bore diameter with this type of reamer, then a larger reamer was used to cut the bore behind that left for the choke. The final diameter armory reamer had a taper at the forward end in order to cut the choke forcing cone taper that leads into the smaller-diameter choke area.

Using a reamer to add choke to an existing choke, it is necessary to enlarge the entire bore diameter from end of the chamber forcing cone to the beginning of the choke forcing cone. The armory reamer will do the job nicely, but while a relatively simple tool, its use requires a lot of skill and knowledge.

To decrease choke constriction by removing choke diameter, an armory reamer can be utilized. With the added paper shims controlling the amount of each cut, it can be inserted from the chamber end of the barrel and powered via a long rod, or it can be inserted from the muzzle end of the barrel using a short rod between the reamer's rear and the power source. The latter system was used by gunsmiths to a great extent for choke regulation until the beginning of World War Two and still is used to some extent. The armory reamer works well, but few gunsmiths know how to make or use one today.

The second method for removing excess metal from the choke diameter rather quickly is with fixed-diameter, solid pull-through reamers. The only current source for these is the Poly Choke. These reamers are used to remove the choke completely when a Poly Choke is to be added to the barrel and the owner does not want the barrel cut or wants overall length to be even greater than original.

These solid-type reamers have built-in cutting flutes. The reamer is inserted from the chamber end, pushed or pulled through the bore up to the choke area, then attached to a power source at the exiting end. Power rotates the reamer as it is pulled through and exits the muzzle of the barrel. During its passage it cuts the choke area to the diameter of the solid reamer thus increasing the diameter

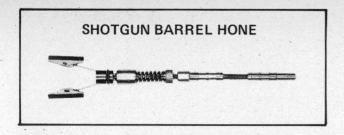

SHOTGUN BARREL HONE

and decreasing constriction. The reamers are made with variations in diameter from one reamer to the next of two-thousandths-inch (0.002). So to remove ten-thousandths of metal in choke diameter, you would use five of the pull-through reamers with each enlarging the diameter 0.002 inch. It is possible to use a fewer number of reamers with each taking more of a cut, but the only danger in this method is that the large cut could change the centerline of the choke area and cut to one side.

This is not a cheap set of tools. The last figure I had for a similar reamer was $30 each and since five are required for only a 0.010-inch conversion, think what the price for a set would be with a range from the smallest 12-gauge specification for extra-full choke back to a straight cylinder bore. Roughly fifteen reamers are needed, not including bores less or more than standard! The whole set was about $800 and this was for one gauge!

The problem with the solid pull-through reamer is the amount of metal removed with each reamer — a minimum of 0.002 inches. As little as 0.0005 or one-half-thousandth will influence the pattern. The obvious answer is an expanding-type reamer to allow less diameter reduction, but the regular expanding reamers will not do the job as their dimension must be set before they can be placed in the barrel for a cut. Also they are straight, with no taper.

Faced with this problem some years ago, I tried reamer after reamer in a search for an answer. Some worked, some did not, and it was an expensive quest using a lot of junk barrels for testing. One company had a possible answer: This was a tapered reamer with a spiral twist designed primarily to ream an electric motor bushing to match the shaft. The only problem was that, being of pull-through configuration, the reamer must be set to the desired diameter, inserted into the bore from the chamber end, pushed to the choke area, hooked to a power source, then the cut made. A slow, not too efficient method, the advantage was that the reamer was tapered so that it was self-centering; the angled cutting blades made a thin slicing cut, allowing less than one-half-thousandth diameter reduction for added control.

I convinced the manufacturer he should make a special set for me for choke work. The taper was reversed with the cutting blades. This allowed the reamer's small end to be inserted from the muzzle of the barrel with the power source attached. Being self-centering during the cut, the larger diameter made the final dimension cut of the choke. I had perfect control with diameter reduction settings fully visible prior to the cutting stroke. Thus I could cut as little as one-quarter-thousandth if desired or make a larger cut simply by adjusting two settings on the reamer. The angled blades could be removed for restoning the edges to assure a clean surface cut.

Bob Brownell liked the reamer and made arrangements to purchase them from the manufacturer in the configuration for barrel choke work. They are now offered to the trade with each gauge reamer costing less than that of a single pull-through solid type! I wrote the instructon manual for Brownell's that fully explains the reamer's use on chokes. Since its introduction, thousands of gunsmiths have purchased the set, which will work for 28-, 20-, 16-,

This simple set of bore calipers was designed by author and has found favor with gunsmiths due to their simplicity.

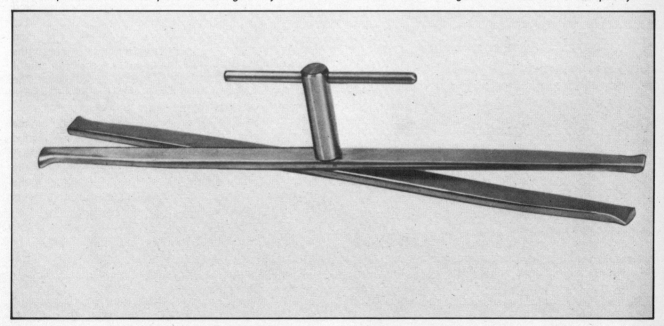

12-and 10-gauge barrels with chokes ranging from cylinder to extra-full. The copyrighted instructions are available through Brownell. I suggest those interested read the instruction manual as we cannot cover all details in our limited space.

Since the instructions were written some gunsmiths have reported a problem in getting a clean cut on each flute. This is simple to solve. The cutting flutes are subject to wear from use. Like all reamers, they must be honed occasionally with a good stone. If one flute has a lot of chip build-up in front of it, this is an indication that it is doing most of the cutting. Simply remove this cutter flute and stone it until it is exactly the same as the other flutes. When reinstalled, all flutes should cut equally. While the instruction manual clearly states one should remove the cutters and clean the surface directly under them to remove any and all foreign residue, some gunsmiths skip this and the cutters are pushed upward by this residue.

As each of these adjustable Brownell reamers slightly exceeds the specifications for any single gauge, they overlap in dimension with one reamer beginning where the other ends. This gives a full range from a tight 28-gauge to an open 10-gauge so that regardless of barrel or choke diameter, the set of five reamers can handle the requirement. Price is relatively low and the Brownell set requires only one reamer per gauge.

Based on experience of quite a few years, anyone interested in choke change or experimentation can now do the work with only a few tools. The set of Brownell expanding reamers, the choke hone tool, a measuring instrument and a good padded bench vise — with of course the Brownell instruction manual, which should be read carefully — cover the needs.

I cannot overemphasize the importance of taking just a small cut each time, then test patterning with the chosen shotshell. It is a slow process, but one will gain a lot of practical knowledge as to what will and what will not change a pattern. Use junk barrels for practice and, if possible, do the first job on an inexpensive single-barrel shotgun with plenty of test patterns.

The reamer will remove metal rapidly. I recommend removal of no more than one-thousandth-inch initially. A heavier cut requires added power and more control to prevent cutting off the centerline. This is not hard to overcome, but the only way to learn is practice, practice and more practice.

Always finish up the choke alteration with the dry hone, first to remove any surface blemish left by the reamer. Then flood it with cutting oil for the final smooth cut. I finish the last one-thousandth-inch with the hone, always.

You can do a really mirror-bright job by using a 0000 steel wool bob as described in the chapter on bores. Simply make a shorter shank on the tool. Insert the bob from the muzzle after the oil-and-hone step. Use the same electric hand drill for a power source. By burnishing both the choke forcing cone and the choke surface with the bob, there is nothing to retard the exiting shot and its plastic protective wad.

There is another way of achieving the effect of change in

After the initial reaming, the choke is miked with calipers. The size of the bore corresponds at the other end of instrument.

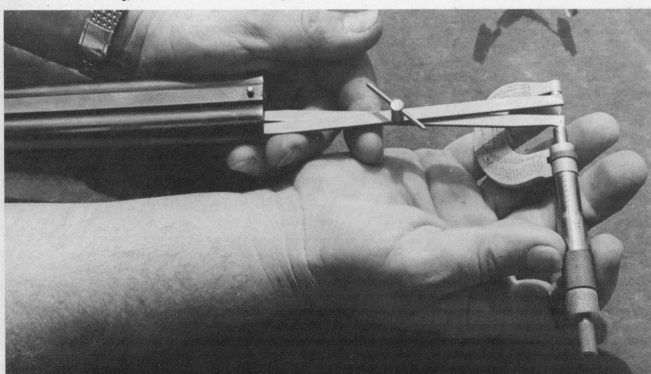

Number Of Shot Pellets Per Shot Weight Per Pellet Size

Shot Charge Weight (oz.)	Shot Sizes								
	2	3	4	5	6	7	7½	8	9
7/8	77	91	120	147	196	259	301	357	511
1	90	106	135	170	225	299	345	410	585
1-1/16	95	112	144	180	239	317	369	435	621
1-1/8	101	119	152	191	253	336	388	461	658
1-3/16	105	124	159	200	267	353	401	435	693
1-1/4	112	132	168	212	280	374	421	512	731
1-3/8	123	145	186	233	309	*	*	*	*
1-1/2	135	159	202	255	*	*	*	*	*
1-5/8	145	171	220	275	*	*	*	*	*
1-3/4	156	190	234	296	*	*	*	*	*
1-7/8	167	197	255	317	*	*	*	*	*
2	180	212	270	340	*	*	*	*	*

(*) Not normally loaded in this shot size.

Shot Size	Diameter in Inches
BB	.18
B	.17
2	.15
3	.14
4	.13
5	.12
6	.11
7	.10
7½	.095
8	.09
9	.08
10	.07

A simple way to remember this is to subtract the shot size number from the key number .17 for shot pellet diameter.

Example: Shot size 6 subtracted from key number .17 equals .11-inch diameter.

a choke without any actual change in the dimensions. This is done simply by taking advantage of the number of pellets in any given shot charge weight.

Remember that pellet percentage — the number of pellets within the thirty-inch circle — is dependent on the number of pellets originally in the unfired shotshell. Also remember that a full choke at forty yards will give seventy percent of the pellets within the thirty-inch-diameter circle, a modified choke will deliver sixty percent and the improved-cylinder choke will deliver fifty percent.

This means that if we start with one hundred shot pellets in the unfired shotshell, then seventy will strike within the thirty-inch-diameter circle with a full-choke barrel. Sixty will strike in the circle with a modified choke and fifty with the improved-cylinder choke. But what if we have a modified barrel and we increase the number of pellets in the shotshell to 150? Then we would have sixty percent of the 150 pellets in the thirty-inch circle, or a total of ninety pellets striking the target. This is more than the seventy pellets with the full choke and the original one hundred pellets.

If we are using #5 shot, a 1⅛-ounce load in the shell will have 191 pellets. Seventy percent would give 133 pellets within the circle with a full choke at forty yards. If we use the modified choke and change to shot size 6 in the same 1⅛-ounce load, there would be 253 pellets in the unfired shotshell. If we get sixty percent of this within the thirty-inch circle at forty yards we would have a total of 151 pellets within the circle. So with the first load we are getting 133 size 5 pellets with the full choke and 151 size 6 pellets with the modified choke. As there is only one-hundredth-inch-diameter difference (0.01), little is lost from a practical standpoint, plus you have eighteen more usable pellets!

This is not a perfect system, but it works and is worth remembering. Even simpler is to use a spreader-loaded shotshell to obtain a less-choke pattern with a full-choke gun. If you are handloading, you can change choke results by simply cutting off the plastic shot protector petals.

An angle blade reamer in the proper size is a must for reworking a shotgun choke. There are several manufacturers.

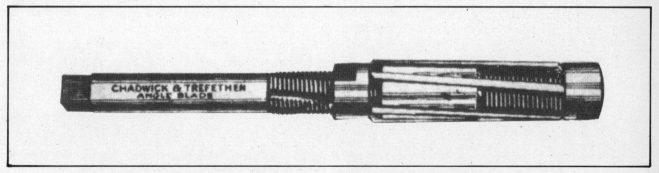

Chapter 16

THE EXTERNAL CHOKE

There Have Been Numerous Variations With Different Degrees Of Success And Acceptance

---

THE IDEA OF some form of mechanical device attached to the exterior of a shotgun barrel to give the shooter an instant choice of choke sans extra barrels is definitely not new. It began virtually with the birth of the self-contained shotshell and I would not be surprised if someone came up with a muzzleloading shotgun with such an external attachment.

The earliest known example was designed and patented by Sylvester H. Roper on April 10, 1866, and marketed through the Roper Repeating Rifle Company of Amherst, Massachusetts, as a component for the Roper repeating shotgun. This consisted of a wide ring that screwed on to the muzzle of the barrel. The idea was that with several rings available you could change the choke from full to quarter choke.

The example I examined in a private collection was with a bore diameter of .740 inch and the one available full-choke ring was in the form of a very abrupt conical-type choke with a diameter at the front of .710 inch, thus giving .030 constriction when screwed on to the barrel end. Without the ring in place there was no choke and the barrel was straight cylinder. If it followed the English system, a

Cutts Compensator, mounted here on a Winchester Model 12, still offers admirable service on many shotguns.

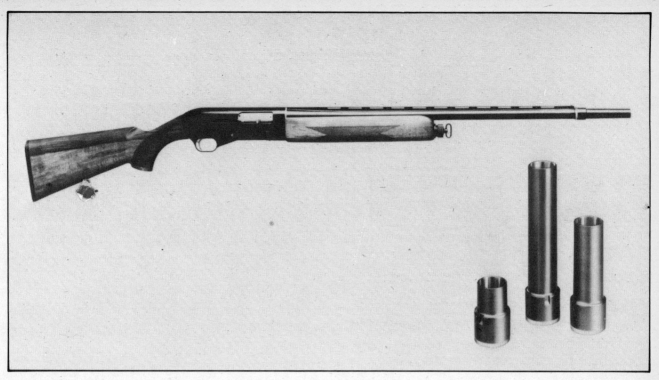

The KFC semiautomatic has been one of those models that featured interchangeable chokes attachable to the muzzle.

complete set of rings would be ¼ choke, ½ choke, ¾ choke and full choke.

Apparently the Roper choke device was the only one on the market for quite a few years. A search of old shotgun catalogs for any mention of a choke device has been unsuccessful, nor does any exist in the large shotgun library I have accumulated.

There is only one such reference to a choke device attached to a shotgun. This is found in Oberfell's & Thompson's classic book, *The Mysteries of Shotgun Patterns* in the form of a not-too-clear statement concerning four side-by-side shotguns now housed in the museum of arms at Liege, Belgium. The museum catalog lists the four guns with the dates 1880 to 1885 and state that they are "equipped with double adjusting concentrators." The one photograph shows each barrel with some form of device externally fitted to muzzle. What it does and how it works are not known.

Probably one reason for lack of engineering development of a choke device is that from around 1880 through World War I the side-by-side shotgun virtually dominated the available market. As the gunner had a choice of two chokes, one per barrel, there was simply not enough demand for such a device to warrant attention. True, there were pumps and even semiauto shotguns around during the period, but they were in a minority. After WWI they gained favor rapidly and eventually assumed their current position.

There are two basic types of external-mounted choke devices with the difference being in the method utilized for the choke action. The first uses a fixed tube to provide choking and, as the tubes are detachable, the shooter sim-ply removes one choke tube and installs another of his choice as circumstances dictate. The second version consists of one unit with a section performing the choke action from open to tight constriction without removing any part or component.

The tube type device is the simplest of the two and has been popular with shooters. The major advantage is that it allows employment of the more efficient, in my opinion, conical-parallel type choke due to the length of the choke tube. The second type has the advantage of offering full choice simply by turning some form of device with one's fingertips. They are predominantly of the simple conical type of choke.

In the early 1920s Colonel Richard M. Cutts of the Marine Corps and his son, Captain (later general) R.M. Cutts, Jr., developed what they called a "compensator" for military application and carried the device to Springfield Armory and Maj. Gen. Julian S. Hatcher. The intent was to utilize the gas that exited the muzzle of a gun to push the barrel down, thereby reducing gun climb and at the same time pushing forward on a series of cuts that in essence "pulled" the barrel forward and compensated partially for recoil.

It was tested at Fort Benning, Georgia, on the '03 Springfield rifle and the Browning Automatic rifle. It did the job well, but the side blast was more than the military cared for and so it turned thumbs down on the device. It is an interesting note that today's military rifles utilize a similar device to great extent. It was adopted, however, for the then new Thompson submachine gun for a 1928 model and a "tommy gun with a cutts" became common in the Roaring Twenties.

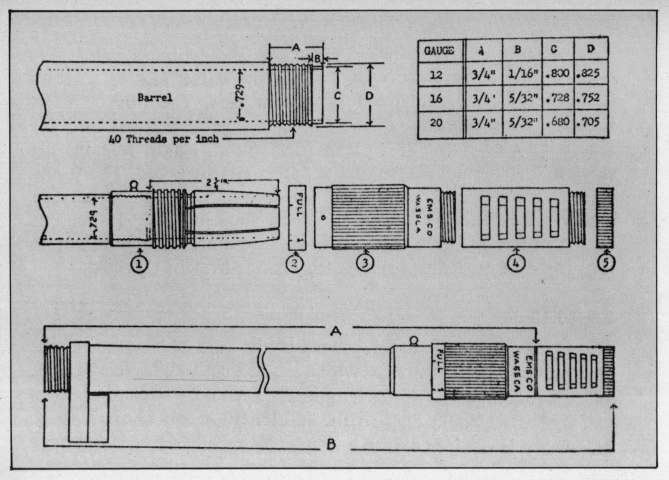

GAUGE	A	B	C	D
12	3/4"	1/16"	.800	.825
16	3/4'	5/32"	.728	.752
20	3/4"	5/32"	.680	.705

The Emsco adjustable choke was one of the earlier models, but it required factory installation on all three gauges.

In 1928 Colonel Cutts and his son interested Lyman with a version of the compensator for shotguns. In essence it was the same as the military version, but with gas vents both top and bottom to exert more forward pull and consequently diminish recoil to a greater extent. A series of choke tubes screwed into the forward end of the recoil chamber.

The Cutts Compensator consists of three basic components. The adapter, as the name implies, adapts the unit to the barrel. This is done by silver soldering it in place to a diameter-mated and machined forward section of the barrel. The recoil chamber screws on to the adapter and is secured by a lock screw on the bottom. The recoil chamber is of sufficiently larger internal diameter than the shotgun bore and accepts the exiting gas. The gas presses against a series of slots, top and bottom, to exert the forward pull which gives about twenty to twenty-five percent recoil reduction. The actual choke tubes screw into the recoil chamber and are locked into position with a wrench. Substitution of choke tubes gives the shooter a variety of constrictions to choose from as field or shooting conditions dictate.

In 1929 Lyman introduced this device in its #17 catalog in 12-gauge with these tubes to choose from: .675 inch, .680, .690, .705, .725 and .740 tube inside diameter. The

.675 and .740 tubes were dropped in 1938 and a .755 tube added. In 1932 two additional gauges were added, 16 and 20. This was the year that Lyman purchased all rights from the two Cuttses. A .410-bore was added in 1938 and the 28-gauge in 1939. Complaints about the weight of the attached unit on the end of the barrel resulted in an aluminum version. Today the Cutts Compensator is available only in 12- and 20-gauge.

For over fifty years it has been a choice of many shooters, but enjoyed most of its popularity in the 1930s due to its availability as a factory installation on various pumps and semiauto barrels. The .755 tube has been called the "spreader" and with the old-style shotshells with the nitro wad and felt wads it really spread the shot. Basically the exiting gas entered the recoil chamber and in addition to providing the recoil-canceling push, exerted rearward pressure on the shot column. The tube, being larger than bore size, offered little resistance to the shot and "spread" it quite rapidly for close-range shooting such as on the skeet field.

The recently touted Russian "Tula choke" is nothing new because the Cutts is similar in basic design. On the opposite end of the choke parade, the Magnum Full choke tubes provided maximum range.

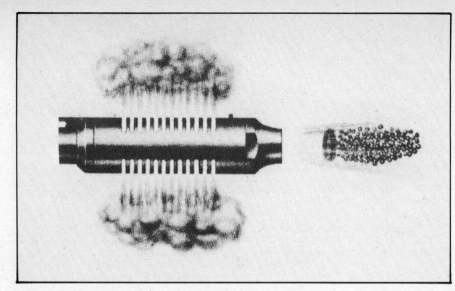

This stop-action photo of the Cutts Compensator, obviously enhanced by an artist, illustrates its workings.

The success of the Cutts Compensator inspired Lyman to develop a choke which is somewhat similar in general appearance, but with several notable differences.

Available in 12- and 20-gauge the Lyman choke, like the Cutts Compensator, uses an adapter to attach the unit to the shotgun barrel and like the Cutts this is silver soldered into position. It also uses a recoil chamber, but with a ring of round holes for the gas exit which makes it not as effective a recoil combatant as the Cutts. The choke tubes, full, modified, upland, then screw on to the exterior of the forward portion of the recoil chamber. As the recoil chamber is threaded internally on the rear to screw on to the adapter and threaded externally for the choke tube to screw into, it offers the shooter a choice of two variations.

First, he can screw the recoil chamber to the adapter and the choke tube to the recoil chamber or he can remove the recoil chamber completely. The thread arrangement allows the choke tube to screw directly on to the adapter. Lyman markets the latter arrangement as the "Economy Choke" and due to the low cost it has been a favorite with shooters and those who simply do not like the recoil chamber arrangement and term such in the South as a "minnow bucket" for its obvious appearance.

The Lyman Choke like the Cutts has enjoyed a long popularity and is still available. In 1980 the Lyman company appointed Walker Arms as a factory authorized installer for both the Cutts and Lyman chokes after the factory withdrew installation service. Both are still available from distributors as well as Walker Arms for individual gunsmithing installation.

In June 1940 Bill Weaver of Weaver Scope Company fame introduced perhaps the simplest of all the externally attached choke-tube devices. It consisted of two components, the chamber and the tubes. There was no separate adapter to solder to the barrel. Instead the chamber was attached via a forty-thread-per-inch arrangement directly to the shotgun barrel. This required factory installation, but was later released to qualified gunsmiths. As the forward end of the barrel was turned and then threaded, this eliminated the weight of the adapter, but in the case of the Weaver choke this mattered little because the whole unit was made from a tough aluminum alloy.

Inside the chamber was a series of circular recesses to trap exiting gases. Like the Lyman Choke, the Weaver used round holes to exit the gas, but these were directly led into the recesses and were a series of holes the length of the chamber body instead of the one circular pattern of the Lyman choke recoil chamber.

The choke tubes screwed directly into the chamber and were available in extra full, full, ¾, ½, ¼ and skeet. I have shot several Weaver Choke-equipped guns and they delivered excellent patterns. The only criticism is that the

The Cyclone choke was a collet-type choke featuring a ventilated sleeve. It was similar to the Poly-Choke.

WEAVER-CHOKE INSTALLATION

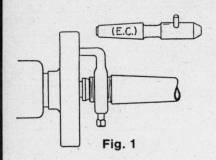

Fig. 1

Installation of Weaver-Choke was complicated. A lathe dog was clamped to the barrel or an extension center (E.C.) was used.

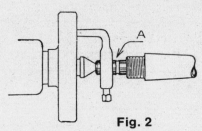

Fig. 2

Lathe dog was placed on a special arbor (A), which pushed in barrel's breech.

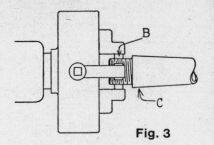

Fig. 3

Breech is held directly in lathe chuck. Small pieces of brass or lead (B) are used to protect barrel. Indicator (C) is used to adjust the chuck properly.

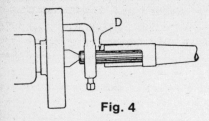

Fig. 4

Special arbor (D) is used for autoloader barrels. One end has slight taper to push into gun chamber.

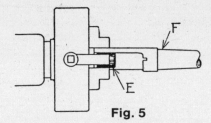

Fig. 5

With autoloader barrel in lathe chuck, short, round plug (E) is laid in the barrel extension. The indicator (F) assures the barrel is running true.

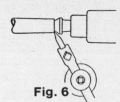

Fig. 6

The end of the barrel is faced perfectly true as it bears against the shoulder of the Weaver-Choke unit.

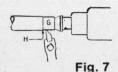

Fig. 7

End of barrel (G) is turned ⅝″ where it'll be threaded. Chase thread to 1/16-inch of the shoulder at (H).

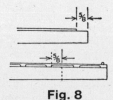

Fig. 8

For installation on ribbed barrel one must remove ⅝″ of the rib. For vent rib, cut next to support.

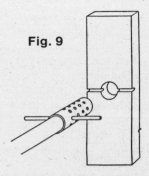

Fig. 9

To screw on vent tube, rod is run through vent holes, and wooden handle used to turn and tighten the tube.

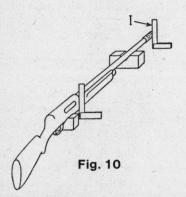

Fig. 10

To install front sight to baffle tube, place gun in V blocks, then use squares to determine right spot.

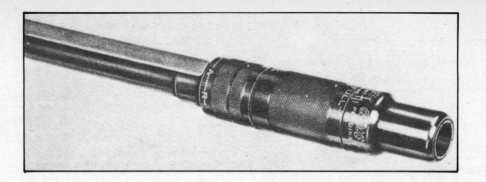

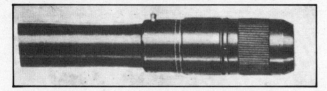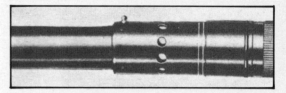

The Jarvis Flex-choke (top) is considered the world's first automatic self-switching shotgun choke device. At lower left is the Lyman choke, while at lower right is the Lyman adjustable choke with its recoil chamber.

black anodized chamber and interchangeable tubes wore to bright aluminum in a short time. One major advantage was weight elimination which resulted in the barrel's giving the same weight distribution instead of being muzzle heavy.

Regrettably, the Weaver Choke is dead due simply, as Weaver puts it, "from lack of sales" and not from any unit lack of quality or efficiency. A shooter with a Weaver Choke attached normally is usually sold on the device and will have no other. I have been told that a company in Texas still manufactures the tubes.

Another tube type device that enjoyed a somewhat brief but full life was the Pachmayr "Power Pac" starting around mid-1950s and lasting through about 1965. While resembling the Cutts Compensator externally, except that the Power Pac had chevron-type gas exit slots, the insides were quite different.

With the Cutts Compensator, the recoil chamber is clear internally with the choke tube screwing into the end and extending forward. The Power Pac tubes screwed into the recoil chamber also, but extended rearward toward the barrel muzzle. The idea was to allow the shot to enter the choke tube, but with the exiting gas escaping out and around the choke tube for the recoil reduction. The placement of the rear end of the choke tube close to the muzzle end supposedly allowed better recoil reduction. Its main problem was clearing accumulated powder residue.

While both factory installed and distributed to selected gunsmiths for installation, the Power Pac with its three tubes — long, medium and short range — was best known for its use on the well-known Sears Roebuck pump shotgun of the period. Most gunsmiths see it in this manner on used shotguns with no seeming end in sight, although it has been discontinued for more than fifteen years.

Another tube-type device introduced in 1961 exited the scene two years later. The Simmons Choke was basically the Lyman Economy choke in a new guise. The choke tube — either full, modified, or improved cylinder — screwed directly to the adapter, which was in turn soldered to the barrel end. The one good change was that the rear end of each tube was knurled for a better grip.

There are probably one or more choke devices of this type, but these were or are the most common encountered. The Cutts Compensator and the Lyman choke are still available and going strong.

There is a slight variation of this type choke device that does not use an adapter, but simply screwed the choke tubes directly on to the barrel via a threaded section of the barrel near the muzzle. This has numerous advantages such as weight and cosmetic appearance. Several companies have used it at one time or another, but only two are relatively well known.

The least of these is the Breda semiauto manufactured in Italy. It was widely distributed some years ago, but is seldom seen today except on the used gun market, although IGI Domino of New York imports a few each year. It came equipped with what was termed "quick choke," this being a barrel around twenty-four inches and three screw-on tubes in improved cylinder, modified or full choke. I test-fired one of these guns for a magazine and, if memory serves me right, the tubes delivered good patterns.

By far the best of this system to come down the pike in quite a few years is the K.F.C. model 250 semiauto with interchangeable choke tubes. No, it does not stand for Kentucky Fried Chicken (and I suspect this joke is getting a bit thin), but rather Kawaguchiya Firearms Company, Ltd. It is an amazing shotgun dead on seven pounds. I became so infatuated with the gun during a test report that I ordered one custom made for me at the factory in Japan.

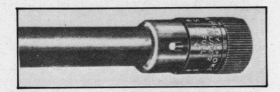

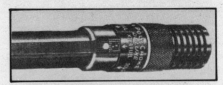

A number of variable chokes have been manufactured in this country over the years, some now obsolete. In the left column (from top) are Herter Vari-choke, the Poly-Choke Super model, the Poly-Choke deluxe version. At right (from top) are Emsco, Poly-Choke vent sleeve version, the same maker's deluxe version and Multy-Choke Dyna-Magic.

There are four chokes, and at first this is confusing. Due to the threads on the barrel being set back about ⅜ inch from the muzzle, it is intended to be used as a cylinder choke sans any tube. Next comes the short quarter-choke tube, a slightly longer half-choke tube and the longest being full choke.

I requested a skeet-1 in the first tube and as tight as possible in the longer tube using #9 shot for the first and #7½ for the latter two at 1200 feet per second (fps) with a 1⅛-ounce load. That extra-tight tube will consistently deliver seventy percent or better at forty-five yards! The choke-tube length is seldom noticed, but was specifically designed that way...short tube for short range, medium for medium and long for long range. One of those little gems of simplicity for the shooter.

While the screw-on choke tube looks simple, it is difficult to manufacture to be completely in centerline with the bore and beyond the average gunsmith's capability or pocketbook in machinery. As to popularity, the president of La Paloma marketing recently told me that his orders for the K.F.C. were seventy-five percent with interchangeable choke tubes.

EXTERNAL ADJUSTABLE CHOKE DEVICE

In the question of who invented what and when, there is no problem in providing a firm answer as to the adjustable choke device for shotguns. What is surprising is that the man responsible is not as well known as he rightfully should be.

It is a story of a man with a good idea and the determination to carry it through when others laughed at his invention. He not only succeeded but also founded a well-known company in the process.

E. Field White in about 1927 or '28 was a skeet and trap shooter who simply wanted a device that would allow him to use his favorite pump shotgun under varying conditions that required different chokes. Being somewhat of a mechanical genius, he designed such a device and made a prototype. On the test field it performed exactly as he had wished. With a background in developing the modern oil burner and major improvements in the field of hydraulics for the automotive business, White thought first of licensing the device. Making his rounds of the gun industry, he encountered the well known N.D.H. (Not Developed Here) mentality and was promptly advised by a series of factory engineers of a thousand and one reasons why the device would not work.

Having somewhat of a stubborn streak, he started a small company in 1929 in Hartford, Connecticut. Using the Latin word for many or multiple, he named the device the Poly-Choke. The device proved so popular that a factory was built to contain the equipment needed for production. White died in 1954, but not before seeing many of the very gun companies that had turned thumbs down on the device offer it as a standard item on their barrels.

In addition to factory installation there are 135 authorized installers scattered over the world. In 1981 they produced and sold the seven millionth Poly-Choke!

What is remarkable is that the current Poly-Choke is improved over the original in some details, but the original concept and design remain unchanged. Over the years several variations have been introduced and discontinued, but the original sells like ice cream on a hot July afternoon year after year.

There are two ways to attach the Poly-Choke to a shotgun barrel. In one the barrel exterior close to the muzzle is machined to a point that it is parallel with the bore line. Then this section is threaded in a lathe. This is called the primary method.

The secondary method is basically the same except that a threaded adapter is soldered to the machined section of the barrel. I have installed Poly-Chokes with both methods, but personally prefer the secondary method. The reason is that threading the barrel end results in barrel-wall thickness being reduced.

The only time I have ever seen one of these devices come loose is when the primary or threading method was used. Soldering an adapter to the machined section of the barrel end results in a thicker wall section and if done correctly is just as accurate as the primary method.

In both methods the choke element is then screwed into place on the end of the barrel. The rear of the element is solid and the front looks somewhat like a set of steel fingers. If pressure is exerted on the tips of the fingers, being spring steel they close. In doing so they form a cone, smaller at the front than at the rear, and become a conical-type choke.

The part of the device that performs this closing pressure is the sleeve. Internally it is also a taper, so in the act of screwing it further on to the element, the taper moves back toward the muzzle and in doing so exerts pressure on the element's steel fingers and closes them slowly. Unscrewing the sleeves results in its internal taper decreasing pressure and as the steel fingers are springs, they return to their normal position and form less of a cone for the choking effect. In order to provide choke settings that will not move, a spring clip goes into the inner surface of the sleeve and locks into the cuts or slits between the steel fingers of the element section. So, by screwing the sleeve inward, a click is reached at every slit and the element's fingers are closed by the sleeve's internal taper. Reverse this and naturally the fingers open for less choking effect.

It is really a simple device in which operation is simplicity itself, yet it provides the shooter with nine separate choke settings. All great designs are simple.

This stop-action photograph was used by Poly-Choke in promotions to illustrate their product in action.

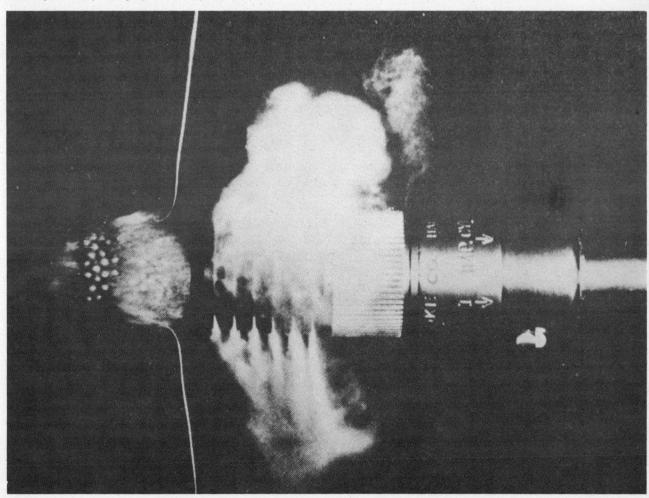

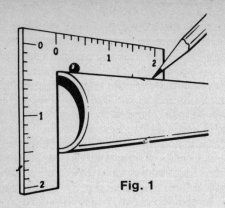

Fig. 1

To install the Multy-Choke, the first step is to run a sight line of 6" on the barrel. All inbuilt choke must be removed either by cutting it off or by use of a reamer.

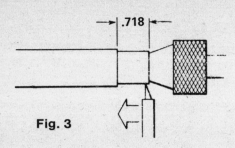

Fig. 2

Chuck
T-Bolt
Machinist Clamp
Live Center
Drive Arbor

For the lathe setup locate the centers, then install the clamp on the chamber end of the barrel; install the T-bolt on the lathe chuck, then use live center in tail stock

.718

Fig. 3

In turning the barrel to clean up a distance of .718, the interior dimensions will not be concentric with the outside dimensions. Latter is turned to .807/.808 inch.

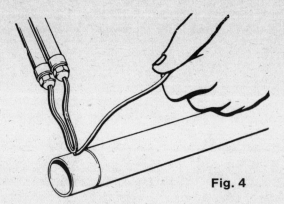

Fig. 4

In soldering the adapter to the barrel, one uses the solder gun to tin the turned portion of the gun barrel.

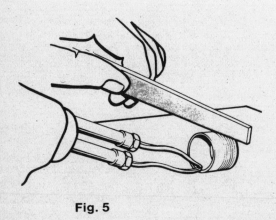

Fig. 5

Using the soldering gun again, the interior dimension of the adapter is soldered, turning it with a file. The file serves as protection against generated heat.

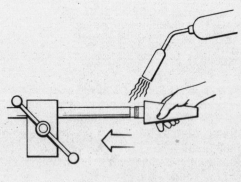

Fig. 6

To start the adapter onto the barrel, apply heat with propane torch to flow solder. Adapter is pushed fully onto turned portion using wooden stick or hammer handle.

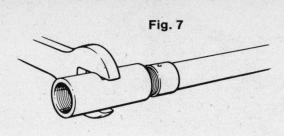

Fig. 7

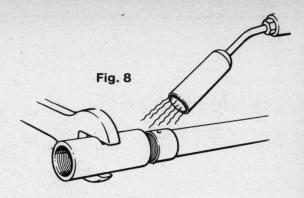

Fig. 8

After the adapter is in place, clean, spread Loctite on the threads; start choke element on adapter by hand, then use installation tool to tighten till choke bottoms.

With installation tool in place, reheat the body until solder flows, rotate until the sight hole is centered on top. Then allow the unit to cool before continuing.

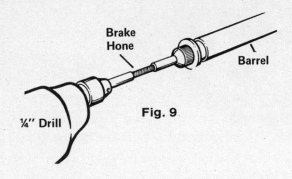

Brake Hone

Barrel

¼" Drill

Fig. 9

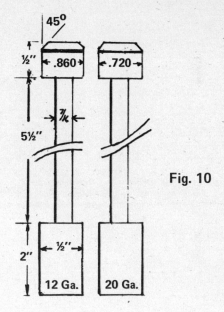

Fig. 10

Once the installation has cooled completely, lap and polish. A brake cylinder hone, which is available at almost any automotive supply store is ideal for this. Final step is to install the front bead sight. (Right) Using the dimensions shown, it is a simple task for a gunsmith to make his own drive arbors for this work.

What few shooters know is that the internal section of the Poly-Choke element is a close match to the actual bore dimension. The 12-gauge element, for example, is available in bore size .716 to .746 inch, the 16-gauge from .658 to .588 inch, and the 20-gauge from .608 to .632 inch. Thus, with the correct element and internal dimension to match the bore's internal dimension, choke construction can be accurately controlled. Remember that choke constriction is the choke's internal diameter subtracted from the bore's internal diameter. When you change the bore's internal diameter you must change the choke's internal diameter to achieve the desired same choke constriction specification.

Availability of Poly-Chokes is strictly limited to the factory or an authorized installer because special tooling is required. Do they work? Yes, and this is from over twenty years of both installing them and shooting them.

They do suffer from one thing, which is the fault of the shooter, not the choke device. That is, with any choke, just because it says *full* does not mean full choke with every size of shot and every shotshell. Any choke, or any setting will work perfectly with one size shot and one shotshell. Another shotshell or shot size will require a different choke or choke setting. The trick is to find the setting that will deliver the desired choke effect with a chosen shot size or shotshell.

The last Poly-Choke I used to any degree required the full setting for #9 and #8 shot, but it was necessary to go back to improved modified settings to get a full choke effect with shot size #7½ and back to modified to get the same choke effect with #6 shot. This is no different from an inbuilt choke on any barrel. While I shot shells loaded for 1200 fps with 1⅛-ounce shot, any variation would have

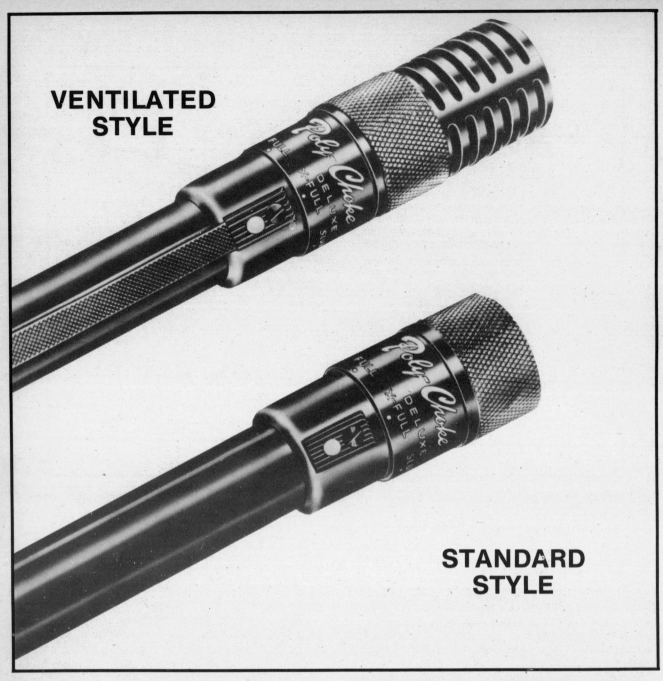

VENTILATED STYLE

STANDARD STYLE

Poly-Choke makes an external adjustable choke in several configurations, but standard and vent styles prevail.

given different results. The Poly-Choke's nine different choke settings allow complete control with any shot size or shotshell. They do not advertise this, probably because the general public would not understand it, but a knowledgeable gunsmith or shooter can take full advantage of those nine settings!

About the time that the Poly-Choke patents expired, around the mid-1950s, there was a rash of similar devices on the market. In 1959 there were no less than eight variable-choke-device manufacturers turning out a multitude of chokes of various names to say nothing of gun

manufacturers turning out their versions under their names or having them made outside of the factory. Usually they were just copies of the basic Poly-Choke design with a few exceptions. They all failed, but did do one positive thing in the years that they were in business: Their combined advertising convinced the shooting public of the advantages of the adjustable or variable choke device. As a result, the concept is more popular than ever.

One of the lookalikes marketed touted the fact that it could be installed by anyone, thus eliminating the gunsmith. Attachment was via the use of the then-new epoxy

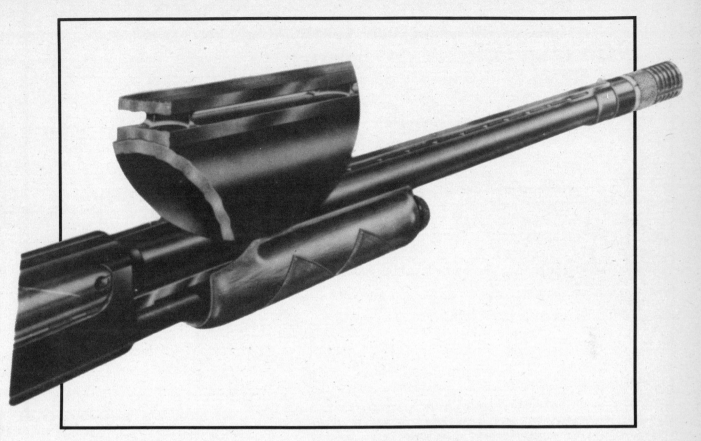

Poly-Choke has gone to a great deal of work to simplify installation of their own vent rib with adjustable choke.

glue. Obviously the designer did not do much testing for epoxy will not withstand heat or expansion and contraction of metal such as in a gun barrel end.

At a local informal skeet shoot, one character who had purchased one of these same choke devices let it be known to all that he had saved the installation cost.

Everything went fine at stations 1, 2, and 3 with a clean broken bird. At station 4 with all of us on the sidelines, the individual fired off a round at the low-house exiting clay bird. Like in slow motion, we watched as the choke device blew off the muzzle of his barrel and sailed outward and, surprisingly, shattered the clay target. One unknown wit shouted, "Hey, that was a neat trick. Let's see you do it again on the next bird!"

One of the lookalikes that did offer something new was the "automatic choke." The idea was that the device functioned normally while in manual setting offering various preselected chokes. Then, when the automatic feature was engaged through some device, the gun fired an open choke, then a tighter choke on the second and even on the third shot without any manual setting between shots.

The most complex of these was the Jarvis Choke of Wichita, Kansas, called the Flex-Choke. This one would start with an improved cylinder on the first shot, switch automatically to a modified choke on the second shot, then automatically to a full on the third shot. It worked as advertised, but fell into disfavor due to its roughly six-inch length and added weight on the end of the barrel.

Next in popularity was the Ajustomatic made by the Hartford Gun Choke Company. This was similar to the Jarvis in function. Even Poly-Choke entered the field with the Poly-Matic, although it was on a slightly different principle and offered a single tighter choke setting for the second shot. Alas, by 1969 the choke crowd had thinned out and only the old standby standards were left. This year also saw the demise of the automatic chokes.

The automatic-type choke was actually quite simple. It had the element and sleeve as previously described in the Poly-Choke. In addition, the rear of the element, which contains the steel fingers, was tapered down toward the muzzle of the gun. In other words, its forward taper engaged the taper of the sleeve for normal choke selection manually. The rear taper of the element operated the automatic feature. In a simple explanation, there was also a third component in the form of a ring. As the ring moved forward, it compressed the rear taper of the element and thus

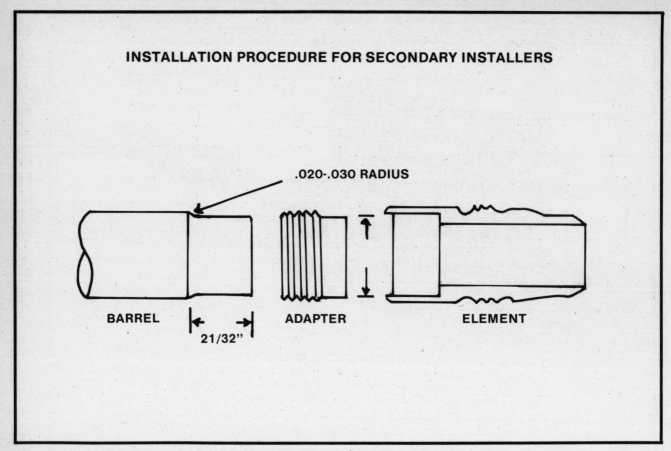

INSTALLATION PROCEDURE FOR SECONDARY INSTALLERS

.020-.030 RADIUS

BARREL

21/32"

ADAPTER

ELEMENT

The installation procedures for the Poly-Choke are simple, if one follows directions, makes precise measurements.

caused the steel fingers to close, thereby increasing choke constriction. The ring was put in motion by the gas from the shotshell as it exited both via the muzzle and through a vent. The first shot went out the choke at the open setting. The gas, following behind, pushed the ring forward and in doing so closed the steel fingers via the rear taper on the element. Now exit the shot from the second shell. Then the gas following again pushed the ring even farther forward setting the choke tighter for the final and third shot. When this was completed, the ring was moved back to its starting point manually for a repeat of the sequence. The device provided a method of locking the ring and allowing the manual setting for each shot also as desired.

The basic idea was that the first shot was at birds at close range, then there was more choke for more range and even more for the third shot. A problem arose if the bird was coming toward you. No one ever figured out a way to reverse the system from full to modified to improved cylinder nor a way to set up the device as game and circumstances of coming in or going out dictated.

The Poly Matic utilized a sliding sleeve to perform the tightening of the choke for a second shot minus the normal steel-finger-type choke system. The idea was that the sleeve, being close to the muzzle, offered an open choke. Then as gas pressure pushed it forward, the choking effect was a bit

tighter for the second shot. It failed to catch the public eye as did the Poly-Streak and Poly-Skeet which went the way of the carrier pigeon.

Lyman climbed aboard the adjustable choke bandwagon about the same time as the others. Their version simply allowed an adjustable choke device to be installed instead of their usual single fixed-choke tube. Both the Cutts Compensator and The Lyman Choke adjustable devices are still on the market. In essence they work identically to the Poly-Choke system, but offer a continuous choke adjustment up or down in constriction. Those who like them swear by them. Those who do not like them are vocal in condemnation with no middle ground. I have used both and have found them, in my opinion, to be devices that will deliver as stated. They have never enjoyed the popularity of the Poly-Choke, probably because they came on the scene so late in the ball game.

Several years ago the Poly-Choke Company selected a couple of distributors,— Brownell's and Walker Arms — to handle a version of its choke called the Multy-Choke without the requirement of the authorized installer arrangement. They are available to anyone, gunsmith or individual, and come with a set of instructions for installation that is within the capabilities of any good gunsmith or machinist.

The Multy-Choke functions identically to the Poly-

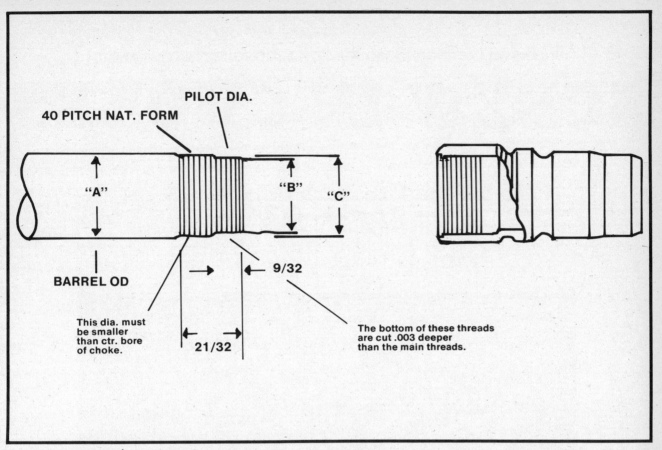

In the drawing above, A indicates the outside diameter of the barrel; B indicates the pilot; C is thread diameter. Choke counterbore may be opened up for oversized barrel outside diameter. Upper right is completed assembly.

Choke in operation, with adapter, element with steel fingers and the sleeve. In fact it is in reality the original Poly-Choke with settings of cylinder, improved-cylinder, modified and full choke. The current Poly-Choke has a selection of nine settings, the Multy-Choke is a four-choke selection. This is the major difference between the two.

Its main advantage is a lower price and installation by anyone with only one special installation tool suggested, although it can actually be installed without the special tool with reasonable care on the part of the installer. It has proven quite popular by its simplicity and price.

All the external choke devices offer numerous advantages to the shotgunner, for with them he can virtually change the choke of his barrel at will either by the substitution of another choke tube or by twisting a sleeve in the case of the variable or adjustable choke. Most of the bad publicity of being a "knot on the end of the barrel" is due to using such a device with a plain barrel. In this case it is like an ugly wife — they look better as time goes by. You get used to the appearance. It is a different tune with a ventilated rib barrel and with such a choke, if installed correctly, the shooter simply does not see the device because his eye is concentrating on the rib leading out to the shotgun sight bead as the ultimate visual target.

The adjustable or variable choke device such as the Poly-Choke or the Multy-Choke requires only trial and error with any shot size or shotshell loading to arrive at a setting that will give the best desired pattern results — be it close or far in range. Simply try different sleeve settings with the preselected shot size and shell loading and let the pattern results be the deciding factor.

With fixed-tube-type chokes there is also a way to arrive at a desired pattern result, yet oddly enough it simply never occurs to anyone! Just as you would ream or hone or both on an inbuilt-type choke to arrive at the desired results, do the identical thing with a choke tube. Reduce its internal diameter and this will reduce the amount of choke constriction, thereby "opening up" the choke. Just go slow and remove a wee bit of metal at a time, then test pattern and repeat until you have a pattern that meets your approval.

If you have access to a lathe, you don't even need a reamer. Just chuck the tube in a four-jaw chuck, index on the choke tube, and use a boring bar to remove a thin strip of metal from the internal diameter. Go out to the range for test shooting, then back to the lathe, without changing set up, for more metal removal. Why this is not done more by gunsmiths has been a mystery to me as I have used it for quite a few years to "custom choke" a tube.

Chapter 17

SCREW-IN CHOKES

The Several Variations Bring Us Closer To The All-Around Shotgun!

Ralph Walker ponders his Winchester Model 101 equipped with the screw-in Winchoke. He found interchangeable feature ideal during this dove hunt.

THE SCREW-IN CHOKE, in my opinion, is the wave of the future. It offers several advantages over any other system in the quest to provide one all-purpose shotgun with various chokes to meet changing target and field conditions.

First, if correctly installed, the screw-in choke tubes are positioned directly against the ending of the bore, thus eliminating any gap that forces the shot charge to "jump" across and in the process deform shot pellets. Deformed pellets, as has been pointed out numerous times, are the root cause of pattern percent decrease. The loss of pellets outside of the working thirty-inch circle of the pattern, at

any range and any choke, simply does not aid in the ultimate goal and they are lost for all practical purposes. The seating of the choke tube against the face of the bore does more to prevent this than any other device to my knowledge.

The correct positioning of the choke tube also allows the shot charge to exit the bore and enter the forcing cone of the choke in an orderly manner. This does more for the ultimate choke effect than many people realize and is quite easily proven. If the choke tube is installed correctly, there is one key factor that has equal effect on pattern performance: If the centerline of the choke tube closely

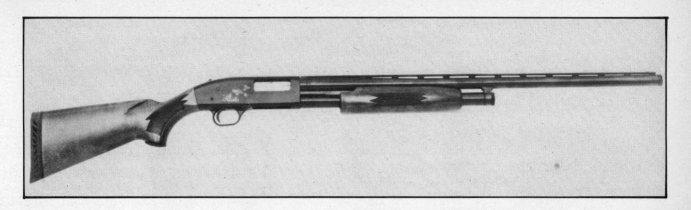

Above: Mossberg Model 500 equipped with the maker's AccuChoke. (Right) Tubes were included with a spanner wrench for installation or removal. Device was introduced in 12-, 20-ga.

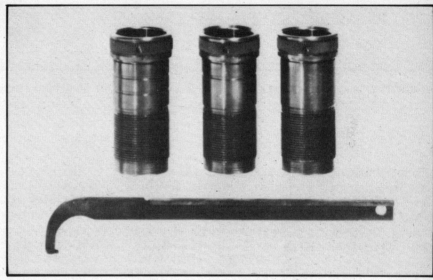

matches the centerline of the bore it is as though the choke were inbuilt and part of the barrel.

With most choke devices, the choke centerline is simply not aligned with the centerline of the bore and you loose choke efficiency and deform individual shot pellets. If at the same time the shooter can exchange one choke tube of one constriction with another selection, it is the closest thing possible to installing another separate barrel with its inbuilt choke.

With three or more choke tubes of varying constriction, you have the same ability as carrying three or more complete barrel units around — each with its own inbuilt choke. For the shooter this is a great advantage because such a load of extra barrels is simply not practical. The extra choke tubes are. If the shooter has the ability to change the choke of his barrel prior to leaving for the field, he or she has the same advantage as access to several barrels.

What is of equal importance, especially with rising costs, is that he only has to purchase one barrel with his choice of shotgun. In reality, the cost of a barrel with the screw-in choke feature and one without is a mere fraction of difference in the total gun cost. Price of individual choke tubes vary with each manufacturer but are generally around $12

to $15 which is a lot less than the cost of an extra barrel, regardless of manufacturer!

Steel shot has been a constant worry as to wear on the choke of a shotgun barrel. While this is still being debated, the fact remains that with the screw-in choke tube, even if a choke becomes worn, it is easily replaced with another screw-in tube. The same solution is always available for the shooter who, after using the newly purchased shotgun, decides that he wants another type of choke. Out with the tube, in with another selection.

The twice-barrel shooter, such as an over/under shotgun, has always had the advantage of his instant choice of two separate chokes to meet conditions. If the gun is an over/under and also equipped with the screw-in choke tube system, his advantages are virtually unlimited in choke constriction choices. For instance, he can install a full choke in each barrel for consistent long-range shooting. In a few seconds he can change to two modified tubes or two improved cylinder tubes for upland game shooting. If he decides to mix them he can have a full and modified choke in place, a full and improved cylinder or modified and improved cylinder. With other than these tubes, such as improved modified, cylinder, extra full, skeet-1, skeet-2, et cetera, the choice selection is virtually unlimited.

Weatherby also has introduced choke tubes which they call the Multi-choke in some models including Model 92 pump.

Until Winchester introduced choke tubes in 1982 for their Model 23, there were no screw-in choke tubes for a side-by-side shotgun. There certainly is no reason similar tubes will not make their appearance for competing models in due course. There are two manufacturers offering an over/under with the system, the Winchester Model 101 and the Lanber, both being in the usual over/under field gun price range. There are a couple of others available such as the Perazzi and the beautiful stainless steel Swedish Caprinus, but both carry a healthy price tag simply beyond the average shooter's wallet.

To the best of my knowledge, Winchester originated the screw-in choke tube system with its Model 59 semiautomatic in 1959. This was a lightweight version of its Model 50 semiautomatic which utilized the floating chamber system with the Model 50 having a steel receiver and sans anything but a built-in choke. The Model 59 had an aluminum receiver and also the floating chamber system of operation.

What was different was the lightweight barrel. In essence this was a steel tube with layers of fiberglass wound around it, not unlike a modern fishing rod with a steel tube liner. To provide a choke system for the WinLite barrel, Winchester came up with a screw-in choke tube that was detachable. The choke tube simply screwed into an enlarged portion of the barrel's steel liner. By inserting different choke tubes the new Model 59 owner in essence had three choke selections instead of three separate barrels.

The Model 59 with its interchangeable Versalite tubes was discontinued in 1965 to make way for the new Winchester semiautomatic shotgun, the Model 1400. The 1200 pump, which used many of the same parts as the 1400, was introduced about the same time. Both of the new models were with the standard inbuilt choke system.

This was changed in 1970 when Winchester offered both the semiauto Model 1400 and the pump Model 1200 with a redesigned version of the old Model 59 Versalite screw-in choke tubes. The new WinChoke tubes were designed to eliminate some minor problems with the older tubes and in the process the ventilated section of the Versalite tube that supposedly reduced recoil was eliminated. The WinChoke tubes extended roughly one-quarter inch past the muzzle of the barrel and were for all practical purposes invisible to the shooter.

The WinChoke required a few years for shooters to fully realize the advantages it offered, but slowly the acceptance grew and the demand increased rapidly. The redesigned Model 1400 Mark II semiauto also sported the option of the WinChoke. It was offered also in the 1500 XTR, a dressed-up version of the 1400. It was the same story with the dressed-up version of the pump 1200, the 1300 XTR. In 1981 Winchester offered the WinChoke system for its Model 101 over/under and its variations and it became an overnight success story winning the design award of 1981 from A.F.I.

One of the success stories in shotguns has been the Mossberg pump Model 500 and its many variations. The firm virtually built an empire on this one gun with little left undone in choice of available models for the consumer. In 1978 the company wisely added the screw-in choke system on the Model 500 following the established lead of Winchester. Its Accu-Choke is totally interchangeable with the WinChoke tubes; one time a manufacturer thought of the shooter and did not bring out a version of an established design that was different only to please corporate pride!

In 1982 Smith & Wesson followed the path and offered its Model 1000 gas-operated semiauto and also the look-

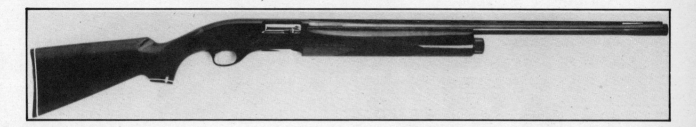

Smith & Wesson also has seen the wisdom of choke tubes and has incorporated them in their Model 1000 autoloader and in the Model 3000 pump action. The interchangeable tubes adapt the gun to different challenges in the field.

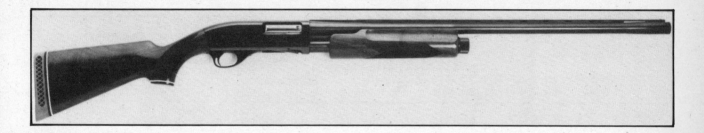

alike Model 3000 pump with the same standard screw-in choke tubes termed the MultiChoke. Difference of tubes is name only as they also will interchange with the WinChoke and Accu-Choke. In late 1982 Weatherby offered the screw-in choke system, also called MultiChoke, on its semiautomatic Model 82 in different variations. There is no difference in their tubes and the system remains interchangeable.

There is little doubt that other shotgun manufacturers have not been asleep and are aware of the increased demand and acceptance of the screw-in choke system among the consumers. There is little doubt that they will join the ranks shortly. One can only hope that they follow the lead of the current manufacturers who adopted the established standard choke tubes Winchester designed twelve years ago.

This covers the new guns and the potential growth on the available market. What about the zillion-odd shotguns that are out there among hill and dale without the screw-in choke tube system?

Stan Baker, one of the best shotgun gunsmiths in the country, has been modifying barrels to accept both his own produced tubes and those of others for several years. All his tools are of his design and every barrel he turns out is precision workmanship. He utilized the "swelled barrel" system which, while not cheap, lacks nothing in quality. If any one gunsmith is to be credited with installing the screw-in choke tube system on barrels not originally equipped, I nominate Baker for the honor.

Jess Briley is best known for his insert barrels that are well known to anyone in the skeet game. In the last few years he has been installing a screw-in choke tube system using tubes of his design. Unlike the WinChoke system tubes, his are very thin with square threads and much longer.

Most important is that he removes existing chokes and then machines the barrel bore to accept his screw-in tubes without changing the exterior of the barrel near the muzzle. This system, in a double-barreled gun, requires extremely precision machining because there is no room to "swell" the muzzles of the barrels. Even in a single-barreled gun, the identical system is utilized. Every job that I have seen can be best described in two words — top quality. His tubes, being of stainless steel and internally of his own design, deliver beautiful patterns!

Most screw-in choke tube gun manufacturers use a barrel in which the forward few inches are of greater diameter than the following rear of the barrel to provide room for the screw-in choke tubes. When done correctly and with precision, it is unnoticed by the shooter. Existing shotgun barrels without the system are simply too small in exterior diameter to allow the forward end of the barrel to be reamed and threaded to accept the choke tube. To do so would end with a barrel much too thin for safety reasons. There are exceptions, of course, such as when a barrel is cut off and the remaining barrel end is of sufficient wall thickness to accommodate reaming and threading. Generally, the wall is just too thin.

Two systems to eliminate the problem have been developed by gunsmiths and are marketed by B-Square. One is to insert a hardened steel plug into the muzzle of the barrel with the choked section being removed. As the plug is pushed or pulled inward toward the muzzle, it cold swages

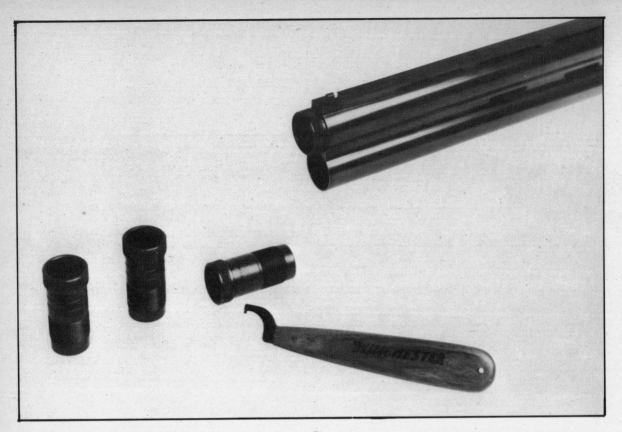

Winchester introduced the Winchoke interchangeable choke system in the pigeon grade trap gun in 1980. The gun comes with four tubes — modified, improved-modified, full and extra full — plus spanner wrench.

the barrel end to a larger diameter. The wall thickness is reduced slightly in the process, but not to a degree to make final wall thickness unsafe.

Unfortunately most barrels do not have the same wall thickness around their circumference. That is, one side will be thick and the other thinner. The steel plug follows the path of least resistance as it is pushed or pulled into the barrel. The result is that the "swell" is more toward the thinner wall and consequently off the bore centerline. Often this results in a split or a wall thinner than safety dic-

tates. If the gunsmith proceeds to ream and thread the off-center "swell" the end result is a choke out of alignment with the bore centerline.

There have been attempts to ream the existing choke out, using the bore centerline to guide the operation with a bushing following the centerline. This is an expensive operation and does not totally eliminate the problem. Other attempts have been made to hot forge the "swell" by heating the barrel end prior to inserting the steel plug. This

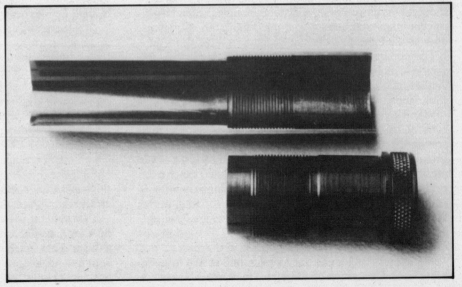

This cut-away photo shows how S&W Multi-choke is mated to barrel. The wall thickness of barrel is increased to accommodate choke tube. Mating of barrel and tube bores eliminates the shoulder where residue can build up.

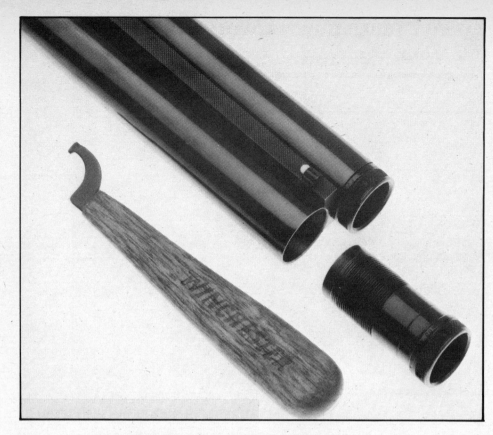

The latest Winchester shotgun to have the WinChoke device incorporated is the Model 23 side-by-side double gun.

helps but again does not eliminate the primary problem, plus it creates the need for rebluing the barrel due to discoloration from the heat.

The second method, and in my opinion far superior, is to machine the forward end of the barrel using the bore centerline as an index. This assures that the machined section near the muzzle is exactly parallel with the bore thus eliminating the problem of uneven barrel wall thickness. In the process of machining more metal is removed from the thick side, little from the thin side, which equals the exterior all around its circumference in thickness.

Next an adapter is soldered onto the machined section of the barrel. The adapter is reamed and threaded to accept the screw-in choke tubes. This eliminates the uneven wall thickness, assures centerline of bore and choke alignment and most importantly the safety factor of wall thickness is not compromised. The end result appearance, if done correctly, is no more than a "swollen barrel end" and even on a non-rib barrel almost unseen by the shooter. Pattern performance wise, it is equal to a factory barrel manufactured with the screw-in choke tube system.

While there is nothing new about an adapter system solving the problem of barrels without the system of screw-in choke tubes, the quality of steel in the adapters available plus consistent quality of manufacture has left much to be desired. Those gunsmiths specializing in this type work invariably machine their own adapters from an old barrel section or other steel which jacks up the price to the consumer due to labor/machine time involved. The gunsmiths of my own company used this method for years.

Recently I developed an adapter manufactured from the best steel available which translates into as small a profile as possible. It is precision manufactured to close tolerance. In addition, I designed a screw-in choke tube of the standard size that is completely different internally. They are reamed to within .002 inch final dimensions. The last .002 inch is then diamond honed to close tolerance final specifications. This results in an extremely smooth surface.

Additionally, the design is of the conical-parallel type choke, not conical only. This results in a superior pattern regardless of degree of choke constriction. The length of the parallel section and the conical section is the result of numerous and lengthy testing both by myself and others. Finally the constriction selection is all the way from wide-open no-choke straight cylinder to a very tight maximum full which is tighter than the full and extra-full constriction offering.

The installation tool assures that the choke tube is backed smack up against the end of the bore of the barrel with a .002-inch clearance between the end of the adapter and the choke tube rear shoulder to keep this snug fit. The tool also assures centerline of bore, adapter and the choke tubes are within .001-inch alignment. It is a system I feel is the final solution for the barrels originally made without the screw-in choke tube system.

Factory installation is available from Walker Arms, Highway 80 West, R-2 B-73, Selma, AL 36701. In addition, the adapter, installation tool and the choke tubes will be made available to any gunsmith from two sources: Walker Arms and Brownell's Inc., Montezuma, IA 50171. Indidivual choke tubes are available to consumers from both companies.

Now It's Possible To Install Interchangeable Tubes In Your Standard Shotgun

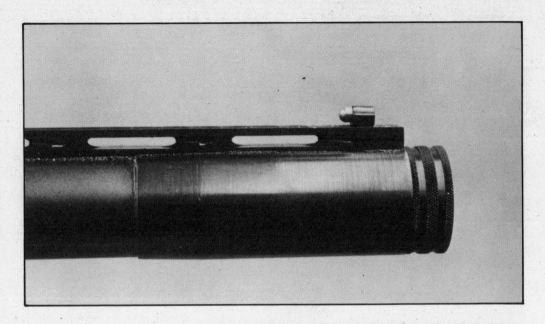

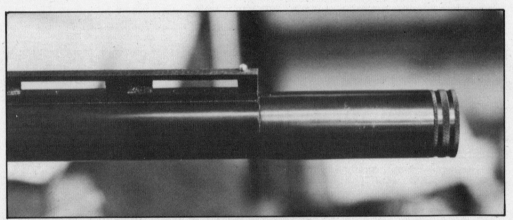

The adaptor unit for the WalkerChoke can be installed in several different ways. At top, the barrel has been shortened, the adaptor added and the vent rib soldered to it. In lower photo, cylinder-bore gun has had this adaptor simply added to the properly prepared barrel end.

WINCHESTER PIONEERED the modern screw-in choke tube system with their Model 59 WinLite barrel. Based on the experience gained, they then developed the current, well known WinChoke. This was first used in their Model 1200 and 1400 shotguns and in several variations of these models. They later incorporated the screw-in WinChoke into their M-101 over/under shotgun and its variations.

Mossberg began manufacturing a version of their Series 500 shotguns with the AccuChoke. Smith & Wesson also adopted the same system for their shotguns under the name MultiChoke. Weatherby has also adopted the same system. Various European manufacturers such as Krieghoff, Perazzi and Lanber utilize this system. Several custom gunmakers such as Baker and Ljutic also utilize the screw-in choke tube system. There is no question as to its wide acceptance and approval by the shooting public. There is also no question that more manufacturers will adopt the system on their shotguns in the future.

All of this has created a market for a screw-in choke tube system to be installed in shotgun barrels made without the system. There have been numerous attempts to achieve this in the past. Except for a few custom shotgun barrel-

With the adaptor properly installed, WalkerChoke tube is easily screwed into the adaptor as the first step. (Lower photo) Tools used in installation are simple, compact.

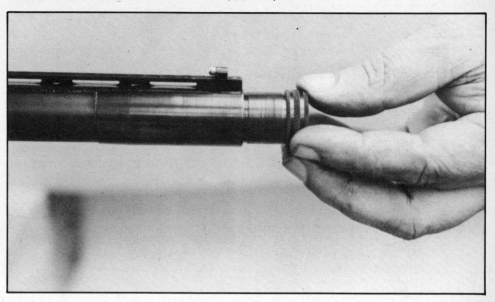

makers, the market has been beyond the average gunsmith in tooling cost and in the complicated technique of correct installation.

The WalkerChoke is not a new system; rather it is a refinement of a time- and field-proven existing system. It was specifically engineered not to be different just for difference's sake, but to be as compatible as possible for maximum versatility and interchangeability.

The WalkerChoke allows the gunowner to quickly change the choke in his shotgun barrel to match changing field or target conditions. Only finger pressure is required for quick installation or removal. The wrench should only be used for removing the tube. It should not be used to install a tube! If a WalkerChoke will not screw into the adaptor easily and without pressure, the threads are clogged with residue and should be cleaned. The adaptor, once fitted, will automatically position the rear of our tubes to index correctly against the face of the bore. To assure this there is a .002-inch clearance between the front of the adaptor and the rear shoulder of the choke tube. This feature totally eliminates any gap between the rear of the tube and the bore. This zero tolerance eliminates the accumulation of lead, plastic and other residue that can jam some choke tubes in place, making removal extremely difficult.

With the barrel held firmly in a vise, it is marked with a pipe cutter at the proper point for the cut-off.

The shot column does not have to "jump" a gap between bore and choke which occurs in some systems. This prevents shot pellet deformation.

These choke tubes, while of the same exterior dimensions as other chokes for the purpose of interchangeability, are completely different internally. Made from quality steel, the design assures maximum pattern efficiency. The choke forcing cone is .800 inch in length for channeling the shot from bore to choke. The tube's choke section is one inch in length and is based on extensive test results. This is the conical-parallel choke design found in quality shotgun barrels. It is not a conical choke tube without a parallel section.

The tubes are bored and reamed initially to within .002 inch of their final dimension. The last .002 inch then is precision diamond-honed for accuracy and smoothness.

The wide range of constriction selection for each gauge in the Walker Choke tubes allows complete pattern control at any known shotgun range to meet changing target requirements. This also allows the same amount of precise control in barrels with a bore diameter above or below standard dimension.

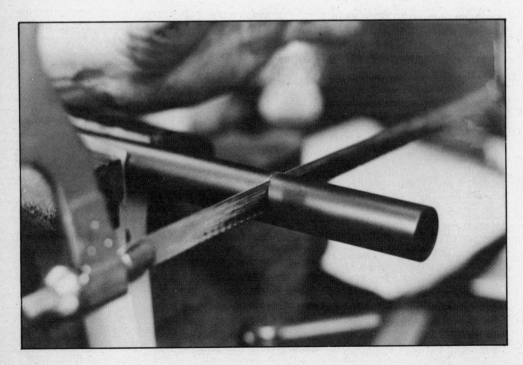

Using the line made with pipe cutter, a hacksaw is used to cut off gun barrel.

With the end of the barrel removed with the hacksaw, it now is necessary to true muzzle end with a lathe.

The simple installation tool is used to align both adaptor and choke tube to within .001 inch tolerance with the shotgun bore. That is, the adaptor centerline and tube centerline will be within .001 inch parallel with the bore centerline.

If used correctly, the installation tool will automatically space the necessary clearance between the forward end of the adaptor and the rear shoulder of the WalkerChoke tube. This installation tool prevents any gap between the rear of the choke tube and bore of the barrel.

The same degree of installation accuracy is achieved in various nonstandard bore diameters on each gauge via the interchangeable bore guide bushing supplied as a component of the installation tool.

It is assumed that the installer will have access to a good accurate lathe and the usual common gunsmith tools. Special tools are as follows:

1. WalkerChoke installation tool to match gauge available in 20-, 16-, 12-, 10-gauge).

2. Poly Bore micrometer available from Walker Arms, Brownell's choke dial caliper, or Brownell's choke comparison caliper. An inside micrometer or common dial caliper also may be used, once the choke section of barrel is removed, to secure the correct bore diameter specification.

3. Propane torch. I recommend the Bernzomatic, but any similar unit can be utilized.

4. A good solder and matching flux such as Brownell's #44.

5. Equipment to install the front sight bead.

6. A hacksaw with fine-tooth blade.

7. A secure bench vise with padded jaws to avoid marring the barrel.

The overall barrel length of a shotgun is measured from a closed breech or bolt to the edge of the barrel muzzle. This includes the chamber. We recommend twenty-six inches for a general-purpose barrel.

The section of the adaptor that will extend past the barrel muzzle to the adaptor's forward edge is 1.513 inches in length. The exposed knurled end of the WalkerChoke tube is .317 inch in length. This gives a combined length of 1.83 inches. For example, if a twenty-six-inch overall barrel length is desired, then the final overall length of the barrel prior to installation would be twenty-six inches, less 1.83 inch, or 24.17 inches total overall length.

To allow for final truing of the muzzle end of the barrel, initially cut the barrel with a hacksaw at 1.5 inches less than the desired overall length. Then true the barrel end with lathe or file to exactly 1.83 inches less than finished overall length.

With vent-rib barrels, the position of the rib must be taken into consideration. The rib must always terminate on a rib support post. Otherwise a twig or similar obstruction will catch under the protruding rib end and bend or tear the rib.

A compromise must, therefore, be made in the overall barrel length. A barrel section .750 inch in length must extend past the chosen rib support post. This .750-inch section will be later machined to accept the rear inside diameter of the adaptor. It is a good idea to make the initial hacksaw cut .800 inch past the chosen rib support post. This will then allow .050 inch for final truing of the muzzle end.

It is important that the hacksaw cut not be at any angle! A simple method to prevent this is to use a common pipe tubing cutter to lightly score the barrel around its diameter, then cut directly on the scored line.

A four-jaw chuck holding the chamber end of the barrel and tailstock center holding the muzzle end can be used to true the muzzle and also to turn the adaptor section on the barrel. Adjust chuck jaws and the tailstock as necessary to obtain a true-running barrel. Remember, you will be using the barrel bore centerline as the index, not the exterior of the barrel which is often not parallel with the bore centerline.

The Brownell Expanding Bore Mandrel, size ½ to 11/16 inch, will handle 20-, 16-, 12-, 10-gauge barrels. This tool securely grips the inside wall of the bore of the barrel. The extended end of the tool engages the tailstock live center. The muzzle end of the barrel is thus fully exposed for truing and also for machining the adaptor section on the

barrel's exterior or a live center utilized after truing.

Another method is to grind away one-third of the forward end of a dead center. This recess section will allow space for the lathe tool bit to true the barrel muzzle. This altered center also may be utilized to hold the muzzle end while the adaptor section is being machined.

With the muzzle true, scribe a line across the barrel exactly .750 inch from the muzzle end. The scribe line will match the length to be machined to accept the adaptor. With a clean-cutting lathe tool, turn the barrel end section to accept the adaptor rear inside diameter. This section of an adaptor is made in several sizes so as a final check carefully measure its inside diameter.

To provide clearance for the solder, machine this section of the barrel .002 inch undersized. For example, using an adaptor with .810-inch inside diameter at its rear, the barrel would be machined to .808-inch outside diameter.

Remember that final centerline alignment is determined by the installation tool's bore guide bushing outside diameter in relation to the barrel bore inside diameter. This provides a .001-inch centerline tolerance alignment. Consequently, this outside turned section on the barrel is of

Once the muzzle has been trued, the barrel then must be machined to accept the adaptor.

The machined section of the barrel is tinned; a pencil is used to graphite the blued section beyond machined area. This will keep tin from adhering to the bluing. (Left) The adaptor also is tinned on interior surface.

secondary importance in the final centerline alignment of bore, adaptor and choke tube.

To prevent a visible gap between the turned barrel section and the rear of adaptor, the turned section must be exactly .750 inch in length. Measure it carefully. Excess of .750 inch will create a visible gap in the finished installation. Less than .750 inch will prevent correct installation of the adaptor and create a gap for the shot to jump across between muzzle end and rear of choke tube!

The installation tool exactly indexes the adaptor to this correct length; however, poor machining can destroy the built-in accuracy of the tool and entire system!

Remove any metal burr or ridge left from machining that would extend down into the bore line of the barrel at the muzzle. This is important for good pattern results. A hand-held scraper works well for this task. Check the fit of the rear of the adaptor to the newly machined section of the barrel. It should slide onto the machined barrel section easily.

Correct installation and the accuracy of matching centerlines depends on correct tool use.

1st Step: Measure the inside diameter of the cleaned barrel bore carefully.

2nd Step: Select the bore guide bushing that is of the closest match between its exterior diameter and the barrel bore internal diameter. These are furnished with .002-inch step variations of external diameter. Check selection by trial insertion of bore guide bushing into barrel bore. This should be a snug fit. Final centerline accuracy depends on your choice!

3rd Step: Remove the lock nut and install the selected bore guide bushing beveled end toward lock nut. Snug fit the nut to lock bore guide bushing to tool.

In preparation for soldering the adaptor to the barrel, both the barrel and adaptor are heated equally by torch. (Left) Installation weight pushes adaptor onto barrel.

4th Step: Tin the turned section of the barrel with Brownell's #44 solder using a liberal amount of matching flux.

NOTE: Solder, through chemical action, actually alloys with the steel. The strongest solder joint is the one with the minimum amount of solder! A correct "tinned" surface is achieved by wiping away excess solder with a clean cloth.

The final tinned surface should look as though it was nickel or chrome plated!

5th Step: Use a piece of aluminum oxide cloth to remove the bluing from the inside rear of the adaptor that will mate with the turned barrel surface. This allows better solder bonding to its inside surface.

6th Step: Tin the inside rear of the adaptor with Brownell's #44 solder using a liberal amount of matching flux. Wipe away excess with a clean cloth. Solder can be prevented from adhering to a metal surface by simply covering the surface with graphite. A common lead pencil works well. We recommend this protection on the blued barrel exterior and blued adaptor exterior near their junction. It can also be applied to the bore bushing guide for this purpose.

7th Step: Screw the installation tool into the adaptor firmly! Remember that the tool is specifically designed to install the adaptor onto the barrel in such a manner that when a choke tube is installed in the adaptor there will be a clearance of .002 inch between the rear shoulder of the knurled section of the choke tube and the forward face of the adaptor. This will assure that the rear of the choke tube is firmly indexed to the face of the barrel muzzle, thus

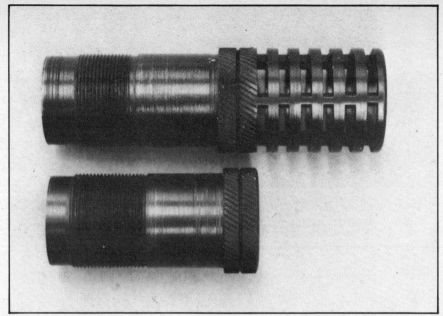

The WalkerChoke is available in standard insert version or as a ventilated unit.

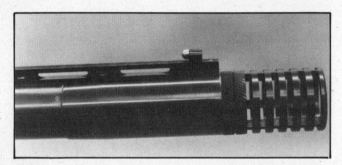

The ventilated version of the WalkerChoke has a Buck Rogers look when inserted in the choke adaptor unit.

Other than the obvious line where the adaptor has been soldered, WalkerChoke resembles other types available.

eliminating any gap that the shot charge would have to "jump" across, damaging shot pellets in the process which in turn would distract from the shot pattern percent! This is extremely important to final performance.

8th Step: Secure the barrel in a padded vise, muzzle toward the ceiling, with six to eight inches of barrel protruding past the top of the vise jaws.

9th Step: Apply a small amount of flux to the tinned barrel section. This assures the strongest bonding.

10th Step: Insert the bore guide bushing into the barrel bore. Push the unit down by hand as far as possible.

11th Step: Install a two-pound weight on top of the installation tool stud that matches the hole in the weight. Be sure barrel and tools are vertically straight in the vise.

12th Step: Use the propane torch to heat the adaptor rear and the forward end of the barrel equally around their circumference. Equal heat is very important. Excess heat is not necessary and will cause discoloration and burn the solder. Apply the heat slowly only to the temperature necessary for the solder to reach its molten state.

When this is achieved, the two-pound weight will automatically push the installation tool down the correct amount to perfectly seat the adaptor to the machined barrel section.

Inspect the joint of the barrel and adaptor rear to assure firm, close seating. Use a clean cloth to remove any extruded solder while it is still molten.

13th Step: Allow the tool and adaptor to cool in its own time period. Application of cold water to a solder joint in an effort to speed cooling crystalizes the solder and also weakens its bond strength in the process. It may also warp the installation tool!

14th Step: When cool, remove the two-pound weight. Unscrew the installation tool from the adaptor. If necessary a steel rod may be inserted into the cross hole provided in the installation tool top for added leverage for tool removal.

For cleanup carefully inspect the bore for any solder that may have been extruded down into it during installation. A stiff wire bore brush or a steel wool bob powered by an electric hand drill may be used to remove it. The Brownell choke hone tool can also be utilized for this purpose. Solder or residue left in the bore can result in severe damage to barrel and adaptor. All that's left is to install whatever sight you favor.

Installation is now complete and the selected Walker-Choke tube can be installed into the adaptor. I recommend test firing, then additional close inspection of each installation.

Chapter 18

A NEW LOOK AT RUST

Modern Plastic Ammo Seems To Contribute To Rusty Chambers; Here's What To Do About It!

How well your shooting goes in the field can depend greatly upon the shape of your gun's bore and the damage from rust.

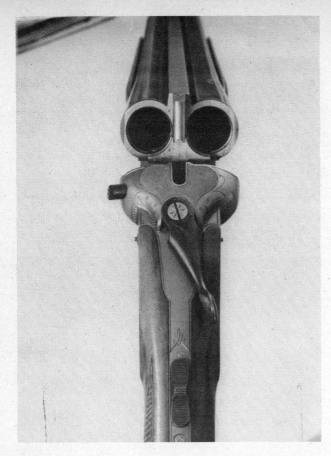

Due to the chemical composition, some of today's plastic ammunition tends to cause rust in chamber and bore.

There is an old saying that "an ounce of prevention is worth a pound of cure." However, to prevent something, you first must understand its cause, then take the necessary steps to eradicate that cause.

When paper shotgun shells were in common use, rusty chambers were about as scarce as rooster teeth, except when someone went to extremes in neglecting a shotgun. Then came the plastic shotgun shell and the shotgun world was plunged immediately into an epidemic of rusty chambers. Just about everything imaginable was blamed for the rusty chambers ranging from the ink used to stamp the shot size on the shell to atomic fallout.

Today the uproar has subsided somewhat, but the rusty chambers continue and, to the best of my knowledge, no one has ever pinpointed the cause. If I am wrong, I bow in humble ignorance.

In the humid Deep South, where I live, this problem is a serious one, far more so than in the northern parts of the country. I don't know whether it was just curiosity or not being able to answer my customers when they asked what caused the rusty chambers, but, whatever the reason, I decided to see if I could find the answer.

After trying every test I could think of and reading everything I could find about the ingredients in plastic, I decided it was way beyond my ability to find the answer. Then one evening I stumbled across the answer while soldering a loose rib on a double-barrel shotgun.

I finished the job, oiled the outside of the barrel and went home. Next morning while cleaning the barrels, I noticed that the insides of the bores were covered with a light film of rust. It occurred to me that this rust was similar in appearance to that found in the chambers of the guns brought into the shop. The answer to the rusty chamber plague is an obvious and simple one; so simple that, while it is a well known metallurgical fact, it had been overlooked completely.

All steel has a high affinity for oxygen; that is, the metal absorbs a small amount of oxygen constantly, which slowly turns it into ferric oxide — red rust — unless the surface of the metal is covered to prevent its exposure to oxygen.

If the steel is heated, the rate of oxygen absorption is increased rapidly in direct proportion. This, by the way, is

O F EVERY five shotguns that come into the average gun shop for repair, at least two of them will be suffering rusty chambers. This, in turn, is either totally or partially responsible for most of the malfunctions in these guns, which may include such things as failure to extract, broken extractors, poor ejection, failure to feed and others. Disregarding the necessity of replacement of broken parts, just about all of these malfunctions can be corrected by removing the rust and polishing the chamber.

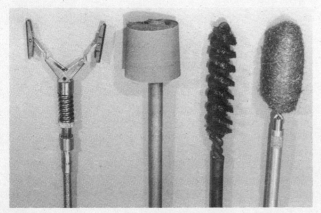

Chamber cleaning tools (from left): a barrel hone; a strip of aluminum oxide cloth over a foam rubber wad; brush for 20mm cannon bore and a steel wool bore brush.

The chamber can be cleaned thoroughly with a bore brush and steel wool held in the forward section of shotgun cleaning rod, which is turned by an electric hand drill.

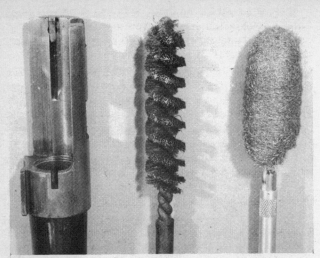

Steel wool in 00 grade, wrapped around bore brush and 20mm cannon brush soldered to rod aid against rust.

the reason for applying the flux to the surface of steel before heating it, when you are soldering. The flux prevents the surface from being exposed to oxygen, which prevents oxidation and contamination of the surface to be soldered. The principle of oxygen absorption by steel is the reason for applying a light coat of oil to your gun to prevent rusting. The same principle is put to positive use with the welder's cutting torch. A high, concentrated flow of oxygen is directed against metal that has been heated to a high temperature. This causes the metal to absorb the oxygen at such a high rate that it oxidizes so fast it actually burns and turns to slag, which is blown free of the surrounding steel.

So what has all this to do with rusty shotgun chambers?

Well, let's go back a few years to those paper shotgun shells. These were wax impregnated to seal out moisture and herein lies the answer. When the paper shell was fired,

Hoppe's powder solvent has a long history and has been a favorite gun-cleaning item with some for many decades.

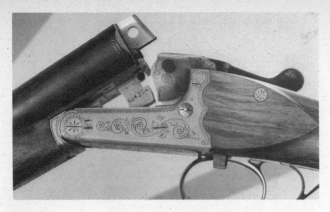

Simply because the exterior surfaces of a shotgun are clean and bright doesn't mean there isn't internal rust.

the heat from the burning powder melted a small amount of the wax which, in turn, was deposited on the walls of the chamber. This thin coating of wax sealed the metal of the chamber from exposure to oxygen, while the chamber was at a high temperature and remained there after firing, still preventing exposure.

The plastic shells are not wax-impregnated nor wax-coated. When fired in a chamber, they do not deposit any protection; in fact, the heat melts or burns away any protection that you have placed in the chamber. When you have finished firing, the walls of the chamber are hot, naked of protection and absorbing oxygen like mad.

If you live in a high-humidity area, the problem is intensified by moisture condensing in the chamber after it has cooled. This mixes with the powder residue to form a mild acid that really gets things going in the rust department.

If left unattended for any period of time, the chamber is left uncleaned. If the gun is fired in this condition, the shell swells against the rough, rusty walls of the chamber, which prevents or retards extraction of the empty shell, often resulting in a broken extractor. If the shell is extracted from a semiauto shotgun with a rusty chamber, part of the power to work the action has been absorbed by the effort, which results in poor ejection as well as feed problem.

I have yet to find anything that will prevent rusting of an unattended chamber completely, unless it is chrome plated or the barrel has a high nickel-steel content. You can, however, prevent the rust from forming simply by thoroughly cleaning the chamber and bore immediately after you have finished shooting. This cleaning should include bore solvent, bore brush and a series of dry patches followed by a final patch lightly oiled.

If you do this after every firing session, even if it is only one shell, you will have cleared away any lingering powder residue, any moisture and the light coat of oil prevents the metal from absorbing oxygen.

The chamber that is already rust coated is another problem and there is no stock answer as to method of correction, for this depends on how much rust is present and if the walls of the chamber are pitted. The best way is to assume

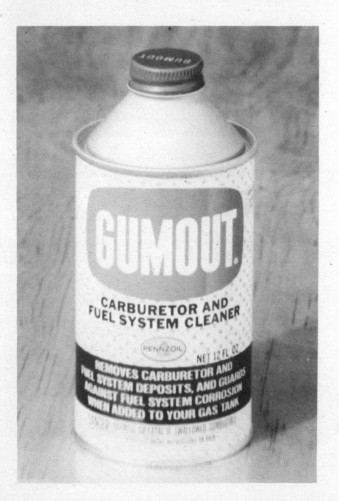

that the rust is light and go to the more drastic measures only if needed. A good scrubbing with a bore brush will help, but a wad of 00 steel wool wound around the bore brush, which is held in the forward joint of the shotgun cleaning rod and turned by an electric hand drill, will break away the rust much faster and more thoroughly.

A 20mm cannon bore brush soldered to the end of a rod and turned in the drill will do the same thing as the steel wool, but the brush will dig out heavy rust better. Regardless of which of these you use, you are only removing rust and not removing any metal from the chamber, so the method is safe even when used by a beginner.

After you have broken the rust free, wipe the chamber thoroughly with dry patches, then give it a good scrubbing with the bore brush of correct gauge that has been dipped in bore solvent. Follow with additional dry patches and inspect the chamber carefully. A flashlight or bright sunlight should be directed into the chamber to provide a clear view. If the walls of the chamber are smooth and clean, consider yourself lucky and next time clean the gun im-

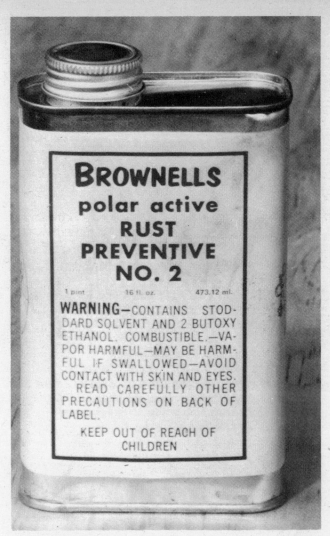

mediately after firing and don't forget to finish up with a light coat of oil in the chamber.

If your inspection reveals pitting in the chamber, you will probably still have trouble with extraction of fired cases. The reason is that the walls of the shell will be forced into these pits by the internal gas pressure and offer resistance to being extracted. If the shell is extracted, a small amount of plastic will be torn from the shell and form a small mound over the pit. Each time a shell is fired, this mound will build up larger, until extraction is completely

The chamber is lapped with a piece of aluminum oxide cloth which is wrapped around a foam rubber wad.

stopped. If left unattended, the metal down in the pit under the plastic will continue to rust and grow deeper.

To eliminate the pitting, it is necessary to hone or lap the chamber until it is smooth and free of pits. This requires removing a small amount from the walls of the chamber and, naturally, there is a limit to the amount that can be removed safely. This must be done carefully to assure that the taper of the chamber is not changed and that the same amount of metal is removed from all sections of the chamber.

To make a tool to lap the chamber, first split a three-eighths-inch metal rod for about two inches on one end with a hacksaw and polish the edges of the cut to remove any burrs. A strip of 400-grit aluminum oxide cloth about six inches long is inserted with one end in the cut and the remainder wrapped around a short piece of foam rubber.

The purpose of the foam rubber is to keep the aluminum oxide cloth pressed lightly against the walls of the chamber. The wad on the end of the metal rod is placed in the chamber and turned with an electric hand drill. If the drill bogs down, you have too much foam rubber backing. Keep

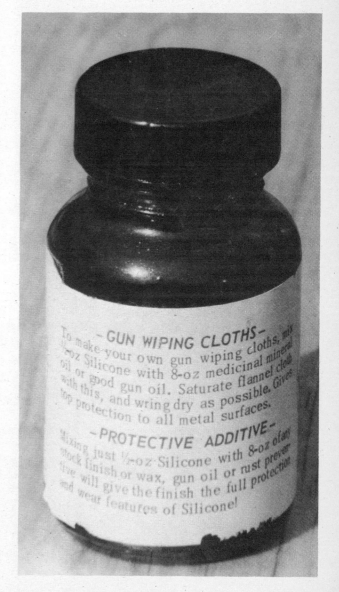

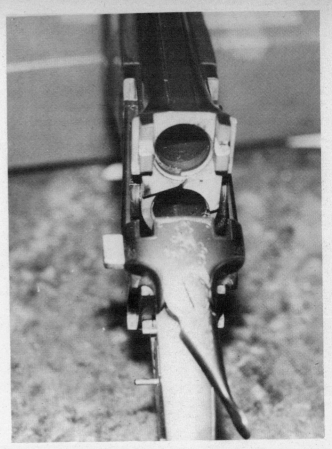

Automatic ejectors are out of time on this over/under. Rust can contribute to such problems, but the solution and retiming is best left to a professional gunsmith.

Usually, rust is an obvious problem and, once noticed, can be handled before one gets to the patterning board.

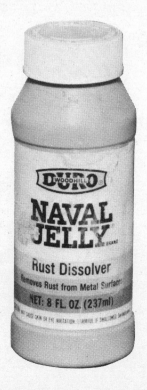

the wad turning and move it steadily back and forth the full depth of the chamber.

This method will remove only a small amount of metal, but it will eliminate most pitting. Use it sparingly, removing the wad often and inspecting the chamber in strong light. For deeply pitted chambers, you can use 240-grit aluminum oxide cloth, but it is best to use as fine a grit as you can and still get the job done.

A barrel hone — available from Brownell's — will do the job slightly better and maintain a more even surface. It does, however, remove metal much faster than the aluminum oxide cloth and must be watched closely. The hone will remove metal more quickly if left dry, but it can be slowed down by liberal amounts of cutting oil applied in the chamber while it is turning. The hone will not leave the chamber walls highly polished, so it is best to follow the hone with aluminum oxide cloth in 500-grit or crocus cloth to assure a high polish.

The average shotgun chamber can be honed or lapped only two or three times before it becomes so enlarged that it reaches the danger point. So, unless you enjoy buying replacement barrels, take that ounce of prevention and clean and oil the chamber after each session of firing.

Chapter 19

BORE BUILD-UP
& WHAT TO DO ABOUT IT

*Few Shotgunners Recognize This Problem
And Its Effect Upon Accuracy!*

Buildup of plastic from the wads of modern shotshells is visible in choke of this shotgun. In firing the gun, the author discovered that this can affect the pattern. He tells what can be done to alleviate the problem.

MOST BEGINNERS ASSUME that if the words *modified choke* are stamped on the barrel of a shotgun, this means the barrel will deliver a modified pattern regardless of whether they shoot 00 buckshot or #9 bird shot. The experienced shotgunner soon discovers that unfortunately this just does not hold true, as the choke will deliver a perfect modified pattern with one shot size only.

They also learn that the choke usually will deliver every-

thing from an improved-cylinder pattern to almost a full-choke pattern, depending upon the shot size used. Adding to the confusion is the fact that different powder loads even using the same size shot will deliver varying patterns. This generally holds true with just about any choke from skeet 1 to extra full.

Somewhere along the line, either by accident or careful patterning with different loads and shot sizes, the shotgunner finds the correct load and shot size to match his choke.

Once he discovers this and learns what the choke will do at various distances, his shooting quickly improves. He gains confidence in his ability and this, in itself, further improves his shooting. Then for some unknown reason he starts to miss shot after shot and begins to wonder if fault lies in himself or the gun.

Everybody has his off day when his coordination just doesn't seem to click and about all he can do when this happens is to try to settle down, shoot slower and hope for a better day. However, most of the time the trouble will be caused, either totally or partially, by changes in the choke dimension. This is not due to wear and diminishing of the amount of choke constriction but just the opposite — increased constriction!

Before the days of the plastic shot protector we all were familiar with unprotected shot smearing against the sides of the choke walls, sticking there and slowly closing the choke dimension with each succeeding shot. Knowing shotgun shooters carefully cleaned the choke with bore solvent and a wire brush to remove this lead build up.

With the advent of plastic shot protectors, we have been swayed by advertisements and no longer take this precaution, or the new shooters coming along are not familiar with the old procedure. Truth of the matter is that the plastic shot protector is more an offender than the naked shot in causing build-up as the shot protector is pressed against the walls of the choke. To this are added small particles of lead smear as a few shot always will be pushed through the walls of the plastic shot protector by the gas pressure behind the shot column. The amount of build-up on the walls of the choke will be determined not only by the number of shells fired, but by the amount of choke constriction, plus the smoothness of the walls of the choke.

The end result is that the choke constriction is closed slightly with each shot fired; this, in turn, affects the pattern delivered. The amount of build-up is small, in most cases

The effects of plastic buildup in this bore are obvious in this photo of a shotgun barrel that has been split.

To accomplish the same mission, these steel wool bobs have been wound on standard bore brushes. From left are bobs wrapped on a 12-gauge cleaning rod; 16 and 20-gauge brushes similarly wrapped.

around .002 inch. In cases of rough choke walls and prolonged neglect, the constriction can total .005 inch, but this is the highest that I have recorded.

This may not sound like much, but any choke specialist will tell you that as little as one-thousandth-inch constriction has quite an effect on the pattern percent and effectiveness. For this reason the custom choke is always honed rather than cut with a reamer for the last few thousandths of constriction with the gunsmith making shooting tests every step of the way.

Factory chokes in mass-produced guns are built to a set standard with plus-or-minus tolerances rather than cut by hand, which is the main reason two barrels for the same model gun with the same choke marking quite often will deliver different patterns. Even with a factory choke the shotgunner soon learns what the choke will do and depends on the choke to deliver this same pattern consistently. With the build-up from the plastic and lead smear, the choke cannot deliver the consistency, for it has been changed in dimensions!

An added bee in the butter is that this build-up is not equalized, but usually will be thicker on one side of the choke wall than on the other sides, which produces a ragged and uneven pattern. Half of the effectiveness of any shotgun pattern is determined by the even distribution of the pellets which, in turn, is determined by the roundness of the choke to a great extent. This same smearing plastic and lead build-up will be found also in the bore behind the choke, even extending clear back to the chamber.

I am not certain exactly what effect this build-up in the bore itself has on a pattern, but I do know that the smoother the bore preceding the choke constriction, the more even the pattern and the higher the percent of pellets in the pattern. From examining innumerable barrels with slight bulges on one side, I have a sneaking but unproven suspicion that this build-up in the bore is a contributing factor in producing these bulges.

So what can we do about all of this build-up? A good scrubbing of the bore with your regular shotgun cleaning rod equipped with a bore brush after a good soaking with bore solvent will help. J-B Compound and WD-40 are excellent lead removers, but they will not remove all of the plastic build-up even with intensive scrubbing. There is an easier and simpler way that will remove the whole mess in

The end of a wooden dowel can be cut and roughed with a knife to hold the steel wool without turning.

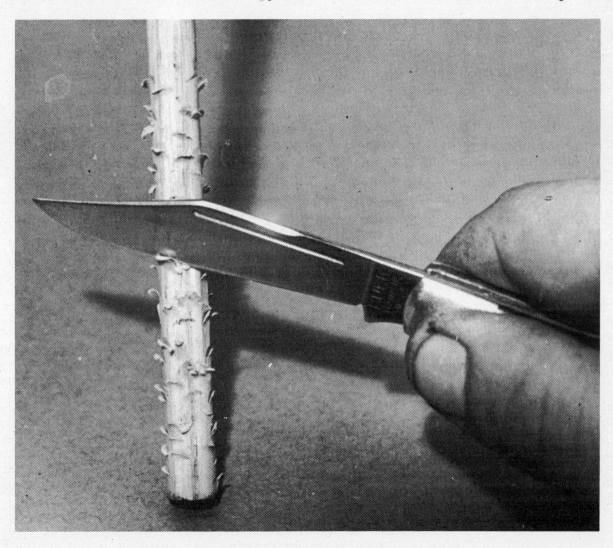

a matter of a few minutes at a cost of around a quarter. I have used it daily for a good many years both commercially and in my personal guns.

Purchase a hardwood dowel at your local hardware store, three feet long and three-eighths inch in diameter. While you are there, pick up a pack of three-aught (000) steel wool. Take out your knife and carefully cut lightly into one end of the dowel, raising small slivers of wood, but not removing the slivers with the dowel. Make these cuts all the way around the dowel end for about a three-inch-long section.

Next, tear a pad of steel wool in half and carefully unwrap one of the halves. If you do this correctly, the steel wool will come off in an even layer. Lay this flat on a table, pick up your dowel and place its cut end on the left end of the steel wool. Press down lightly and rotate the dowel clockwise, winding the layer of steel wool evenly around the cut end of the dowel. The rough dowel end will hold the bob of steel wool securely without allowing it to slip.

The dowel with the steel wool bob on one end can be pushed back and forth through the bore of your shotgun by hand to clean the plastic and lead build-up from the bore and choke, but it is a slow process. A much better way is to rotate the steel wool bob rapidly, as you push and pull it through the bore. This can be done best by using the dowel chucked in a three-eighths-inch electric hand drill, but in a pinch you can use a hand egg-beater drill or a carpenter's brace.

Press the rotating steel wool bob into the barrel and note how tight it is in the chamber before easing it up into the bore. If you have too much steel wool on the bob, the drill will slow down and almost stall. If this is the case, remove the dowel and unwrap about one layer of steel wool from the bob and try again. If you do not have enough steel wool on the bob, the drill will turn at full speed and the dowel will flop around in the bore. The correct amount of steel wool

Steel wool of the correct texture described in text is laid flat, then rolled onto the dowel.

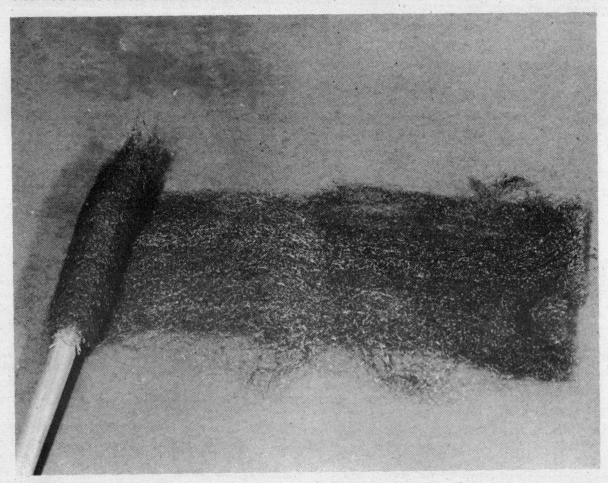

As the steel wool comes out of the gun's muzzle, it brings with it the plastic, lead build-up in choke.

will slow the drill slightly, but you will feel it turning easily. Move the bob down the bore slowly and allow only about one-third of it to exit from the muzzle. If you allow much more than this to exit, you cannot pull it back into the bore and will have to unchuck it and push the dowel on through the bore by hand. Remove the dowel and bob after you have made about five or six trips back and forth through the bore. Follow with a clean patch through the bore to clear any lingering loosened residue. Your bore will be shining like a mirror, free of any plastic or lead build-up as well as any light rust, if you have neglected to clean the gun for a longer period.

A more refined version of the dowel and polishing bob can be made by removing the handle from a regular aluminum or brass shotgun cleaning rod and using this as a substitute for the wooden dowel. A standard shotgun bore brush of correct gauge is screwed into the rod's recess and the steel wool wrapped around the brush. By using a bore brush, only a small amount of steel wool is required around the brush and you can switch from one gauge to another simply by switching brushes.

What effect does the steel wool have on the bore? Absolutely none except to burnish it lightly and make it smoother. As a test, I used this method on a personal Beretta over/under shotgun for over two years, constantly measuring both the bore and choke with a bore micrometer. There was no change in the bore or choke dimensions. The amount of crud this simple system will remove from a bore and choke is amazing. Even rusty and rough bores can be cleaned up considerably with the steel wool bob, but if it is used in conjunction with WD-40, Break Free or Tuf-Oil, it will do a far better job.

Chapter 20

THE ALL-AROUND REPLACEMENT

By Accident, The Author Discovered A Shotgun Barrel That Unscrambles Numerous Problems!

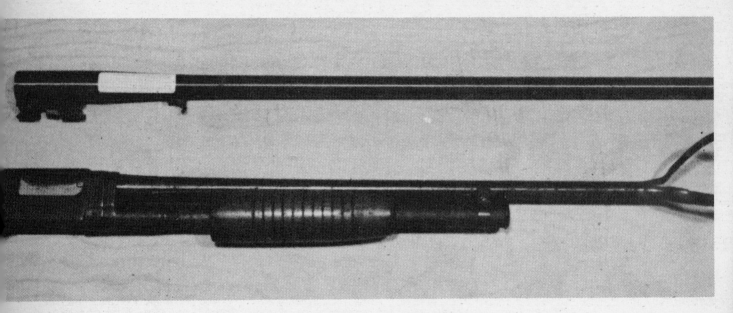

When some shotgun barrels suffer damage, repair tubes can run into great expense, but there are substitutions that can be used at nominal cost.

EACH YEAR A gunsmith can count on a dozen or more shotgun customers coming into the shop with the ends of their barrels altered into something resembling a metal bird cage. In the majority of cases the blown barrel is the result of some foreign matter such as leaves, small sticks, even water, having been lodged in the bore when the gun was fired. One of the most common occurences involves the owner falling and filling the bore with mud. Usually the owner is not aware of the mud-lugged bore and fires the gun with interesting results, but I have known a few who actually tried to shoot the mud out on purpose!

The gunsmith faced with solving the problem is limited mainly by exactly where in the barrel the damage occurs. If it is on the extreme end of the barrel and the gun is not a double barrel, the best answer is to install a choke device such as the Poly-Choke, Cutts Compensator or Lyman choke. If the gun is a double-barrel model or the owner dislikes a choking device, the gunsmith can only cut the barrel off behind the damaged area which will result in a cylinder-bored barrel without choke. The legal barrel length of eighteen inches always must be taken into consideration and quite often this will dictate a new barrel, regardless of the model or type of shotgun.

When used as a replacement barrel for the Winchester Model 12, the locking lug of the Stevens Model 94 barrel is removed by melting silver solder.

After the locking lug has been removed from the barrel of the Model 94, the forend lug also must be removed, using an abrasive cutoff wheel.

If the gun is of recent manufacture, a replacement barrel usually will be available from the original manufacturer or from one of the independent barrel dealers. The real tough problem is when the gun is an old, out-of-date model for which replacement barrels either are not available or are extremely high priced. A few companies offer replacement barrels for some of the old classic doubles such as the L.C. Smith, Parker, etc. Barrels for the non-doubles is another question that is not easily answered, for unlike rifle barrel blanks, shotgun barrel blanks in various gauges, chokes and lengths are hard to find. Swapping barrels from one pump or semiautomatic to another model is limited in that

the barrel already will be threaded and little or no metal will be available for cutting a new set of threads.

Part of an answer accidentally came to me one day in the form of a customer's Savage-Stevens Model 94 single-barrel shotgun with the locking lug blown off the barrel. These lugs are silver soldered to the barrel at the factory and will remain firmly attached unless someone, such as the owner of this particular shotgun, decides to reload a shell and try for the Olympic distance record.

It occurred to me that here was the barrel blank I had been looking for, as plenty of metal was available for any type of threading needs. A check in the Savage parts

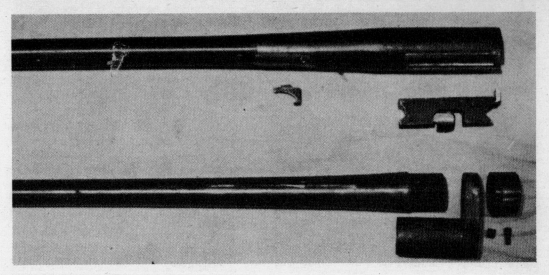

At top, the Model 94 barrel has been stripped to become a barrel blank. Beneath it, the Model 12 barrel is disassembled with parts to be used.

With the Stevens Model 94 barrel chucked in the lathe, the extractor cut for the original extractor is machined in barrel.

catalog revealed that a new barrel was available at $14, including the extractor assembly. After installing the new M-94 barrel on the customer's shotgun, I decided to rework the old barrel and install it on one of the guns waiting in the shop for a new barrel.

The first conversion was as a replacement barrel for a Remington Model 11 semiauto which was discontinued about twenty-five years ago. Replacement barrels for these guns have become as scarce as rooster teeth due to the large number of surplus military riot models released a few years ago, each needing a longer tube. The M-11 owner was surprised when he saw the reworked Savage M-94 barrel and requested that I cancel his order for the regular M-11 replacement barrel. This decision I welcomed, as all efforts to locate one had failed. Since then I have reworked these Model 94 barrels and fitted them to various makes and models and, in each case, the installation has proved successful and economical. Savage is the parent organization of the Stevens, Springfield and Fox brands and any of their single-barrel break-open shotgun barrels can be used for this purpose, with the exception of the Model 95. The barrels are available to any qualified gunsmith in 12-, 16-, 20-gauge and .410, and in various chokes and barrel lengths.

I never had used one of these barrels to replace a Winchester Model 12 barrel as factory barrels are still available. The only hitch is that the current Winchester catalog price is $71.50 for the barrel. Added to that is the labor of fitting the barrel, receiver extension and adjusting sleeve. The total price can easily mount up to the cost of a good used Model 12. The owner of a 20-gauge Model 12 with a badly damaged barrel asked me to try fitting one of the Model 94 barrels to his gun, as he did not want a factory replacement barrel at this cost, but did want a special choke.

Preliminary investigation revealed that this would be the hardest conversion of them all, as it would cover the entire procedure quite thoroughly. There are slight variations with other types and brands, of course, but the basic procedure will remain the same and anyone equipped with a good lathe should have little trouble with the Model 12 or any other model.

The replacement Model 94 barrel comes from the factory equipped with the complete extractor assembly, which must be removed as the first step. After disassembling all of the extractor components, the barrel is held in a vise and a propane torch used to melt the silver solder and allow the locking lug to be removed. Incidentally, the Savage parts catalog lists the extractor components at $2.55 and, if you subtract this amount from the $14 cost of the barrel, your actual barrel blank price is reduced to $11.45.

Next, remove the forend lug which is attached directly in front of the locking lug. This can be broken off with a hammer, but as it is arc welded to the barrel, such an effort will leave a small hole in the barrel. A better solution is to cut

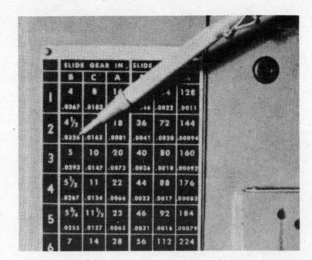

The lateral feed ratio is listed just below the thread listing on quick change gear boxes.

The barrel is turned down to the largest diameter of the original Winchester Model 12 barrel. Note that the short small thread cutting tool is being used in this particular operation.

After the threads have been cut in the replacement barrel, the shoulder area of the barrel is contoured to match that of the original tube from the Winchester Model 12 shotgun.

The author sets up to polish the Model 94 barrel with strips of aluminum oxide cloth. This will be done, when lathe is started, with the tool turning at high speed for the operation.

the lug off with a Dremel abrasive cut-off wheel. The lug is discarded and any remaining stub on the barrel is filed flush with the surface. Your replacement barrel blank now is ready to be fitted to your shotgun.

In the case of the Model 12, the barrel is disassembled and, with the adjusting sleeve and receiver extension removed, the barrel is measured and a sketch made, listing all dimensions. All Model 12 barrels are a bit on the thin

side and you have the choice of copying this contour or taking the easy road and leaving the replacement barrel a little thicker. You will find that one problem immediately rears its ugly head: the barrel thread dimensions. Winchester chose thirty threads per inch, which is an odd size. This probably was due to the wide variety of thread types and sizes in use in 1912 when the gun was first produced. Unless your lathe is an old one, you will not find thirty threads per inch listed on the gear box. Most modern lathes will list twenty-eight and thirty-two threads per inch as the closest, but these cannot be used as the difference is too great, even with extensive thread chasing.

There is, however, a solution to the problem. The "leed" of a thread, which is identical to the "pitch" in a single-cut thread, is the amount the thread will advance a screw with one complete revolution of the screw. The Model 12's thirty threads per inch is a single-cut thread with a pitch of .0333 inch. Lathe threading gears are designed to cut threads in specific threads per inch ratio, but the lathe also is equipped with direct gears to provide a lateral feed of the cutting bit forward slowly as the work is revolved in the lathe and are listed as so much lateral feed per revolution.

The direct lateral feed gears can be utilized to cut the odd thirty threads per inch if your lathe has a lateral feed close to .0333 per revolution. My Clausing delivers .0326 inch lateral feed in one direct gear and this is close enough, as the small difference between .0333 and .0326 can be compensated for with a little careful chasing of the threads with a triangular file. The only trick in using the lateral gears is that, during the thread-cutting operation, the lathe must be kept in gear in at all times. This is necessary as the regular thread-cutting dial cannot be used with any degree of success. Actually all that is necessary is to make a threading cut, stop the lathe, then reverse the lathe back to the starting point, stop the lathe, and make the next threading cut, all without disengaging the gears. But I would recommend that you make a few practice cuts on scrap before you cut the threads on the barrel.

The first matching step is to face off the breech end of the barrel to eliminate the cut made for the original Model 94 extractor. All Model 94 barrels in 20- and 12-gauge are chambered for the three-inch shell. Therefore the facing off of the barrel back beyond the extractor cut will leave a chamber still slightly in excess of the normal 2¾-inch length. This excess length will create no problem with the 2¾-inch shells, for they commonly are fired in guns chambered for the three-inch shell.

The other gauges will require deepening the chamber after the barrel is fitted to most model pumps and semi-automatics with the exception of the Model 12 Winchester. Rechambering in any gauge is not necessary with the Model 12, as the chamber ring, which is a part of the chamber, is fixed to the receiver and the actual barrel chamber

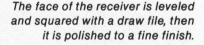

The face of the receiver is leveled and squared with a draw file, then it is polished to a fine finish.

Forging the new magazine band lug is done around a steel rod, which must have the correct diameter of the barrel.

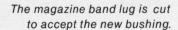

The magazine band lug is cut to accept the new bushing.

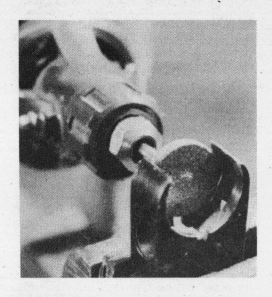

depth is less than 2¾ inches. The thickness of the chamber ring will more than compensate for the amount the original M94 chamber is shortened in the removing of the extractor cut.

Normally a barrel is turned between centers, but as all factory shotgun barrels have a slight upward bend to compensate for the shot drop at forty yards, this is not possible with the Model 94 barrels unless the barrel is straightened. The Savage barrels are rolled to final shape and the outside is closely parallel with the chamber and bore. It is a lot simpler to chuck the barrel with approximately a foot of it extended and supported by a center in the lathe tailstock. The next machining step should be to turn the barrel down in the shoulder area to the largest diameter listed on your sketch. Next, turn the outside thread diameter and space the shoulder of the barrel according to your sketch dimension, but adding .05 inch to the length to allow for tight breeching of the barrel to the chamber ring.

Select your correct lateral gear and, with the lathe in the slowest spindle speed possible, begin your threading. You will find a regular commercial threading tool too large for this job and a short, specially ground threading tool will be needed. A short "free turn" area cut next to the barrel shoulder will be a big help when you stop the lathe at the end of a threading cut. Don't forget to reverse the lathe back to the starting point without disengaging the gears and begin the next depth cut of the thread. Make your cuts light and take your time. Use the receiver extension to check the thread fit and to determine when the threads have been cut to sufficient depth.

After the threading is completed, contour the shoulder area to match the original Model 12 barrel. If you have decided to match the original full-length contour, it will be necessary to straighten the barrel and probably use a steady rest or a follower rest. Otherwise the barrel can be polished for bluing, using strips of aluminum oxide cloth held in the hands while the barrel is being turned at high speeds.

The barrel shoulder now is machined to line up the receiver extension with the front sight. Remove the chamber ring from the receiver and fit the receiver extension and adjusting sleeve to the receiver for a tight fit. One advantage of machining a new barrel is that the adjusting sleeve can be regulated to give a full draw capacity to allow for future wear. Most Model 12s will have battered receiver faces, so it is a good idea to draw file lightly and polish it for a snug fit of barrel and receiver extension to the receiver.

When the barrel assembly is aligned correctly and snug with the receiver, you are ready for the all important breeching. Remove the barrel assembly and install the chamber ring in the receiver. Your barrel assembly should now strike the chamber ring and fail to turn into place in the receiver. The breech of the barrel is now carefully machined, removing only a small amount of metal at a time until the barrel assembly turns into the receiver with a firm and snug fit against the chamber ring. The inside of the chamber ring and the barrel chamber should line up perfectly.

The Model 12 barrel has a forward half-circle lug underneath that fits into a recess in the magazine band and band bushing to hold the magazine assembly securely to the barrel. There are several ways to attach this lug to the barrel and any that gets the job done is acceptable. The simple way is to forge a small strip of metal around a steel rod of correct barrel diameter, then file it to correct shape. The lug then is silver soldered to the barrel at the correct

position on the barrel. If the barrel has not been contoured to the same diameter as the original barrel at this point it will be necessary to open up the magazine band and band bushing with a small round grindstone. The magazine band bushing screw recesses are then cut into the band lug and the magazine assembled to the barrel. All that remains is to blue the barrel.

Other models such as the Remington Model 11 require that you remove the barrel forward ring from the old barrel and silver solder it in correct position on the new barrel. With few exceptions, all forward lugs are silver soldered to the original barrel and are easily removed with a propane torch. If you run into one that is arc-welded to the barrel, it will be necessary to cut it free with a hacksaw and file the old barrel stub away.

Fitting Savage Model 94 barrels to various shotguns is not as difficult as it may sound and is within the capability of many a home gunsmith. In many cases they will return a good shotgun to service that would otherwise end up on the junk pile.

The magazine band and the band bushing must be enlarged in order to fit the larger diameter of the replacement.

The forged magazine band lug, once properly filed and shaped, is held for silver soldering to the barrel.

Chapter 21

MODERNIZING THE OLDER SIXTEEN

A Bit Of Work Can Bring A Classic Up To Modern Ammo Standards

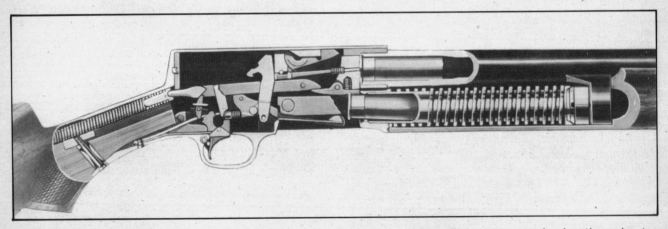

No matter what the gauge, the functioning of the Browning Auto 5 is the same, utilizing same mechanism throughout.

IN USED GUN RACKS all over the country, a gem of a shotgun bargain gathers dust for want of a buyer. Would you believe a Browning five-shot automatic in excellent condition for a price under $150? Its a fact and the low price is not unusual by any means.

The catch is that the Browning is a 16-gauge and chambered for the obsolete 2-9/16-inch shell, instead of the current and longer 2¾-inch shell. If 2¾-inch shells are used in the gun the results are rather disappointing. Jam-

med shells, failure to feed and failure to eject are the general order of the day. Worse, the longer shell unfolds past the forcing cone of the chamber and up into the bore itself thereby creating a bottleneck. The shot then must squeeze past this constriction and it becomes battered in the process; this results in a ragged and scattered pattern. In addition, breech pressure is raised considerably and shoulder-bruising recoil increases in direct ratio.

The 2-9/16-inch 16-gauge shell was standard length until 1929, when the Sporting Arms and Ammunition

With depth gauge in the chamber, the front line designates short chamber, while rear line marks the 2¾-inch depth. The T-handle with a threaded front section aids removal of gauge.

Manufacturing Institute (SAAMI) changed the length to our current 2¾-inch shell. All guns manufactured after 1929 have the designation *16 gauge 2 ¾ Inch* stamped on the barrel. Those with the shorter 2-9/16-inch chamber will be stamped *16 gauge*. The Browning also is used in Europe and those made for that market will be marked *16/ 65* for 16-gauge, 65mm. The last figure designates the case length, 65mm being 2-9/16 inches. The longer chamber will be marked *16/70* with 70mm being the longer 2¾-inch shell.

The old short-length shell was available until World War II, but after the war ammunition production was resumed only on the 2¾-inch 16-gauge shell. Dealer shelves had been virtually emptied during the war years and the 2-

Gunsmith Jack Ashworth uses a large T-handle to turn reamer during rechambering operation.

This Auto 5 has been fully rechambered to 2¾-inch depth as shown by position of depth gauge.

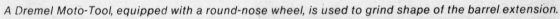

A Dremel Moto-Tool, equipped with a round-nose wheel, is used to grind shape of the barrel extension.

The Dremel Tool also is used to cut the oval slot in the ejector. Cut is accomplished here, using a dental burr.

9/16-inch shells were almost impossible to find. Many of the guns struggled along trying to digest the longer shells amid strong language from their owners, but most were confined to the attic or sold to unsuspecting buyers.

Browning Arms worked out a conversion procedure and thousands of the short-chamber guns have been converted by that company and many thousands more by gun shops across the country. Unfortunately, many of the independent convertors failed to obtain the dimensions and procedure from Browning, resulting in some weird conversion attempts. Most of the better gun shops still perform the conversion for a gunsmithing bill of $75 to $85, but the home gunsmith can save more than half the price by doing the job himself. It is not a conversion that requires a basement full of machine tools. In fact, you can do the job without using power equipment. However, a Dremel Moto-Tool will simplify the process and produce a much neater job. The job looks complicated at first glance, but really is quite simple once you get into the actual work.

Assuming you are the owner of a 16-gauge 2-9/16-inch Browning, completely disassemble the gun down to the last part. Thoroughly scrub every part to remove the dirt, grime and dried oil accumulated over the years. No step should be taken toward conversion until the gun is absolutely clean, otherwise you will fit and adjust parts that no longer will fit if the gun is cleaned after the conversion. Common mineral spirits is a good cleaning solution that is both cheap and has a low flash point. After cleaning take a close look at each part to be sure none are broken or worn excessively.

The chamber must be cut deeper to accept the longer 2¾-inch shell and a chamber reamer will be necessary. You may choose to have your local gunsmith do this for you at a price of $25 to $35 or you can buy a reamer of your own. There are quite a few on the market and most will do a good job for beginners. I would suggest you select a reamer with angled rather than straight flutes as the angled flutes cut much cleaner when the rechambering is hand-powered. You will also need a chamber depth gauge available from several commercial sources. However, any good machinist can turn one on a lathe in a few minutes from a section of three-quarter-inch-diameter rod.

The gauge is turned straight without a taper, but the front end must measure exactly .732 inch in diameter. Have the machinist turn the gauge to around .735-inch, then polish the front end down to the desired .732-inch diameter. The length can be exactly 2¾ inches or you can just cut a groove around the gauge at this length and leave the gauge longer to facilitate handling. The one shown in the photographs has the first groove cut at 2-9/16 inches and the second groove cut at 2¾ inches. The rear of this gauge was tapped to receive a "T" handle so that the gauge could be inserted and removed quickly. These are refinements made on a gauge that sees a lot of use and are not necessary for the home workshop. A little white chalk in the grooves will make them much easier to see when the gauge is being used.

The first step in the conversion is to remove the ejector which is pinned to the barrel extension. Look closely and you will see the faint outline of a pin about half-way down the ejector's length in the recess of the ejector. Use a pin punch slightly less in diameter than the pin and, with the barrel extension supported on a wood or metal punch block, drive the pin out the rear of the barrel extension. Place the pin and the ejector in a safe place, as they will be needed later.

With the barrel held vertically, chamber toward the ceiling and at eyeball height, insert your homemade depth gauge and note how much the chamber must be deepened to accept the 2¾-inch shell. Remove the chamber depth gauge and secure the barrel vertically, again chamber to the ceiling, in a good bench vise and begin the rechambering. Doing this by hand will create no problems provided you exert pressure straight downward and do not exert side pressure. Make your cuts all the way around in a clean and smooth rotation while the reamer is kept flooded with cutting oil. Make three or four complete rotations of the reamer, then lift it free and clean both it and the chamber of all oil and chips.

Insert the depth gauge and bend down until you can look directly across the edge of the barrel end to see if it is lined up with the 2¾-inch mark on the depth gauge. Chances are that you will have to make several cuts with the reamer before the mark on the gauge and the barrel edge are aligned. After full depth has been reached, the chamber must be polished. The easy way to do this is to hacksaw a one-inch slot in the end of a foot-long three-eighths-inch-diameter metal rod. Next insert a short length of 400-grit aluminum oxide cloth in the slot and back it with a piece of foam rubber to form a polishing bob. The rod is turned with an electric hand drill and the aluminum oxide cloth is kept pressed tightly against the chamber walls by the foam rubber. Keep the polishing bob moving at all times and polish

The upper barrel is in the original short-chamber version with the ejector in position. Lower barrel shows ejector in the new oval slot at the full back position. This will allow the longer shell to clear the shotgun's chamber.

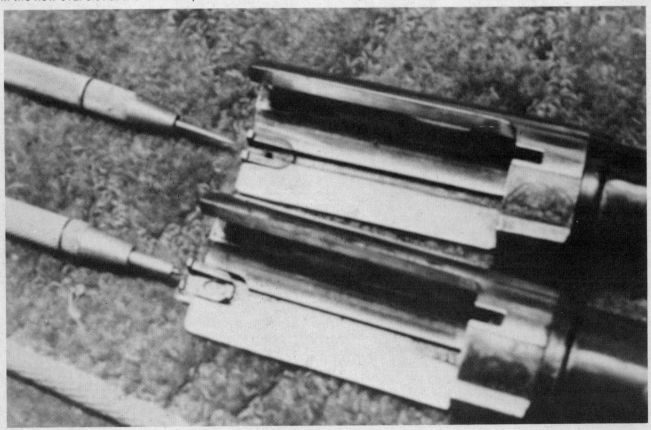

Lines for enlarging the ejection port have been laid out. All metal inside lines must be removed.

In filing away excess metal to lengthen the ejection port, one keeps the top and bottom lines continuous with the original lines. After polishing, the author recommends the use of touch-up blue, thus avoiding complete rebluing.

The rear of the link must be filed back 3/32 inch at the point indicated, maintaining thickness of the link arms.

the entire chamber. A smooth and highly polished chamber is a tremendous asset to getting correct extraction of a fired shell.

The next step in converting the barrel is to assure that the end of the fired shell will not catch on the side of the chamber and the barrel extension when it is being ejected. To achieve this grind a slope on the open side of the barrel extension. This slope must extend from the outside rim of the barrel extension down to the inside rim recess of the chamber. Take your time, keep the slope even and maintain the original edge of both the outside and the inside of the barrel. Use a polishing point in the Dremel Moto-Tool to smooth the grind marks and to polish the slope as slick as glass.

The original fixed ejector must be altered to a sliding type that will move freely in its recess in the barrel extension. A little careful filing on all sides of the ejector will accomplish this in short order. The original hole in the ejector must be lengthened into an oval slot ¼-inch long with a 5/64-inch web of metal left at the front end of the ejector. A dental burr in the Dremel Moto-Tool and a few strokes of a small round file will get the job done best, although a drill can be used as a makeshift milling cutter to cut the slot.

When finished, install the ejector in the barrel extension and tap the ejector pin back into place. Check to be sure that the ejector slides easily to the rear and is stopped by the ejector pin. This sliding of the ejector to the rear more

Although a file can be used, an abrasive wheel is faster for cutting back shell stop, maintaining bottom ledge lines.

than original will allow the end of the longer 2¾-inch fired shell to clear the end of the barrel as it is ejected. If it should catch on the edge of the barrel, the slope that you ground will allow it to slide out and be ejected without jamming.

The ejection port of the receiver must also be lengthened to clear the longer shell. Measure 17/32 inch from the front of the receiver and draw a line opposite the ejection port front. Connect the front line with the top edge of the ejection port to another line. Repeat the same on the bottom edge with another line joining the front line. Round the edges slightly where the lines intersect. The metal inside of the lines must be removed to lengthen the ejection port. You can do this quickly with a carbide cutter in the Dremel Moto-Tool or you can get the job done a little slower with just a file. Either way, stop dead on the lines and polish your edges to match the rest of the lines of the ejection port. A little dab of touch-up blue can be applied to the edges, if the gun is not to be reblued.

The next part to alter is the link that connects the breech bolt with the action spring. If left unaltered, the breech bolt will go forward more than originally and override the safety sear, preventing the gun from firing as the safety sear blocks the main sear. The inner rear section of the link must be filed back 3/32 inch while maintaining the original inner lines of the link arms. After the conversion is completed, if the gun should fail to fire or the breech block binds when pulled to the rear, you will have to cut this section back a bit more, but this seldom will be necessary.

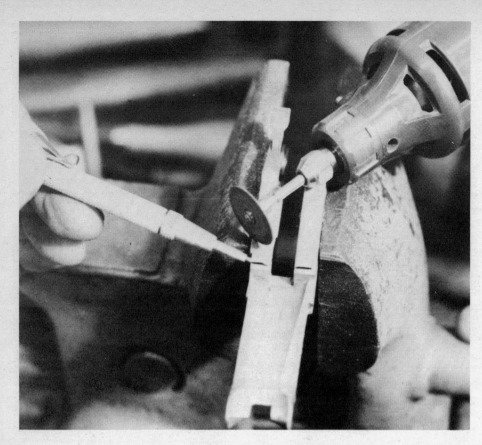

Shell carrier must be cut back 1/16 inch at rear shoulder to handle length of longer shell.

With the rear cut made, the excess metal is being removed by moving the cut-off wheel back and forth in even motion.

Walker utilized a shop-made cutter fashioned from one-inch pipe and a connector to cut forward top edge of forearm.

The carrier that lifts the shells from the magazine for feeding into the chamber must be altered to match the new shell length. Lay a shell on the carrier and note how the rim of the shell presses against the rear shoulder of the carrier. This rear shoulder must be cut back one-sixteenth inch for the longer shell. The easy way to do this is with a Dremel abrasive cut-off wheel. Measure the one-sixteenth inch and scribe a line directly across the rear of the carrier. Now make one downward cut directly on the scribed line with the abrasive cut-off wheel almost to full depth. The excess metal can be removed by moving the abrasive wheel back and forth, grinding a little of the metal away at a time. The thin wheel is easy to break, so keep a steady hand and make light passes. When you have the excess metal removed, continue grinding until you match the new section with the bottom line of the carrier. Finish up with a few light passes full length of the carrier to get the new section smooth and flush with the original lines.

The shell stop is altered next and this also is done easily with an abrasive cut-off wheel in the Dremel Moto-Tool, but it can be filed, if necessary. The front of the shell stop is cut back 3/32 inch, but the bottom ledge line is maintained. Finish it up by polishing the new surface. This alteration is to prevent a shell from overriding the locking block latch during loading and to prevent a shell from getting jammed between the carrier and the breech bolt.

The wood forearm limits how far the barrel goes forward, so it also must be altered to the new shell length. The forward ledge inside of the forearm is what stops the barrel guide ring so that must be cut forward 3/32 inch. You can do this with a chisel or knife, but a simple homemade tool will do a better job.

You need a section of regular one-inch water pipe and a pipe connector for this tool. File one end of the pipe connector flat and cut a series of teeth around the edge. The diameter of the connector then is turned down on a lathe or ground down·until it matches the inside diameter of the forearm. All that remains is to mark off the 3/32 inch on the forward forearm stop ledge and rotate the cutter until the excess wood is removed. You also will have to remove 3/32 inch of wood from the rear upper portion of the forearm to clear the barrel extension and barrel extension guide when the barrel moves forward to the new stop position.

Now assemble the gun and install the forearm. The barrel will move forward 3/32 inch more than it did before the conversion and, if you have measured everything correctly, the edge of the barrel extension at the chamber will be exactly flush with the new edge of the ejection port. Move the barrel back and forth a few times by hand, tripping the breech block with the release button. If everything is working right, you can make your test firing.

Set the gun on heavy loads; that is, with the beveled, steel friction washer (bevel toward the muzzle) on top of the recoil spring, and the bronze friction ring on the top of the steel friction washer. Load the gun with light loads (2½ dram/1 ounce) and with the gun held firmly to your shoulder, fire and see if the gun will eject and reload. Chances are that it will not. Clear the gun and set it for light loads; that is, with the cupped friction washer at the rear of the spring against the receiver, and the bronze friction ring at the front of the recoil spring. Again try the light loads. This time the shells should be jected about three feet from you. Reset the gun for heavy loads and try some medium-loaded shells (2¾ dram/1⅛ ounce) to see if they also will eject. I do not recommend loads heavier than 3 drams/1⅛ ounce of shot in a converted gun, for it must be remembered that

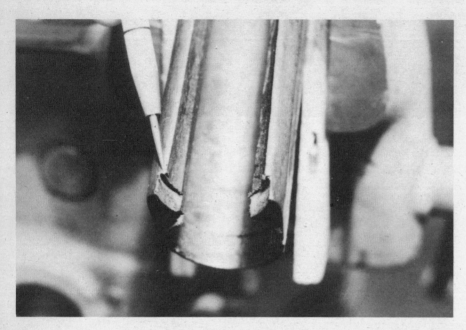

To clear barrel extension, the extension acts as a guide when barrel moves forward to new position. It is necessary to remove 3/32 inch from upper part of forearm for it to work.

Pointer is used to indicate the area in which the wood must be removed on assembled shotgun.

these guns never were designed to handle the modern short magnum 16-gauge loads. Continued firing of the short magnum shells will damage the gun.

Most ejection problems with a Browning five-shot automatic are due either to the shooter not holding the gun firmly against his shoulder or a rough magazine tube. If you are not guilty of the first, disassemble the gun and look closely at the outside of the magazine tube. If it is rough, the friction ring will grab at the rough spots and prevent correct function. Polish the tube lengthwise with 400-grit aluminum oxide cloth. Do not polish it around. This will just create rings and hinder correct function as much as do the rough spots. Apply two or three drops of oil to the tube and spread the oil with your hand all over the tube.

Heavy oiling will prevent the friction ring from doing its job and the gun will be battered badly by the barrel slamming to the rear. The friction ring acts just like the brakes on a car, as the cone on the cupped friction washer and the rear of the barrel guide ring causes the friction piece to be compressed and apply brakes to the rearward recoiling barrel.

A new recoil spring from a modern Sweet Sixteen Browning will fit the older model, if the old recoil spring proves too weak. Replacement ejectors for converted models with a new ejector pin also are available from Browning, but be sure to specify that it is for the converted model, as the Sweet Sixteen ejector will not interchange.

Over the years I have converted dozens of these guns and they all function like a clock as long as the owner does not get magnum shell happy. Maybe you will get as lucky as one customer did and pick up one of these guns in like-new condition with two extra barrels, all with ribs, and in the original fitted case for fifty bucks!

If all measurements have been correct, edge of the barrel extension should match the edge of the new ejection port.

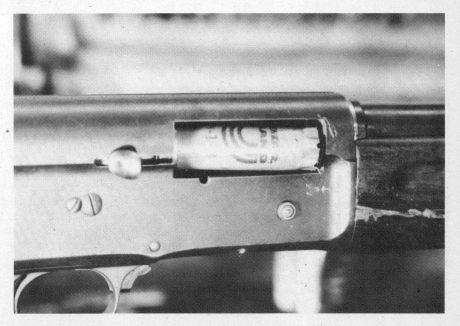

With all of redesign work done, 2¾-inch shell now is ejected from the action without jamming.

Chapter 22

FIT YOUR OWN SHOTGUN STOCK

There's No Such Thing As An Average Stock...You Have To Make It Fit For Accurate Shooting

NO TWO THINGS are ever exactly alike, be they snowflakes or elephants. How then can a five-foot, ninety-pound bean pole of a man be expected to use the same gun stock as a husky 250-pound six-footer? Yet factory stocks, out of economic necessity, are manufactured to an "average man" dimension.

It is quite obvious that the gun owner adapts to the stock rather than reversing the procedure and adapting the stock to the gun owner. More than any other reason, incorrectly fitted stocks are the cause of missed targets.

The only way to achieve an absolutely perfect stock fit is to start with a plank of good wood and custom build the stock. This can get a wee bit on the expensive side, plus a lot of time must be invested in numerous fittings, removing a small amount of wood each time, with test firing between fittings. The other alternative is to rework the dimensions of a factory stock to conform as nearly as possible to the desired measurements. Any good stockmaker can do the

job for you, but with a little know-how, a few good tools and a lot of determination, the job is not beyond the capabilities of a home gunsmith. One of the main problems for the home gunsmith in the past has been measuring for the correct fit. Drop and pull gauges always have been available through some of the gunsmith supply houses, but the price of good gauges has been prohibitive for most home gunsmiths.

Some years ago I made up a simple pull gauge for use in my shop. Over the years it has been used on thousands of gun stocks and is still doing a good job. Quite a few copies were made and used by other gunsmiths, both hobby and professional. Bob Brownell of Brownell's, Incorporated, in Montezuma, Iowa, saw a photo of the gauge and became interested. After working and playing with the sample I made up for him, he modified the design. The result is quite an improvement and the commercial model offered by his company is made of good oil-finished walnut with inlaid metal scales. With this gauge the home gun-

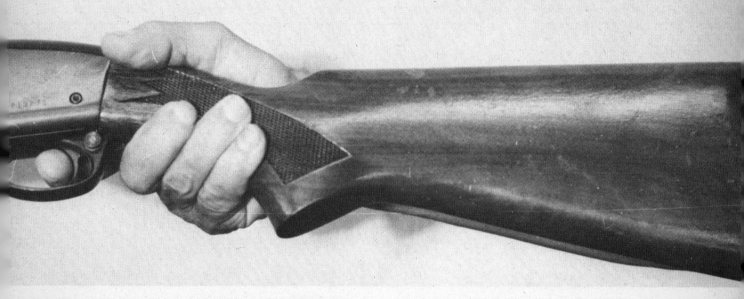

One can check for proper length of stock by what's known as the arm method. It's simple and relatively precise. This example is quite close to the perfect stock fit.

smith can measure his stock and determine the exact measurements needed to adapt the stock to fit his particular carcass.

The major stock dimension is the "length of pull." This is the measurement from the center of the trigger of a gun to the back edge of the butt plate at a point half-way between the heel (top) and the toe (bottom) of the butt plate. If the length of pull is too long, the stock will have a tendency to ride off the shoulder and onto the arm muscle during the recoil. The result is a black and blue muscle and a missed target, as the sliding gun usually will hit to the left. This is reversed, of course, for a southpaw shooter.

If the length of pull is too short, the tendency is to pull and to shoot to the right or, in some cases, to hold the stock loosely against the shoulder. Repeated use of a short stock will pound a shooter's shoulder into a mass of black and blue welts in short order.

There is an old and simple method of determining whether a stock has the correct amount of pull for an individual provided he does not swing through the trees or walk around with his knuckles dragging in the sand. Drop your arm to your side, then bring the forearm up waist high and place the butt of the gun stock against the inside of your upper arm just above the elbow. Next, place your finger on the trigger while the stock is pressing against your arm. If the stock is too long, you will have to stretch your finger to

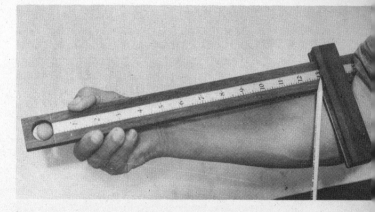

This measurement is with Brownell's Pull & Drop Gauge. Note that the proper length is read from the rear of the bar, otherwise it will be an inch or more short, as indicated by the length reading shown by the pencil.

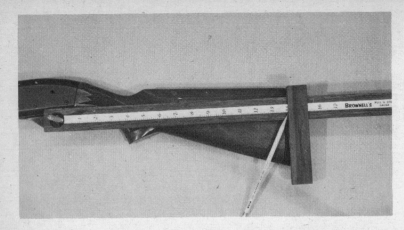

Using the Brownell gauge to check stock length, note that the measurement is taken at a point midway between the heel and the toe of the shotgun's butt.

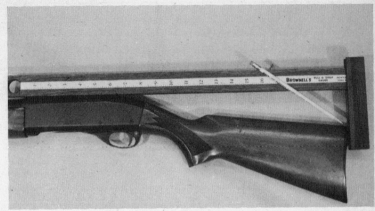

To measure the drop at the heel, press the front of the gauge against top of the receiver. The measurement then is taken at the point indicated by pencil.

reach the trigger. If the stock is too short, the trigger finger will reach the trigger, but will overlap past the second joint of the trigger finger. The correct finger placement on the trigger is half-way to the first joint on the pad of the finger. The trigger should not be positioned in the joint between the first and second sections of the finger. The reason is that the maximum sensitivity and consequently the maximum control is in the tip of the forefinger. On two-trigger guns the correct pull should be taken from the front trigger. The reason is that the front trigger should be pulled first, then the hand slipped back to allow the finger to catch the second trigger. If the back trigger is pulled first, it is much harder to reposition the hand forward to engage the front trigger. This method of determining if a stock fits gives only a rough idea of the stock pull length; it does not tell you exactly how much to alter the stock, if the fit is not correct.

Trying to measure this with a tape or a yardstick is difficult, but is rather simple with Brownell's pull and drop gauge. Reposition your arm, but this time without the gun. Position the pull and drop gauge sliding bar to around ten inches on the scale, then insert your trigger finger in the hole that is at the front of the gauge. This hole has approximately the same curvature of a trigger and will give about the same feel as a trigger. Next, slide the bar toward the rear of the gauge until it touches the inner part of the upper arm exactly where the butt stock of the gun touched the arm. Without disturbing the sliding bar, remove the gauge and note the measurement at the rear of the sliding bar.

Write the arm pull measurement down on a piece of paper.

Lay your gun on a flat surface and slide the bar of the gauge fully to the rear. Position the hole in the gauge directly over the gun's trigger and line up the back of the hole with the curvature of the trigger. You can do this by eyeball alignment or, better still, use a pencil held vertically through the hole and pressing against both the trigger and the rear of the hole in the gauge. Now, slide the bar forward until it fits firmly against the butt of your gun while the pencil still is keeping the hole and the trigger aligned. Remove the gauge and note the measurement on the scale in front of the bar. Write down this stock pull measurement.

By subtracting the smaller of the two measurements from the larger, you will have the answer to the total amount the stock must be altered. If the stock pull measurement is the larger of the two, the stock must be shortened. Just don't forget to take the arm pull measurement reading from the rear of the sliding bar and the stock pull measurement reading from the front of the sliding bar.

Do not jump in and start whacking away at your stock!

This is a mechanical measurement solution, but is not necessarily the absolute and final solution to how much the stock must be altered. Quite a few things must be taken into consideration such as shooting form, how you hold your head in relation to the stock, even the type of clothing you will be wearing when using the gun. Hedge your bet and make temporary alterations to the stock.

If you are a long-armed cuss and the measurements indi-

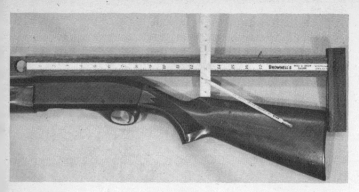

Use a small ruler across the gauge to measure the drop at the comb. Reading is taken at bottom of the gauge.

cate that the stock must be lengthened three-quarters of an inch, install one of those inexpensive slip-on recoil pads and do your test firing to see if you have the correct length figured out. If the measurements dictate one-half-inch more pull, first remove the original butt plate before you slip on the recoil pad as the butt plate of most guns will be around one-fourth-inch thick. Additional alterations for one-eighth or one-fourth inch can be obtained temporarily by cutting out a spacer filler from heavy cigar-box cardboard and inserting the filler between the stock and the butt plate. Most of these cigar box tops will be one-eighth-inch thick, but check to be sure. The butt plate screws will pull up fairly tight, but take care and do not strip them out trying to get the butt plate skin tight. You will be surprised how much an alteration of one-eighth-inch will make.

If a shorter stock is indicated, this also should be a temporary alteration first, then followed by a thorough test firing. As stated before, you can shorten the stock one-fourth inch by removing the butt plate. Shoot the stock naked and see if this length is sufficient. If even more shortening is necessary, cut the butt stock off one-fourth inch and test fire again. Make the shortening of the stock no more than one-fourth inch each time and shoot the stock again in the test firing. The butt plate, when reinstalled, will add one-fourth inch; thus you can add this much back, if you find you have cut a little too much off after test firing.

Your test firing should be as natural as possible and, most important, done while wearing your regular hunting clothes. Position a target at a short range and bring the gun up in a quick natural snap shot. Repeat this several times and note whether the stock "feels better" than it did before you made the temporary alteration. Your hits or misses on the target will provide even more information as to whether the stock is fitting better, as your accuracy should improve. To be positive your temporary length is correct it is a good idea to adjust the stock one-fourth inch longer and one-fourth inch shorter than your final length and test fire at these lengths. These two extra test runs should settle the question as to the final correct length. Take your time and do the job right, as it is important that the stock feels as comfortable as an old shoe without any muscle strain.

Stocks that require additional length usually can be altered permanently simply by installing a good recoil pad of sufficient thickness. Extra sections of matching or contrasting wood can be glued between the butt stock and the butt plate to achieve the length, but this can be tricky and, unless done carefully, will stand out like a plow mule at the Kentucky Derby.

Shortened stocks are much easier as about all that is required is to cut the stock to the desired length and reinstall the original butt plate or adjust the length to accept a recoil pad. Whatever the final method of stock length alteration, the end product will be a more comfortable gun to shoot and more accurate shooting.

The second important stock dimension is the amount of drop, the drop at the heel of the stock and drop at the comb of the stock. If an imaginary line is drawn down the line of sight and extended back to the butt plate of the stock, the distance between the heel (top) of the stock and this line is known as the "drop at heel."

The distance between this imaginary line and the top of the comb at the beginning of the comb of the stock is known as "drop at comb." The less the distance of these two measurements from the imaginary sight line, the more the tendency will be to shoot high and consequently the more the distance of the measurements the more the tendency to shoot low. On a rifle the front and rear sight or scope will require correct head placement on the stock and drop may

Here one can see the scale on the short leg of the gauge which is used in measuring the drop at heel of the stock.

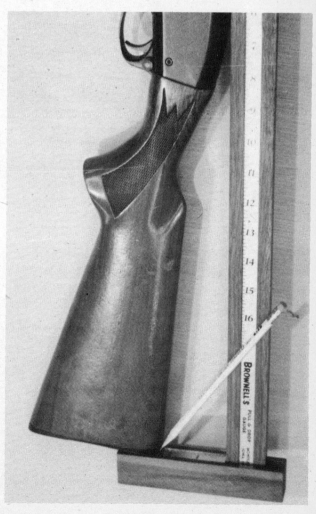

The Pachmayr Gun Works of Los Angeles has issued these detailed instructions on proper cutting of a stock for recoil pad installation as well as the instructions on the adjoining page for actual installation. Illustrations are the average shotgun dimensions for proper trigger pull length and drop at the comb and heel as well as dimensions from trigger to heel and toe. Stocks having more drop at heel and comb require less down pitch at the muzzle.

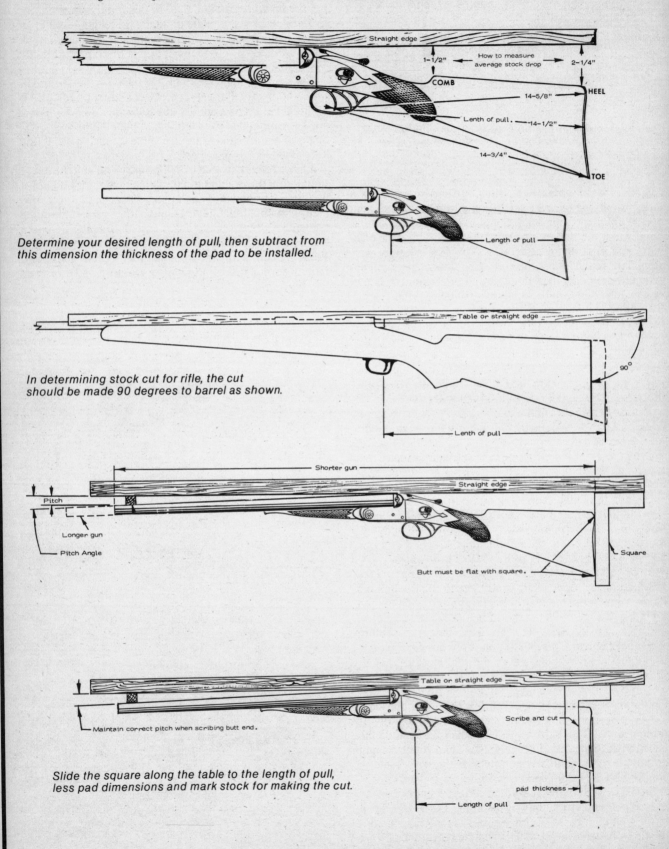

Determine your desired length of pull, then subtract from this dimension the thickness of the pad to be installed.

In determining stock cut for rifle, the cut should be made 90 degrees to barrel as shown.

Slide the square along the table to the length of pull, less pad dimensions and mark stock for making the cut.

METHOD A

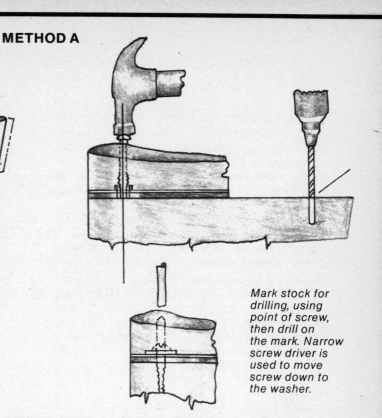

Insert screw through bottom of pad until it raises pad, then mark. Then put vaseline on screws and push through soft rubber until it hits washer.

Mark stock for drilling, using point of screw, then drill on the mark. Narrow screw driver is used to move screw down to the washer.

METHOD B

¼"

Use same method as above to mark the stock as shown above, then drill and insert dowel pins. They are glued in, then protruding pins are glued into pad. Adhesive should be used between stock and the pad.

Pad is centered on the stock. It will be larger than wood, allowing material for grinding rubber down to same dimensions.

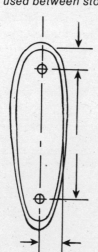

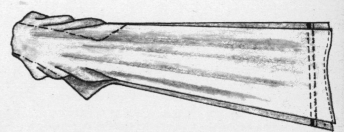

To hold pad in place while it dries, stretch an old piece of inner tube over the pad. This will apply pressure while the adhesive is drying.

be uncomfortable but will not materially affect the accuracy except by shooter fatigue. Shotguns are entirely another matter for the positioning of the head in relation to the line of sight will directly affect the accuracy as the eye in effect is the rear sight of a shotgun.

To measure drop with the Brownell pull and drop gauge, slide the bar fully to the rear and place the inside of the sliding bar against the butt plate. With your other hand press the bottom of the gauge against the top of the receiver, lining it up with the line of sight. Next, look at the inside of the sliding bar and read the scale exactly where it meets the top of the butt plate (heel of the stock). This measurement gives the drop at the heel. The sliding bar can be repositioned up the stock and held next to and slightly to one side of the beginning of the comb to read the drop at comb. A correct and accurate measurement is hard to read with this arrangement. A much simpler method is to lay a short metal rule directly aross the gauge with the zero edge of the rule touching the stock at the beginning of the comb. Read the measurement where the rule exactly crosses the bottom edge of the gauge. This is the drop at the comb.

Shotgun drop is measured with the gauge pressed against the top of the receiver. On iron-sighted rifles you can add one-half inch to the measurement to compensate for this sight height if you want to get real fancy and technical about measuring. For scope sighted rifles add 1½ inches for the same reason.

Quite frankly this is a matter of personal opinion and is really not necessary due to the many variations of sight height. Most stockmakers forget the fancy stuff and stick to reading drop using the top of the receiver as the imaginary line of sight. The drop at the comb then is adjusted to compensate for the desired height of the sights.

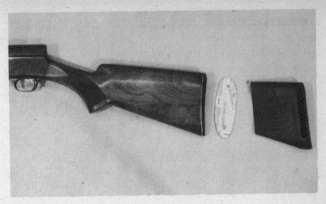

Cardboard, with a slipover rubber pad, is used here to lengthen stock temporarily in checking the proper length.

There are no hard and fast established rules about drop at heel and drop at comb, as personal opinion, old shooting habits and a dozen other things get involved in the final dimensions. Most shooters have a gun that is comfortable to shoot and one with which they can shoot accurately. The trick is really simple: Just measure the drop at comb and heel of this "right feeling" stock and then modify the "wrong feeling" stock to these dimensions.

Modifying a stock to change the drop at the heel is a tough nut in ninety-nine percent of the guns with which you will come in contact. It will require refitting the butt stock

Top gun has original factory stock for Remington Model 11-48, while gun beneath has a custom-fitted stock that was made for a shooter who holds his head unusually high. Custom pad has a full inch of added drop, while the angle of the butt plate has been changed, as well.

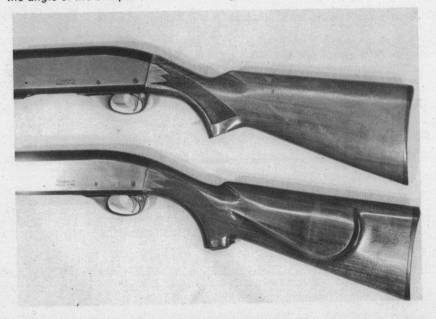

to the action, thereby dropping or raising the butt of the stock in the process on guns with a separate butt stock. On one-piece stocks it is almost impossible without gluing a separate piece of wood on the bottom of the stock, blending it with the rest of the stock, then cutting the top of the stock down to obtain the desired additional drop.

I have found that most shooters who complain about the drop of a stock are those whose shooting days began with one of the old guns with a lot of drop in the stock. They learned to shoot with their head held high and slightly away from the stock. Today's stocks, with less drop, cause them invariably to shoot high and the comb pounds their cheek during recoil. Altering the drop at the heel is difficult, as I have explained, but altering the drop at the comb is much easier and quite often is the real problem; not the drop at heel.

For those desiring more drop the matter usually can be solved by just shaving the top edge of the comb down a small amount, thereby increasing the drop at comb. If you do this, make the alteration a wee bit at a time with shooting tests every step of the way. Less drop can be solved only by gluing a section of wood to the comb and whittling it away until the desired drop-at-comb dimension is achieved.

The most important factor of all is simply whether the gun fits you. When it is right it will be comfortable to shoot and will come up to the same position on your shoulder each time with the sights directly in line with your eye without adjusting either the gun or your head.

Anything less is an incorrect fitting stock.

A properly fitting stock can mean more quail or other game birds in the field or a better score on claybird range. Some shooters don't know whether stock fits!

Hunter appears to be pondering the lack of a ventilated rib on his shotgun, wondering whether addition will improve his luck in the field.

Chapter 23

VENTILATED RIBS & HOW TO INSTALL THEM

Poly-Choke Has Simplified An Often Complicated Procedure

I WOULD NOT own a shotgun not equipped with a ventilated rib! Obviously others feel the same way because there is not a shotgun on the market, to my knowledge — except single-barrels and bolt-actions — which is not available with a factory-installed ventilated rib. This seems to be one subject on which shotgunners are in full agreement.

The solid rib found on some older shotguns is, the name implies, solid from breech of the barrel to muzzle end. It is seldom seen today because the ventilated rib has taken its place, primarily due to the ventilated rib's being simply much lighter in weight. A plain barrel and a ventilated or vent-rib barrel are close to being the same in weight, but not the same in price!

To those who doubt the advantages of a vent rib, a simple illustration may change their minds. All that is required for the demonstration is a common three-foot wooden rule or yardstick. For purposes of the demonstration the yardstick becomes the shotgun barrel.

Hold the yardstick to eye level with its flat side up. Sight

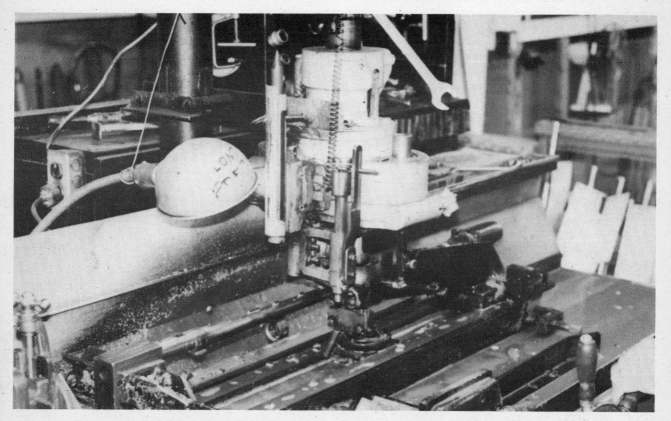

Equipment at Simmons Gun Specialties is set up to handle the drilling of the posts prior to vent rib installation.

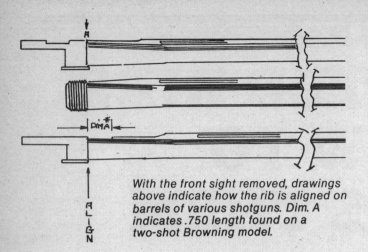

With the front sight removed, drawings above indicate how the rib is aligned on barrels of various shotguns. Dim. A indicates .750 length found on a two-shot Browning model.

The underside of the rib is sanded with 00 emery cloth, but it is not necessary to completely remove the anodizing. For proper mounting, surface should show some brightness.

down its length the same as you would a shotgun barrel and at a selected target. This is the view one gets with a plain non-rib shotgun barrel. Now turn the yardstick with the edge upward and again sight down its length at an imaginary target. This is similar to the view of a vent-rib-equipped barrel. Obviously the thinner edge of the rib gives the impression of a much longer barrel and increases sighting accuracy.

I have used this demonstration for quite a few years and have yet to find a shooter not impressed. With today's shorter shotgun barrels, the vent rib is a definite advantage in every phase of shotgun shooting.

There are quite a few shotgun barrels not equipped with a vent rib due to lack of choice at time of purchase or lack of knowledge on the part of the purchaser. Whatever the reason, the problem evolves into how to put a vent rib on a plain shotgun barrel.

The early leader in this field was the rib from the Simmons Gun Company, which requires roughly the same installation procedure as most manufacturers. Basically a series of studs is silver soldered onto the top of the shotgun barrel. As the barrel is contoured, the attached posts or studs end up at different heights. To solve this, the barrel is positioned in a milling machine correctly, then a milling

cutter is passed over them shaving each to a parallel height.

In order to attach the rib itself, a dovetail or notch is cut into the studs or posts. The rib slides onto the studs or posts and is locked into place. One other method is to drill the top of each post to accept a rivet. A flat section of steel is placed into position and riveted to individual studs. A thin rib, resembling a section of sheet steel with the edges on each side turned under, then slides onto the flat attached section of steel. Other companies use other systems, of course, but one way or another the rib is silver soldered onto the barrel and, in some cases, arc-welded in position.

All this requires extensive machinery and specially designed holding fixtures. Most gun shops and about all hobbyists find themselves out in the cold if they are interested in attaching a vent rib to their plain barrel.

There is one other way that, in my opinion, does not lack in appearance or quality. This is the installation and the vent rib developed by the Poly-Choke Company. I have installed them for years and never have had a single one

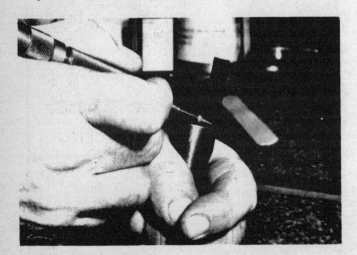

One of the initial steps in installation of Poly-Choke rib is to scribe muzzle cut-off on underside of rib.

As described more fully in the text, with the rib held in fixture, Allen head screws are tightened. One must be certain that rib bottoms entire length of fixture.

The adhesive furnished with the kit is applied to underside of the rib with a thickness of up to a quarter-inch with no voids anywhere on the rib's inner surfaces.

To hold the rib for drying, glass tape is applied at the muzzle end. It is pulled tight so there is equal pressure the full length of the barrel from chamber.

come loose under the most adverse conditions or thousands of rounds fired through the barrel.

In addition to authorized installers, Poly-Choke released them to Brownell's about ten years ago and recently to Walker Arms for distribution. If the instructions are followed, any knowledgeable gunsmith can complete the job as can any individual who so desires. One special accessory is a necessity for proper installation. This is the rib-holding fixture that holds the rib straight during the installation. Without it, the job is impossible if quality is expected.

When the Poly Rib was released for distribution by Brownell's, I wrote a set of installation instructions that differs considerably in the technique of installing the rib. So much so that I would advise anyone interested to purchase these instructions from Brownell's in addition to those from Poly-Choke that follow.

The Poly Rib is machined from extruded aluminum, hence it does not add to the weight of the barrel to any degree or change the balance point of a shotgun. The top is

specially machined to break up any light reflection or shadow. It comes with two sight beads, the front and the smaller middle bead. Both go into predrilled and pre-threaded mating holes in the rib.

The bottom of the rib is specifically contoured to exactly mate with that of a shotgun barrel. This is important to remember. The rib must be ordered to exactly match the barrel on which it is to be installed; that is, manufacturer, gun model, gauge and the barrel length. Omit any of this and the underside of the rib will probably not match the barrel's exterior contour.

The rib is held to the barrel by two things. The front sight bead extends through the rib and into the barrel metal. This adds extra strength at its front, but I doubt if it is really necessary. A special epoxy bonding agent was developed by the Poly-Choke company and is simply not available from any other source. This is the key.

When mixed in correct proportions it sets up but never hardens! When a barrel is fired any number of times it heats up and the metal expands. When cool, it contracts

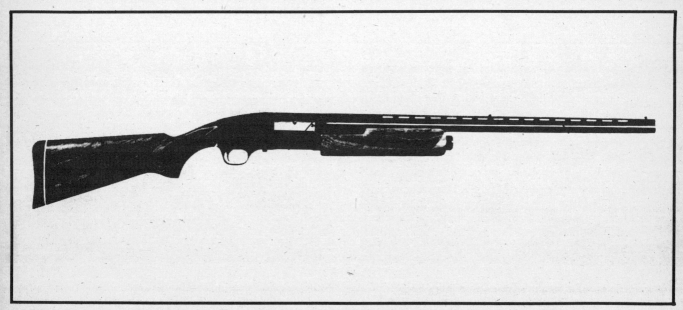

Once the Poly-Choke rib is installed properly, it offers a custom touch to the shotgun that even adds value.

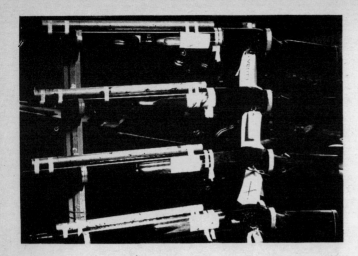

Poly-Choke ribs have been added to each of these guns and they have been placed in a rack to dry overnight.

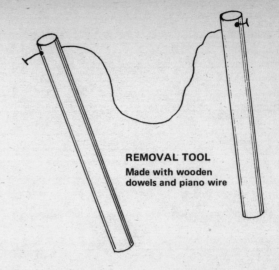

REMOVAL TOOL
Made with wooden
dowels and piano wire

If it becomes necessary to remove the rib at a later time, this simple tool can be used as described in the text. Wire cuts through adhesive, popping off the rib.

back to original dimensions. Without the non-hardening special epoxy, this flexing of dimensions quickly breaks any bond.

This is not so with the bonding material supplied by Poly-Choke for this purpose. It flexes with the metal! Shear strength is in excess of five thousand pounds per square inch (psi). You can tighten a bench vise on a Poly rib and pull on the barrel until you bend it and the rib will remain bonded to the barrel.

There is a special technique that allows removal; this is covered in the instructions included in this chapter.

Quite recently Poly-Choke made one welcome change. Previously the bonding material was purchased separately by the gunsmith and had a habit of hardening on the shelf when not used quickly. Currently the bonding material is supplied with each rib and is sufficient to do the job with a bit extra for those who are sloppy.

According to the manufacturer, here is what you need to install a Poly-Choke vent rib:

- Holding fixtures (provided)
- Front sight jig (provided)
- Adhesive/catalyst (provided)
- Toluol, a solvent that must be purchased locally because, as a red-label liquid, it cannot be shipped through the mails. Try your paint store.
- Cleaning tools (make them yourself or order from Poly-Choke).
- Wooden applicators (medical tongue depressors can be used to mix and apply adhesive).
- Glass filament tape (provided)

The manufacturer cautions against installing a Featheraire vent rib for forty-eight hours if the barrel has been reblued. In addition, the company says not to blue a barrel that has a Featheraire vent rib installed.

The adhesive used in installation is a Poly-Choke product and the company says it cannot be responsible for rib installations with any other material.

Poly-Choke also recommends the exclusive use of toluol solvent in the cleaning. This has excellent cleaning qualities, but does not attack the main holding bond. While other solvents may seem to work as well, they eventually may have a damaging effect on the main bond, the company warns.

Poly-Choke maintains an inventory of ribs for most popular brand guns in various lengths. But some brands are not carried because of limited demand. A rib can be contoured for any gun, but the gun must be sent to the factory.

Abbreviations are used to identify ribs. The marking will be found on the underside of the rib at the chamber end. The abbreviations are:

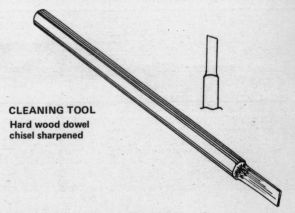

CLEANING TOOL
Hard wood dowel
chisel sharpened

This simple tool can be used to aid in clean-up of the rib after it is installed, removing extra adhesive.

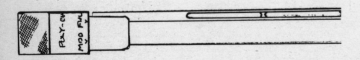

If the rib is to be added to barrel with Poly-Choke-equipped muzzle, the rib must be trimmed at muzzle end. The trimmed end is touched up with flat black paint.

Remington	REM
Winchester	WIN
Browning	BROW
Ithaca	ITH
High Standard	H.STAN
Harrington & Richardson	H&R
Savage	SAV
Franchi	FRAN
Mossberg	MBRG
Noble	NOBLE
Sears	SEARS
Montgomery Ward	MW
Beretta	BERT
Breda	BREDA
Marlin	MAR
LaSalle	LAS

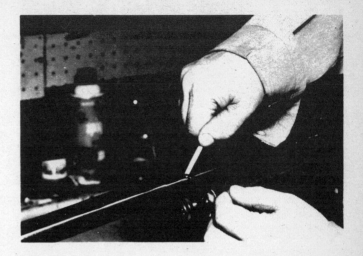

Using the chisel-sharpened length of hardwood dowel, the extra adhesive that has squeezed from beneath the rib usually comes off in a long ribbon without any problem.

When ordering, order by the brand name, model number and overall barrel length to ensure correct match and quicker delivery. If the barrel has a Poly-Choke or other muzzle device mounted, the length will be shorter. A tip: Measure from the chamber shell rim to the rear of the choke element.

There are seventeen steps for the installation of a rib on a plain barrel:

In the shop at Simmons Gun Specialties, great amounts of raw stock are in reserve to fit old or current models.

The average home workshop or even professional gun shop is not nearly as ambitious as Simmons' shop, but author found one does not need expensive equipment or tooling to do a good job of mounting the Simmons ventilated rib.

- Remove the front sight. With ramp-type sights, remove the bead, drill through the bead hole with a 3x56 tap size drill (#46) and remove the ramp with acetylene and vise grips. Tap hole 3x56. The ramp also may be ground flush. But be sure you protect the barrel.

- Align the rib on the barrel at the chamber end. Tape it in place.

- Scribe the muzzle cut-off line on the underside of the rib.

- Cut the rib to length, and check the length after cutting. Dress the end square with a file.

- Tape the rib to the barrel slightly off center so the sight hole is clear. Pick up and mark the sight hole selection on the rib ramp. Use a white pencil for clarity.

- Using a scissors sight jig, pick up the front sight location and drill through with a 3x56 (#37) or 6x48 (#26) depending on the original sight tap size. The holes are body size. The rib is not tapped.

- Tighten the front sight through the rib to check the length and rib fit at both the muzzle and chamber ends. Allow 1/64-inch, at chamber, between the rib and receiver.

- Place the rib in the fixture. Tighten the Allen-head screws tightly and ensure that the rib bottoms the entire length of the fixture.

- Sand the underside of the rib with 00 emery cloth or other rough emery. It is not necessary to completely remove the anodizing, but the surface should show brightness.

- Wipe the underside of the rib with a clean cloth, then clean with a generous amount of toluol. Do not touch the attaching surface after cleaning.

- Assemble the gun. Close the bolt, hold in vise and clean the barrel thoroughly with toluol. Mix adhesive according to instructions.

- Apply adhesive to the underside of the rib. The bed of the adhesive should be ⅛ to ¼ inch thick and evenly applied, with no voids, along the entire length of the rib.

- Put the 5/16-inch shank sight into the front sight hole in the rib and tighten into the barrel. With the front sight used as a pivot, align the rear of the rib with the serrated top of the gun receiver. Squeeze the rib/fixture assembly to the barrel with your hands, starting at the muzzle and continuing rearward to the chamber end.

- Apply glass tape to the muzzle end. When applying the tape, pull down hard using equal pressure with each hand, cross and secure.

- Check the alignment at the chamber, and apply tape at the chamber end. Check edges of the rib where it meets the barrel. An approximately 1/16-inch bead of adhesive should be along the entire length of the rib on both sides. If voids exist, the rib/fixture assembly has not been squeezed down tightly enough on the barrel. Squeeze to eliminate the voids and check to see that the tape has not loosened.

- Check again to ensure that movement has not caused misalignment.
- Place the completed assembly on the rack horizontally. Allow it to cure overnight, with the minimum twelve hours at a temperature not lower than 70F.

For fitting the rib to a Poly-Choke-equipped barrel, the manufacturer recommends:

- Tighten the sleeve of the Poly-Choke as tight as it will go. Remove the Poly-Choke sight. Select the rib that will provide not less than ½ inch of solid stock from the end of the element to the first vented area of the rib.
- Check the height of the rib. Be certain the rib is high enough.
- Trim the rib at the muzzle end. The trim line should be scribed on the ramp at a point 1/16 inch from the Poly-Choke sleeve. Check the length at the muzzle and receiver.
- Blacken the trimmed end of the rib with aluminum touch-up or black paint.
- Tape the rib to the barrel in proper position, letting

the forward end overlay the choke element. Scribe short light lines on both sides of the rib at a point where the choke element and the barrel meet. The scribe lines should not be more than 1/16 inch to ensure their being removed when the rib is milled to overlay the choke element.

- Determine the difference in height of the choke element and the barrel according to this procedure: Mike outside diameter of the barrel. Mike outside diameter of the choke element. Subtract the outside diameter of the barrel dimension from that of the choke element. Divide by two. The resulting dimension is the depth of the milled portion.
- With the milling cutter, machine rib to overlay the choke element. Be certain that the milled portion is finished to correct depth. The rib ramp must be perfectly flat.
- Tape the rib to the barrel in correct position. Check the contour and length of the milled section. Pick up the center of the sight hole in the Poly-Choke element and scribe a light line in the center of the rib.
- Using a scissors sight jig, pick up the scribe line on the rib and drill a #26 hole through the rib.
- Place the rib in proper position and insert the front sight. Check the fit.
- Proceed with regular mounting instructions.

The clean-up can be easy once the barrel is removed

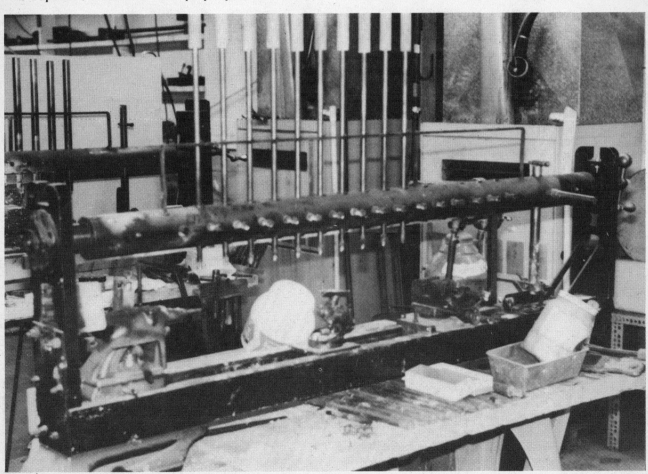

With an idea of saving time and making the job easier, Simmons has special jig for soldering rib posts to barrel.

A milling machine is utilized to prepare a shotgun for installation of a rib.

from the action. All that is required are cotton swabs, cleaning tools and fine steel wool.

Remove the holding fixture, tape, etc. Using a cotton swab, saturate the area where the adhesive has beaded out from under the rib with toluol solvent.

Starting at the chamber end, place the cleaning tool at the bead and push forward the entire length. Hold the sharpened edge of the cleaning tool at the point where the rib and barrel meet. The excess cured adhesive will be removed in one long string.

The stubborn areas not removed by now should be eliminated with a toluol-saturated piece of fine steel wool. Repeat on the opposite side. Run the tap into the threaded mid-rib sight hole. Use the 3x56 size. Install the middle sight.

Shear the shank of the front sight in the bore, file and polish flush. Position the adhesive Poly-Choke nameplate into the milled section of the rib ramp at the chamber end.

The end of a Poly-Choke rib is milled so that a Walker choke adapter can be installed at the gun's muzzle.

Inspect to ensure that all adhesive has been removed, especially between the rib vents. Do not oil.

For removal of the rib, remove the front and mid-rib sights. Tighten the 3x56 tap into the mid-rib sight hole until the rib has raised off the barrel at that point.

Using a removal tool, punch piano wire through the raised area. Reattach the holding dowel and pull forward to the muzzle then rearward to the chamber. The rib will pop off. The shim stock also may be used for removal instead of the piano wire.

With toluol, remove all adhesive from the barrel and underside of the rib. The rib then can be reinstalled utilizing regular installation procedures.

In mixing the adhesive, use five parts of black to one part catalyst by weight. Place a clean sheet of paper on the scale. With a wooden applicator place approximately 100 grains of black adhesive on the scale.

Advance the counterweight twenty percent. For example: If the scale weight is 100 grains, advance the counterweight to 120. Add small amounts of catalyst until the scale balances.

Mix thoroughly with clean applicator. Mix until all the brown streaks have disappeared and the mixture has an even black-colored consistency.

The shelf life of the catalyst is only six months. The catalyst must be removed from its foil container when received. Place the contents in a small glass jar (baby food containers are ideal). Each time the catalyst is used, mix thoroughly. The substance separates naturally and must be mixed.

For your inspection, check for voids in the adhesive bed. Reassemble the gun and check alignment of the rib. Some guns, particularly recoiling automatics, allow the barrel to float. Closing the bolt usually aligns the barrel to a true shooting position.

With recoiling-barrel automatics, manually push the barrel back to ejection position to be certain the rib will retract under the action housing.

Before delivering the gun to customers, gunsmiths should review these points:

- Are the sights installed? the shanks sheared?
- Has the Poly-Choke nameplate been mounted?
- Has all the adhesive been removed?
- Has the rebluing tag been tied to the barrel advising against rebluing the barrel with the rib installed?
- Is the alignment with action correct? No bends or dips?

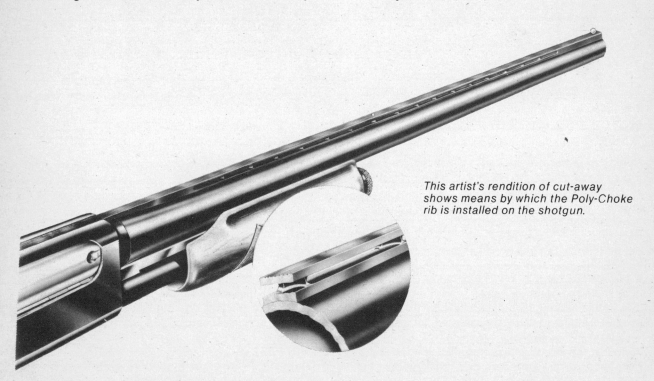

This artist's rendition of cut-away shows means by which the Poly-Choke rib is installed on the shotgun.

GUNSMITH SUPPLIERS

Alley Supply Co., Carson Valley Industrial Park, P.O. Box 848, Gardnerville, NV 89410/702-782-3800 (JET line lathes, mills, etc.)

Ametek, Hunter Spring Div., One Spring Ave., Hatfield, PA 19440/215-822-2971 (trigger gauge)

B-Square Co., Box 11281, Ft. Worth, TX 76110

Jim Balar, 490 Halfmoon Rd., Columbia Falls, MT 59912 (hex screws)

Al Biesen, W. 2039 Sinto Ave., Spokane, WA 99201 (grip caps, buttplates)

Billingsley & Brownell, Box 25, Wyarno, WY 82845/307-737-2468

Blue Ridge Machine and Tool, 165 Midland Trail, Hurricane, WV 25526/304-562-3538 (machinery, tools, shop suppl.)

Bonanza Sports Mfg. Co., 412 Western Ave., Faribault, MN 55021/507-332-7153

Briganti Custom Gun-Smithing, P.O. Box 56, 475 Route 32, Highland Mills, NY 10930/914-928-9816 (cold rust bluing, hand polishing, metal work)

Brookstone Co., 125 Vose Farm Rd., Peterborough, NH 03458

Brownell's, Main & Third, Montezuma, IA 50171/515-623-5401

W.E. Brownell, 1852 Alessandro Trail, Vista, CA 92083 (checkering tools)

Burgess Vibrocrafters, Inc. (BVI), Rte. 83, Grayslake, IL 60030

Chapman Mfg. Co., Rte. 17 at Saw Mill Rd., Durham, CT 06422

Chase Chemical Corp., 3527 Smallman St., Pittsburgh, PA 15201/412-681-6544 (Chubb Multigauge for shotguns)

Chubb (see Chase Chem. Co.)

Chicago Wheel & Mfg. Co., 1101 W. Monroe St., Chicago, IL 60607/312-226-8155 (Handee grinders)

Christy Gun Works, 875 57th St., Sacramento, CA 95819

Classic Arms Corp., P.O. Box 8, Palo Alto, CA 94302/415-321-7243

Clover Mfg. Co., 139 Woodward Ave., Norwalk, CT 06856/800-243-6492 (Clover compound)

Clymer Mfg. Co., Inc., 14241 W. 11 Mile Rd., Oak Park, MI 48237/313-541-5533 (reamers)

Dave Cook, 720 Hancock Ave., Hancock, MI 49930 (metalsmithing only)

Delta Arms Sporting Goods, Highway 82 West, Indianola, MS 38751/601-887-5566 (Lightwood/England)

Dem-Bart Checkering Tools, Inc., 6807 Hiway #2, Snohomish, WA 98290/206-568-7536

Dremel Mfg. Co., 4915 21st St., Racine, WI 53406 (grinders)

Chas. E. Duffy, Williams Lane, West Hurley, NY 12491

E-Z Tool Co., P.O. Box 3186, 25 N.W. 44th Ave., Des Moines, IA 50313 (lathe taper attachment)

Edmund Scientific Co., 101 E. Glouster Pike, Barrington, NJ 08007

Emco-Lux, 2050 Fairwood Ave., P.O. Box 07861, Columbus, OH 43207/614-445-8328

Forster Products, Inc., 82 E. Lanark Ave., Lanark, IL 61046/815-493-6360

Francis Tool Co. (formerly Keith Francis Inc.), 1020 W. Catching Slough Rd., Coos Bay, OR 97420 (reamers)

G.R.S. Corp., P.O. Box 748, Emporia, KS 66801/316-343-1084 (Gravermeister)

Gilmore Pattern Works, P.O. Box 50084, Tulsa, OK 74150/918-245-9627 (Wagner safe-T-planer)

Glendo Corp., P.O. Box 1153, Emporia, KS 66801/316-343-1084 (Accu-Finish tool)

Gold Lode, Inc., 1305 Remington Rd., Suite A, Schaumburg, IL 60195 (gold inlay kit)

Gopher Shooter's Supply, Box 278, Faribault, MN 55021 (screwdrivers, etc.)

Grace Metal Prod., 115 Ames St., Elk Rapids, MI 49629 (screwdrivers, drifts)

Gunline Tools, Box 478, Placentia, CA 92670/714-528-5252

Gun-Tec, P.O. Box 8125, W. Palm Beach, FL 33407

Half Moon Rifle Shop, 490 Halfmoon Rd., Columbia Falls, MT 59912/406-892-4409 (hex screws)

Henriksen Tool Co., Inc., P.O. Box 668, Phoenix, OR 97535/503-535-2309 (reamers)

Huey Gun Cases (Marvin Huey), Box 98, Reed's Spring, MO 65737/417-538-4233 (high grade English ebony tools)

Paul Jaeger Inc., 211 Leedom St., Jenkintown, PA 19046

John's Rifle Shop, 25 N.W. 44th Ave., Des Moines, IA 50313/515-288-8680

Kasenit Co., Inc., 3 King St., Mahwah, NJ 07430/201-529-3663 (surface hrdng. comp.)

Terry K. Kopp, Highway 13, Lexington, MO 64067/816-359-2636 (stock rubbing compound)

J. Korzinek, RD #2, Box 73, Canton, PA 11724/717-673-8512 (stainl. steel bluing)

John G. Lawson (The Sight Shop), 1802 E. Columbia Ave., Tacoma, WA 98404/206-474-5465

Lea Mfg. Co., 237 E. Aurora St., Waterbury, CT 06720/203-753-5116

Lightwood (Fieldsport) Ltd., Britannia Rd., Banbury, Oxfordshire, OX16 8TD, England

Lock's Phila. Gun Exch., 6700 Rowland Ave., Philadelphia, PA 19149/215-332-6225

John McClure, 4549 Alamo Dr., San Diego, CA 92115 (electric checkering tool)

McIntyre Tools, P.O. Box 491/State Road #1144, Troy, NC 27371/919-572-2603 (shotgun bbl. facing tool)

Michaels of Oregon Co., P.O. Box 13010, Portland, OR 97213/503-255-6890

Miller Single Trigger Mfg. Co., R.D. 1, Box 99, Millersburg, PA 17061/717-692-3704

Frank Mittermeier, 3577 E. Tremont, New York, NY 10465

Moderntools, 1671 W. McNab Rd., Ft. Lauderdale, FL 33309/305-979-3900

N&J Sales, Lime Kiln Rd., Northford, CT 06472/203-484-0247 (screwdrivers)

Karl A. Neise, Inc., 1671 W. McNab Rd., Ft. Lauderdale, FL 33309/305-979-3900

Palmgren Prods., Chicago Tool & Eng. Co., 8383 South Chicago Ave., Chicago, IL 60167/312-721-9675 (vises, etc.)

Panavise Prods., Inc., 2850 E. 29th St., Long Beach, CA 90806/213-595-7621

C.R. Pedersen & Son, 2717 S. Pere Marquette, Ludington, MI 49431/616-843-2061

Richland Arms Co., 321 W. Adrian St., Blissfield, MI 49228

A.G. Russell, 1705 Highway 71N, Springdale, AR 72764 (Arkansas oilstones)

Schaffner Mfg. Co., Emsworth, Pittsburgh, PA 15202 (polishing kits)

SGW (formerly Schuetzen Gun Works), 624 Old Pacific Hwy., S.E., Olympia, WA 98503/206-456-3471

Shaw's, 9447 W. Lilac Rd., Escondido, CA 92025/619-728-7070

Shooters Specialty Shop, 5146 E. Pima, Tucson, AZ 85712/602-325-3346

L.S. Starrett Co., 121 Crescent St., Athol, MA 01331/617-249-3551

Texas Platers Supply Co., 2453 W. Five Mile Parkway, Dallas, TX 75233 (plating kit)

Stan de Treville, Box 33021, San Diego, CA 92103/619-298-3393 (checkering patterns)

Turner Co., Div. Cleanweld Prods., Inc., 821 Park Ave., Sycamore, IL 60178/815-895-4545

Twin City Steel Treating Co., Inc., 1114 S. 3rd, Minneapolis, MN 55415 (heat treating)

Will-Burt Co., 169 S. Main, Orrville, OH 44667 (vises)

Williams Gun Sight Co., 7389 Lapeer Rd., Davison, MI 48423

Wilson Arms Co., 63 Leetes Island Rd., Branford, CT 06405

W.C. Wolff Co., Box 232, Ardmore, PA 19003 (springs)

Woodcraft Supply Corp., 313 Montvale, Woburn, MA 01801